POWER
FROM
EXPERIENCE

POWER
FROM
EXPERIENCE

Urban Popular
Movements
in Late
Twentieth-Century
Mexico

PAUL LAWRENCE HABER

The Pennsylvania State University Press
University Park, Pennsylvania

Library of Congress Cataloging-in-Publication Data

Haber, Paul (Paul Lawrence)
    Power from experience : urban popular movements in
    late twentieth-century Mexico / Paul Lawrence Haber.
        p.   cm.
Includes bibliographical references (p.   ) and index.
ISBN 978-0-271-02708-1 (pbk : alk. paper)
1. Social movements—Mexico–History—20th century.
2. Political participation—Mexico—History—20th century.
3. Mexico–Social conditions—1970– .
4. Mexico—Politics and government—1988– .
I. Title.

HN113.5.H26 2005
322.4'4'07209045—dc22
2005013858

The Pennsylvania State University Press is a member
of the Association of American University Presses.

It is the policy of The Pennsylvania State University
Press to use acid-free paper. This book is printed on stock that
meets the minimum requirements of American National
Standard for Information Sciences—Permanence of Paper
for Printed Library Material, ANSI Z39.48–1992.

CONTENTS

Preface and Acknowledgments   vii

List of Acronyms   xiii

Introduction: Introducing the Terrain of
Struggle   1

1 Theory and Method for a Phenomenological and
   Institutional Study of Social Movements   15

2 Mexico at the Zenith of the 1980s Protest
   Cycle   47

3 The Seesaw Political Economy of Recovery, Crisis,
   and Democratic Transition, 1988–2000   85

4 The Comité de Defensa Popular de Francisco Villa
   de Durango   123

5 The Asamblea de Barrios of Mexico City   173

6 Comparisons and Conclusions   213

   Appendixes   241

   Bibliography   251

   Index   271

In memory of
my mother,
Agnes Marie Jensen Haber,
1922–2000

y mi compañero
Juan Francisco Salazar Álvarez,
1962–2000

Seriously persistent students of social movements are an interesting lot. We tend to come to our subject not just out of intellectual curiosity. Nor are we drawn to our subject only by force of conviction that these actors are fundamental to our understanding of history, which we most certainly believe them to be. Neither is it simply the drive for publication that is the currency of recognition (not to mention survival) in the professional academic environment where many of us reside. These motivations certainly exist in some combination for the university-affiliated scholar. But as explanations, they are not so much wrong as incomplete. For there is something else motivating the willingness to do what turns out to be relatively arduous, time-consuming, often frustrating fieldwork. There are easier ways to get tenure.

Underlying the history of internal battles and antagonistic relations with local and national power holders, the details of public-works projects, and the complexities of political campaigns is the original idea of the Left: we want to live differently. For many of us, this has meant pursuing a socialist ideal, a democratic socialism in which the values of solidarity with and care and concern for others, equality, dignity, and freedom for all would be at the core, rather than the periphery, of collective experience. This ideal has instructed many of us to work for the creative destruction of the capitalist world. Capitalism is indicted as the sponsor of alienation, selfish individualism born out of fear, the need to survive by achieving advantage over others, inequalities legitimated under the false gods of individual incentive and god-given abilities, and a lack of efficacious concern for our fellow human beings—especially those in trouble.

Social movements are attractive in part because they very clearly proclaim that there is something terribly wrong about how we are living and that something can and should be done about it. The focus of critique and of the suggested alternatives is often outward, toward existing forms of socioeconomic, cultural, and political structures and relationships that are judged to be repressive, exploitative, and authoritarian. Lived experience in a social movement or careful ethnographic research of those living such experiences often reveals a deep consensus among activists that these structures are so very wrong because of what they do to people's quality of life, to the quality of relationships between people and the ways in which we interact with our environment. Movements derive their power in part from the occasions of solidarity they provide. People are motivated to join movements that create spaces in which they can experience common cause and thereby overcome some portion of their alienation. Movement activists are motivated to create counterhegemonic cultural acts and meanings when the existing political culture does not produce the dignity and joy to which people aspire. We sense that we can do better. Movements, at least those with staying power, demonstrate an array of capacities in their efforts to effectively respond to the interests and values of those they claim to represent. This book tells the stories of movement organizations that have done exactly this.

Certainly, movements for liberation from oppression, repression, and exploitation and that follow visions of freedom and equity do not always succeed in making substantial progress in realizing their ideals. But they try, and it is this vulnerable and courageous effort that attracts many students of culture, politics, and social relations. I know that I am attracted to movements for help in the praxis that derives from my own sense that some things in the world are terribly out of whack with my most cherished values. I too, just like many of the movement people who enliven the history I have attempted to write here, am trying to gain the sense of dignity that arises as alienation is partially overcome via the making of meaningful connections. Participating in the power of movements, and even studying them—if one does so in a deeply personal way—provides the opportunity to struggle with values and meaning in the company of others with similar sensibilities.

This book is the culmination of more than a decade's worth of fieldwork, reading, writing, teaching, conversation, and solitary reflection. The project began as a dissertation in the Department of Political Science at Columbia University. Fieldwork started in the summer of 1988, in time for me to witness the extraordinary elections in which Carlos Salinas officially won the Mexican presidency but only amid widespread and credible claims of massive fraud. I lived mostly in Mexico during 1989 and 1990 and thus was able to observe closely some of the dramatic events that transpired during these years, most notably the formation of both the Democratic Revolutionary Party (PRD) and the Workers' Party (PT). The creation of these two political parties radically transformed the politics of social movements in general and the two case studies presented here in particular: the Asamblea de Barrios of Mexico City and the Comité de Defensa Popular of Durango. I moved between Mexico and the United States through the end of 1991 and thus was able to observe firsthand the famous 1991 midterm elections in which the dominant political party, the Partido Revolucionario Institucional (Institutionalized Revolutionary Party [PRI]) achieved "la recuperación oficial" (official recuperation).[1] Key to the Salinas administration's political success was the effectiveness of an extremely controversial and high-profile antipoverty program known as the Program of National Solidarity (PRONASOL). Particularly because a significant percentage of resources were targeted at the urban popular movement, PRONASOL became a primary focus of my research.

Between 1992 and 1999, I returned to Mexico each year to conduct research that focused on a major reorientation of strategy, as key leaders and organizations of the urban popular movement moved into electoral politics and then achieved office and embarked on governance. My initial understandings of these complex dynamics, particularly in relationship to the situation in Durango, were recorded in a series of publications (P. Haber 1989, 1990, 1993, 1994a, 1994b, 1996a, 1996b, 1997a, 1997b, 1998a). Throughout this period, I studied and taught social movement theory and followed closely the development of the Latin American social movement literature. I owe a great debt to those who have published their books before me.[2] This book is my best effort to combine my own evolving theoretical understanding of movements for socioeconomic, political, and cultural change with what I have learned from observing the politics of Mexican urban popular movements.

I have had the great fortune of getting to know other fellow travelers, without whom there would be nothing to report. In Durango, I want to single out Juan Salazar Álvarez, Mayela Mercado Gallegos, Gonzalo Yáñez, Gabino Martínez Guzmán, and Miguel Palacios Moncayo. I also want to thank the thousands of CDP*istas* with whom I mingled for a decade and to single out the dozens of CDP members who took the time and risked their trust to explain the basics to *el gringo*. In Mexico City's Asamblea de

---

1. *Official recuperation* refers to the electoral recovery of the Mexican political machine. One of the key elements of this recovery was President Salinas's purported antipoverty program, directed in large part at the urban poor and those who claimed to represent them, including urban popular movements. See, in particular, Gómez Tagle 1993.

2. Works on Latin American social movements that have been most influential on my thinking include Bennett 1995a; Cook 1996; Foweraker 1993; Gay 1994; Harvey 1998; Oxhorn 1995; Rubin 1997; Stokes 1995; Street 1992; Schnieder 1995; Alvarez, Dagnino, and Escobar 1998; D. Camacho and Menjívar 1989; Escobar and Alvarez 1992; Eckstein 1989b; and Foweraker and Craig 1990.

Barrios, I owe special gratitude to Francisco Saucedo, Yolanda Tello, Marco Rascon, Bete Baños, and the many movement militants who not only allowed me to attend their meetings, participate in their marches, and wait with them outside the doors of countless government officials but also, in that unique *chilango* movement style, demanded that I also hazard answers to the complex questions that history was posing.

In addition to offering me those individuals who were directly tied to the Asamblea de Barrios, Mexico City bestowed on me—as it has so many others—an abundance of quality activist scholars. These men and women shared with me their experience, reflections, and example, all of a quality that I will never be able to adequately reciprocate (unless, perhaps, they end up on my activist doorstep in the United States someday). Amongst this august crowd, I single out for special mention those who exhibited the most patience, and in so doing, taught me the most: Julio Moguel, Luis Hernández, Alejandro Luevano, Martin Longoria, and Sergio Zermeño. Alejandro showed great kindness and support for the graduate student just off the boat, orienting me towards the movement organizations with those all important introductions that got my foot in the door. As I matured, so did our conversations. Alejandro's profound insights continue to inform me and force me to rethink my positions. Julio and Luis gave me great perspective on the post-1968 Left and seriously engaged me in my evolving interpretations of the CDP, which they both know better than I. Both Martin and Alejandro shared with me their years of experience in one of Mexico's most enduring and important urban popular movement organizations, the Union de Colonias Populares (UCP), as well as their experiences as PRD federal deputies. It is hard to think of more experienced teachers on the questions of movement-PRD relations. Sergio encouraged me and gave me opportunities to publish in Mexico.

And now turning to my colleagues in North America, I sincerely thank fellow movement students whom it has been my pleasure and benefit to come to know and learn from and with: Vivienne Bennett, Jonathan Fox, Maria Cook, Judy Hellman, Kenneth Greene, Jeffrey Rubin, Neil Harvey, and Janet Finn. I owe a very special thanks to those who took the time to read the entire manuscript a number of times and provide me with detailed, smart, and demanding editorial comments, which were indispensable in the work of turning a draft into a finished product: Vivienne Bennett, Linda Farthing, Judy Hellman, and Mark Nechodom.

Reaching far back in time to when this project began, I would also like to thank the members of my dissertation committee at Columbia University, especially Doug Chalmers, Dick Cloward, and Al Stepan, who in their different ways supported me through challenge and example. During the early stages of dissertation writing, Barbara Epstein of the University of California at Santa Cruz graciously allowed me to sit in on her stimulating graduate seminar on social movements, which gave me some of my early conceptual bearings.

At two critical stages I was given safe haven to write. The Proctors in Watsonville, California, gave me a place to write at the beginning stages of this project; and Joyce Campbell in Tacambaro, Michoacán, provided a home in which I was able to write the first draft of the book. Thank you for your generosity.

I would also like to give thanks to the Fulbright Foundation, the John D. and Catherine T. MacArthur Foundation, and the University of Montana Foundation for their generous financial support. I am also grateful to Sandy Thatcher, Romaine Perin, and everyone else at Penn State University Press for helping this book to see the light of day.

And, finally, I would like to thank those with whom I have been the closest—the friends and family who listened and questioned and, above all, loved, believed, imagined, and sparred with me. Thank you, Olivia, Rafa, Ellie, Agnes, Eric, CT, Mark, Terry, Juan, and Marilyn.

LIST OF ACRONYMS

AB	Asamblea de Barrios (Assembly of Neighborhoods)
ACNR	Asociación Cívica Nacional Revolucionaria (National Revolutionary Civic Association)
ANOCP	Asamblea Nacional de Obreros y Campesinos Popular (National Popular Assembly of Workers and Peasants)
CANACINTRA	Cámara Nacional de Industrias de l Transformación (National Chamber of Manufacturing Industries)
CDP	Comité de Defensa Popular (Popular Defense Committee)
CIOAC	Central Independiente de Obreros Agrícolas y Campesinos (Independent Confederation of Agricultural Workers and Peasants)
CLIC	Comité de Lucha Inquilinaria del Centro (Committee of the Downtown Renter's Struggle)
CNC	Confederación Nacional Campesina (National Peasant Confederation)
CNOP	Confederación Nacional de Organizaciones Populares (National Confederation of Popular Organizations)
CNPA	Coordinadora Nacional Plan de Ayala (National Coordinating Committee of the Plan de Ayala)
CNTE	Coordinadora Nacional de Trabajadores de la Educación (National Coordinating Committee of Education Workers)
CNUP	Convención Nacional Urbano Popular (Urban Popular National Convention)
COCEI	Coalición de Obreros, Campesinos y Estudiantes del Istmo (Coalition of Workers, Peasants, and Students of the Isthmus)
COFIPE	Código Federal de Instituciones y Procedimientos Electorales (Federal Code of Electoral Institutions and Procedures)
CONAMUP	Coordinadora Nacional del Movimiento Urbano Popular (National Coordinating Committee of the Urban Popular Movement)
CONANACO	Confederación de Cámaras Nacionales de Comercio (Confederation of National Chambers of Commerce)

CONCAMIN	Confederación de Cámaras Industrialies (Confederation of Industrial Chambers)
COPLAMAR	Coordinación General del Plan Nacional de Zonas Deprimidas y Groupos Marginados (Central Coordination of the National Plan of Economically Depressed Regions and Marginalized Groups)
CTM	Confederación de Trabajadores de México (Confederation of Mexican Workers)
CUD	Coordinadora Unica de Damnificados (United Coordinating Committee of Earthquake Victims)
FDN	Frente Democrático Nacional (National Democratic Front)
FNOC	Frente Nacional de Organizaciones y Ciudadanos (National Front of Organizations and Citizens)
FPTYL	Frente Popular Tierra y Libertad (Popular Front Land and Liberty)
IFE	Instituto Federal Electoral (Federal Electoral Institute)
IMF	International Monetary Fund
ISI	Import Substitution Industrialization
MAP	Movimiento de Acción Popular (Movement of Popular Action)
MRP	Movimiento Revolucionario del Pueblo (Revolutionary Movement of the People)
NAFTA	North American Free Trade Agreement (Tratado de Libre Comercio de América del Norte)
OIR-LM	Organización de Izquierda Revolucionaria–Línea de Masas (Revolutionary Left Organization–Mass Line)
PAN	Partido Acción Nacional (National Action Party)
PARM	Partido Auténtico de la Revolución Mexicana (Authentic Party of the Mexican Revolution)
PCDP	Partido del Comité de Defensa Popular (Party of the Committee of Popular Defense)
PFCRN	Partido del Frente Cardenista de Reconstrucción Nacional (Party of the Cardenas Front of National Reconstruction)
PMS	Partido Mexicano Socialista (Mexican Socialist Party)
PMT	Partido Mexicano de los Trabajadores (Mexican Workers' Party)

PPS	Partido Popular Socialista (Popular Socialist Party)
PRD	Partido de la Revolución Democrática (Party of the Democratic Revolution)
PRHP	Programa de Renovación Habitacional Popular (Program of Popular Housing Renovation)
PRI	Partido Revolucionario Institucional (Institutionalized Revolutionary Party)
PRONASOL	Programa Nacional de Solidaridad (National Solidarity Program)
PRT	Partido Revolucionario de los Trabajadores (Revolutionary Workers' Party)
PSUM	Partido Socialista Unificado de México (Unified Socialist Party of Mexico)
PT	Partido de Trabajo (Workers' Party)
SAM	Sistema Alimentario Mexicana (Mexican Food System)
SEDESOL	Secretaría de Desarrollo Social (Ministry of Social Development)
SEDUE	Secretaría de Desarrollo Urbano y Ecología (Ministry of Urban Development and Ecology)
SNTE	Sindicato Nacional de Trabajadores de la Educación (National Union of Education Workers)
SPP	Secretaría de Programación y Presupuesto (Ministry of Programming and Budget)
UCP	Unión de Colonias Populares (Union of Popular Neighborhoods)
UNAM	Universidad Nacional Autónoma de México (National Autonomous University of Mexico)
UNORCA	Unión Nacional de Organizaciones Regionales Campesinas (National Union of Autonomous Regional Peasant Organizations)
UPEZ	Unión de los Pueblos de Emiliano Zapata (Union of the People of Emiliano Zapata)
UPI	Unión Popular Independiente (Independent Popular Union)
UPREZ	Unión Popular Revolucionaria Emiliano Zapata (Popular Revolutionary Union Emiliano Zapata)

INTRODUCTION

Introducing the Terrain of Struggle

We know that the kind of history one writes depends very much on the kind one wants. History shares a quality with all scientific classifications: it is composed for some specific *purpose*. So long as it does not willfully distort facts and events, it must be judged on the basis of whether it meets the historian's intentions. No history can be true or false in an abstract or absolute sense. Consequently, it is very important to be explicit about one's aims.
—ERNEST BECKER, *The Structure of Evil*

Poor people are, in general, too ignorant to be trusted. Democracy needs an active and participatory middle class that strives to improve its condition and cares about politics and the national progress.
—PORFIRIO DÍAZ

The July 2000 electoral overthrow in Mexico of the twentieth century's longest-lasting authoritarian regime cannot be properly understood without an accounting of the significant role played by the mobilization of the urban poor during the 1970s, 1980s, and 1990s. The nonunionized urban poor have become the most populous social class: they are more numerous than unionized workers and the peasantry, and they far outstrip what by Latin American standards is a significant middle class.

The regime's failure to incorporate this large number of people into Mexico's political, economic, social, and cultural institutions made it possible for them to become the political base for the radical students who survived the regime's violent repression of the student movement in the late 1960s and early 1970s. Beginning quietly, so quietly that they eluded significant comment or in some quarters even detection, these student leaders enabled the urban poor to become significant actors in the left-wing reawakening of Mexico's civil society during the 1970s and 1980s. These urban social movements played a key role in the contentious presidential election of 1988, when Carlos Salinas of the Partido Revolucionario Institucional (Institutionalized Revolutionary Party [PRI]) was declared the winner, but only over loud accusations of massive fraud.

Throughout the turbulent Cold War period, most political actors on the revolutionary left perceived elections as exercises designed to legitimate authoritarianism through the staging of democratic farces: electoral contests that yielded no substantial benefits to those challenging the authoritarian regime at its core. Where elections existed but were perceived thus by the Left, it attempted to locate itself within the sites of power that had the capacity to destabilize existing institutions and practices, thereby creating the possibility of democratic reforms. These democratic-reform social movements tended to wither during the transition phase of democratization, that is, when the authoritarian regime was being replaced by a new and incipient democratic order. This scenario can be seen in many recent cases, including those of Brazil, El Salvador, Poland, South Africa, and the former Czechoslovakia. However, once political parties and the holding of public office become viable options, movement leaders often turn their attention to playing the new democratic game. This has happened all over the world, as social movements that played vital roles in democratic transition have created or been incorporated into Left and Center-Left political parties.[1] Mexico is no exception: by the end of the 1980s, the new urban popular movement organizations debated participation in electoral politics, with the majority opting for political party affiliation by the 1990s.

A primary purpose of this book is to examine this widespread historical trend through an exploration of the Mexican experience, considering what the transformation from urban low-income movement to party politics has meant for the country's democratic transition and its future consolidation. I examine the implications for neoliberal political and economic restructuring of these transformations on the left and what the close association between most of the large urban popular movement organizations and political parties has meant for the evolution of the Mexican party system. Finally, I explore the implications of this change in terms of power, material rewards, and identity for those who moved these movements forward, the rank-and-file members and sympathizers.

Most people who study politics agree that elite interactions are critical in an analysis of political outcomes. However, as Joseph Klesner argues, "the study of elite interactions alone, of strategic pacts in which elites

---

1. Three trends dominate this process. First, movements turn to party politics when they calculate that their interests behoove them to do so; second, this decision causes movements to either disappear or fade from a central role as protagonists; and finally, when movement leaders join political parties promising to represent the interests and values of their social base, they find themselves in new institutional settings forced to compromise with others representing other interests and values, both nationally and internationally.

promise to protect each other's interests or existence, ignores the social bases of the elites who are negotiating" (1998, 478). In his review of the literature on Mexico's democratic transition, Klesner notes that "[t]here is a crying need for systematic exploration of the extent of recruitment of civic organization leaders into the opposition parties" (491). In this study, I aspire to help fill this gap, by detailing the strategic decisions made by movement leadership to seize the new political opportunities promised by electoral participation in the post-1988 period.

As Pamela Oliver and many others correctly point out, movements should not be equated with any particular organization or organizations. They function more as networks occupied by both organizational and nonorganizational actors (1989, 4). However, as Snow and his colleagues (1986) observe, lead organizations can tell us a great deal about a social movement. The two cases chosen for this study represent extremely important organizations, both of them in the leadership of Mexican urban social movements. The first, the Comité de Defensa Popular (Popular Defense Committee [CDP]) of Durango, has a rich and influential history dating back to the 1970s, when it influenced the entire popular movement by becoming one of the first organizations to participate in electoral politics. It is the most important organization within the Partido de Trabajo (Workers' Party [PT]), a new political party that emerged in the 1990s. Sergio Zermeño has written that "The CDP is without a doubt the urban popular movement with the most tradition, power, and continuity in Mexico" (1997, 9). The second case study, that of the Asamblea de Barrios (Assembly of Neighborhoods [AB]) of Mexico City, represents the most important urban popular movement affiliated with the Center-Left Partido de la Revolución Democrática (Party of the Democratic Revolution [PRD]). By studying these two movement organizations and their trajectories into electoral politics, we are in a strong position to reflect on the complexities of urban movement and political party relationships.

Few accounts of Mexico's long political transition from being ruled by an authoritarian regime overseeing a highly regulated and nationalist capitalism to being governed by a fledgling democratic regime implementing a market-oriented and internationalized capitalism, make reference to the urban poor. If they are mentioned, it is often in the capacity of passive or second-class citizens. One of my goals is to dispel this unfortunate myth and interpret Mexico's thirty-year history of urban-poor social activism in terms of how it was experienced by its participants, from top leadership to midlevel activists to the rank and file, examining their ability to change the policy content and policy style of the country's particularly durable authoritarian regime.

In this book, I aspire to contribute to an appreciation of the magnitude of change that has occurred in the politics of the urban poor. What I claim and document is that the presence of the urban popular movement shaped the consciousness and political activity of millions of people across Mexico. These movements were crucial to the events of 1988 and the multiparty system that has begun to take shape in Mexico in subsequent years. The story that unfolds here also illustrates the persistence of authoritarian qualities in the workings of Mexican politics (renovated corporatism, clientelism, and co-optation). Authoritarianism in Mexico has never been static or monolithic in its exercise or its results. In particular, in many parts of Mexico, power has long been hotly contested, and the national regime, based upon the continued domination of the PRI, was significantly and repeatedly challenged. From the late 1970s to the mid-1990s, in some cases, the opposition won elections, took office, and contributed to building a more robust federalism. In others, social movement organizations deeply influenced the operations of the PRI government, as well as altering the authoritarian power structures in civil society.

Methodology

While different theoretical and methodological approaches have created the tremendous diversity that characterizes the Latin American social movement literature of the past decade, these approaches are significantly shaped by what can realistically be researched. Accessibility to people involved, political sensitivities, and the quality of available information all interact with the temperament and the theoretical and methodological inclinations and capabilities of authors to influence the written literature in ways that are sometimes unrecognized. In my case, fieldwork was fundamentally shaped by the fact that I was both inclined to work closely with movement leadership and that they were willing to work with me.[2]

2. This sharply contrasts with the experience of Jeffrey Rubin (1997) with another Mexican movement organization, the Coalition of Workers, Peasants, and Students of the Isthmus (COCEI) of Juchitán, Oaxaca, to which he was not given access. I want to emphasize that I am in no way assuming this to be negative. In fact, my reading of Rubin's work is that his lack of access to leadership encouraged him to rely more on community members, and this

The results of my investigation would have been very different indeed had not the early suspicions, sometimes expressed openly in my presence, that I was likely to be associated with some form of undercover surveillance not given way to significant levels of trust on the part of top and midlevel leadership in both Durango and Mexico City. This network of trust grew over the many months that I spent living within the urban popular movement, and the trust I gained with top leadership spilled over into my interactions with midlevel leadership, whose members had close ties with much of the rank and file. Despite assurances to the contrary, I remained firm in my intuition that maintaining this trust required that I carefully limit the relationships I developed with government officials. This has resulted in an analysis in which the state is viewed from the perspective of the movements; this would not have been so had I felt freer to develop relationships with elected officials and government administrators.[3]

This book is also influenced by the fact that the published regional history of nineteenth- and twentieth-century *durangueño* history is, to be charitable, very thin indeed.[4] The lack of a rich historiography combined with my training as a political scientist and not as an historian pushed me toward the contemporary period very early on in my research. In this my work also contrasts sharply with that of Jeffrey Rubin, who drew on the rich historiography of Oaxaca to develop deep historical sensibilities. While our differences are in part a reflection of our divergent passions, insights, and convictions, they also stem from what we had to work with. Social science research in radical social movements is, at least in many cases, influenced as much by contingencies met on the ground as it is by the dictates of one's discipline or theoretical orientations.

In writing this book I was strongly motivated by a desire to convey to the reader the political experience of participants in the Mexican urban social movement, without getting lost in abstract discussions of structures.[5]

---

resulted in a nuanced account of community-movement relationship unparalleled in the Mexican urban movement literature. The point here is that research is profoundly influenced by access, and access is never perfectly controlled by the person doing the research. Creative adaptation to the realities of access is important.

    3. The advantages of greater access to state officials is well demonstrated by the work of Vivienne Bennett (1995b).

    4. The major exception is the revolutionary period. See, in particular, Martínez Guzmán and Chávez Ramírez 1998 and Katz 1998.

    5. My approach is a response to Melucci's (1989) imperative that the structuralist view "which starts from the analysis of a social condition to explain a group's action must be

While it was essential to stake out a position regarding the political implications for policy formation and outcomes at both the regional and the
national levels, I did not want the prose to take on the style of a public policy text. The experience of social movements is too rich a story to get lost,
as it often does, in social science renditions. The experience of participants
as it is articulated in their own words not only makes for interesting reading but also opens an engaging lens through which the reader can better
understand movement politics. The passion and insight expressed by
movement participants is key to understanding why people joined, stayed
in, and drifted away from the movement at various points in its history;
they convey how it felt and what it meant to participate in these events that
changed Mexico's history.[6] The story that unfolds in the following pages is
the result of my effort to combine their various perspectives.

Historical interpretation can entail a significant degree of controversy
and contention. The reader will notice that rather than write this history
in a single voice, I have often opted to present in the form of conversation
or debate "what really happened." At other times, because of the nature of
the data, the logic, or even admittedly simply my own intuition, I move
more aggressively and take a strong interpretive position. I advise the
reader of such interpretive interventions, particularly when strong analyses
are presented.

In this book I seek to convey what I have termed "the experience of
movement"—that is, the phenomenology of being in the movement as
seen from a variety of perspectives, from those of the rank-and-file mem-

---

reversed. The action of a group and the level of the system which it affects must become the
basis for analyzing the composition of a social condition, which may facilitate the formation
of conflictual actors" (48). It is also consistent with Piven and Cloward's "judgment that *the
most useful way to think about the effectiveness of protest is to examine the disruptive effects on institutions of different forms of mass defiance and then to examine the political reverberations of those disruptions*" (1979, 24; emphasis in the original).

6. While writing this book, I often pondered a remark made by that great teacher of
comparative mythology Joseph Campbell (1988) that I interpreted as both warning and suggestion: "What we're learning . . . is not the wisdom of life. We're learning technologies,
we're getting information. There's a curious reluctance on the part of faculties to indicate the
life values of their subjects" (9). Wisdom means to me deep insight. I am attracted to social
movements because they have a habit of offering such insights both to participants and those
who study them. How could it be otherwise? Social movements are about challenging power,
introducing new normative visions and conceptualizations. In their doing so, they encourage
us to imagine the possible—not only utopic visions but also strategies for making headway
toward them.

bers to those of top leadership. This experience of movement is extremely varied both over time, as the movements went through various stages from emergence to decline, and as dictated by one's particular position within it. It is extremely important to convey both the headiness generated by active participation in a particularly dynamic type of public life as well as the factionalism, bossism, and clientelism within Mexican urban popular movement organizations. The story that unfolds in the following pages is the result of my effort to combine these various perspectives. This ethnographic orientation is combined with a more traditional political science power analysis that focuses on social movements as pressure groups that influence policy in both style and outcome. This analysis draws from a review of the policy record as well as the interpretations of movement participants and state actors.

This method is applied to two of the most important urban popular movement organizations of the 1970s–1990s: the CDP in Durango and the AB in Mexico City, neither of which have received the kind of detailed analytical treatment they deserve. By exploring them in depth, this study also aspires to make a contribution to the growing and rich literature on Mexico's regional histories. The two case studies show that movement strength is due to successful institution building within movements simultaneous to continued social mobilization, skillful negotiation with elites, taking advantage of political opportunities, and the types of strategies movements design to exploit these opportunities.

Assessing the Importance of Social Movements

From a political science perspective, the most important questions are the most difficult to answer: Did the movements affect power relations and policy outcomes? If so, how did they do it and why were their achievements limited? The challenge of isolating and assessing the causal influences of social movements is an old and contentious issue. As expressed in one literature review, "The interest of many scholars in social movements stems from their belief that movements represent an important force for social change. Yet demonstrating the independent effect of collective action on social change is difficult" (McAdam, McCarthy, and Zald, 1988, 727). Perhaps in part because of this very difficulty, few analysts have been willing to tackle the problem of assessing the systemic political implications of Latin American social movements. Clearly, "part of the problem lies in conceptualizing 'effects' or 'impact' of movements on state institutions given the principle of multiple causality" (Street 1989, 7). Assessing the independent causal weight of social movements in a cycle of protest that by definition involves many crucial individuals, groups, movements, political parties, state institutions, and international actors—while most certainly difficult—is not insurmountable. Well-argued and empirically supported interpretations are both possible and desirable, and my goal in this book is to offer them.

Social movements often have emancipatory revolutionary goals. Sometimes, movements are judged to be failures because they fail to achieve these goals. While movements usually fail to achieve their more far reaching goals, limiting their historical importance on this basis is not only a disservice to their creativity and bravery—often in the face of fantastic odds—but also bad history. Manuel Castells, in his influential work on urban social movements, is representative of a wide body of opinion among sympathetic movement analysts in the sociological tradition when he responds to this problem:

> [The importance of urban social movements] is not limited to their great victories, which, alone, would be exceptional, but to the impact they had, even in defeat. Their lasting effects are present in the breaches produced in the dominant logic, in the compromises reached with the institutions, in the changing cultural forms of the city, in the collective memory of the neighborhoods, and, ultimately, in the continuing social debate about what the city should be. (1983, 71–72)

Learning more about how social movements have influenced political outcomes contributes to reducing the wide gap in our understanding of Latin America. "Our current knowledge of Latin America is painfully inadequate and centered primarily on elite concerns and perspectives. As a consequence, we know much more about state structures, political parties, and interest groups than about the lives and preoccupations of 'popular groups'" (Eckstein 1989a, 2). From the political science perspective, we should be troubled by how relatively little we know about these movements, despite their importance in both the historical trajectories and the contemporary developments of Latin America. The high regard we give to

state structures, political parties, and elite groups is warranted. But the lack
of attention to popular movements is not.

The Study of Mexico's Urban Poor

Massive rural-to-urban migration in Latin America during the 1960s and
1970s meant that both those who feared and those who hoped to find revolutionary potential among the urban poor were motivated to explore this
possibility. Influential social scientists such as Karl Deutsch (1961) and
James Coleman (1960) predicted that this sudden migration carried with it
the very real possibility that these "peasants in cities" might well shed their
rural conservatism for the new dress of political mobilization. Later in the
decade, Samuel Huntington warned that the most likely source of political
destabilization in Latin American cities surely was to be found among the
urban poor: "On the surface, the most promising source of urban revolt is
clearly the slums and shantytowns produced by the influx of the rural
poor. . . . At some point, the slums of Rio and Lima . . . like those of
Harlem and Watts, are likely to be swept by social violence, as the children
of the city demand the rewards of the city" (1968, 283, cited in Handelman
1975, 37). During the 1970s, Fagen and Tuohy (1972), Cornelius (1975),
Montaño (1976), Eckstein (1977b), and Lomnitz (1977) all undertook
extensive empirical investigations and found the concerns expressed by
earlier social scientists to be unfounded.[7]

7. Books containing broadly similar conclusions regarding the capacity of state regimes
to effectively guard against the revolutionary potential of urban shanties were undertaken in
a number of Latin American countries. Perlman 1976 on Brazil and Collier 1976 on Peru are
two of the most widely read. Perlman makes explicit that she began her fieldwork in the early
1960s very much aware of the "revolutionary expectations" that many have for the urban
poor. "The long-awaited 'revolution' arrived on April 1, 1964—not from the left as anticipated, but from the right in the form of a military coup" (xvi). Many of the urban poor
shocked the world by not only failing to resist the coup, but also "[descending] from their
hillsides and [marching] alongside businessmen and housewives in support of law and order,
tradition, family, and private property" (ibid.). In Eckstein and the majority of other influential 1970s studies on the urban poor, the term *social movement* does not appear. Perlman
(1976) notes, "The most important political organization in the favela is the Residents' Association" (163). As Eckstein (1977a) and Cornelius (1975) report for Mexico, these organizations typified clientilist patterns of interest bargaining, with access to state elites and the ability to extract resources key to the local political boss's power. The major exceptions appear in
reference to Chile and Cuba, where large sectors of the urban poor participated in radical
politics in the 1960s and early 1970s. On Chile, see Castells 1972 and Vanderschueren 1971a,
1971b. On Cuba, see Zeitlin 1970 and Fagen 1969.

While the 1970s literature addressing the politics of the urban poor is not uniform, prevailing images exist. For Mexico, authors write of a national corporatist regime that is capable of incorporating rural to urban migration so as to effectively prevent system-threatening behavior. The image that emerges from these studies is that of an urban poor conforming to the demands of national regimes. Wayne Cornelius (1972), with reference to not merely the Mexican urban poor but Latin America more generally, describes new arrivals to urban settings as fundamentally conservative, too fearful to risk dissent. Larissa Lomnitz finds a "nearly complete lack of influence and control over urban and national institutions" (1977, 181). While there is some participation, is—to use Lomintz's term—almost entirely "passive." There is no mention whatsoever of opposition politics.

Evelyn Stevens wrote an influential study of three major protest movements in Mexico from the late 1950s to the late 1960s. She concluded that state responses to these protest movements resulted in a strengthening of Mexico's authoritarian regime (1974, 13).[8] Not only were "decision makers . . . adamantly opposed to making any accommodation with the protesters which would have required even minimal modification of their preferred policies" (258): they were able to get away with it. As Stevens goes on to say, "Not only that, but they made plain their refusal even to concede that the protesters had any right to present demands and to be given an explanation as to why the demands would not be granted" (ibid.).

During the 1970s, Eckstein aimed to demonstrate "how [urban poor] residents in newly formed low-income neighborhoods become associated with groups which, in effect, extend the regime's legitimacy where political order had not previously existed" (1977b, 24). Opposition parties emerging from the 1970s *apertura democrática* (democratic opening) strengthen Mexican authoritarianism by creating the illusion of democracy without

---

8. Stevens details three case studies: the railroad strikes of 1958–59, the doctors' strikes of 1964–65, and the student strikes of 1968, and discusses the failure of each to achieve progress toward any fundamental goals. Organizers were blacklisted, jailed, and exiled. Laws that had been challenged as undemocratic or inappropriate in a Mexican republic committed to the revolutionary ideals of social justice were not only not repealed, but also sometimes strengthened. A key example is the Law of Social Dissolution, which provided for severe prison terms for persons convicted of promoting ideas deemed to "disturb the public order or affect the sovereignty of the Mexican State." The repeal of this law was one of the demands listed in the student's original six-point petition. While the law was repealed in 1969, a subsequent change in the Penal Code reinstated all the infractions and increased the penalties (253–54).

providing the substance. The political importance of regional variation is dismissed, for all local politics is "subordinated to the President through his control over patronage, political recruitment, and budgetary allotments" (24). Almost all "groups" are affiliated with the PRI, "and even the nominally independent ones are subject to PRI and government influence because the leaders overtly or covertly associate with PRI or government groups or persons associated with such groups" (27). Even nominally independent groups are encouraged to show their support for the regime at public events, as there are simply no other avenues to power and to the distribution of public goods and services. Patronage directed at the urban poor unambiguously strengthens the regime, and poor residents have no alternative but to associate themselves with PRI-affiliated political entrepreneurs.

The conclusions reached by Wayne Cornelius, on the basis of fieldwork done about the same time and also in the Mexico City area, are, in broad outline, quite similar. Cornelius interviewed community leaders and was told that "if a need of their community were particularly acute and the government had ignored community petitions regarding the need, they would try to organize a protest demonstration outside the office of some high-ranking government functionary; but none were able to document an instance in which this kind of action was actually taken" (1974, 1139). Cornelius documents that this should come as no surprise, because the majority of new urban migrants believed that no good could come from such efforts.

Montaño's (1976) study of Mexico's urban poor has a somewhat different cast. While he encountered an urban poor made up of recent migrants who, for the most part, were effectively incorporated into the inclusionary political regime, he chronicles some independent opposition, particularly composed of alliances between the urban poor, student movements, and the progressive wing of the Catholic Church. He quotes a federal deputy of the PRI from Nezahualcóytol in the Mexico City area who suggests that progressive Christian leaders were influencing an independent politics among at least some small sectors of the urban poor:

> These Jesuits that publish that small paper are not really priests, they are looking for and causing problems, using their influence with the people to try to turn the people against the government. As you can imagine, this is against the law and we are not inclined to accept this, if they want to cause problems we are going to teach them a lesson real soon. I know that the people are extremely

angry at the behavior of these so-called priests, especially now
that "el señor Presidente" has given us water, electricity, paving,
which furthermore, we could lose [if this kind of insubordinate
activity does not cease]. (102)

Despite such examples, Montaño concludes that these instances of
rebellion remain local, affecting only a relatively small number of people.
He stresses that independent organizations, whether social movements or
oppositional political parties, play no decisive role in the lives of the overwhelming majority of the urban poor. When resistance exists, it is almost
always the result of an independent leader or small number of leaders acting on local issues (104). He concludes, on the basis of survey data, that the
urban poor tend to view all politicians in negative terms, which, he argues,
results far more often in fatalism than in rebellious acts (154). Clearly,
Montaño is not describing any kind of widespread culture of resistance or
systemic threat, although he does devote an entire chapter to some "radicalized exceptions." He focuses on two *colonias* (neighborhoods), Colonia
Pancho Villa in the state of Chihuahua and the Colonia Rubén Jaramillo
on the periphery of Cuernavaca (which is close to Mexico City), both
being well-known examples of what would soon become identified as the
national urban popular movement.

By the 1980s, the term *quiescence* was no longer adequate to describe the
politics of the urban poor as new urban popular movement organizations
emerged and preexisting organizations grew, as favorable changes in the
structure of political opportunities were seized. Many popular movement
participants had previous experience with the PRI and were drawn to independent movement organizations because of the PRI's failure to adequately
respond to their needs (Bolos 1995, 241).[9] Movement politics gave way to

9. In June 1994, a three-day seminar titled "Social Actors and Urban Demands" was held
at the Universidad Iberoamericana in Mexico City. Representatives of Mexico City's urban
popular movement, including what are widely considered to have been the three most important urban popular movement organizations in the Mexico City area—the Assembly of
Neighborhoods (AB), the Union of Popular Neighborhoods (UCP), and the Popular Revolutionary Union Emiliano Zapata (UPREZ)—were all present. Also attending were representatives of the most important NGOs working with the urban popular movement, such as Casa y
Ciudad and the Centro Operacional de Vivienda y Poblamiento (Operational Center of
Housing and Population). The entire three-day seminar was taped; the proceedings were
then transcribed and assembled in book form under the coordination of Silvia Bolos (1995). I
refer to the book frequently because it supports and, "in the public record," expands on many
of the claims I make on the basis of observations and confidential interviews.

opposition parties that emerged at the end of the 1980s and that relied heavily on the urban poor vote. As momentous as these changes have been, it is important to point out that the majority of the Mexican urban poor did not actively participate in the 1979–89 heyday of the urban popular movement. What does emerge is the presence of an urban popular movement that shaped the consciousness and political activity of millions of poor people in many cities across the nation and that were crucial to the events of 1988 and to the party system that took shape in subsequent years.

Organization of the Book

In Chapter 1, I consider the theoretical debates that are pertinent to the key questions of this study, introducing the assumptions, perceptions, and intuitions that guide the subsequent historical account. My major theoretical claim is that social movement theory benefits greatly from a close relationship with the actual experience of social movement history. I construct theory from the many disparate elements that contribute to movement existence, from birth to decline. At a minimum, theory must be developed with a close eye on the structure of political opportunities that history provides the movement, the strategy developed to exploit these opportunities, the experience from the perceptions of differently situated participants both within and outside the movement, and the changes in these variables over time. Authentic social movements, while often including members of the elite, grow from the bottom up. So should the theory that seeks to illuminate them.

Chapter 2 provides a historical overview of Mexico from the Spanish conquest to 1988, focusing on those events, ideas, and institutions that have had the most impact on urban popular movements. I analyze in depth the period between 1979 and 1988, when mass mobilization and radical politics put pressure on the regime to reform specific policies and move toward democratization. The year 1979 saw coalition politics being developed by sector: teachers, peasants, and the urban poor created national coordinating bodies. These instilled and symbolized a period of dynamic social movement activity in Mexico, culminating in the important role played by movements in the dramatic presidential elections of 1988.

In Chapter 3, I explore the decline of the protest cycle from 1988 to 1994. The lessening of activity is understood in relation to interacting factors: a decrease in the elite splits that predominated during the earlier protest cycle; a mitigation of the economic crisis that had racked the nation; an increase in policies implemented by the Salinas administration, designed in part to roll back multisectoral movement solidarity; and a related shift in the political-opportunity structure to favor party involvement by key movement players. Throughout this analysis, the focus remains on the politics of the urban poor in relation to other key actors, including civil society, political parties, and the state.

In Chapter 4, I narrate the history of the CDP in Durango, from its Maoist origins in the late 1960s to the successful election of the CDP candidate to the Municipal presidency of 1992–95. Chapter 5 tells the story of the AB of Mexico City, a movement whose roots are in the 1985 Mexico City earthquake and that grows to hold key administrative and PRD party offices in the capital. Its history is contrasted to that of the CDP in Durango.

In Chapter 6, I take a focused look at the 1988–91 period, an extremely important chapter in Mexico's long democratic transition. I examines in detail the split between the urban popular movements that sided with Cuauhtémoc Cárdenas and the PRD and those who incorporated into the PT and openly embraced the Programa Nacional de Solidaridad (National Solidarity Program [PRONASOL]). PRONASOL was a high-profile and controversial antipoverty program initiated by President Carlos Salinas de Gortari in 1989, designed at least in part to split the Left and undermine its appeal among the electorate. The AB and the CDP took opposite positions in what became the most consequential and highly publicized debate between urban popular movement organizations in the 1988–91 period. Because the two organizations are leaders within their respective camps, contrasting their differences and the political outcomes of their strategies provides a fruitful vantage point from which to examine the role of Solidarity in exacerbating divisions within the Mexican Left. It also presents an important window through which to view the changing relationships between the state and popular movements during the Salinas administration (1988–94) in comparison to the administration of Miguel de la Madrid Hurtado (1982–88). This chapter ends the book with reflections on the immensely complex question of what happens when a movement culture is largely disbanded because of entry into party politics during a democratic transition.

ONE

Theory and Method for a Phenomenological and Institutional Study of Social Movements

La teoría no es más que una caja de herramientas: tú sacas la que te sirve y dejas el resto.
[Theory is nothing more than a toolbox: you take what serves you and leave the rest.]
—BENJAMÍN ARDITI

Combining the political process model with the interdisciplinary approach known as New Social Movement theory greatly enhances our understanding of social change organizations. The political process model, strongly identified with traditional political science analysis, especially in the United States, focuses on the power of social movements to alter both the content and the process of public policy. This permits an assessment of their capacity to effectively exploit available political opportunities. Joining this approach to New Social Movement theory, developed largely in Europe, incorporates the cultural meaning and workings of social movements, traditionally the province of cultural anthropology in the United States. My particular synthesis of these approaches is designed to convey the lived experience of the participants, what I refer to as the phenomenology of movement.

This phenomenology of movement is illustrated in part by the direct testimony of those who experienced the movement firsthand: movement participants and those close to the movement, including its adversaries. Changes in institutional behavior are demonstrated through use of the classic methods of political science, including archival research of the public record and, in the present cases, direct observation over a ten-year period. The experience of movement and the institutional changes it creates are deeply related: when people experience a movement as working well and are hopeful about its possibilities, it is most likely to achieve the greatest changes in public policy. In some cases, these changes can extend to replacing regimes, as has occurred all over the world in the later part of the twentieth century, with minimally defined democratic regimes emerging from authoritarian regimes of the Left and Right.

In the first section of this chapter I summarize the field experiences that convinced me to use a synthetic approach incorporating both political science and ethnography. This is followed by two other key orientations of my research: the political process approach and a focus on relationships. Next I discuss how best to define social movements, so that we can clearly demarcate the subject. The subsequent section elaborates the ideas of political culture. Over the course of my fieldwork a limited set of key categories emerged as most critical, and the remainder of the chapter is organized around these: repression and co-optation, autonomy, internal organization, and alliances.

Developing a Syncretic Model

Do what you can to give the reader an opportunity to peer into the day-to-day practices of Mexican urban popular movements. Provide words that will encourage him or her to imagine participating in a politics of transformation. This self-imposed directive both motivated and intimidated me throughout my research and writing. How could I achieve this goal given that my education in political science had trained me to define the political in terms of institutional processes, measured in terms of institutional or policy outcomes? The underlying assumptions were that (1) certainty should be and could be measured regarding the causal weight of the relationship between powerful actors in civil society and the state and (2) if it could not be, then in most cases it should be abandoned, because to do otherwise was to enter into the forbidden territory of the "subjective."

While some social scientists may have trouble finding positive value in the currency of "subjective experience," readers whose passions go first to understanding individual experience may find themselves stretching to appreciate how individual experience "affected" the neoliberal project, the party system, and other institutional reforms. Those most interested in power as defined by institutional change may find some relief in the focus on social movement organizations that are politically significant in a particular sense: they changed institutional and policy politics at both the regional and the national levels.[1] Further, the historical chapters of this book

1. This contrasts with the definition of politically relevant social movements introduced by Offe (1985). Offe and many other New Social Movement theorists locate relevance more in the transformative potential of social movements, while I locate it more in changes realized in institutions and policy.

remain true to traditional social science by making the best possible case for causal connection. However, I no longer feel so tightly limited to always having to draw measurable connections. Sometimes one must speculate on the connections or simply leave them as questions to be pondered or possibly to be studied more systematically later.

The movement experience, perhaps especially during a period of ascendancy, profoundly alters the consciousness of those who live it, whether at the level of leaders, of neighborhood activist, or of scholarly observer. The opening line of Philip Oxhorn's engaging study of popular movements in Chile reads, "It is impossible to study the urban poor without becoming emotionally attached to their cause (1995, ix). It has certainly been true in my case. I would add that it was impossible for me to study urban poor politics without becoming convinced of the importance of not losing the magic in the telling of the story by overemphasizing classic social science concerns (why and so what) to the exclusion of the experience. Some refer to this as movement culture; I call it the phenomenology of the movement.

My use of the term *phenomenology* is really quite simple. Inclusion of the phenomenological means that an effort is made to represent or describe people's experience and assumes a sincere effort to be faithful to the quality of that experience. For the past twenty years or so a debate has raged, perhaps most notably in cultural anthropology, between those who argue for the superiority of oral history and those who prefer a more objective social science interpretation. My effort is to bridge these points of view by combining them.[2]

In my conversations with movement participants and those journalists, scholars, politicians, and administrators who have interacted closely with them, I have been struck by how little political action or interpretation takes place solely on the basis of textual analysis. Rather, textual analysis is understood and made sense of through images that serve as the primary referents in the mind. Even the most hardened empiricist will present statistical evidence to create a persuasive image. Although it is not always recognized, data selection itself is driven by images, both those favored and those deemed inferior, flawed, or somehow undesirable. I am not implying or defending the notion of an unmediated human observation of objective

2. The introduction of phenomenological sensibilities has made inroads in a number of scholarly fields in which the pursuit of "objective" scientific understandings was once dominant if not hegemonic. In the words of one of archetypal psychology's most important architects, James Hillman, "I'm simply following the imagistic, the phenomenological way: take a thing for what it is and let it talk" (1983, 14).

reality. Rather, the theoretical suggestion is to encourage a method that allows the phenomenon to speak in its varied voices and meanings, without undue disciplinary constraints. *Methodological success depends more on close listening by the investigator than it does on sophisticated empirical methods.* I have found that to allow the people of the movements to express a diversity of images, variable meanings, and contrasting interpretations requires a disciplined resistance to the dictate of reporting the objective, reproducible, verifiable truth. In some places, I come down hard on a particular interpretation; in others, I am in agreement with a particular organizational or individual's perspective; in others, in sharp disagreement. I have attempted to articulate why this is so and what political, theoretical, or historical imperative(s) drive me to take particular stands. At other times, I refuse to take a particular position but, rather, endeavor to tell the story from a variety of directions and subject positioning, demonstrating the complexity of the act or historical period.

The great diversity of movement experience is not something that can be kept neat and tidy via theory. I have cast the net widely to include sympathizers of similar and diverse class origins, other similar or relevant movements, political parties, and state actors. Other writers might focus on actors not given detailed empirical attention here: print and electronic media, intellectuals, and domestic and international nongovernmental organizations (NGOs). My choice, however, was influenced by the relationships that were given the most importance by movement actors themselves, in part as expressed by the frequency of interactions I observed.

The ethnographic components of the present study explore what the experience of urban popular movements has meant to members and those close to them, whether allies or foes. This material is presented traditionally, through interview quotes and assessments derived from close observation and participation. Except in rare circumstances in which the informant's identity is important and permission was granted to cite names, those who are quoted remain anonymous. My routine promise of confidentiality at the outset of the interview was particularly important, as I spoke with many participants with clandestine backgrounds and met with state actors operating in an authoritarian political setting. Moreover, leaking comments about strategically important issues—at least in some instances—clearly risked political disadvantage. I also found, through some trial and error, that if a respondent were assured that a conversation would not come back to haunt him or her, a more honest and deeply felt rendition of the truth would be forthcoming.

Social movement scholars have long debated the possibility of integrating the more mechanistic approaches associated with the "United States" school of Resource Mobilization (RM) theory—of which the political process approach is an outgrowth—and the "European" school of New Social Movement theory.[3] Pessimists argued against the likelihood of being able to synthesize the utilitarian interest oriented approaches of RM with the value-centered identity perspective of what is called New Social Movement theory.[4] My position is that since social movements combine both identity and utilitarian logics, scholarship must strive to interpret how they intersect and interrelate.

An example is found in the issue of solidarity between movement participants. Those employing the political process approach often recognize solidarity, but it can be discussed in rather antiseptic terms, as a movement resource. What is oftentimes missing is a nuanced attention that conveys the experience of this solidarity. What is solidarity, in addition to our observation of its functional utility to the power of movements? Why is solidarity so prized by movement participants, often enabling people to overcome the obstacles to participation? What difference does it make to a middle-aged, low-income woman living in a shantytown if she refers to her neighbor as *señora* or *compañera?* Exploring the experience and consciousness of the creation of community not only deepens our appreciation for the experience of movements; it also contributes to our analytical understanding of how this resource is generated and its power implications. As Jaime Rello of the Unión Popular Revolucionaria Emiliano Zapata (Popular Revolutionary Union Emiliano Zapata [UPREZ]) argued, the project may be housing, but the process is a school of community building and solidarity.[5] To assess the movement and its organizations only in terms of the houses constructed and changes in government policy is to miss a fundamental dimension (Bolos 1995, 301).

3. Proponents of Resource Mobilization theory contend that available resources and the ways they are employed are absolutely indispensable explaining the relative degrees of success and failure of particular movements or movement organizations. For social movements, the most important resources enable them to disrupt established elite practices and force concessions. Popular movements use a number of tactics, including sit-ins, office takeovers, boycotts, mass demonstrations, threats of or actual use of violence, and public embarrassments to disrupt business as usual. See McCarthy and Zald 1977 and Garner and Zald 1985.

4. For examples of such arguments, see the work of Cohen (1985), writing from a New Social Movement perspective, and of Jenkins (1983), from an RM perspective.

5. UPREZ is an important urban popular movement organization operating in and around Mexico City.

The Left in Mexico and elsewhere tends to emphasize the importance of shifting from individual needs to the collective, and the urban popular movement is certainly no exception. The goal of this study is to understand this process, both as a movement resource and as experience. As the study covers the period of movement emergence in the 1970s through to its decline in the 1990s, we can witness the peaks and valleys of this process. As noted by Elías López of UPREZ, the movement did not simply encourage the collective; it purposely engaged in institutional practices that addressed individual rights and obligations more democratically than did the dominant culture. UPREZ, like many popular movement organizations, created judicial commissions empowered to settle individual problems, including land tenure and boundary disputes, youth gangs, and matrimonial discord (cited in Bolos 1995, 284).

Solidarity at all levels of relationship in an organization played tremendously important roles in the power of both the CDP of Durango and the AB of Mexico City. As leadership in both organizations was motivated by changing political opportunities to increasingly identify with political parties, experiences of solidarity declined markedly, contributing to decline in the organizations. The ensuing alienation has undermined the capacity of party leaders to mobilize their bases, which in turn has had negative implications for both the PRD and the PT.

Ethnography provides the richest mechanism for conveying the experience of movements and their *unique* patterns of subjectivity and the construction of subjects.[6] The ethnographic imagery here derives from hundreds of formal and informal interviews with movement participants at the top-leadership, middle-leadership (*cuadro*), neighborhood-activist, and base levels over the course of a decade.[7] Added to these are my own personal observations of formal and informal decision-making processes and of relationships within specific movement organizations and between them and other movement organizations, political parties, NGOs, state agencies, political officeholders, and the media. Liberal use of ethnographic material guards against an inclination sometimes present in political science: the implicit or explicit assumption that political decisions are

6. Survey data can provide interesting information that is useful in the understanding of political processes. However, survey data is incapable of generating significant insight into the deeper issues of consciousness that subject construction implies.

7. *Base* is the most commonly used term in the Mexican popular movement lexicon to refer to the rank-and-file membership.

made on the basis of rational, objective calculations of narrowly defined interests. I do not share this assumption and, in fact, present empirical evidence to the contrary.

The most exciting challenge posed by the study of Latin American social movements since the 1980s has been how to combine institutional politics with the cultural experience and meanings of the movement.[8] Writing this book has brought me face to face with the immense demands of this effort. My concern has most consistently been to avoid an overly romanticized presentation that falsely celebrates and exaggerates the transformative achievement of Latin American social movements (P. Haber 1996a; 1997a). Social justice concerns demand a recognition that the social movements of the 1980s and 1990s operated during a time of economic crisis and that the implementation of neoliberalism failed to improve the lives of the majority of the hemisphere's people.

The contemporary "boom" in poststructural analyses of capitalism, power, and resistance has stimulated recent thinking on social movements in valuable ways.[9] By refuting determinism and resuscitating agency, the social movement literature has become much more interesting, hopeful, and, I think, accurate. However, there is a tendency to obscure the fact that while the agency of resistance certainly affects the actualized contours of capitalism and power relationships, the poor are still the poor. Power, while being more complicated and diffuse than the structural analyses of the past suggested, is still experienced as exploitation, domination, and repression by many peasants, shantytown dwellers, and low-paid workers. In fact, despite democratization and the growing cornucopia of multiplying vibrant identities, for many the situation is getting worse. Failure to acknowledge this has in many instances resulted in a misguided celebratory tone in much of the New Social Movement research, doing a disservice to the movements themselves and to our collective effort as scholars to ascribe historical significance to them.[10]

Some perspectives on the urban popular movement either do not make their way onto the following pages or remain on the periphery. Scholarly

8. Sonia Alvarez and Arturo Escobar (1992) eloquently express this challenge in the introductory essay to the first of their two edited volumes on Latin American social movements.

9. For a good introduction to critical social theory, see Agger 1998.

10. Much of the high-quality analysis of the new democracies in Latin America confirms that democratic practices do not characterize the lives of the region's poor majorities. See, for example, Oxhorn and Ducatenzeiler 1998 and Aguero and Stark 1998.

treatments by others whose intellectual home base is where I only attempt to visit (the sociological, economic, geographic, or artistic) would no doubt deliver a contrasting phenomenological treatment. While I made a conscious effort to expand the boundaries of my training as an empirical political scientist, clearly this bias remains and deeply influences the telling of the story in subsequent chapters.

The practice of recounting Latin American case studies by incorporating consciousness and identity into the definition of the political without losing sight of the institutional is gaining momentum. This is true for efforts such as mine on a relatively established category (urban poor, labor, peasantry, elites) as well as for those telling the stories of marginalized minorities (gays, lesbians, environmentalists, feminists, indigenous peoples, Pagans, and Protestants, among others).

The Political Process Approach

This analysis is informed by a theoretical orientation known as the political process approach, which is designed to reveal the political importance of social movements and which makes a number of important contributions to theory and method that are embraced in this study. I also identify the limitations of this approach that the present study attempts to address.[11]

The political process approach encourages the study of complex movement networks over time.[12] Snapshot analyses of dramatic episodes in a

11. In his study of the U.S. civil rights movement, Doug McAdam's (1982) use of the phrase "political process model," which he took from a 1975 article by Rule and Tilly, touched off its widespread usage. For other early works on this approach, see Eisinger 1973; Piven and Cloward 1979; and Tilly 1978. Elements that I am grouping together under the political process model other scholars differentiate. For example, Mueller (1992, 9) refers to Piven and Cloward's approach as "break-down theory" and to Tilly's as "polity model." Certainly differences exist between these authors; see, for example, Piven and Cloward's (1992) criticism of the work of Tilly and his associates. However, I choose to group them together because they all focus on the relationships of conflict and alliance between social movements and other political actors. In the 1980s and 1990s, Sidney Tarrow, perhaps more than anyone else, developed and promoted the approach as "a broad framework for understanding the social movements, protest cycles and revolutions that began in the West and spread around the world over the past two centuries" (1994, 2). While Tarrow once spoke in terms of a formal model (1988, 428), by 1994 he was explicitly rejecting this, which he determined to "have added more heat than light to this area of study" (1994, 2).

12. Tarrow includes longevity as a defining characteristic of the social movements: "Long before there were organized movements, there were riots, rebellions and general turbulence. It is only by sustaining collective action against antagonists that a contentious episode becomes a social movement" (1994, 5).

movement's history are discouraged, and longitudinal studies are prized; ideally, the analysis covers the entire life of a movement. Such a history can be seen through the life cycle metaphor: from the movement's birth, through its formative years, to middle age, old age, and death. This approach stresses that "[m]ediating between opportunity and action are people and the subjective meanings they attach to their situations" (McAdam 1982, 48). In other words, political consciousness and decision making are highlighted and structural determinism is deemphasized, although this does not suggest ignoring environments in which movements exist. Piven and Cloward (1979), for example, emphasize the structural socioeconomic shifts represented by industrialization and massive rural-to-urban, south-to-north immigration for the emergence and sustainability of the U.S. civil rights movement. However while structure may enable or discourage movement life, it does not determine outcomes.

Consistent with this approach, assessing a movement's impact on political institutions and policy must be understood in relation to the mobilization of resources by key actors (movements, parties, and state agencies), as understood by RM theory. Resources include money, repression, mass mobilizations designed to disrupt business as usual, values and ideals that legitimate those who promote them as well as discredit those who do not, electoral skills, media access, efficacious internal organization, and relationships with state actors. The power of these resources is determined not only by their possession but also in the strategic ways they are used. One of the key puzzles in the study of social movements is how they are able to exist in hostile environments. Part of the answer is found in how good their members are at developing strategies that legitimate them and change conditions for others.

Considerable care to avoid applying one's interpretations onto movement outcomes characterizes the use of the political process approach by emotionally and politically committed authors. This has been perhaps most forcefully addressed by Piven and Cloward, who in their pathbreaking book, *Poor People's Movements* (1979), persuasively critiqued those who faulted movements for not living up to the ideals of the analyst. From my perspective, the analyst's primary task is, rather than defining the "objective" political opportunity structure, to determine the various movement perspectives and to describe and interpret their implications. It is also crucial that the analyst be explicit about the basis of any critique. Does it reflect the author's perspective of what goals should have been pursued? Or is it taken from the perspective of contending positions within the movement? This can become enormously complicated if the author is also a movement participant.

Two concepts at the heart of the political process approach are *political opportunity structure* and *cycles of protest*. The political opportunity structure helps to explain how collective action overcomes the long list of constraints on movement power such as the free-rider problem, a relative lack of key resources vis-à-vis opponents, the absence of political participation as a valued activity in civil society, repression, and so on.[13] The puzzle of movements is not so much why they fail but how they manage to emerge, sustain themselves, and influence political outcomes in what are very often extremely hostile environments.

The definition of political opportunity structures is of course also the subject of intense debate, and these structures change over time, often as a result of collective action itself. "Political opportunity structure can help to understand variations in the strategies, structures, and outcomes of similar movements that arise in different places" (Tarrow 1988, 430). However, as Cloward and Piven note, with reference to what they term the problem of "indeterminacy," history reminds us that "objective" structures of opportunity do not determine movement behaviors (1979, 654; 1989). It is important to discern distinctions in the opportunity structure. For example, even different organizations within the same social movement sector often face quite distinct opportunity structures. In the two case studies considered here, the differences in their opportunity structures help to explain the variations in their strategies and their relative successes.

Determining how best to exploit political opportunities is at the core of movement strategy. Strategic decisions are often characterized by strong disagreements, which highlights the importance of decision making that governs dispute resolution. From my perspective, the study of social movements would profit from increased attention to the particulars of movement strategy, analysis of attempts to seize and expand these opportunities, and the role of strategy in mobilizing resources to exploit opportunities. Given the day-to-day importance of strategy, it is striking that it does not gain more nuanced and detailed attention in even many empirically based studies. Movement theory is furthered by debates between

13. The term "structure of political opportunities" was first used by Eisinger (1973) and its meaning has remained largely unchanged since. It has been succinctly defined by Brockett to be "the configuration of forces in a (potential or actual) group's political environment that influences that group's assertion of its political claims" (1991, 254).

scholars and activists over the power and liabilities of particular strategies in varying opportunity structures. Longitudinal studies allow us to observe and analyze these changes, and they suggest possibilities for comparative work.

The key variables of the political opportunity structure that determine opportunities for movement action are degree of openness of the polity and level of repression; stability or instability of political alignments and elite splits; alliance structure; economic performance and the way in which accountability is distributed during times of rapid economic downturns; and the policy-making capacity of the state. As Cook correctly points out, "For dissident movements in authoritarian political systems, the most likely facilitator of political space short of systemic crisis is elite conflict or disunity" (1990, 11).

The concept of cycles of protest is also key. Protest cycles are those times when conditions lead elements of civil society to mobilize in an attempt to realign power relations.[14] These periods are when most change takes place, when interests and demands are redefined, and when the public discourse becomes infused with voices of social groups that under more "normal" conditions are muted or simply silenced. Protest cycles are the antithesis of political silence, or "apathy," as it is misleadingly called.[15]

While the term *cycles of protest* suggests no precise territorial limitation, it clearly implies something beyond an isolated region or population sector. Some periods clearly qualify: that of Europe in 1848, that of the youth movements of the 1960s, and that of the 1980s democratization wave in the Eastern bloc and Latin America. The democratic discourse that generated such enthusiasm in Mexico during the 1980s and 1990s was definitely influenced by events and discourses far beyond its borders.

The political process approach offers a set of analytical concepts that act as effective tools for interpreting the politics of social movements. It orients

14. Tarrow observes that protest cycles occurring since the 1960s in Europe and the United States demonstrate certain key features: heightened conflict, broad sectoral and geographic diffusion, the expansion of the repertoire of contention, the appearance of new movement organizations and the empowerment of old ones, the creation of new 'master frames' linking the actions of disparate groups to one another and intensified interaction between challengers and the state" (1994, 155). The Mexican case is broadly consistent with these characteristics. "Master frames," a concept introduced by Snow and Benford (1992), refers to a movement motif that captures the imagination of dissenters.

15. For a cogent and, in my view, devastating critique of "apathy" as an effective concept for the explanation of political participation or nonparticipation, see Gaventa 1980.

us to the political and institutional histories. It asserts the importance of understanding the political implications of the relationship between movements and other political actors. By emphasizing the making and implementation of political strategy, it stimulates our sensibility that political outcomes are neither inevitable nor derivative of set-in-stone structural forces. The focus on strategy also stimulates the political imagination of the reader, by suggesting possibilities of how things might have gone differently.

The political process approach is also capable of incorporating the Gramscian insight that the struggle for successful transformative change must take place in the battlefield of cultural meaning.[16] Power to maintain the existing order is derived not just from control over the means of production, or from a monopoly over the legitimate use of force, but also from the collective consciousness of a people, from their cultural beliefs and actions. Movement strategy ignores at its peril the cultural terrain, the terrain of consciousness and the common sense of people. For as powerful as ideas can be, at times reaching a stage that Gramsci theorized as one of "ideological hegemony," the fact is that legitimating ideas and common sense are social constructions, and thus must be constantly re-created. This is where the potential for ideological disruption lies, with the making of new cultural understandings and common sense based on a different set of images, conceptions, and values. Certainly, some of the most interesting efforts to probe how movements attempt to "frame the discussion" have been produced by a number of social movement theorists who use an explicitly Gramscian approach.[17]

The political study of social movements is greatly enhanced by extending the analytical lens to encompass the processes by which movements and specific movement actors define what is wrong and why, and what remedies are to be pursued and how. It is crucial to pay attention to the promotion of competing paradigms and to how ideas and actions are

16. The principle referent for Antonio Gramsci is a selective collection from the extensive prison notebooks edited and translated by Hoare and Smith (1971).

17. David Snow and his colleagues (1986) wrote a particularly influential article in which they described the process of issue framing in four stages: bridging, amplification, extension, and transformation. In the first three, the movement links existing understandings, or "frames," to images of change. In the last, the movement actually attempts to reinterpret already existing understandings in a kind of wholesale manner. For other related contributions, see in particular Klandermans 1988, 1992 and Gamson 1988. Gamson (1992a) makes the helpful observation that frames are "a close relative if not a synonym" for what Thomas Kuhn (1962) called paradigms.

disseminated.[18] Overlooking this area of struggle undermines the phenom-enological portrayal of movements as well as the analysis of their political import. The ability or inability of movements to promote cultural dis-courses and images that resonate with what already exists and to link new ideas and images to people's felt grievances and aspirations is an important determinant in how well they will exploit existing political opportunities.[19]

Mobilizing acts are those "words or deeds that further the mobilization process among some set of potential challengers" (Gamson 1992a, 72). Organizing acts are a subset of mobilizing acts in this typology, and they further the ability of the movement's or movement organization's mem-bers to work together. Divesting acts are those mobilizing acts that effec-tively challenge authority in such a way as to encourage dissent. Reframing acts are those that further the adoption of a paradigm of injustice, some-thing that is extremely difficult to achieve. One well-known example of this was the successful adoption of injustice as a frame with which to stim-ulate an energetic multiclass and multiracial demand for challenging the withholding of equal voting rights to black people in the U.S. South. As we will see, this expression of political will and pressure was far more success-ful than the Mexican urban popular movement's framing of increasing poverty and inequity during the 1980s economic crisis.

A key question arises in connection with the changes in political oppor-tunity structure that occurred in Mexico in the late 1980s. From the late 1970s through the election of 1988, the urban popular movement bene-fited from a national cycle of protest in which political opportunities expanded to the advantage of dissenters. In the wake of the 1988 elections, the political opportunity structure shifted to make electoral involvement and party construction more favorable, a shift adequately anticipated by political process approach theory. The consequent shift of urban popular movement actors away from protest contributed to the end of a national cycle of protest. The challenge remains of proposing political meanings for this shift in various locations: for those most closely tied to the movements (top leaders, midlevel leadership [cuadros], the base); for the Mexican

18. Unlike movements in the past, contemporary popular movements in Mexico must now contend with the electronic media, prevalent in rural as well as urban areas as primary sources of political education. As is true in many countries, the electronic media is heavily biased toward status quo positions. For insightful discussions regarding the relationship between the media and social movements, see Gitlan 1980; Kielbowicz and Scherer 1986; and Gamson 1988.

19. Gamson, Fireman, and Rytina's (1982) typology of mobilizing acts is particularly instructive, and I adopt it in the case study chapters.

party system and democratization; and for the neoliberal project initiated in the mid-1980s.

My primary reservation concerning the political process approach is that its institutional and policy emphasis can result in the "experience of movement" being given short shrift. As suggested above, this need not be, given the approach's openness to political consciousness and the importance of political perception in the strategic implementation of normatively ambitious visions that is central to the definition of social movement. My own particular challenge was to combine my training in political science with a subsequent appreciation for and ability to incorporate ethnography.

The political process approach views the political opportunity structure as creating opportunities and setting the limits of movement potential, even though these change as a result of movement actions. The exact degree of flexibility can never be known, even historically (although persuasive counterfactuals can be presented). The use of ethnographic detail in reconstructing key strategic decisions emphasizes that possibilities and limitations are often far from obvious to the actors themselves. The internal politics of social movement organizations is an interplay of diverse and competing perceptions.

Relationships

The study of social movements is largely an examination of relationships, which are primarily of two types. The first type are those between and within the hierarchy of top leadership, midlevel management, and the rank and file in the movement itself. The second set are relationships that movement entities form with others: relationships between organizations of the same identity (within, for example, the peasantry or the feminist movement); between different social movements (for example, autonomous peasant leagues); and between movements and political parties, the state, NGOs (that provide funding, ideas, and training), and international institutions of all sorts.

My underlying perspective holds that relationships are the key to the political experience of movements.[20] The rubric of *relationship* allows for

20. Taking a cue from the physicist Werner Heisenberg, "Modern science classifies the world . . . not into different groups of objects but into different groups of connections. . . . The world thus appears to be a complicated tissue of events, in which connections of different kinds alternate or overlap or combine and thereby determine the texture of the whole" (quoted by Lawrence LeShan in "How Can you Tell a Physicist from a Mystic?" *Intellectual Digest*, February 1972).

the integrated consideration of a number of concepts that have deservedly found a central location in social movement theory: repression, autonomy, alliances, and internal decision-making processes. This emphasis on relationships as an organizing principle here requires that they be well mapped, that their stories capture the complexity and often subtle nuances of interactions, and that their political interpretation relay both what they meant for the actors themselves and for politics more generally. Ethnographic data allows the reader to better appreciate how these relationships were experienced, how this experience contributed to outcomes, and how the relationships are detailed and "measured" with reference to policy and institutional outcomes.

Relationships are at the heart of any analysis of politics. Even authors whose theoretical perspective prioritizes shifting structures and forces that eclipse individual agency are describing relationships. Much of what I have learned about the importance of relationships stems from my own political experiences in the United States; teaching the politics of dissent to university students; and, last but not least, engaging in fieldwork in Mexico, where participants consistently described their experience and the power of their movement in relational terms.[21]

The choice to use relationship as the archetypal motif of this study also derives from my conviction that considerations of theory and method should be directed, at least in part, by concern over how the resulting discourse affects the intended audience. The intention of this book is to communicate with existing and potential students of social movements and of Mexico. Since relationship is at the center of most of our political, love, and work lives, it is my hope that using relationships as a way of organizing material and suggesting meaning will position the story in such a way as to resonate with the already developed sensibilities of most readers.

Further, I chose this approach because it underlies a basic assumption I entertain regarding theory and method. So much of the current debates over social movement theory and method, and searches for the new revelatory paradigm, are misguided, because they assume that the goal is to find the ideal cognitive map. The fallacy of this approach is not that it is

21. During the 1990s I was involved in the creation of a political party in the United States called the New Party, which was focused on building relationships (P. Haber 1999). The ability to develop strong internal relationships, build relational alliances with others, and prevail in relational engagements with political adversaries was in part the measure of the New Party's political legitimacy. In 2003, I worked as a lobbyist for higher education. This experience reinforced my conviction concerning the importance of relationships.

driven by an overly ambitious vision of how to deepen our knowledge, but rather that there is the notion that theory building is the key to understanding the complexity of social movements. I believe that the potential of social movement scholarship would be enhanced if we were to value more the relationships between and with those who do this special form of collective action. After all, the best work comes from those who invest their hearts and souls, as well as their analytical minds, in the work.[22]

The Thorny, Necessary Process of Definition

The definition of *social movement*, especially when it comes to the distinction between traditional and "new" movements, has been a major preoccupation of scholars from the 1980s to the present.[23] While I do not share the desire of some for a single definition, or am concerned about the absence of a comprehensive theory of Latin American social movements that can serve as the basis for comparative analysis, I fully concur that studies should define their terms and then use them consistently.

The political practice of movements is dramatically distinct from that of interest groups. Thus, this distinction must be at the heart of any workable definition. Latin America's current democratic consolidation only makes this distinction all the more relevant. Also key is the sometimes confusing distinction between social movements and popular movement. In Mexico, the term *popular movement* was used during the time period of my study to refer to social movements that were independent from the PRI and from the broader authoritarian regime.[24] Almost always, the description referred

22. This controversial assertion can be illustrated with an anecdote. For twelve years I have taught an upper-division university course on twentieth-century U.S. social movements, using Piven and Cloward's *Poor People's Movements* (1979) as a primary text. Year after year the fourth of four case studies they employ—that of the welfare rights movement—most engages a majority of the students. Why? Because Piven and Cloward were personally involved in this movement, and their discourse brings to life the complex relationships that existed and determined the movement's life course.

23. As is well known, there is substantial debate about the use of the term *new*. For example, Arturo Escobar and Sonia Alvarez (1992) created a splash when they emphasized and celebrated the emergence of an identity politics that was no longer oriented to taking state power. Critiques of this approach arose from a variety of perspectives; see, for example, P. Haber 1996a.

24. Manuel Castells has long distinguished between popular movements—which are oriented toward improving services and other basic material needs on the basis of established

to low-income movements, as distinct from middle-class-run human rights movements, urban feminist movements, and the like. However, sometimes the lines became blurred when people used the term to refer to a movement that did not neatly fit this definition.

With this in mind, I offer the following definition: The defining characteristic of social movements is that they always seek to disrupt. They disrupt existing politics based on their normative assertion that they have been deprived of an entitlement, be it recognition, rights, or economic justice. Social movements disrupt not only public policy but also the way in which that policy is made. They challenge dominant modes of perception that discriminate against particular identities and ways of being in the world, and they are composed of people who assume that if they work with like others, they can accomplish things that they cannot achieve alone. What differentiates social movements from public-interest lobbies or formal interest groups is not only the "radicalness" of their demands but also their ability and willingness to use noninstitutional forms of political participation. Social movements are groups of people who define themselves as marginalized, question the legitimacy of existing decision-making processes, and demand that civil society and its representatives be given a greater voice in a fundamentally changed system. Social movements may seek to secure distributive benefits for their members, but to maintain their status of a social movement rather than an interest group, they must not lose the drive to make transformative social change beyond benefiting their own members. The more prominent the state is in affecting the quality of life, the more likely that it will be the primary focus of critique and confrontation. While private-sector representatives (slumlords, polluting factories) may be the target of specific actions, the goal of most contemporary social movements is to reform or revolutionize the state so that it better promotes and defends their interests and values.[25] Finally, movements are not short-lived occurrences, but rather exhibit the capacity to generate

rights (*reivindicaciones*)—and social movements, which produce social effects (particularly changes in class relations) that are qualitatively new and capable of transforming social structures (see, for example, Castells 1983). In Mexico, this distinction went unobserved by most people most of the time. Thus, the terms were used rather interchangeably. However, there were times when the distinction became important, and this will be noted in the narrative.

25. As indicated by Tarrow, "National states are so central a focus for the mobilization of opinion today that we often forget that this was not always so. The major change took place between the late eighteenth and the middle of the nineteenth centuries" (1994, 62).

solidarity over time based on some combination of mutual interest and identity.[26]

Conceptual clarity requires that we distinguish between a social movement and a social movement organization. Social movements are complex networks lacking central command. While there are lead organizations and influential, often charismatic leaders, "it is misleading to equate a social movement with any kind of single collective decision-making entity" (Oliver 1989, 4).[27] This book centers on the politics of two urban popular movement organizations that played leading roles but in no way fully represent, let alone controlled, the Mexican urban popular movement.

As for "new" movements, it is certainly true that movement identities have multiplied since the 1970s in Mexico. Furthermore, peasant and worker movements oriented to Marxist revolutionary ideals certainly no longer dominate Mexican social movements. However, the definitional distinction that Susan Berger (1997) makes, that "new social movements do not seek to take state power" is not the crucial issue affecting the new types of movements that are discussed here. Those movement organizations that were at the heart of Mexican politics during the turbulent 1980s directed their efforts toward the state. While their rhetoric at times may have advocated "taking power" in the revolutionary sense, their realistic aspirations had to do with reforming the content of policy and the way that policy was made. They were also dedicated to the proposition of doing whatever they could to undermine the existing regime and replace it with a democratic government with socialist principles.

This strategy cannot be understood without appreciating how much it resulted from calculations of the balance of power. The movement leaders of the 1980s either participated in or were deeply influenced by the 1960s student movement. They concluded that an armed revolutionary strategy was incapable of success.[28] Such calculations of power, as the case studies show, have always been fundamental to strategy and identity formation. This was true of those urban popular movements in the 1970s that were deeply influenced by not only the repression of the student movement

26. Under the definition of *social movement* used here, some labor organizations would be defined as elements of movements and others would not. For example, CNTE, a Mexican dissident union, represents a movement, while the larger confederation within which it exists, the SNTE, does not.

27. Many analysts have singled out the myth of the unitary actor. For a particularly influential salvo on this issue, see Melucci 1989.

28. This strategic assessment is, of course, in sharp contrast to the calculations made in many other Latin American countries, from Argentina to Guatemala.

but also the crushing of the guerilla movement, led by such dramatic figures as Lucio Cabañas. They may have named their neighborhoods and streets after the martyrs, but they knew not to pick up arms if they were to survive.[29]

Two developments in the politics of Latin American social movements in the 1980s and 1990s are crucial here. First, the revolutionary Marxist discourse of the past has been largely displaced by the democratic discourse of the present. Second, identity movements have emerged whose primary daily operation focus not on state powers but rather on the creation of autonomous spaces. The proliferation of identities and "causes" influence discourse and cultural meanings at play in both social relations and politics. The urban popular movement in general, and the two case study organizations in particular, focus on both state power and identity.

We are of course still left with the problem of discerning when a movement or movement organization ceases to be so. Organizations such as the CDP that joined in the creation of the PT and made use of funds from the state's Solidarity fund were considered by many movements and intellectuals to have "lost their movement credentials." This illustrates how determining definitional boundaries is confounded by the use of different definitions for social movement, co-optation, and other key terms. Differences exist not only among scholars but also, as this study makes clear, within and among movement organizations themselves.

Political Culture

The concept of political culture fell out of favor in Mexican political studies after the beating it took during the 1970s, when dependency theory became the reigning intellectual fashion.[30] However, beginning in the

29. It is certainly true that the discourse of the "new" Zapatistas is innovative in its poetic insistence that they are not interested in taking state power under their own banner. However, there are two points that often go unmentioned. First, while the Zapatistas disavow an interest in taking power from the state, they have engaged in protracted negotiations with the government to change the nature of state power and policy. Second, it seems reasonable to at least speculate that their relationship to state power, like their decisions on military engagement, have been at least somewhat influenced by power calculations.

30. Dependency theory effectively challenged modernization theory as the paradigm of choice for many, if not most, students of Latin America from the 1970s through the 1980s. A central tenet of modernization is that Latin America's conservative Catholic Iberian culture is responsible for poverty, inequity, and authoritarianism. Dependency theory challenged this and argued that the root cause of these problems was economic and political.

1980s and continuing throughout the 1990s, many authors resuscitated culture as an explanatory category as they sought "to understand the motivation, sense, and meaning of the people's political life" (Venegas Aguilera 1995, 98). Mexican authors as diverse as Soledad Loaeza, Carlos Monsiváis, José Pacheco, Roger Bartra, Javier Guerrero, and Héctor Aguilar Camín contributed to this effort, inspiring others to reconsider the importance of political culture in Mexican politics and making it easier for those who were less known and who promoted even more unconventional approaches to be heard.

Are movements rational or irrational? The empirical evidence presented here supports the following: "To attempt to divide the actions of individuals into 'rational' versus 'emotional' or 'irrational' types is to deny the complexity of human behavior" (Turner and Killian 1987, 14, as cited by Gamson [1992a, 54]). My training as a political scientist ensured that I spent years trying to ascertain whether a particular intra- or interorganizational conflict was a product of strategy, philosophy, or interpersonal relationships. The answer to such questions almost inevitably resembled something akin to *huevos revueltos* (scrambled eggs), an image suggested to me by a social movement activist not long after my research began.

Are movement leaders and followers driven by emotions or by calculated strategies designed to maximize, by instrumental means, the benefits of power and interest? I take a position now widely accepted on both sides of the Atlantic and in the North and South—that social movements are politics by other means. While movement politics are a particular kind of politics, with defining characteristics that differentiate it from other forms of political activity, and are not essentially driven by the same logics and images as interest groups or political parties, on the question of passion versus interests, rational versus irrational, and the like, it is empirically incorrect to assert a priori that movements are of a species different from other political forms.

The theory and method adopted here demand an investigation and detailed reporting of the movement's cultural practices. These cultural practices, the day-to-day discourse and practice of organizational life, are assessed in terms of their political significance for those who participate at various levels within the movements (top leadership, cuadros, and bases) and for those who interact with them. The story is deeply influenced by the motivations and meanings of people's political engagement.

Repression and Co-optation

The threat and exercise of official coercion and repression are such an important resource of the state in its efforts to control collective dissent that they deserve to be singled out for special analytic treatment. They often determine whether a social movement will emerge at all and always shape the movement's form and substance. This is clearly illustrated in the post–World War II histories of Eastern Europe and the Soviet Union, where collective dissent was difficult if not impossible because of high levels of repression. As these same countries experienced political openings, collective dissent rose sharply.

Repression is one of the most important variables differentiating the way in which all types of regimes, whether democratic or authoritarian, shape protest. Exclusionary regimes rely heavily on the use and threat of repression, sometimes using violence to such an extent that *state terrorism* ceases to be an inflated term. Democratic regimes find it more difficult to exercise state repression in a prolonged fashion within their own borders, while inclusionary regimes are renowned for their expert use of co-optation and selective repression. Whatever the regime type, most social movements face both "the iron fist of repression [and] the velvet glove of co-optation and limited concessions" (Carson 1981, 257–58).

The challenge for the analyst is to determine the precise combination of repression and co-optation and the strategic logic underlying repressive state behavior. While there may be a dominant state logic, regional differences and variations between state agencies can be extremely important to particular social movements. And while the state is almost always a central actor, often this calculation must also be applied to nonstate elites, who also direct co-optation and repression toward popular movements, often in collusion or even coordination with official actions. Thus, the analytical task requires an understanding of the way the logics of all these actors intersect and influence one another; also needed is an evaluation of the effectiveness of movement response to particular combinations of co-optation and repression.

Piven and Cloward argue that repression becomes more costly to regimes when the "troublemakers" have gained the support of or at least sympathy from groups whose continued support the regime desires for

itself and deems important: "Unless insurgent groups are virtually of out-
cast status, permitting leaders of the regime to mobilize popular hatred
against them, politically unstable conditions make the use of force risky,
since the reactions of other aroused groups cannot be safely predicted.
When government is unable to ignore the insurgents, and is unwilling to
risk the uncertain repercussions of the use of force, it will make efforts to
conciliate and disarm the protestors" (1979, 29).

We need to complicate this picture. First of all, state actors are not unified actors, and while one part of the regime may act repressively, another
may act quite differently. An example is the repressive actions by local and
state governments against civil rights demonstrators in the southern
United States as contrasted with the federal government's methods of
quelling these same acts. The state's use of violence against non-outcast
groups is quite common.[31]

Furthermore, despite the fact that repression is correctly understood as
a crucial state resource, history provides numerous examples of state
repression actually encouraging or further radicalizing collective dissent.[32]
The use of violence against high-profile opposition movements in Mexico,
from the urban popular movement during the 1980s to the well-publicized
Zapatista movement during the 1990s, was moderated by concerns over
the potential for loss of legitimacy among the public. Political elites are
often well aware that the historical record clearly indicates that the use of
repression can backfire against the interests of those who use it.

Mexico's location in the international system of nation-states and super-
power relations limited the extent to which the government could resort to
repression without risking costs in its relations with the United States.
While it did not prevent repression, it no doubt mitigated its use, in
comparison to other countries in Latin America, most notably Chile,
Argentina, Uruguay, and Guatemala. Such constraints on the ability of
regimes to use repression can generally be interpreted as a movement
resource.

31. Two contemporary examples from Bolivia are the Cochabamba water wars of 2000
and the February 2003 rebellion against tax hikes in La Paz (Farthing and Kohl 2001).

32. Wolf (1969) illustrates this in discussing a number of peasant movements, and Womack (1969) describes how repression stimulated the Zapatista movement in the Mexican Revolution. Some of the collective action described by Tilly, Tilly, and Tilly (1975) was encouraged by the misuse of repression. Indiscriminate repression is seen as one reason why people
rebel (Gurr 1970). Lichbach (1987) focuses directly on how the use of repression can deter or
escalate dissent.

The protest cycle in Mexico emerged because the political opportunity structure allowed for a wider range of disruptive mobilizations and organizational behaviors than a more repressive state would have permitted. Limited recourse to repression forced the regime to develop effective mechanisms of co-optation. The de la Madrid administration's (1982–88) failure to reform and revitalize critical government institutions encouraged the cycle's momentum just as Salinas's (1988–94) success in this area contributed to its decline.

Autonomy

The crucial issue of whether an existing social movement has been co-opted or has maintained its autonomy is frequently debated in provocative and polemical terms. Collective dissent needs a minimum level of autonomy in which to form. Autonomy is a fundamental category of analysis because of its importance to the identity, strategy, and the very survival of social movements. Without it, they become arms of the state, political party or whatever has absorbed them.[33] Jonathan Fox provides a helpful analytic distinction: "Autonomy, defined as an organization or movement's degree of control over setting goals and making decisions, offers a more flexible approach [than that of defining groups as either official (progovernment) or independent (antigovernment), as is unfortunately a common practice in Mexico and elsewhere]. While autonomy is an inherently relative notion, the key threshold here is whether group decisions, *on balance*, are made internally or externally" (1990b, 3; emphasis added).

Determining what is "on balance" is the challenge. While it is certainly the case that some movements insist on more autonomy than do others, autonomy varies over time, and movement organizations vary in terms of which decisions they are willing to subject to outside interference. Also, while it is the state that most often threatened and compromised social movement autonomy, it can also be impinged upon by other actors, such as political parties, other social movements, or foreign intervention. In the Mexican case, the corporatist status of unionized labor made independent

---

33. Castells's (1983) influential research demonstrates the importance of autonomy for an extremely diverse set of urban movements ranging from grassroots movements in sixteenth-century Spain to the contemporary gay movement in San Francisco, California.

opposition either impossible or extremely difficult.[34] The relatively higher level of autonomy among students, peasants, and the urban informal sector helps to explain why these groups were the focal areas of collective urban dissent during the 1980s.[35]

The costs of attaining and maintaining autonomy is an area that has received relatively less attention from scholars, despite its importance. These costs are paid by individual movement organizations when they refuse to negotiate for political or material benefits. This insistence on autonomy can lead to problems such as rank-and-file discontent and movement isolation. Further, a rigid insistence on autonomy can be a serious impediment to forming coalitions, which require of movements that they enter into a politics of articulation that inevitably changes their individual identities and diminishes their autonomy. An inability to form or maintain coalitions often undermines the strength of the opposition.

Clearly there is a delicate balance between autonomy and close relationships. The ideal is to attain some degree of relative autonomy from powerful actors that are determined to shape the behavior of movements to their own interests and values. The most likely suspects are state actors, from the president to local planning boards, and the political parties. However, relationships with other social movements can also raise concerns. In Mexico in the last quarter of the twentieth century, coalition efforts were frequently undermined by a failure both to maintain adequate levels of autonomy and to form a coherent front that combined power resources in synergetic ways.

The ability of popular movements to maintain a relative degree of autonomy from the state was indispensable to the emergence of the protest cycle in the 1979–82 period. Without it, they would have been simply contained within the corporatist system and thus become system strengthening rather than threatening. Maintaining autonomy between 1982 and 1988 was integral to the individual gains that movements were able to make and to the formation of the Frente Democrático Nacional (National Democratic Front [FDN]), a temporary coalition in support of

34. One of the most distinctive characteristics of Mexico's authoritarian regime was the institutionalization and routinization of relationships with important sectors. This system of interest bargaining is known as state corporatism and will be more fully discussed in Chapter 3.

35. The simple explanation for why the peasantry had more independent organizations than did labor is that peasant corporatist mechanisms are in relatively greater disarray in more areas of the country than are those linked to labor.

Cárdenas's presidential bid. The decision by many movements to forfeit a significant degree of autonomy in order to gain concessions from Salinas contributed to the overall decline in the protest cycle in the 1989–91 period.

Internal Organization

The political process approach encourages an examination of how movement organizations are run internally and how decision-making processes influence their political efficacy. Many use this approach to highlight ways in which the internal organization of the movement is itself a strategy and a resource. For example, one of Cook's (1996) main arguments is that the internal democracy of dissident Mexican teachers was fundamental to whatever success the movement enjoyed. In my own emphasis on internal organization I consider not only how it shaped the organizational fortunes of the AB and CDP but also how it influenced broader institutional and policy-making processes. To what extent did it reflect the dominant authoritarian culture and to what extent did it subvert it by practicing a democratic alternative? Not surprisingly, very different answers are generated, depending on the level of movement considered. In general, movement leaders tend to claim higher levels of internal democracy than is observed by NGO actors who interact with movements or scholars.[36] From the movement leadership perspective, the major impediment to internal democracy is information. As articulated by one movement leader from Mexico City:

> One of the basic aspects of democracy is information. The making of decisions requires information, a lot of information—information that the people who comprise the base of the organization do not possess. This situation means that decisions pass to the leadership, naturally. The leader should, in addition to organizing, in addition to generating programs, inform the members. This is very complicated in practice. It requires an extremely developed structure determined to provide high levels of information to the bases (Sergio García Díaz of UPREZ, cited in Bolos 1995, 113).

36. This tendency was in evidence at a 1994 seminar that brought together movement leaders and NGO representatives and scholars; its results are presented in Bolos 1995. See, in particular, 109.

Some organizations have addressed this issue, by creating structures that disperse information so as to expand the number of informed decision-makers. Responding to the issue of why leadership so often does not empower others, Victor Aguilar of UPREZ explained, "Because the question of power is very strong, and gaining it has cost a lot, perhaps too much to then give it up. Let's be clear on this: there are many interests at stake and it will take a lot of work to put them aside. There are economic interests and those of prestige" (cited in Bolos 1995, 251). Given this tendency, how do we explain the differences that are found?

In his historical summary of the Unión de Colonias Populares (Union of Popular Neighborhoods [UCP])-Naucalpan, Alberto Oviedo demonstrates that it is critically important to remember that the leadership structure can change over the life of an organization.[37] "The early history of our organization is a history of *caudillismos*. In Naucalpan, the organization was constructed by a group of priests; in reality, internal democracy was based on what the leaders said. Although there were plenaries of the neighborhoods involved, they always performed in line with the wishes of the leader. Although there were discussions, the decisions taken were always in line with the wishes of the leadership" (cited in Bolos 1995, 279).[38] Three years later, leadership struggles for control of the organization caused internal ruptures, a pattern repeated some years later. By 1994, Oviedo described an organization experimenting without "maximum leaders" and working to create an organizational culture of shared power, with the natural tendency to accumulate power being checked by rotating the project leadership.

While no one statement adequately describes democratization from the perspective of the urban popular movement, the following is one that most movement actors would agree with:

> The problem of democracy has a very real and concrete content: It is disabling authoritarianism, the impunity of functionaries that have a patrimonial vision of public resources, meaning, and the application of public policy at the discretion of the leadership. [This can be and has been done by both] the opposition and the PRI. The leader becomes defined as the authoritarian manager.

37. Naucalpan is an area of Mexico City.
38. A *caudillo* is a type of political boss whose leadership style is authoritarian and who bases his power largely on a charismatic personality and the dispensing of personal favors.

This is constructed with the assistance of official authority. But it also requires the servitude of the bases, they arm him with the power of obedience. (Rafael Alvarez as cited in Bolos 1995, 228)

Leaders, especially movement leaders, maintain their positions in large part because they know how to get things done. According to Alvarez, this type of deferential, clientelistic, resolute leadership is favored and is virtually "the only kind of leadership Mexico knows" (cited in Bolos 1995, 229). Bolos reports, however, on the bases of extensive interviews with rank-and-file urban popular movement participants, that leadership's entry into politics has altered their view of politics; having once seen it as something dirty, they begin to view it as having beneficial possibilities for the good (Bolos, 1995, 236).

My own general observation is that many Mexicans who experienced the politics of popular movement leaders—both rural and urban—were convinced that leadership could in fact further their interests and values. However, the existence of authoritarianism within Mexican popular movements weakened democratization, which what was billed by the movements themselves as part of their reason for being.

Alliances

Social movements not only mobilize their own resources in their struggle; they also combine forces whenever possible to minimize confrontation with other social and political forces. This is especially true for entities, such as the Mexican urban popular movement, that lack the kind of strong structural position that is afforded industrial labor or the middle class.

Many, if not most, studies of social movements have noted the importance of alliances between social movement organizations and political parties, the state, cross-class organizations, outside advisers, and so on.[39]

39. See, for example, Jenkins 1985 and Jenkins and Perrow 1977 for the importance of alliances to the development of the U.S. farm workers movement and McAdam 1982 for their role in the development of the U.S. civil rights movement. Popkin (1979), Migdal (1984), Wolf (1969), and Moore (1969) all explore the importance of alliances to "successful" peasant movements of varying size and importance. Adams (1970) has noted the role of outside organizers and advisers in Guatemala, and Castells (1983) has done so for urban social movements, while it is one of the main insights of Carrillo's (1990) work on Mexico. J. C. Scott (1985) emphasizes the fact that without such support, the poor are unlikely to mobilize.

Alliances—the pooling of resources—is often theorized to have immense potential by both scholars and activists. Alliances are extremely difficult to form and even more difficult to maintain. One of the most contentious, and important, debates among poor people's movements and their supporters is on the pros and cons of alliances with the middle class. Because governments are more reluctant to repress the middle class, its participation (or even active sympathy) affords a degree of protection. However, the historical evidence suggests that alliances with the middle class create the risk that the interests of the poor over time will be subordinated to those of the middle class. In Mexico, this concern is close to the surface for popular movement participants because they often associate the limited achievements of the revolution with the multiclass alliances formed during the 1930s. Furthermore, the authoritarian political system that emerged out of the revolution was legitimated and sustained for many years through recourse to alliances that, in the view of popular movement activists, turned out to be co-optation.

Alliances among popular movements in Mexico have generally proved to be very difficult, because of their heterogeneous character.[40] The problems associated with heterogeneity are particularly difficult to overcome in a country such as Mexico, where the opposition for so long had such low resource levels. In addition, alliances of relatively homogenous movements, such as the Coordinadora Nacional del Movimiento Urbano Popular (National Coordinating Committee of the Urban Popular Movement [CONAMUP]), the national umbrella urban popular movement organization, also have proven impossible to sustain as differences emerged over key strategy decisions, most notably electoral participation.

Alliances were made with state reformers who were able and willing to negotiate with movement actors and treat them as legitimate interlocutors. Alliances with reform minded people within state agencies and sometimes with reform-minded elected officials were essential to the survival of popular movement actors. These alliances functioned as working relationships, wherein the goals of state reformers and the popular movement actors coincided. Some of them existed for rather long periods of time, while others were episodic. The motivations of state reformers varied.

40. Heterogeneity often leads to fragmentation within the social movement sector, as is well documented by Mainwaring (1987) in the case of Brazil. While temporary heterogeneous groupings are not uncommon, they are extremely difficult to sustain over time in the social movement world. Political parties have proved themselves much better at doing this.

Sometimes it they acted out of a personal conviction that working collabo-
ratively with movement organizations effectively fit their definition of
pursuing good public policy. Other times they participated because collaboration furthered their desired political goals, such as legitimating the
regime or state agency or undermining the opposition. Sometimes these
goals coincided.

Alliances formed between popular movements and political parties but
were severely complicated by the contradictory organizational imperatives
of movements and parties. This situation was only resolved by the decline
of movements and the ascendancy of parties in the 1990s, when many
prominent urban popular movement organizations had essentially merged
with parties.

During the 1990s, a very important identity shift occurred that affected
the nature of alliances. Whereas during the 1970s and 1980s, the politics
of dissent was most powerfully defined by mobilization and organization
by sector, during the 1990s, as elections took on more importance, the
notion of citizen became increasingly central. The AB of Mexico City was
an early harbinger of things to come, when it emphasized this concept
beginning in the mid-1980s. As Mexico moved into the 1990s, it became
increasingly clear that the most important social formations were no
longer sectoral, but rather were defined by citizenship, with bold efforts to
achieve multiclass, multiethnic, and gender-sensitive alliances, such as
those called for by the Zapatistas.

Vision and Survival

One of the recurring problems with the New Social Movement paradigm
is that scholars who rely on it tend to employ a neat dichotomy between
strategic or instrumental rationality (old movements) and normative (new)
movements that distance themselves from the state and political parties. In
the social movement worlds I know best, those of Latin America and the
United States, I have rarely seen such a sharp distinction on the ground.
Social movements most often focus both on the state and on civil society,
and where political parties are relevant, they most certainly enter into the
mix. Social movements and their organizations contain elements of not
only strategic rationality in their dealings with administrative power but
also the promotion of normative visions.

Power and ideals coexist and neither drops out for long. The relation-ship is complex and highly dynamic and, in my view, should be emphasized by movement scholars just as it is by movement participants. If power drops out too far, the movement ceases to develop knowledge and practice capable of changing society. If ideals fall out of daily life too far and for too long, the movement ceases to have any dynamism or motivation with which to change society, and it disintegrates. Over the life of a movement or movement organization, extremes can occur temporarily without extreme outcomes. But if either persists, the movement loses its dynamism and its raison d'être.

Social movements work for both stability and dynamic change. Power-ful movements seek to preserve that which is of value and to advance val-ues that had been absent or insufficiently expressed. Often, movements and movement organizations can be seen both preserving values under attack and simultaneously endeavoring to change existing practices. The balance between stability and change varies within movements (including at the individual and organizational levels) and over time.[41]

While movements are committed to significant change, they also must survive in the world as it is, and the story of movements is incomplete without attention being given to this. Poor people's movements stake much of their identity on the fact that their members are poor—and ille-gitimately and unnecessarily so. Participants in poor people's movements explicitly devote themselves to encouraging a change in consciousness, from one of acquiescence, fatalism, and powerlessness to one that pro-duces an assertive, even aggressive, stance and claims on new rights and conceptions of justice. In ostensibly democratic polities, the movements can point to the gap between proclamations in the constitution and the day-to-day reality. In the process, movement leaders are in large part cho-sen and retain their positions because they translate this consciousness into material results. If they fail to do so, they will lose legitimacy over time. Movement leaders know this; the bases know this and remind the leaders of this basic reality; and state functionaries know this. In my experience, the most likely people to miss this "essential fact" are ideologically driven party functionaries and movement scholars.[42]

41. The very dynamism of movements means that snapshots in time are a very weak basis upon which to make judgments.

42. Jeffrey Rubin's (1997) work on the cocei is extremely interesting on this point. He tells a story of a movement that gained and maintained legitimacy with its bases not so much

Another basic element of movement survival is the ability for movement leaders and cuadros to survive economically. While some have lived
on the generosity of the bases, most rely on outside financing. As anybody
who has received a salary knows, such remuneration does not come without expectations, or "strings." The specific expectations of "funders"—
whether they are state actors, closely tied to state actors, or autonomous—
influence movement leaders, a fact that gets very short shrift in the
literature.

Most movement organizations exhibit the tension between political and
material survival on the one hand and the pursuit of visionary ideals on the
other. How they manage this tension is at the heart of their experience and
to a significant degree spells out the meaning of their politics. In subsequent chapters, I present this drama.

---

through the successful acquisition of material improvements, but through the artful depiction
of asserting strong Zapotec identity in the pursuit of such goods. Interestingly, despite this
apparent difference, COCEI leadership was willing to participate in Salinas's antipoverty program PRONASOL in order to gain access to substantial material rewards. They were strongly
criticized by those who argued that PRONASOL was designed to destroy the autonomy and
power of the democratic movement that had come together under the banner of the FDN in
1988.

TWO

Mexico at the Zenith of the 1980s Protest Cycle

The emergence of a protest movement entails a transformation both of consciousness and of behavior. The change in consciousness has at least three distinct aspects. First, "the system"—or those aspects of the system that people experience and perceive—loses legitimacy. Large numbers of men and women who ordinarily accept the authority of their rulers and the legitimacy of institutional arrangements come to believe in some measure that these rulers and these arrangements are unjust and wrong. Second, people who are ordinarily fatalistic, who believe that existing arrangements are inevitable, begin to assert "rights" that imply demands for change. Third, there is a new sense of efficacy; people who ordinarily consider themselves helpless come to believe that they have some capacity to alter their lot.
—FRANCES FOX PIVEN AND RICHARD CLOWARD, *Poor People's Movements: Why They Success, How They Fail*

When Spanish adventurers invaded Mexico in 1519, their primary goal was simple: to extract the vast mineral wealth of the country and take over the best lands for the benefit of themselves and the Spanish Crown.[1] As Cockcroft recounts, "Death became the Indians' daily companion. Killings, floggings, overwork, malnutrition, poor hygiene, starvation, and disease caused more than 90 percent of the Indian population to be wiped out by 1650" (1998, 19).

The conquerors took over a land with a complex of diverse and competing indigenous societies, some of which were extremely sophisticated. Foremost among these were the Aztecs, who dominated most of the area of what is today Mexico from A.D. 1319 until the Spaniards arrived in their capital of Tenochtitlán, located where Mexico City is now situated. The Aztecs constructed a highly centralized state ruled by military elites and a secular nobility. In the south, from 325 to 925, the Maya controlled territory that extended into Central America. Contemporary Mexican social movements often make reference to the glories of this indigenous past, drawing on its legends for both their inspiration and their legitimization.

Hierarchy was an important characteristic of these societies. Cockcroft explains that "social stratification, class conflict, and state systems of complex

---

1. The Spanish conquerors set up vast land holdings. For example, Hernán Cortés established a twenty-five-thousand-square-mile hacienda in the southern state of Oaxaca.

social organization had developed and flourished in Mexico long before the arrival of the Europeans" (1998, 14). The Spanish built on and strengthened this social stratification and political authoritarianism, establishing a caste-conscious, class-based society ruled by a brutal authoritarian regime dominated by secular authorities who were loyal to the Spanish Crown, which was in league with the Catholic Church. While the details of this highly unequal and authoritarian society have changed in important ways over the centuries, discrimination based on race, extreme inequalities in wealth, and the institutionalization of antidemocratic political relationships have remained central to Mexico throughout its history.

This historical context is key to interpreting contemporary Mexican social movements and the country's process of democratization, as its current political culture is deeply influenced by centuries of authoritarian public power. This history makes efforts to institutionalize democracy more difficult, whether within social movement organizations or in the political system in general. Although democratic exercises of power have taken place in Mexico and their expansion is possible in the future, the momentum of a long authoritarian past is an important factor in contemporary efforts. Those who ignore the power of this history are prone to repeat it, whereas those who have made an effort to understand it can learn from it in working to deconstruct authoritarian sensibilities, practices, and institutions.

The War of Independence

Mexico gained formal independence from Spain in 1821. Agustín de Iturbide, who led the triumphant military forces into Mexico City, established a conservative order that was fundamentally at odds with the more radical visions of the original independence leaders, Miguel Hidalgo and José María Morelos. In different ways, these two men sought a social revolution, to undermine the racist caste system and highly stratified class structure, and a political revolution, to democratize authoritarian institutions. Instead of pursuing this plan, the new regime kept authoritarian structures and practices in place. A major shift in social relations marked a formal end to discrimination against persons of Spanish blood who had been born in the colony (*criollos*) by those of Spanish blood born in Spain (*peninsulares*). Most Mexicans, who were *mestizos*, of mixed Spanish and Indian blood, remained relatively unaffected. They neither participated in nor were deeply affected by independence from Spain. "The nineteenth century would vindicate the general apathy of the rural Mexican, for his life would change little, if at all" (M. C. Meyer and Sherman 1995, 297).

Mexican social movement intellectuals often argue that the failure at independence to achieve fundamental changes is an important contributory factor in contemporary injustices. The utopian-based practices of the independence leaders—Hidalgo, Morelos, and their associates—are also important reference points for contemporary social reformers. Both Hidalgo and Morelos were parish priests; as such, they are symbols of a very different face of the Roman Catholic Church from that of the institution, which throughout its history has most often supported the ruling classes over the working class and poor.[2]

The Mexican Revolution

It is not unusual for a new republic to experience a protracted period of political instability as new constellations of power are consolidated and Mexico was no exception. Agustín de Iturbide declared himself emperor of Mexico in 1822 but was deposed from power the following year. Between 1823 and 1855 there were more than thirty new governments formed, with different heads of state. Political instability finally came to a decisive end with the rule of Porfirio Díaz, who governed the country as a dictator between 1876 and 1911. The Porfirians destroyed strongmen and economic groups associated with previous regimes and replaced them with loyalists (Aguilar Camín and Meyer 1993, 11). Díaz moved aggressively to build the Mexican economy, with the aid of substantial foreign investment. The ruthlessness and prejudices of the Porfiriato eventually led to armed rebellion by a diverse group of dissidents.

In 1911, a new period of political disruption began with the Mexican Revolution, which led to fundamental changes in governance but once again failed to produce substantial changes for the majority of Mexicans. The first revolutionary surge was led by a parish priest, Francisco Madero, who, drawing on the tradition of Hidalgo and Morelos, articulated sweeping

2. It is important to recognize that the church has continued to give birth to individuals and movements that are supportive of progressive change.

radical change, before he was caught and executed. After his death, the agrarian radical Emiliano Zapata, the renegade Pancho Villa, and the fundamentally conservative forces known as the Constitutionalists joined forces to overthrow the state. Once they won, a lot of the radicals' rhetoric was incorporated into the postrevolutionary order and some of its demands put into practice, but the postrevolutionary government did not shift fundamental resources away from the wealthy or establish a democratic polity.[3] As Judith Adler Hellman argues, a new ruling class was established, "composed of (a) the new elite of recently landed revolutionary generals, (b) industrialists and businessmen who had prospered during and immediately after the revolution, and (c) members of the old land-owning oligarchy who had become aware that they could pursue their pre-Revolutionary interests and preserve much of their pre-Revolutionary status by declaring their adherence to the new regime" (1988, 15).

The Mexican Revolution led to a new constitution that, on paper, is one of the most progressive documents of its kind. Particularly noteworthy is its emphasis on the rights of working people and the peasantry and on the state's obligations to provide substantial resources to the Mexican majority. While shifts in Mexico's class structure did occur over the course of the twentieth century—most notably in the growth of the urban middle and working class—the kind of social justice or political democracy called for in the new constitution did not occur, in part because the constitution and constitutional law have very different standing in Mexico from that of their equivalents in other countries. In the United States, for example, while scholars, politicians, and the public may dispute specific decisions taken by the courts, all agree that the constitution is to be followed to the letter. In Mexico, while critics certainly have attempted to force adherence to the letter of constitutional law, until quite recently the entire legal system, right up to the Supreme Court, always acted in accordance with the executive branch's wishes.[4]

3. Three of the most well known radical revolutionary demands were adopted by the new order, albeit in practice they were far more moderate than their advocates originally intended. They were, first, Zapata's call for land redistribution through the breakup of the hacienda system and large church holdings; second, Pancho Villa's demand for the establishment of a free and universal system of public education; and third, the demand made by many union leaders that protections for workers be incorporated into the new Mexican Constitution.

4. President Zedillo introduced a constitutional reform in 1994 designed to increase the independence of the federal judiciary up to and very much including the Supreme Court. See, for example, Domingo 2000 and Magaloni and Zepeda 2004.

The high ideals of the revolution, established by the constitution, have always provided the single most important referent for most of the nation's political parties and social movements that organized and mobilizing in the twentieth century. Social movements in Mexico, as in many other countries, concern themselves primarily with holding the state accountable to its own rhetoric. In Mexico, as is true elsewhere, the constitution serves as a primary tool in this struggle.

The Inclusionary Authoritarian Regime

The structure of political institutions and their management of Mexico's capitalist economy were consistently at the heart of Mexican popular movement critiques and reform proposals. Mexican popular movements often portrayed the regime that was established by the winners of the Mexican Revolution as having betrayed the real revolutionaries, the most famous of whom was Emiliano Zapata.

Between 1915 and 1934, while Mexico slowly ended the fighting between the major revolutionary combatants, the so-called Northern Dynasty of revolutionary generals ruled the country. The most notable were Venustíano Carranza (1914 and 1915–20), Alvaro Obregón (1920–24), and Plutarco Elías Calles (1924–28).[5] The new leadership focused on national reconstruction and promoted economic growth that primarily benefited the ruling class. Less than one in twelve peasants benefited from land reform, and although opposition to granting favorable concessions to foreign capital motivated the revolution, Calles in particular worked to reestablish the close ties with foreign capital that had been disrupted during the war.

The new leadership was also preoccupied with consolidating power as regional forces resisted the regime's tendencies to centralize power, notably in the Office of the President. In 1929 Calles responded by creating a political party—in the name of the revolution—which was to be a broad-based multiconstituency party that would centralize power in the executive branch while establishing effective lines of communication, dispute resolution, and patronage with the provinces. Although Calles initiated

5. Calles continued to direct national affairs through a series of puppet presidents between 1928 and 1934, when Lázaro Cárdenas became president and threw Calles out of the country.

the party and its basic logic, it was President Lázaro Cárdenas (1934–40) who is regarded as the primary architect of the postrevolutionary political order.

Cárdenas was first and foremost a nationalist, who believed deeply in the idea of a unified Mexico, which led him to move decisively to end the provincial rebellions. Unlike the generals of the Northern Dynasty, he recognized that for the peasantry and the workers to be loyal to the new order, they had to receive substantial benefits, so he directed more resources to them than they had ever been given. Many historians, and Mexicans in general, believe that this was motivated by sincere convictions about social justice; in any case, his decisive action to institutionalize class compromise stabilized the existing, unequal system. When he left office, the limited gains in the political and economic share made by the poor and working class declined once again in favor of the middle and especially the upper classes.

The key institutions of the class compromise Cárdenas brokered were the state (dominated by the executive branch) and political society (dominated by the official revolutionary party—the Institutionalized Revolutionary Party [PRI]).[6] A key role of the "official state party" was to legitimate the system through regular elections that had the veneer of democratic procedure but were rigged to ensure that the official party or one of its close allies won. Many political careers included posts in both the state and the party, and political elites moved between these posts in the same way that many U.S. political elites move between administrative political appointments and business.

President Cárdenas recognized four groups as legitimate interlocutors: the peasantry (at the time the largest social group); organized labor; the military; and a more heterogeneous grouping known as the popular sector that was composed primarily of state employees, professionals, and small merchants and workers operating in the informal economy. All these groups were considered critical because each had the ability to disrupt national consensus if left unchecked and to legitimize the system if effectively incorporated. Notably absent from this list were the Catholic Church and business organizations, but these groups influenced the state through institutional arrangements and other means.[7] Cárdenas believed that the

6. The previously named Revolutionary Party went through several changes in structure and name before the name Institutional Revolutionary Party was finally settled on in 1946.

7. Business influenced the regime through a variety of formal and informal channels. It created giant umbrella interest group organizations, including the Confederation of Industrial Chambers (CONCAMIN), the Confederation of National Chambers of Commerce (CONCANACO), and the National Chamber of Manufacturing Industries (CANACINTRA).

business class posed the most significant threat to state autonomy and sought to limit its excessive power and influence by augmenting the power of the peasantry and working classes, which became his active support base and continued to serve this role for the PRI for decades to come. Even when their influence over state policy dwindled in the post-1940 period, the majority of peasants and working class retained their loyalty to the regime.[8]

The essential aim in this kind of system, known widely as "state corporatism," is to institutionalize a regime of hierarchical interest mediation (Schmitter 1974). Peasants who wanted something from the state were generally required to work within the official peasant wing of the party known as the Confederación Nacional Campesina (National Peasant Confederation [CNC]). Normally, peasants would bring their concerns to local-level officials, who would take them up the chain of command. Similar arrangements existed for the other sectors, most notably labor and low- and moderate-income members of the popular sector. Cross-sectoral alliances—as in, for example, joint reform proposals by the peasantry and labor—were actively discouraged. While this system never achieved an absolute monopoly, its success was premised on there being a low chance of gaining access to power or patronage outside it. The low success of independent efforts discouraged others from even trying.

Several major types of capitalist authoritarian regimes exist in the world. The most common are personal dictatorships, such as that of Manuel Noriega in Panama, Anastasio Somoza in Nicaragua, or Ferdinand Marcos in the Philippines, and exclusionary authoritarian regimes, often headed by military officers, such as those in Uruguay, Argentina, and Brazil during the 1970s. In contrast, Mexico developed a relatively rare form: an inclusionary authoritarian regime, which differs from exclusionary authoritarian regimes in its institutionalized capacity to effectively incorporate new actors and, in the process, moderate their original demands.[9] Importantly, this includes actors who begin in the opposition or

---

8. The Cárdenas presidency was a vital period in twentieth-century Mexican history. Many refer to Cárdenas as the single most important architect and implementer of the inclusionary authoritarian regime. Thus, there are many detailed treatments. See, for example, Cornelius 1973; Córdova 1974; Anguiano 1975; Hamilton 1982; S. Haber 1989; and Knight 1994.

9. For clarification on the distinction between exclusionary and inclusionary forms of authoritarianism, see O'Donnell 1973; Malloy 1977; and Stepan 1978. For classic elaborations on Mexico's distinctive form of authoritarianism, see Purcell 1975 and Reyna and Weinert 1977.

who threaten to join it. For example, while an effective grassroots organizer with roots in the Communist Party in Chile during the reign of General Augusto Pinochet is likely to be hunted down and probably murdered, the same person in Mexico might well find the state offering him or her a government position with a budget. The Mexican inclusionary authoritarian regime was the longest-lasting authoritarian regime of the twentieth century because it was dynamic in responding to the demands of inclusion, as well as flexible, at the regional as well as national level, in incorporating new actors and changing both policy making and content as a result.

Almost all analysts concur on several other key attributes that have contributed to the regime's longevity. High on the list is the steady and significant growth of the Mexican economy between 1940 and 1980, when the state adopted Import Substitution Industrialization (ISI) policies, also implemented in many other low-incomes countries, which were designed to encourage the domestic production of manufactured goods that previously had been imported. The so-called Mexican Miracle of 1940–70 is often used as a dramatic demonstration of the ISI model's success. The economy grew an average of 6.5 percent a year, making it one of the fastest-growing economies in the world; the peso remained relatively stable; government deficits and public borrowing were tightly controlled; and average inflation rates were low. Although wealth became more concentrated, the majority of the population, particularly urban dwellers, experienced increases in their standards of living. New Mexican industries, the so-called infant industries, were protected through a combination of tariffs and import licensing. Although problems began to emerge during the 1970s, up until the economic crisis of 1982 difficulties with excessive government spending were widely thought to be manageable as a result of the mid-1970s discovery of large oil reserves in the Gulf of Mexico.[10]

For the purposes of this study, particularly important is the PRI regime's use of significant government resources to foster opportunities for social mobility, as often as possible through its corporatist institutions, thereby legitimating the party and the power structure. A second critical factor is that ISI actively encouraged rapid rural-to-urban migration as part of its modernizing project. During the 1930s, two-thirds of Mexico's population lived in the rural areas; by 1980 two-thirds lived in urban areas of twenty-five hundred people or more. Much of this growth occurred in Mexico's

---

10. For a summary statement of Mexico's economic development model at this time, see P. Haber 1998a. For more detailed treatments from a variety of perspectives, see González Navarro 1965; Reynolds 1970, 1978; Vernon 1963; and Villarreal 1977.

largest cities. Official government statistics state that the population of Mexico City grew from less than 2 million people in 1940 to almost 13.5 million in 1980. During the same period, Guadalajara grew from less than 300,000 to more than 2 million and Monterrey grew from about 200,000 to almost 2 million (cited in Bennett 1995b, 8). While through the 1960s and early 1970s the urban economy's growth rates were high enough to absorb much of this massive migration, by the 1980s urban areas had lost this capacity. Continuing migration led to a massive growth in the construction of shantytowns and in urban poverty, underemployment, and the informal economy. While the PRI's popular sector organizations were ostensibly poised to incorporate this population influx, it has never has been as effective as either the labor or the peasant sector in monopolizing political control. This is where the urban social movement moved in and established its base.

Most interpreters conclude that Mexico has been an unusually stable example of political authoritarianism; however, according to the official discourse of the regime throughout this period, Mexico was a democracy. Minimal definitions of democracy usually focus exclusively or almost exclusively on regular, competitive, and fair elections. As has been pointed out for years by dozens of analysts and countless Mexican citizens, elections in Mexico are regular, but at least until recently, they were not impartial, fair, or competitive. Another common critique challenges official claims that Mexico functions as a federalist system modeled on that of the United States. This line of argument claims that while on paper and by official proclamation Mexico has three autonomous branches of government (executive, legislative, and judicial), in practice power is highly concentrated in the Office of the President. As many have pointed out, Mexico's system functions without the necessary level of checks and balances. By law, Mexican state and local governments have high levels of autonomy, but in practice the executive branch controls the majority of the budget and decision-making authority.[11] Moreover, commentators challenge Mexico's official claim that basic human rights are respected, demonstrating the substantial evidence amassed by independent observers and human rights organizations that contradict this.[12]

11. For an early and widely read classic on this point, see Fagen and Tuohy 1972. For a more recent work, see Rodríguez 1997.

12. America's Watch published a report with the particularly revealing title *Human Rights in Mexico: A Policy of Impunity* (1990). Over the past decade, the systemic discrimination and violence employed against indigenous people has only served to reinforce this view.

For the cases examined in the present study, it is important to understand how the Mexican political regime actually worked up through the year 2000. The price for receiving favorable responses to individual and group demands was to remain loyal to the regime by voting for PRI candidates, showing up for PRI-sponsored rallies, and avoiding the appeals of regime opponents. As long as the majority of Mexicans stuck to this, the continuation of the inclusionary authoritarian regime was guaranteed. Despite some important exceptions, such as the famous railroad-worker strike of 1959 and the student movement of 1968, the majority of Mexicans were unwilling to challenge this way of doing politics until the early 1980s.

Mexico in the 1970s and 1980s

During his presidency (1970–76), Luis Echeverría was preoccupied with incorporating new actors and demands, as the legitimacy of the Mexican inclusionary authoritarian regime had been badly damaged by the brutal 1968 military repression of the student movement that resulted in hundreds of deaths. Echeverría was minister of the interior in 1968, and many were concerned that the repression would continue during his presidency. Instead, consistent with the inclusionary authoritarian regime's dependence on resolving conflicts peacefully, Echeverría moved decisively toward reconciliation. His administration increased social spending, directing funds to infrastructure and to the peasantry and urban poor. When the first urban social movement organizations led by those associated with the student movement began to develop in some areas, including Durango, Echeverría helped to establish rather favorable working conditions for them, even intervening on their behalf in conflicts with local and state officials.

President López Portillo (1976–82) was a different kind of president: he reversed the accommodating stance of Echeverría and replaced it with a much more repressive policy toward what he apparently perceived to be radical detractors. America's Watch reported that more than five hundred people disappeared during his administration (1990, 35). Largely in response to the repression, sectoral networks, known as *coordinadoras*, established national organizational structures encompassing a broad range of local groups, including the urban poor, small rural producers, and teachers, and assumed a key role in opposing the regime. While the individual organizations maintained their autonomy at the local level, they benefited from the strength in numbers provided by the coordinadoras and created significant hubs of power for low- and moderate-income people. The origins of the coordinadoras are detailed by one urban social movement leader:

> López Portillo was busy capturing film clips of grandiose public-works projects, while in the shadows out of sight or interest of international and national presses he was either ordering or by process of benign neglect encouraging brutality against the popular forces. This had of course a stunning impact on our ability to continue aggressive actions, for we are no good to anybody if we are dead or in prison. We would get together and talk, having to admit that we had been put in a defensive position. And here the country was booming and our people were getting poorer. We had to do something. It was out of such concerns that the coordinadora was born. (Interview by the author, national meeting of CONAMUP, Jalapa Veracruz, 1989)

The coordinadoras were organized in direct opposition to the corporatist system, which was explicitly mandated to prevent exactly the kind of cross-sectoral working relationships that they established. They represented what in Mexico is called the social Left, made up of individuals who were active in social movements and political currents, as distinguished from those involved in party politics. Even though the success of individual coordinadoras and relationships between them was uneven, their very presence and their ability to function over time were a victory for the opposition, even if efforts to fuse them into something bigger were frustrated.

The contrasts between Echeverría and López Portillo were commonly drawn in my conversations with social movement leaders, cuadros, and rank-and-file members:

> Look, I'm not saying that everything was great for us during the Echeverría years. Those in the administration had neither the will nor the ability to encourage us, but they tolerated us. What could they do? Here were all these people coming in from the countryside with no place to live. Rents were high and getting higher. Neither the PRI nor the government was able to effectively

respond. So, when we starting really picking up steam with the land invasions, the so-called political opening had some affect. . . . Echeverría let his people make deals with governors and local bosses to allow us some latitude, to work with us.

When the López Portillo people came in, they had a different idea. They were all about helping business people and using their newfound riches to enforce social control and giving all initiative to the state. . . . If we did not go away, if we continued to act independently, they made it clear that they were willing to bust heads. What could we do? We had to do something to defend ourselves, to build ties between us that would make it harder to pick us off one by one. It was either that or give up. (Movement cuadro, interview by the author, national meeting of CONAMUP, Jalapa Veracruz, 1989)

In 1977 López Portillo introduced a political reform in an attempt to induce the social Left and the leftist political parties to enter electoral politics.[13] Reformers within the regime, notably a well-known and respected intellectual named Jesús Reyes Heroles, spurred by the absence of debate during the 1976 election, felt that the regime's longevity and its highest goals—continuing to make progress on realizing the ideals of the 1917 Constitution—were endangered by the lack of a significant opposition. The regime's original proposal called for significant changes but these were watered down by those cautious about submitting the PRI to anything approaching real competition. While the final reform legalized the Communist Party and provide certain financial incentives for the creation of new parties, it did not substantially level the playing field by removing the structural advantages enjoyed by the PRI.

At the time of this political reform, the coordinadoras were led by the segment of the social Left that rejected the allure of the electoral reform, which it viewed as a ploy to subvert its transformative aspirations through incorporation and co-optation. This leadership was convinced that the reform initiative was designed to avoid the violent confrontations occurring in many parts of Central and South America (interviews by the author). Some analysts have also argued that the social Left opposed political party

13. For details of this and other reform initiatives of the 1970s and the first half of the 1980s, see Middlebrook 1986.

formation because of concerns that competition between existing political groupings would become unmanageable within a party framework (Tamayo 1990). The decision at this point of almost all social Left actors not to enter the electoral arena was critical to the emergence of the 1980s protest cycle, just as their later decision to enter electoral politics was central to its demise.

Mexico's economic miracle began to unravel during the Echeverría administration, in part because the president responded to the pressures created by the 1960s student movement through aggressively increasing social spending.[14] Rather than pay for these expenditures through increased taxes or other government revenues, he borrowed. This led to a crisis that forced President López Portillo (1976–82) to sign an agreement with the International Monetary Fund (IMF), as soon as he took office, that required Mexico to limit public spending. However, soon after this, oil was discovered in Mexico and the promise of future revenues propelled him to increase spending and borrowing at levels even higher than those seen under Echeverría.[15] But recession and high inflation gripped much of the world in the late 1970s and early 1980s, producing the phenomenon known as "stagflation" and causing higher rates on the floating interest rate loans that Mexico owed principally to large private U.S. banks. When oil prices dropped sharply in 1982, Mexico's found itself unable to repay its foreign debt and announced that it was about to default, launching what became known as the third-world debt crisis.

Mexico's economy plunged precipitously during the 1980s. Real gross domestic product (GDP) growth rates, which had been 11.8 percent in 1980 and 8.1 percent in 1981, fell sharply to 5.9 percent in 1982, and 3.2 percent in 1983. While GDP growth recovered somewhat in 1984 and 1985, it plunged again in 1986 by 6.8 percent. Inflation rates soared, averaging more than 100 percent a year between 1982 and 1987. Not surprisingly, real wages plummeted. Mexico's distribution of wealth and income,

14. The student movement had two main critiques: lack of democracy and the inequality of benefits from Mexico's growing economy. The students demanded that the regime reprioritize spending toward the rural and urban poor.

15. President Lázaro Cárdenas expropriated all privately owned oil and petroleum holdings in 1938, on a date that remains a national holiday. Since that time, Mexico's vast oil reserves have been monopolized by the state through the national oil company known as PEMEX. For many years, oil remained the primary source of foreign exchange and the number-one Mexican export. In more recent years, the Mexican economy has diversified substantially, although oil remains very important.

already one of the most unequal in the world, worsened.[16] The country was forced to renegotiate its international debt obligations with private banks, in discussions brokered by the IMF and representatives of the Reagan administration and the U.S. Federal Reserve Bank. The debt payment schedule was adjusted so that Mexico could meet its obligations but only after its agreeing to a dramatic structural adjustment program. This included sharp reductions in government spending, including that directed at low-income people.

All this combined to produce classic boom-and-bust politics. Echeverría, and especially López Portillo, had raised expectations of good economic times. Rather than being able to sustain the promise of significant social mobility, material conditions suffered dramatically through declining real employment wages but also through the reduction in the money and services provided through public programs, known as social wages. In 1982, a minimum salary was hypothetically sufficient for supporting a family of four. By 1988, it was only 50 percent sufficient (Rivas 1989, 8). Public spending as a percentage of GDP decreased from 33.8 percent in 1981 to 19.8 percent in 1988 (Consejo Consultivo del Programa Nacional de Solidaridad 1990). By official count, the number of Mexicans living in poverty rose from 18.4 million in 1981 to 41.3 million in 1988 (ibid.). Severe cuts in social spending occurred in both urban and rural areas (Salinas de Gortari 1989).

As real wages tumbled and corporatist relationships became increasingly difficult because of the loss of patronage funds, Mexico's next president, Miguel de la Madrid (1982–88) focused on economic stabilization during the first half of his administration. By 1985, however, his policy choices made it clear that he was moving Mexico in the direction of a new economic-development paradigm known as neoliberalism.[17]

Once President de la Madrid insisted in 1985 that liberalization was to be the government's official policy and Mexico then engaged in a sweeping

16. All figures are taken from Pastor and Wise 2003. This useful analysis summarizes key dynamics of the Mexico's political economy from 1980 through 2001 at both the macro and micro levels.

17. Neoliberalism is the new internationalized "free market" paradigm that has displaced state-led capitalism in most of Latin America over the course of the past generation. While no two countries that have adopted this model of economic development face the exact same policy options, the most common attributes are efforts to maintain a tight money supply and a balanced budget in pursuit of manageable inflation rates. Balanced, or more nearly balanced, budgets are pursued through cutbacks (oftentimes quite severe) in social spending. Neoliberalism is also defined by the liberalization of import/export laws and encouragement

program of economic modernization, structural adjustment, and linkage with the world economy through trade, foreign investment, and the transfer of technology, something analogous to a political avalanche took place, with changes throughout the system sweeping away old obstacles and putting official prices, import permits, and foreign investment limits on the endangered-species list.

Neoliberalism's advocates argued that ISI stifled economic modernization and growth with too much state ownership and regulation. Its adherents propose decreasing state spending, privatizing state-owned enterprises, and ridding the economy of regulations. Neoliberalism emphasizes inflation control through a tight money supply and minimal state borrowing. It promotes the export sector and sharply reduces restrictions on the free flow of investment, goods, and services across national borders.

The de la Madrid administration's paradigmatic shift in direction after a half century of ISI became the primary focus of critique for those at the center and left of Mexico's political spectrum—a very sizable number of people and organizations. The administration was also criticized for its technocratic decision-making style. The ascendancy of a technocratic elite is a widespread phenomenon in Latin America. Technocrats are political elites with graduate degrees, often in neoclassical economics from U.S. Ivy League schools. Frequently, technocratic presidents have no experience in elected office before becoming president. Such was the case with all Mexican presidents from López Portillo (1976–82) through to Ernesto Zedillo (1994–2000).

Some scholars and a portion of the politically engaged public heralded this shift in the background of the leadership and in policy-making style as freeing Mexico from the weight of political cronyism. Others argued that Mexico's decisions were increasingly influenced by neoclassical economics, which disadvantaged the poor and working classes. Technocrats were often critiqued for their arrogance and for further distancing the decision-making process from citizen consultation. The emphasis on technocratic

---

of the export sector through infrastructural development and tax law. Neoliberalism has resuscitated the imperative of pursuing comparative advantage as the principal public policy goal and pushes governments to encourage the exploitation of factor endowments in an international context rather than seek the development of local industries to meet domestic demand. Neoliberal states are noted for an ideological imperative that demands sharp reduction in state ownership (via privatization, or the selling off of state-owned enterprises) and deregulation in the name of market efficiencies. For a more detailed introduction to Mexican neoliberalism, see P. Haber 1998b; Dussell Peters 2000; Teichman 2001; and Williams 2001.

decision-making during the de la Madrid administration had the unintended affect of alienating the administration from the system of alliances that the regime had long relied on for its legitimacy. This aggravated the already difficult situation brought on by the fiscal crisis, which had undermined the regime's ability to fund the corporatist system.

Social Movement Opposition (1979–88)

What occurred in the 1979–88 period in Mexico supports Susan Eckstein's contention that "economic relationships, especially *changing* economic relationships, [are] the principal cause of protest and pressure for change" (Eckstein 1989, 4; emphasis in original). The sudden economic decline in 1982 altered the political opportunity structure in ways that were favorable to many social movements, which successfully framed the regime's reduction of government subsidies to mobilize large numbers of people and put the state on the defensive. De la Madrid's policies and policy-making style also seriously alienated important sectors of organized labor. Not only were the austerity measures strongly opposed by the unions; in addition, the leaders were often the brunt of the anticorruption policies in the early years of the administration (S. D. Morris 1995, 58).

The political opportunity structure of social movements was improved by the elite splits that had begun when the Yale-educated de la Madrid was selected as the PRI's presidential candidate. De la Madrid further alienated important sectors of the political class by refusing to take account of a wide body of opinion and include many with expertise in his inner circle. This homogeneity in policy making represented an important break with past practice and was to become a feature of neoliberal transitions, not only in Mexico but in other Latin American countries as well.[18] While de la Madrid regularly consulted key members of the business community, their support was weak because of the extremely poor economic performance and the hard line that de la Madrid took against the right-wing opposition party, the Partido Acción Nacional (National Action Party [PAN]) (S. D. Morris 1995, 54).

These elite splits, the massive discontent within civil society, and the creation of the coordinadoras all led the social Left to believe that real gains were possible, and alliances became more common, even between

18. For a comparative study of Argentina, Chile, and Mexico, see Teichman 2001.

actors that had previously been at odds.[19] Two aspects of de la Madrid's neoliberalism were particularly vulnerable to challenge. First, the benefits of privatization (selling state-owned properties and businesses to the private sector) benefited a small number of industrial/financial conglomerates, and allegations of collusion between them and high-level officials was widespread (Teichman 1995, 152–53). Second, de la Madrid was ineffective in mitigating the inevitable political liabilities caused by an economic crisis of immense proportions, and, in fact, his actions only served to exacerbate the situation.

The social movements unleashed a cycle of protest, debate, and confrontation during the 1980s in ways scarcely imaginable during earlier decades. While these dynamics had certainly occurred before on a sporadic and regional basis, what differentiates this protest cycle is how widespread it was and how long it lasted.[20] Complex relationships developed between what in other periods would have been relatively isolated events and actors.

The Coordinadoras

During their "golden age," between 1979 and 1984, the coordinadoras oversaw the activities of important popular sectors despite diverse ideologies, political strategies, leaderships, and interorganizational relationships. All these factors meant that individual organizational autonomy was always in tension with the effort to establish a meaningful set of basic principles, positions, and actions to which all members could adhere.[21] But all agreed on what became one of the most important functions of the coordinadoras: the defense of member organizations threatened by repression.[22]

19. This illustrates one of the propositions of the political process approach: in times of shifting political opportunities, calculations of alliance shift accordingly.

20. Cycles of protest can be usefully viewed by means of a biological metaphor of life maturity and death. While cycles of protest, like biological life forms, always end or die, the duration of the life cycle is uncertain and premature death is a possibility. Health is predetermined to an extent by genetics, but environmental conditions can make a big difference. The ability to adapt to change in environmental climate makes a difference and so does luck.

21. For examples of those who assert the fundamental importance of the coordinadoras during this period, see Carr 1986, 15; Moguel 1987; 1991b, 3; Prieto 1986; and Pérez Arce 1990.

22. An example of acting in defense of those facing repression was the decision to hold the 1989 national meeting of urban popular movements in Jalapa, Veracruz, where the urban popular movement had been threatened. The presence of a large number of movement militants was designed to communicate that their sister organization was not without support.

The three most important coordinadoras were the Coordinadora Nacional Plan de Ayala (National Coordinating Committee of the Plan de Ayala [CNPA]), a peasant-based movement; the Coordinadora Nacional de Trabajadores de la Educación (National Coordinating Committee of Education Workers [CNTE]), a movement for union democracy within the larger PRI-controlled teachers union; and, of most interest here, the National Coordinating Committee of the Urban Popular Movement (CONAMUP). Each of these organizations was created as a direct challenge to one of the three official sectoral institutions of the PRI: CNPA in competition with the National Peasant Confederation (CNC); CNTE with the Confederación Nacional de Organizaciones Populares (National Confederation of Popular Organizations [CNOP]) and the PRI-dominated Labor Congress; and CONAMUP with CNOP.

Each coordinadora represented collective efforts to promote a democratic discourse and establish collective voices in civil society that were in direct competition with official regime discourse. As one CONAMUP member told me, "Before CONAMUP, I had never heard a different history, a different analysis. I had never believed that there was any alternative, because frankly in my world there was none. Before CONAMUP, my political choices were limited to the PRI and its cronies. With the birth of CONAMUP, came the birth of new possibilities for many of us" (interview, 1989).

CNPA, formed in 1979, took its name from the famous Plan de Ayala put forward by Emiliano Zapata during the revolution. CNPA represents an important Mexican example of what Snow and his colleagues (1986) refer to as "frame alignment," whereby a social movement links its concerns to existing images, symbols, motifs, rights, and sensibilities in the culture. The positions taken by CNPA closely followed the original Zapatista claims: land reform and local control of resources by those who work the land; respect for autonomous organizations of agricultural workers and small landholders; and just treatment in the allocation of state supports. Resistance to local power structures in many areas of rural Mexico, especially in the south, is often a dangerous business. Solidarity between members was extremely important to CNPA members, whose vulnerability increased with isolation. History is replete with the efforts of CNPA to defend member organizations against state repression and the violence of local *caciques* (political bosses). If nothing increases solidarity like common defense against great odds, then CNPA certainly had no shortage of opportunities. Despite internal divisions over strategy, CNPA successfully resisted countless efforts to destroy it through co-optation and repression.[23]

Although CNPA was successful in broadcasting that small farmers were particularly hard hit by the devastating affects of the 1980s economic crisis in Mexico, it always lacked the political resources to force a significant reversal of government policy.[24] Policy changes advocated by CNPA were often nostalgic, harking back to the 1930s, and when more radical propositions were voiced, they were even less realistic given the relative lack of rural mobilization against the state. The PRI's greatest base of support remained in the rural areas, electoral fraud was easier, and the PRI was skillful in maintaining well-established rural patronage networks. Finally, threats and acts of repression against opponents were less likely to receive media coverage in the countryside than in the cities and towns. While CNPA's record does not include major legislative victories, using Piven and Cloward's concept (1979) that social movement success must be based on what is historically possible, CNPA persistence and success in making common cause with other sectors of the social Left can legitimately be seen as a measure of success, as the material and political obstacles to effective opposition in remote rural areas are formidable.[25]

23. Harvey identifies a main source of division between those organizations that "insisted on maintaining a high level of national mobilization while others argued that it was necessary to concentrate more on solutions at the local and regional levels" (1998, 136).

CNPA endured difficult internal divisions over strategy in the 1979–82 period. By the middle of 1982, it had regained some of its internal coherence and had been strengthened through the establishment of ties to other coordinadoras. Prieto argues that CNPA suffered from a lack of sufficient legal representation in its land disputes that results in part from a flawed strategy, one that overly relied on mobilization at the expense of negotiation (1986, 87–88). The coordinadora's importance began to fade in 1985–86, as other strong independent peasant movements emerged, most notably UNORCA. It diminished even further in the 1989–91 period, as it proved incapable of effectively responding to Salinas's political and economic initiatives. Although it continued to function through the 1990s, it was "but a shadow of its former self" (Julio Moguel, personal conversation, 1999).

24. CNPA was aided in its claim of the farmers' hardship by data and analysis from many mainline institutions, such as the World Bank, which supported this assertion (World Bank 1986).

25. The 1994 armed uprising by the Zapatistas as advocates of not only indigenous rights but the rural poor in general, was the single most important act of rural opposition since the 1930s. However, even the Zapatistas, who have widespread international support and high levels of legitimacy and support within broad sectors of civil society, have thus far failed to negotiate a successful shift in national policy, either before or after 2000.

Organized labor remained vital to political calculations in Mexico. Throughout the postrevolutionary regime period, from the 1920s up until the election of Vicente Fox in July 2000, it exercised a tremendous influence on the stability of the regime. A key feature of the inclusionary authoritarian regime was the official recognition given to specific unions, which conferred a host of both formal (legal) and informal (extralegal) advantages. It is not unusual that strike numbers go down during economic downturns, because of the vulnerability of workers when shutdowns and layoffs can actually be to the owner's advantage (Finn 1998). In Mexico, however, the tight control that the state maintained over the PRI-controlled unions throughout the crisis determined the limited labor response. They were notably absent and played an insignificant role in the protest cycle; despite the 44 percent plummet in real manufacturing wages between 1982 and 1989, the number of strikes decreased by 83 percent, petitions to strike decreased by 58 percent, and the number of striking workers declined by 73 percent during that same time period (Cook 1991, 1). The relative lack of labor unrest explains why the actions of other groups—most notably the urban poor—loomed so large in the overall structure of defiance. It also explains in part why the opposition did not accomplish more: if there had been more active labor involvement, the threat to the system would have been significantly greater.

The most important exception to this dominant pattern was CNTE, a dissident current within the Sindicato Nacional de Trabajadores de la Educación (National Union of Education Workers [SNTE]), which is probably the largest single union in all Latin America, with about a million members (Cook 1996, 2–3). CNTE had its beginnings in 1979, when teachers in the southern state of Chiapas resisted union leadership impositions designed to reduce dissent. Their actions propelled the formation within the SNTE of CNTE, which resisted SNTE cronyism and state neglect of education.

By Luis Hernández Navarro's count, CNTE organized "six successive waves of demonstrations, involving nearly 150,000 educational workers, against their union leadership at both the regional and the national levels" during its first three years (1986, 59). Like the other coordinadoras, CNTE had to defend itself against repressive reprisals, most notably when it mobilized forty thousand people to protest the assassination of CNTE leader Misrael Núñez Acosta in 1981.

The case of CNTE provides graphic evidence for how movement strategy and fortunes change over the course of a boom-and-bust period.[26] While it was able to make a powerful argument for increased wages and work conditions for teachers in the heady days of the oil boom, the onslaught of the 1982 economic crisis reduced the possibility of winning wage demands and led CNTE to shift its focus to political reform within the PRI-controlled union structure, and they subsequently won five seats at the thirteenth National Congress of the SNTE. However, like CNPA, CNTE was unable to achieve structural reform or substantially mitigate the economic crisis for educational employees or for the educational system in general (Street 1992; Foweraker 1993; Cook 1996).[27]

Arguably, the most important coordinadora for the protest cycle was the urban popular movement, the sector where the regime's official organization had far less influence than in either the peasant or labor sector.[28] The urban movement's national coordinating committee (CONAMUP) was constituted through the efforts of a nucleus of four individual recently formed social movements.[29] At its first national meeting, in May 1980 in the

26. As all Mexican unions are legally obligated to be sanctioned by the state, before being able to work in the public school system, a breakaway union would have had to gain recognition through the Ministry of Education. The impossibility of this task effectively blocked the strategy of forming a new union. Despite this obstacle, Luis Hernández "calculated in March 1982 that the CNTE had a solid base of about 100,000 members, a capacity to mobilize 150,000 teachers, and an immediate potential of 200,000" (cited in Moguel 1987, 28). The first figure represents about 16 percent of total SNTE union membership. "After a decline in the mid-1980s, the dissident ranks grew again in both absolute and proportional terms during the mobilizations of 1989. Approximately 500,000 teachers were said to have been on strike in early 1989. The number of members identified with the CNTE after 1989 probably stabilized at around 300,000, or approximately 30 percent of the union" (Cook 1996, 3 n. 5).

27. While some charge that CNTE's emphasis on internal democracy undermined its decision-making capacity and exacerbated internal fragmentation, Cook makes a persuasive argument that its internal democracy is a fundamental strength (ibid.). Moguel argued that the serious problems of the CNPA and CONAMUP in adjusting to changing conditions in the late 1980s was caused, at least in part, by the scam of "direct democracy" that only served to obscure the lack democratic participation (Moguel 1990a, 11). Moguel's argument bolster's Cook's: the limitations of CNTE do not principally derive from the impressive level of internal democracy achieved.

28. The phrase *urban popular movement* was coined during the first two CONAMUP meetings, the second of which was held in Durango.

29. These four organizations were the Frente Popular Tierra y Libertad from Monterrey (founded in 1976), the CDP of Durango (founded in 1979), the Unión de Colonias Populares del Valle de México (founded in 1979), and the Frente Popular de Zacatecas (founded in 1979).

northern city of Monterrey, it created an umbrella organization capable of developing an agenda for the urban poor while also defending individual movements against repression. Although always characterized by some internal stress as a result of its political heterogeneity, CONAMUP managed to contain conflict quite well during the "golden era" of 1979–84.

Urban popular movement organizations affiliated with the political currents of Política Popular and the Organización de Izquierda Revolucionaria–Línea de Masas (Revolutionary Left Organization–Mass Line [OIR-LM])—notably the Frente Popular Tierra y Libertad (Popular Front Land and Liberty [FPTYL]) and the CDP of Durango—argued against electoral involvement during the early 1980s, insisting that the time was not yet right, given the absence of a "real party of the people." Urban popular movement organizations affiliated with the political current represented by Movimiento Revolucionario del Pueblo (Revolutionary Movement of the People [MRP]), particularly the Unión de Colonias Populares (Union of Popular Neighborhoods [UCP]), early on favored electoral involvement, with the aim of increasing visibility and legitimization. CONAMUP was formed with the understanding that this difference would be respected, with each movement organization free to opt for its own electoral strategy.

From the outset, CONAMUP defined itself as a revolutionary movement, identifying itself with the revolutionary struggles in other Latin American countries, especially El Salvador. Like the other coordinadoras, CONAMUP resisted official affiliation with political currents or parties, while formally insisting on respect for the individual decisions of members to affiliate as they chose. Throughout the 1980s, CONAMUP remained steadfast in its refusal to take a unified position on electoral involvement, despite the insistence by some members that the importance of electoral politics had increased so much that the coordinadora had become marginalized (P. Haber 1989). These issues came to a head around the Cárdenas electoral campaign when the conclusion that he had been deprived of victory only through the treachery of the regime was hegemonic within virtually all opposition circles.

The political current the OIR-LM, formed in February 1982, has special relevance to this study because not only was it the most influential new current to emerge during this period but also because the CDP leadership were major players.[30] The formation of the OIR-LM when seen in juxtaposition

30. The OIR was the creation of four Maoist organizations: the Movimiento Obrero, Campesino, Estudiantil Revolucionario (MOCER) de Zacatecas; the FPTYL of Monterrey; the CDP of Durango; and the Seccional Ho Chi Min of Mexico City. The principal leaders of this

to the Partido Socialista Unificado de México (Unified Socialist Party of Mexico [PSUM]) provides a window into the sectarianism of the Mexican Left that extended into the 1990s. The PSUM was created in 1981 in response to 1970s electoral reforms.

The OIR-LM argued that the study of history showed that a "true" workers party must be led by organic intellectuals who would not make a fetish of industrial workers and must favor the formation of a "natural vanguard" in the social movement. The OIR-LM's mission was to build this natural vanguard into a revolutionary one that would be capable of contributing to the transformation of Mexican society (see, in particular, OIR-LM 1982). The OIR-LM based its credentials and capabilities on its long years of grass-roots experience with social movements. OIR-LM leaders were often quick to point out how this experience contrasted sharply with that of most left-ist political parties, notably the PSUM and its predecessor, the Communist Party (interviews by the author). These parties were criticized for being top heavy with university-trained, overly abstract, overly "worker-oriented" intellectuals.[31]

The OIR-LM was formed to complement the coordinadora organizations, which were conceived as mass organizations, but unlike the coordinadoras, the OIR-LM was not constructed directly for the rank-and-file masses. Rather, its meetings were attended by cuadros (second-tier leadership) and those in top leadership positions. OIR-LM meetings and publications were characterized by long debates over how to best interpret "the historical moment," derive "optimal strategy" from it, and better organize

---

organization were Alberto Anaya from Monterrey; José Narro from Zacatecas; Marcos Cruz, Gonzalo Yáñez, and Alfonso P. Rios from Durango; and Julio Moguel, Luis Hernández, Saul Escobar, Jesús Martin del Campo, Francisco González Gómez, Armando Quientero, Benjamin Hernández Camacho, Rosario Robles, and Jorge Isaac from Mexico City.

31. In my preliminary conversations with CDP bases, cuadros, and leaders, I was struck by their constant reference to a movement culture of activities and decision making characterized by opposition to dominant authoritarian norms, or what Gramsci conceptualized in the early twentieth century as "prefigurative politics." Gramsci (1971) insisted that a commitment to prefigurative politics includes resistance to existing cultural norms regarding interpersonal relationships and creates environments that successfully encourage human relationships that transform the commodified and instrumental relationships of dominant capitalist and political society into relationships characterized by solidarity in pursuit of democratic socialist ideals. This Gramscian notion has been very influential for both movement activists and scholars. The primary responsibility of such a politics is "to create and sustain within the lived practice of the movement relationships and political forms that "prefigured" and embodied the desired society" (Gamson 1992a, 62).

Mexico's revolutionary potential. Considerable effort was directed at transforming existing members and budding leadership into revolutionary cadre capable of moving Mexico toward a socialist reality. Once the proper praxis was developed by the revolutionary vanguard, it was disseminated to the rank and file.

The goals of OIR-LM were not limited to honing the rational, instrumental skills of leaders and cuadros, or attempting to read with efficacious precision the lived moment of history. They were *also* a response to what Alberto Melucci (1989) has argued is the pivotal work of social movements: the construction of collective identity. The work of the urban popular movement was not limited to the material struggles of the urban poor, as important as this was; nor was the movement limited to pressuring the state to adhere to its own rhetoric regarding the mitigation of poverty. The urban popular movement was also engaged in redefining the identity of the urban poor within a new vision for the country at large. The OIR-LM was committed to this work.

The importance of the OIR-LM during the early 1980s, as well as other political currents such as the Asociación Cívica Nacional Revolucionaria (National Revolutionary Civic Association [ACNR]) and the Socialist Current, reflects the long history of deep antagonism between political parties and social movements. While the construction of the OIR-LM was a clear step in the direction of building a "true party of the masses," this group did not believe that the time had come to participate in electoral politics (OIR-LM 1982). Its deep suspicions regarding party involvement were to change in the later 1980s in response to changing political opportunities when Cárdenas became a symbol of unity for virtually all Left and populist forces. At that time, the OIR-LM became the basis of the Partido de Trabajo (Workers' Party [PT]), and the ACNR and Socialist Current (both associated with the AB) joined with the Cárdenas-led Party of the Democratic Revolution (PRD).

While the early 1980s witnessed many energetic moves toward social movement unification, these efforts fell far short of party building. Political parties were suspected of wanting to control the resources of these movements for their own goals. Given that social movements did not see the electoral option as a favorable use of their political opportunities, advances by the parties were often not well received. Because of the importance of the movements to overall Left power during the 1980s, the lack of movement support undermined the potential of Left political parties.

This hesitancy and distrust of the political parties is clearly expressed in the following statement:

PAN, PRI, PSUM, they're all the same. Political parties were created by political elites able to manipulate working people to mobilize and organize on their behalf. Urban social movements were created precisely because political parties, at least in this country, are not true and able representatives of the masses. Parties of the Left, who pretend to speak on our behalf, are as bad as the PRI. Succeeding in our revolutionary struggle is dependent upon maintaining a healthy distance from political parties. We should not even negotiate with them, at least until such time as they recognize us as equals if not the vanguard. (Urban social movement leader, interview by the author, 1987)

In June 1983, after much wrangling, a cross section of left-leaning organizations finally agreed to combine forces and managed to create a new organization, the Asamblea Nacional de Obreros y Campesinos Popular (National Popular Assembly of Workers and Peasants [ANOCP]), which, along with the coordinadoras, organized two important *paro cívicos* (civic strikes), one involving well more than a million people. From a political process perspective, the high numbers indicate that large numbers of people anticipated vulnerability in the state's position, leading them to protest. While some important elements of the Left did not participate, the civic strike nonetheless was a dramatic show of coordinated discontent.[32] The mere fact that such coordination was possible generated significant excitement on the left that a multiclass surge could force reforms and perhaps even structural alterations. As one movement intellectual explained:

> As is well known by knowledgeable observers, the Mexican Left had been long hampered by an extremely high level of conformity on the part of civil society to the official ideology of the state and its party, the PRI. . . . The economic crisis, and what was widely

32. Noticeably absent from the strike were independent unions such as the Sindicato Unico de Trabajadores de la Industria Nuclear (SUTIN) and the Frente Auténtico del Trabajo (FAT). Even the Unidad Obrera Independiente (UOI), which had first proposed the strike, withdrew from the effort in the final hours, arguing that the participation of political parties compromised the popular character of the strike. Prieto disputes this, claiming that UOI dropped out in favor of negotiating a separate deal with the state (1986, 92).

Walton's (1989) survey of protests against austerity measures that were implemented throughout Latin America demonstrates that the civic strikes were common during this period of Latin American history.

perceived (and even reported in some of the national dailies) to be the inept management of the crisis, with clear signs of very disproportionate distribution of austerity, allowed us to work—for the first time in my lifetime—in an atmosphere of significant potential for regime change. (Interview by the author)

Repression

Rather than change course, the de la Madrid administration chose to take a more hard line policy.[33] Increased repression on individual movement organizations was at least partially effective in forcing into a defensive position many organizations that had recently become more aggressive. The second half of 1984 witnessed the dismantling of ANOCP—a direct result of increased repression. As repression discouraged openly radical civil disobedience, the electoral option became more appealing to many social movements. The success of increased repression to constrain the creation of powerful multiclass alliances continued into the elections of 1985, when the Left received only 6.02 percent of the vote.[34]

Increased repression spurred intense and divisive debate on the electoral option within organizations such as CONAMUP. Divergent positions were taken by two important member organizations: the Movimiento Revolucionario del Pueblo (Revolutionary Movement of the People [MRP]) and the OIR-LM. The MRP argued that membership should be open to political organizations (including political parties) in addition to urban social movements (Bouchier Tretiack 1988, 92). Important urban movement organizations, most notably the UCP, encouraged CONAMUP to take the possibility of electoral participation seriously. The OIR-LM countered that CONAMUP membership should be limited to urban social movements,

33. While most organizations can document increased repression in the years following the strike, the most publicized incidents include events in Juchitán in which the COCEI lost its bid to hold on to a municipal electoral victory, events at the National Teacher's College in Mexico City, and at the Autonomous University of Guerrero.

34. According to official figures, the 1985 Left vote was divided between three parties: PSUM (3.24), PMT (1.53) and PRT (1.25). This was a serious disappointment to those who had advocated for the electoral arena as a potentially important area of struggle for the Left. The 1985 figure of 6.02 percent was little more than the 5.64 received in the 1982 election or the first election following the 1977 electoral reform in which the Communist Party (PCM) received 4.86 percent of the vote (Moguel 1987, 76).

arguing that its power came precisely from its continued autonomy from political parties. The OIR-LM position won out, and CONAMUP declared its "autonomy in relation to political organizations" (CONAMUP 1983, 146).

While alliances would certainly continue, the right of individual movements to abstain from particular actions—notably electoral behavior—was respected. While this held the coordinadora together, it undermined CONAMUP's ability to take firm positions on national issues (P. Haber 1990). As CONAMUP also decided to limit membership to urban social movement organizations, any chance to host the emergence of a powerful broad-based-movement organization was lost. As this situation suggests, the problems of autonomy are not limited to relations with the state but can and often do include those with political parties and other political organizations as well.

The coordinadora strategy as a response to increased state repression raises an important theoretical point: social movements not only shift strategy to exploit new expanding opportunities but also to adjust to restrictions. The building of network ties was designed in part to protect individual movement organizations so that the movement could be more assertive in pressing its agenda. The coordinadoras successfully challenged the revolutionary credentials of the regime, disputing the PRI/state's appropriation of the most important symbols of the Mexican Revolution—the 1917 Mexican Constitution and the revolutionary heroes Emiliano Zapata and Pancho Villa—and framing their discourses within these already broadly recognized and highly legitimate cognitive frames. They successfully convinced many potential movement activists and sympathizers that (1) the goals of the revolution and its most progressive leaders were legitimate and desirable, (2) the PRI/government's appropriation of these symbols should be delegitimated, (3) that the independent social movements were the legitimate bearers of these goals, and (4) joining forces or at least being sympathetic to the movements was a realistic way to realize these revolutionary goals.

Cascading Earthquakes

The year 1985 was extremely important for the 1980s protest cycle in general and the urban popular movement in particular. Not only was Mexico City afflicted with an earthquake that killed more than fifteen thousand people but the regime's inability to respond competently to the disaster undermined its legitimacy. Also in 1985, the de la Madrid administration took a radical departure from postrevolutionary policy in regard to foreign investment, U.S.-Mexican relations, and the Mexican development model by adopting neoliberalism, which caused splits within the ruling elites.

During the first several days following the September earthquake, which measured 7.3 on the Richter scale, citizens poured into the streets and formed work crews, toiling in many cases around the clock. The scores of heroic deeds that occurred contributed to the human bonding and emotions that are peculiar to crisis situations and transformed social consciousness, at least temporarily. Much of the optimism felt by the opposition immediately following the earthquake derived from the hope that the experience of working with people from other neighborhoods and social classes—which under previous, "normal" conditions would have been avoided and feared—could be built upon to produce a shift in political consciousness against the party/state regime. In contrast to this massive civil response and solidarity, official voices were repeatedly aired over the electronic media, instructing citizens to stay in their houses, announcing that all was under control thanks to government emergency response teams. Few people believed this message, and the appearance, in particularly hard hit areas, of de la Madrid, well groomed and in an expensive leather jacket, further reinforced the already widespread perception that he was out of touch with the realities of most Mexicans.

In the weeks and months following the earthquake, new movement organizations emerged and grew at rates that amazed everyone, not least of all the movement leaders themselves.[35] Preexisting movement organizations were also strengthened, most dramatically in the Mexico City area, but in many other parts of Mexico as well. As one leader from Tijuana explained:

> We were, all of us, in and out of the movement, watching events on the TV, listening to news broadcasts on the radio, and reading about it all in the newspapers. The excitement was contagious. Especially as the people were mobilized in protests at places with

35. In the dozens of interviews I conducted with leaders of urban popular movements between 1987 and 1991, the question of the earthquake's contribution to the protest cycle repeatedly came up. Respondents were almost universal in recounting their overwhelming surprise at the extent of "take-off" generated by the earthquake for collective dissent not only in Mexico City but across the country as well.

high visibility, like the legislature or, better yet, the Presidential Palace, it was felt here not only by us, but [also] by the governor and other political elites here in the border towns. We started, well, in a way, mimicking what was happening in Mexico City. When they started demanding decent housing conditions for all in Mexico City, we said, why can't we do that here as well? And so we did. (Interview by the author, 1988)

Despite internal tensions, up until the earthquake CONAMUP had been capable of containing the overwhelming majority of urban movements under its umbrella.[36] With the earthquake, the newly established colonias on the periphery of existing urban areas where CONAMUP was strongest became less important as social movement activity and national attention focused on areas hardest hit by the quake, in downtown Mexico City. New movement organizations, such as the Coordinadora Unica de Damnifica-dos (United Coordinating Committee of Earthquake Victims [CUD]), which formed in October 1985 with the participation of 27 organizations and 20 affiliates, eroded CONAMUP's centrality. In 1987, the CUD gave birth to the Asamblea de Barrios (AB).

These new movement organizations challenged CONAMUP, arguing that its focus on the construction of *colonias populares* located on the outskirts of urban areas had come at the expense of ignoring the problems of low-income renters and the movement organizations they had constructed.[37] Important movement leaders and other influential individuals argued that the time had come to act as a social, rather than a popular, movement and that CONAMUP had failed to meet the challenge.[38] Organizations responding to the earthquake began to enter into agreements with international agencies, such as the Swiss Red Cross, Catholic Relief Service, and United

36. Vega has carefully calculated that in 1984, 60 percent of all urban popular movements belonged to CONAMUP (1989, 158).

37. The term *colonias populares* (popular-class neighborhoods) is used in two ways. In the first, it means simply any low-income neighborhoods. In the second, it refers to either low-income neighborhoods that have been constructed and organized by urban popular movement organizations or already constructed low-income neighborhoods that have since been organized by such organizations. It is this second definition that will be of most importance in this study.

38. As first discussed in the Introduction, the distinction here is between popular movements, which are oriented toward improving services and other basic material needs on the basis of established rights (*reivindicaciones*), and social movements, which prove themselves capable of generating significant transformations of power and class.

Nations agencies, in reconstruction efforts that included multiclass beneficiaries. This internationalization of relationships and funding and the
building of multiclass coalitions had a dynamic affect. Especially among
downtown movement organizations, this signaled new opportunities to be
seized. It called for a new alignment of the pecking order within the urban
popular movement and new strategies to exploit the new structure of political opportunities. Finally, the leadership of some of the more powerful
movements that the earthquake gave birth to came from outside the ranks
of the OIR-LM and CONAMUP (interviews by the author and author's observations at CONAMUP meetings, national and regional).

The Rise of Cárdenas

The 1985 adoption of neoliberal policies by the de la Madrid administration, most notably through changes in the foreign-investment law, split
the political elite. As predicted by the political process approach, this type
of rupture often greatly expands political opportunities for opposition
forces. In the Mexican case, it was a decisive factor in Cuauhtémoc Cárdenas's ability to gain the support of many longtime PRI supporters when he
decided to split from the PRI and lead a nationalist, progressive populist
bid for the presidency in 1987–88 (Laso de la Vega 1987; Muñoz Ledo
1988).

While inflation rates went down steadily between 1982 and 1984, they
shot up again in 1986 (by 106 percent) and 1987 (159 percent) (Pastor and
Wise 2003, 182). Opposition forces were quick to seize on this development—
austerity measures and a "selling out to the *gringos*" that were sacrificing
national pride and impoverishing the nation could not even achieve their
most important stated goal: controlling inflation. Loudly critiquing the
costs of implementing neoliberal reforms and the austerity measures associated with them through de la Madrid's technocratic fiat fueled the
protest cycle as it reached its zenith in the summer of 1988. Repeated
warnings to the president and his closest associates that his approach was
undermining the regime's stability went largely unnoticed or unheeded.
After all, when a regime has remained in power for six decades, a certain
impression of inevitable stability has a not unsurprising force. However,
within the growing opposition, regime stability and regime continuity did
not feel inevitable. Movement organizations were growing in frequency

and size, mobilizing protests, marches, and large public meetings. To many, Mexico appeared on the precipice of regime change.

De la Madrid's policies split the glue of anti-imperialist nationalism that had bound the PRI electoral and legislative alliance to a set of semiautonomous parties, the Partido Popular Socialista (Popular Socialist Party [PPS]), the Partido Auténtico de la Revolución Mexicana (Authentic Party of the Mexican Revolution [PARM]), and the Partido Socialista de los Trabajadores (PST) together. Until the mid-1980s, these so-called satellite parties were willing to orbit the PRI as long as it maintained a semblance of Left rhetoric in its foreign policy and in exchange were granted limited influence and, more important, government posts and privileges for its leadership. When they cut their ties to the PRI, these parties joined the coalition of social movements and political parties known as the National Democratic Front (FDN).

The origins of the FDN can be traced to 1987, when the Corriente Democrática (Democratic Current) emerged as a dissident group from within the ranks of the PRI. The *corriente* was headed by Cuauhtémoc Cárdenas, son of national hero President Lázaro Cárdenas and a staunch nationalist, and veteran politician Porfirio Muñoz Ledo. The *corriente* agitated strongly against de la Madrid's neoliberalism and the party's lack of internal democracy, particularly in the selection of the presidential candidate; Cárdenas was a serious contender for that role. Cárdenas's decision to run for president after the *corriente*'s expulsion from the PRI provoked a whirlwind of support—the Socialist Party's presidential candidate, Heberto Castillo, bowed out of the race in favor of Cárdenas, and groups that supported Castillo, such as the CDP, followed suit. Additional support came from individuals within the regime—no doubt in part because they realized that the regimen's balance of power increasingly favored "técnicos" over the more traditional *políticos*.[39]

The Cárdenas candidacy was a galvanizing, uniting force that greatly intensified the speed of the protest cycle. At a pace that was truly breathtaking, virtually the entire Center-Left spectrum joined in to work hard on the

39. "In Mexican popular usage the two terms are used to distinguish differences in career patterns (bureaucratic versus electoral experience), qualifications for entry (expertise versus loyal service to party), basis for legitimacy (professional administration versus continuation of Revolutionary heritage), and ideological guidelines (technical versus political rationales). They may also reflect geographical (Federal District versus provinces), generational (post-1940 versus pre-1940), and possibly racial and class differences" (Centeno 1997, 103).

Cárdenas campaign. Within Mexico's "culture of the leader," Cárdenas posed a viable threat to the regime, as he gained a popularity that had not been achieved by any other candidate since the demobilization of the revolutionary forces in the 1930s. It strikes me as poetically ironic that this demobilization of the 1930s that was so fundamental to the consolidation of the regime was accomplished by Lázaro Cárdenas and the most important threat to be posed to this consolidation would come from Lázaro's son, Cuauhtémoc a half century later. To add even further to the complexity of this situation, following his presidency (1934–40), Lázaro often played the role of urging the regime in a left leaning direction, warning that the regime's longevity depended on progressively fulfilling the left-leaning promises of the revolution. And, it would fall to Cuauhtémoc to in a way fulfill his father's warnings by leading a regime destabilizing movement precisely on the grounds that the regime had failed to heed his father's warnings.

Although the FDN argued that the de la Madrid administration had sold out the goals of the revolution, given in to foreign creditors and investors, and increased authoritarianism, many on the left remained wary of Cárdenas's progressive credentials. After all, he was an ex-*priísta* governor of the state of Michoacán and had been a serious contender for the PRI's presidential nomination. However, whatever the leadership reluctance, the surge of grassroots support for Cárdenas gave the movements very little choice other than to support him. As one leader put it:

> In the days following the Cárdenas announcement that he would run for the presidency, it's all the people wanted to talk about. In the independent union halls, and even in many of the *priísta* unions, people could not contain their excitement. Here for the first time was a guy with name recognition who was willing to challenge the PRI. The economic policies were killing people. We were a country with its tail between its legs, cowering from the frequent beatings of the IMF and other international giants. Mexicans are a deeply nationalist, proud people. This was not easy to take. So, along comes this Cárdenas who tells us that he tried to democratize the PRI so that the people's business could be heard and our pride restored, and he was told no. Here was a guy with the guts to walk out of the power circles and take a chance, throwing his hopes to the people. Here was a guy who when he referred

to our movements did not do so with open disdain or complete ignorance of who we were and what we stood for. (Interview by the author, Mexico City, 1988)

Another movement leader added:

We called a meeting and I remember walking toward the park where the meeting was to be held and hearing the chants for Cárdenas. The place was packed and the people were ecstatic. They knew something important was happening. After six years of getting absolutely screwed, well really, after decades of getting screwed, people were finally getting a chance to unleash their enthusiasm for the big fight. Not just a little bit more of this budget or that, but a change of the whole thing. That is what Cárdenas represented to people in 1988. As I walked toward that stage, I knew, we all knew [the movement leadership] that the decision was already taken. People were not waiting to be led on this decision. It was theirs, and they were making it. (Interview by the author, Mexico City, 1988)

Urban social movement organizations in Mexico City were especially important to these dramatic political developments as well as to the signs of institutional reform that took place during the second half of the de la Madrid administration.[40] These included the election of "social movement friendly" representatives to the Federal District Assembly, the electoral onslaught of Cárdenas in July 1988, and the general atmosphere of civil empowerment that pervaded the city that were expressed in concrete proposals (such as that for statehood for the Federal District). However, the relative importance of social movements to Cárdenas's 1988 showing has

---

40. Toward and at the height of the protest cycle, commentators debated the claim that there were more movements or movement participants than in the past, in either real or proportional terms. Alan Knight pointed out that we lacked comparative data for the 1940–65 period (1990, 79). Ann Craig argued that "we may have the impression that there are *more* but that organized groups continue to represent a distinct minority of the population" (1990, 272). However, most movement participants themselves believed that they were part of a rising tide of political opposition, and this belief fueled their willingness to participate energetically in opposition politics. They argued that (1) sympathy was much higher across the class spectrum than in the recent past, (2) the overall numbers of affiliates were up, and (3) the overall movement presence was definitely stronger than in the 1940–65 period.

inspired considerable passionate debate but eludes final conclusions. Some analysts, such as Judy Hellman (1992, 1994), strongly assert that the FDN could not have attained its 1988 successes without the previously constructed social movement sector. Others conclude that the relation between popular movements and Cárdenas in 1988 was relatively unimportant: Cárdenas's impressive electoral showing was the result of spontaneous voting for a popular alternative to the PRI (interviews by the author). Movement organizations certainly made important contributions by promoting Cárdenas as a candidate, providing institutional structures upon which campaign activities could build, and helping in the important task of poll watching and scrutinizing official counts.

There is no doubt about the significance of the Cárdenas candidacy for Mexican social movements. Cárdenas's bid for the presidency provided the national project to which many movement organizations had aspired but which they had not been able to accomplish in the post-1968 era. Previous efforts at broad coalitions were widely viewed as practice runs by activists entertaining visions of multiclass national movements with the capacity to transform Mexican politics. Virtually all aspects of urban social movement activity were deeply influenced by the ideas and type of institution building that was associated with Cuauhtémoc Cárdenas—often referred to in Mexico as neo-Cardenismo—and almost all major social movement organizations supported his candidacy.[41]

The elections of July 1988 marked a watershed in Mexican political history, dealing a severe shock to the PRI. The official announcement that Carlos Salinas de Gortari won was followed by an tidal wave of charges of official fraud. Credible challenges to the official count have been published.[42] Massive mobilizations occurred around the country, most dramatically in Mexico City—where I joined an estimated one million other people protesting the result. At this rally, other opposition candidates—including the center-right PAN candidate Manuel Clouthier—raised their fists in unison with Cárdenas to the thunderous approval of the crowd.

41. Even those few exceptions, such as those movements that supported PRT candidate Rosario Ibarra for presidency, joined forces in defense of Cárdenas's victory against official fraud in the highly mobilized period following the elections that extended into the fall of 1988 and the first quarter of 1989.

42. For analytical scrutiny on the July 1988 elections, see, for example, the collection of essays compiled in Butler and Bustamante 1991. Perhaps the most authoritative study published in Mexico is by the Fundación Arturo Rosenblueth (1989).

Uncertainty and the possibility of major change had permeated the sense of certainty and political stability that were the hallmarks of the Mexican system.

The opposition's areas of strength (both the FDN and the PAN) were in urban Mexico and those regions that have experienced large amounts of recent migration (Barberán et al. 1988, 23–24). The most dramatic victory was in Mexico City and surrounding areas, where the FDN registered a landslide despite its weakness relative to the regime in material and human resources. Members of the urban social movements and students assisted Cárdenas in the cities by promoting the FDN and helping to ensure against irregularities at polling places. Cárdenas's inability to make himself more popular with rural voters, particularly in more remote areas, was combined with a lack of resources to protect voting practices against corruption.

While the presidential election was certainly the focal point, elections for the Senate and the lower house were also significant. While the PRI won 249 of the 300 direct district competitions (31 for the PAN and 20 for the Left and Center-Left candidates), thanks to the 200 seats awarded on the basis of proportional voting, the opposition gained 189 more seats. While this was not enough to reverse major policy directions, it certainly provided the legislative opposition with an important sounding board from which to criticize administrative policies and began the major shift in relations between the legislative and executive branches that is so central to the democratic transition still under way in the first years of the twenty-first century.

These victories greatly stimulated interest in the electoral option among movement leadership. At the time, there was great excitement about this possibility. As one Mexico City movement leader noted:

> There we were watching all these seats go to the Left opposition. And we said, hey, those should be our seats. I mean, if the time had come that the Left was really going to get a seat at the table, if things were finally starting to shift our way, then we reasoned, we should be in those seats. Who really knew the situation on the ground? We did. Why should positions of power go to party hacks whose hands were unsoiled from the work in the barrios. We represented the poor. If the poor were going to get the good representation they deserved in the halls of power, we both

> deserved to give it to them and were obligated to do so. (Interview by the author)

The longevity of the postrevolutionary Mexican political regime is explained in part by its prevention of multiclass and regional alliances strong enough to bring down the regime, either through voting blocs or massive collective dissent. Both the 1988 election and the mass mobilizations and public protest alarmed many regime supporters, as this member of the political elite in his midfifties describes:

> I came of age in the context of the 1960s student movement. The lesson I and many of my colleagues drew was that while the system had liabilities, it more importantly had the capacity to address them. We were proud of this capacity, something very rare among countries at our level of socioeconomic development. We did not deny problems; we fixed them. The 1970s in a sense fixed the 1960s, and when the fiscal imbalances of Echeverría's remedy required attention, the succeeding administration prepared to do what was required until oil discoveries allowed for the postponement of austerity. When the entire development model was called into question in the early 1980s, we did not panic, but rather moved decisively to correct the situation by the introduction of a new, more appropriate model. But nothing prepared us for the massive response of the summer of 1988. This was something we had never seen before. For the first time in my life, I felt the political system to be threatened to the point that I did not know if we could successfully respond. Looking back now, I see that we were able. But, to be honest, this comes only with the benefit of hindsight. At the moment, many of us were very much less certain. (Interview by the author, July 1992)

The PRI, even by official count, lost the urban vote in the 1988 presidential elections, managing its disputed victory only by finishing strongly in rural areas. Regime defenders had much to worry about. Not only had the Cardenista faction's break with the PRI created a strong Center-Left opposition candidate for president, but Cárdenas himself appeared potentially a moral leader for regime transition, in a situation with similarities to of Vaclav Havel in Czechoslovakia or Nelson Mandela in South Africa.

Conclusion

In the land that is now Mexico, political authoritarianism and the concentration of economic wealth has its roots in a time long before the arrival of the Spanish. The colonial system built on this elitism and contributed to it a caste system based on race. The structures of extreme political, economic, and cultural inequalities were incorporated in the founding of Mexico in the early nineteenth century: although there were individuals and movements dedicated to serious egalitarian reform, the independence movement that institutionalized the new nation did not include either these people or the serious implementation of their ideas. The Mexican Revolution, occurring a hundred years later, failed in a similar fashion: the ideals of the more radical reformers were—to be charitable—muted in their implementation. The inclusionary corporatist authoritarian regime established during the 1920s and 1930s institutionalized inequality in a remarkably resilient way. Although there were regional and episodic challenges to this system, and although these challenges often resulted in moderate regime reforms, the fundamental structures of extreme inequalities in Mexico endured. The economic crisis of the 1980s changed in fundamental ways the structure of political opportunities that were available to oppositions that emerged from within and outside the existing regime. These forces came together in 1988 to challenge the regime as it had not been challenged for a half century.

Through effective strategy—and hard work—the urban social movement did a better job of exploiting its newfound opportunities than did the de la Madrid administration did in marshaling the still-vast available state resources to undermine increased protest and pressure for change. In his focus on macroeconomic stabilization and the introduction of neoliberal reforms in consultation with the business community, de la Madrid paid inadequate attention to how these policies were experienced by the majority of low-income Mexicans. This choice of focus put the corporatist authoritarian regime at risk. Implementing unpopular policies without effectively "doing politics" encouraged the development of powerful dissident alliances.

De la Madrid's governing style stimulated the maturation of powerful electoral oppositions led by leaders (popular PAN leader Manuel Clouthier in addition to Cárdenas) who were previously willing to work within the system as well as those "outside" the system (members of social movements).

De la Madrid's policies and detached style of governance not only encouraged leftist popular movements and neo-Cardenismo but also contributed decisively to the increased mobilization of the business class and sections of the middle class around Clouthier, who broke ranks with existing channels of negotiation and interest mediation, resigning his position as president of the Consejo Coordinador Empresarial (Coordinating Business Council), one of the most important negotiating forums for Mexican business with the state.

The economic crisis and subsequent paradigmatic shift from state-led capitalism to neoliberalism provoked in a political crisis that was exacerbated by de la Madrid's failure to renovate the system of political alliances at the same time. For not only did de la Madrid initiate a process of change in an economic-development model long associated with the "perfection of the Revolution," he did so while continuing to pay Mexico's enormous foreign debt and initiating strict austerity measures. Millions of Mexicans realized that paying the foreign debt by cutting social services directly decreased their standard of living while simultaneously damaging their national pride. Clearly, political leadership needed to chart a new course if the regime was to continue.

THREE

The Seesaw Political Economy of Recovery, Crisis, and Democratic Transition, 1988–2000

In previous decades, the PRI could count on *campesinos* who had received land from agrarian reform, and unionized workers who were the product of import-substituting industrialization. Now the country is experiencing a formidable process of transformation. We must seek new bases of support for the party. We must build alliances with new groups, some of which are unorganized now; others are organized for various purposes, but don't want to participate in political parties. We must convince them to participate.
—PRESIDENT CARLOS SALINAS DE GORTARI

The elite fragmentation and civic protest of mid-1980s Mexico could not continue into the next administration without putting the entire regime in jeopardy. In keeping with its traditions of adaptability, the regime's political elite regrouped under the leadership of Carlos Salinas and introduced an extremely effective program of political reconstruction that successfully divided the opposition. The first priority was to separate the conservative PAN from the left-leaning Cárdenas, because regime leaders were well aware that if all major opposition forces unified, the regime would surely be removed from power. Agreements with the PAN leadership, particularly those in legislative office, were facilitated by the fact that both the highest ranks of the PRI and the PAN were neoliberals, while Cárdenas clearly was not. Salinas demonstrated an almost uncanny ability at crucial moments to come to "understandings" with the PAN. Although this exacerbated tensions within the PAN between those in favor of accommodation to the regime and those opposed, the party weathered these disagreements and moved decisively away from Cárdenas.

Salinas was skillful at shoring up legitimacy for the regime throughout his administration and devised ways to put a new, gentler face on economic reforms and austerity measures. Stabilization of the regime during this period was greatly assisted by a modest economic recovery and the decision by the United States to legitimate the Salinas administration at every

The epigraph is a statement made by President Salinas six weeks after he took office. Cited in Cornelius, Gentleman, and Smith 1989, 27–28.

opportunity. Decision making remained highly concentrated within the Office of the President, and many critics charged that under Salinas, it became even more centralized in the person of the president and his very closest advisers.[1]

While Salinas is sometimes criticized by his detractors as a technocrat in the style of de la Madrid, he does not fit the general definition, particularly because he paid far closer attention to the political realities on the ground than did his predecessor. In fact, Salinas's particularly effective style of governance provides a sharp contrast to de la Madrid's. Although the concept of *concertación social* (social reconciliation) was proclaimed to exist during the de la Madrid administration to include civil society in the design, implementation, and evaluation of policy, it was not until Salinas that the idea produced significant political payoff in the hands of an artful practitioner.[2] Although economic policy making was concentrated in the hands of the president and his top aides, Salinas appointed those with ties to the social Left to positions throughout his government. For example, Carlos Rojas, who was close to the urban popular movements (particularly to the OIR-LM), was selected as head of the high-profile antipoverty program called the National Solidarity Program (PRONASOL), a move that legitimized the program for many social movement actors.

The government's rebuilding and refashioning the system of international and domestic alliances with big business, the United States government, the PAN, and social movements, in combination with the partial economic recovery and internal splits within the opposition, reversed the momentum of the protest cycle. In fact, the process was so complete that by 1995, when Mexico suffered yet *another* sharp economic decline, during the first year of the Zedillo presidency, rather than another social movement protest cycle getting under way, pressure increased for electoral reforms starring the political parties as the key protagonists.

In this chapter I focus my analysis on the political recovery achieved by the regime during the Salinas years. Salinas masterminded this recovery

1. The accusations of political opponents have been supported by the academic literature. See, for example, Centeno 1997; Teichman 1995; and Camp 1990.

2. The idea of *concertación social* as a Latin American neoliberal strategy is not unique to Mexico, as witnessed by the implementation of broadly similar policies in Peru, Argentina, Chile, and elsewhere. There are similarities with "developmentalist populism" used to reconcile contradictory goals and social interests during the industrialization phase of the 1950s (see Cardoso and Faletto 1979).

first and foremost by implementing an antipoverty program that was targeted at undermining the unity of the Cárdenas-led Center-Left coalition. Salinas married the seductiveness of gaining access to state resources with the surgical use of repression. The success of this dual strategy was aided by internal weaknesses in the Cárdenas coalition and an economic recovery. Finally, Salinas moved boldly against his internal enemies and in redefining Mexican nationalism so as to allow for a new relationship with the United States, a fact registered most potently through the successful negotiation of the North American Free Trade Agreement (North American Free Trade Agreement (Tratado de Libre Comercio de América del Norte [NAFTA]). Reasserting strong leadership, attention to media spin, and the good fortune of economic recovery all contributed to the regime's regaining support from the poor and working classes, while appealing to the middle classes. In a less detailed way, I discuss here the 1994–2000 period, which culminated in the elections of 2000, which the PAN's candidate, Vicente Fox, won and, by so doing, brought to an end the longest-lasting authoritarian regime of the twentieth century.

The Protest Cycle Declines, 1988–1994

With the Cárdenas threat very much on his mind, President Salinas's first act in office was to implement the antipoverty program known as PRONASOL, which promised to promote "balanced regional development," and more fairly allocate development funds by targeting regions with high poverty rates. Salinas's political logic for undertaking the program was that much of the Cárdenas appeal came from the growing and deepening poverty of the Mexican people. The urban situation was particularly dangerous for the regime because its corporatist mechanisms were weaker there than in the countryside, and voter fraud was easier to accomplish in rural areas than in the cities.

PRONASOL officially declared that it would encourage the active participation of social organizations and of local governments through some cost sharing. As is typical in Mexico, the lion's share of the money came directly from federal coffers, and federal financing of the program grew from U.S.$500 million in 1989 to U.S.$2.2 billion in 1993 (SEDESOL 1994). While many critics noted that this amount was hardly sufficient to fulfill the basic needs of Mexico's poor, it is also true that PRONASOL compares favorably with similar programs in other developing countries.[3]

The program was highly successful and produced a strong electoral recovery for the PRI in the 1991 midterm elections. It deeply divided the social Left, with some movement organizations embracing the opportunities presented by the Solidarity resources (including the CDP of Durango) and some joining with Cárdenas in rejecting the program (as the AB of Mexico City did).

Mexico's macroeconomic recovery, wherein real GDP growth averaged almost 4 percent between 1988 and 1994 and inflation rates were significantly lowered, also contributed to the Salinas administration's popularity and the recovery of governmental legitimacy, which had been so tarnished during the previous administration. Salinas's role in negotiating NAFTA with the United States and Canada was effectively used to frame the president and his regime in a bold light. When a popular armed resistance emerged in southern Mexico in early 1994, Salinas demonstrated political acuity by not succumbing to the advice of hard-liners to initiate massive repression and instead agreed to quickly negotiate a ceasefire. The regime's legitimacy was further strengthened when Ernesto Zedillo won the presidency in 1994 in what was widely perceived to be a relatively clean election.

As noted by Tulchin and Selee (2003), "In the 1980s and 1990s, the Mexican government was eager to show the outside world that it was a nation of laws in order to attract needed investments and to demonstrate that it was an equal partner in NAFTA" (10). While Salinas's major emphasis was on economic recovery, when Zedillo took over in December 1994, he allowed and in fact deepened the momentum of electoral reforms. The most important of these was the Instituto Federal Electoral (Federal Electoral Institute [IFE]). The IFE was originally established in 1990, but Salinas had kept tight reign on it via the chairmanship of the interior minister. In 1994 this changed, as real power was allowed to devolve to nonpartisan staff and the IFE became independent from the Office of the President. This monumental change was reinforced by the electoral reform of 1996, "which brought about a constitutional reform that enjoyed the support of all the parties in Congress, ensur[ing] that votes were counted with the

---

3. It is extremely important to recognize that these numbers are the government's own numbers and that there is ample evidence to suggest that actual spending levels were much higher. This issue is discussed in more detail in the folloinwg Chapter 4. In addition, one study found that PRONASOL spent more per capita than any other social fund program in the developing world (Cornia and Reddy 2001, 15).

utmost care. The controls probably have no parallel in world history. The electoral process of July 2000 was far more equitable than in the past in terms of money as well as access to the media" (Elizondo 2003, 30).

Since 1989, Mexico has been developing what is in essence a three-party system, with two parties emerging in opposition to the PRI. On the center right is the PAN. Formed in 1939, in direct opposition to the policies of Lázaro Cárdenas, the party had long been the major voice of opposition in the electoral arena although unable to win significant elections. This began to change in the 1980s, particularly in the northern parts of the country, when PAN started winning gubernatorial races. On the center left, Cárdenas led the creation of the Party of the Democratic Revolution (PRD), which has run candidates from 1989 to the present, including Cárdenas for president in both 1994 and 2000.

This process culminated in 2000 when presidential elections produced an outcome that many Mexicans thought they would never see: the PRI lost. Zedillo's credibility had been greatly diminished during the economic crisis that began the very month he took office in 1995. Despite the fact that average macroeconomic performance remained strong during the remainder of his administration, the crisis of 1995 always loomed large in people's minds. Particularly damaging was the massive public bailout of the financial sector:

> The privatization of state-owned banks at the beginning of the 1990s in the context of liberalization resulted in a credit boom for consumer goods and real estate. Even the positive expectations that liberalization generated under the Salinas administration, both nationally and internationally, as well as high real interest rates, the crisis of December of 1994 resulted in a massive amount of bad loans for the recently privatized financial sector. The government, however, contrary to its policy on social issues, small and medium enterprises, subsidies, and industrial policy, decided to stage the bailout, with a cost of around 19 percent of Mexico's GDP. (Dussel Peters 2000, 54)

All this, combined with the dynamic campaign of the PAN candidate, Vicente Fox, led to the end of the inclusionary authoritarian regime that had existed in Mexico for more than seventy years, and the beginning of Mexico's experimentation with multiparty electoral democracy. While Fox was certainly not the preferred candidate of most urban popular movement

actors, I argue that the movement played an important role in delegitimiz-
ing the authoritarian regime and laying the basis for the democratic transition that brought Fox to power.

Neo-Cardenismo Post–July 1988

When Cárdenas lost the election in 1988, an intense debate within the
opposition centered on whether he should lead a national resistance movement similar to those under way in Eastern Europe and in other parts of
Latin America, or whether he should refuse to recognize Carlos Salinas's
victory and focus on building a new Center-Left party to compete in
future elections. Even though Cárdenas and his advisors chose the second
option, the initial debate and uncertainty generated confusion, which had
a direct bearing on the future political conduct of popular movements.

The National Democratic Front (FDN) was a loose coalition of parties,
political currents and social movement organizations designed for the
1988 campaign. Shortly after the July 1988 election, Cárdenas made the
decision to begin the process of building a new political party. In early
1989, the PRD was created. Bringing all the FDN forces into the permanent
fold of a single political party proved to be impossible. While all the parties within the FDN had supported Cárdenas for president, they could not
agree on common candidate slates for federal, state, and local offices.
Harsh clashes and factionalism had resulted, and often parties ran competing candidates, which allowed the PRI candidates to win more easily. These
clashes affected efforts to build the new party as well, and the internal balance of power between what were called ex-*priístas*, more-radical party
members (particularly members of the Mexican Socialist Party), and the
leaders of political currents and social movements was unclear.[4]

While some rural and urban popular movement organizations (including the AB) were energetic in their support of the PRD, many others never
made the transition from the FDN to the PRD. Leopoldo Enzástiga of the

---

4. The loose designation "ex-*priístas*," of course, refers primarily to those people who
came from the Corriente Democrática but also referred to members of "semi-state" parties
such as the PARM, PPS, and PFCRN, which joined forces with Cárdenas.

   The PRD is a complex grouping of diverse interests and political orientations. Fierce
battles have raged within the party and been widely reported in the press. There are three
main groupings. The first is the Corriente Democrática, the group of 1980s dissenters from
the PRI led by Cárdenas. Related to them are other PRI members who left the party later,

UCP argued that the "Movimiento Popular Cardenista" was defined as a mass movement that includes but is not limited to the PRD, but he admitted that the "determining influence of Cárdenas" had made the relation between the PRD and the popular movement particularly weak (1990, 11). While Cárdenas had effectively built a strong base for his leadership on the enduring memory of his father, or what was known as Cardenismo, his leadership style represented traditional *caudillismo*, or the cult of personality, which made and to this day continues to make many uneasy. The legacy of his father contributed—at least for a time—to the ability of Cárdenas to present himself as a redemptive myth, capable of reversing social decay, of resuming the abandoned path and promoting democratization, the defense of national sovereignty, and social equality (Tamayo 1990, 121). However, his unrelenting focus on gaining the presidency and his willingness to favor the broad-based incorporation of many ex-*priístas* into the PRD cost him much social movement support.

Many movement leaders maintained their ties to the Cardenista movement because they believed that Cárdenas and the PRD represented the best hope for a leftist front in their geographic location, particularly in and around Mexico City, where the PRD continues to be more powerful than either the PRI or the PAN. Optimism ebbed and flowed between individual movement leaders about the prospects for increasing the popular movement agenda within the PRD, an agenda that is in most ways considerably more radical (in terms of both political and economic orientation) than are the priorities and orientations of the *corriente* leaders.[5] However, the most

including some very high profile leaders. *Corriente* members retain most positions and direction over the party. The second and third groupings are the political and social Left. The political Left is represented by Left parties that are themselves complex. In 1981, the Partido Socialista Unificado de México (PSUM) was born out of the Mexican Communist Party, the Coalición de Izquierda, and the Movimiento de Acción Popular (MAP). In 1987, the PMS (Mexican Socialist Party) was formed out of the PSUM in alliance with other groups. The social Left is made up political currents and social movement organizations. Political currents within the PRD are represented by the Organización Revolucionaria Punto Crítico, sections (most notably that of Mexico City) of the Organización de Izquierda Revolucionaria-Línea de Masas (OIR-LM), the Movimiento al Socialismo, and the Asociación Cívica Nacional Revolucionaria (ACNR). Important movement organizations include the Coalición Obrera, Campesina, Estudiantil de Istmo (COCEI), the Central Independiente de Obreros Agrícolas y Campesinos (CIOAC), the Asamblea de Barrios, la Unión Popular Revolucionaria Emiliano Zapata (UPREZ), and the Unión de Colonias Populares (UCP).

5. The analysis provided here is clearly from the viewpoint of the movements. For an analysis from the perspective of party interests, see Bruhn 1997.

serious rupture within the PRD—between elements on the left and more centrist elements—was not over policy direction, but rather over relations between popular movements and the Salinas administration.

PRD leadership responded to Salinas's concertación by insinuating that signing concertación public agreements, known as *convenios de concertación*, with the president violated basic PRD tenets. These convenios sometimes involved an agreement between a social movement organization, such as the CDP of Durango, and President Salinas to work together to mitigate poverty. Salinas would come to town for a public signing with the governor, mayor, and popular movement leadership. Each would commit some resources, with the federal government kicking in most of the money and the popular movement agreeing to contribute some of the manual labor. This provided the social movement organization with money to provide services, usually for housing, education, or health care, strengthening the leadership's influence with its rank and file. It also often increased the political currency of social movement leaders with local and state authorities, given that the leaders were dealing directly with a supportive president. Many important PRD representatives argued that these agreements legitimated and reinforced the president's power and prestige, a position viewed by those tempted by PRONASOL as extremely moralistic and pedantic. By 1990, a deep split existed between movements loyal to Cárdenas, such as the AB, and movements such as the CDP that made tactical agreements with the Salinas administration. Even though the PRD position on PRONASOL mellowed by 1991–92, by then, Salinas's effort to divide movement unity had succeeded. The split was given important organizational recognition in the formation of the Partido del Trabajo (Workers' Party [PT]), which was made up in large part of popular movements participating, or wishing to participate, in PRONASOL.

From a perspective that places mobilization rather than organization at the center of movement power, one can argue that Cárdenas's window of opportunity came and went in 1988–89.[6] The momentum of regime threatening national protest against could not be sustained and the first formative years of party building were dominated by protesting unfair and corrupt procedures that were alleged to have occurred during the state-

6. For the most influential and well stated argument concerning the importance of mobilization and the dangers of organization building during times of mass protest, see Piven and Cloward 1979. Certainly, many commentators wasted no time predicting the unlikelihood of Cárdenas's ever again enjoying the coalitional support constructed in 1988. See, for example, Lerner de Sheinbaum 1989.

level elections between 1989 and 1991. For the PRD, the results of the fourteen state elections held during 1989 provide a dismal picture that did not
improve during 1990 or 1991.[7] Voter abstention rose from almost 50 percent in 1988 to 66 percent. The total FDN vote in 1988, including all federal, state, and local elections, was 26.46 percent, falling to 17.32 percent in
1989, while the PRI vote increased from 56.55 to 64.58 percent during the
same period.[8] Some of these defeats were particularly painful, such as that
of the Baja California election, as Cárdenas had carried the state in 1988. In
Michoacán, where in 1988 Cárdenas and the FDN had won landslide victories (including both senate races), the combined vote for FDN members
dropped from 60.67 percent in 1988 to 44.73 percent in 1989, with the PRD
receiving only 38 percent.[9] The sound defeat the PRD received in the
August 1991 midterm elections, in which they received less than 10 percent
of the vote, was also a serious disappointment to supporters.

This failure in the electoral arena in the post-1988 period raised serious
questions about the wisdom of this "electoral fraud" strategy by the PRD
for a politics of resistance. The strategy was pursued over the objections of
many popular movement organizations, political currents, and intellectuals who argued that inordinate amounts of time, energy, and resources
were spent on promoting Cárdenas as the lawful president. For many
within the urban popular movement, this strategy was seen as contrary to
their values and interests, as the following quote shows:

> Cárdenas had won our respect in 1988. But here he was afterward,
> spending his time refusing the legitimacy of the guy who was in
> the process of initiating programs vital to our organizational
> interests. It would have been one thing if Cárdenas had managed
> to pull off a revolution, but for whatever reasons, he chose instead
> to take the legal route. OK, he had his reasons, even if I don't
> understand them. But once this decision was made to form a party
> and begin the work of what everyone should have understood was
> going to be a long process of building a party and democratic

7. During 1989, state elections were held in Baja California, Campeche, Chihuahua,
Zacatecas, Durango, Oaxaca, Veracruz, Aguascalientes, Sinaloa, Tlaxcala, Puebla, Guerrero,
Tamaulipas, and Michoacán.

8. The statistic of 17.32 percent actually inflates the PRD showing, for it includes other
FDN participants (PPS, PFCRN, and PARM). The actual percentage of votes cast for the PRD in
1989 is a lower figure, 8.73 percent.

9. All amounts are official figures from the Federal Election Commission as cited in PRI
1990.

party system, then he had to understand that the rest of us needed to survive also. And here were Salinas and Rojas coming at us with the exact kind of program that we had been demanding for years [PRONASOL]. I'm not saying that Salinas had our interests at heart. Hardly. What I am saying is that we had won an important concession. Here was a program with enough money to help us build our organizations and also mitigate the pain our people were feeling from the crisis. Here was a program in which they were essentially saying, we will let you run it and we will even share credit for its accomplishments with you. And all Cárdenas and his people could say was, don't deal with this guy, he is an illegitimate president. Not much of a choice. (OIR-LM and urban popular movement leader, interview by the author, 1992)

Although the PRD controlled a number of municipal governments, they were concentrated in a small number of states, and most of the PRD municipalities were in politically insignificant areas. Lack of funds and the nature of public finances in Mexico (in which the federal government controls the overwhelming majority of resources) further limited the influence of these victories on national politics, although some of them had important local implications.[10]

The Salinas Political Recovery

This entire period of Mexican political history is fundamentally shaped by the way in which Cardenista forces were treated as a common enemy of both the PRI and the PAN. An example is found in the 1990 collaboration between the PRI and the PAN in their successful effort to legislate a significant change in the electoral code (Código Federal de Instituciones y Procedimientos Electorales [COFIPE]). The reform meant that the party receiving the most votes would automatically be guaranteed a majority of seats in the Chamber of Deputies, with the proviso that they must receive 35 percent of the vote, a requirement that at the time posed no serious threat to the PRI. The new law also made the formation of electoral

10. For comparative evaluations of opposition governments at the municipal level, see Rodríguez and Ward 1995; Ziccardi 1995; and Cornelius, Eisenstadt, and Hindley 1999.

alliances in federal elections much more difficult. This change benefited the PAN and the PRI; both wished to avoid the type of electoral alliance that took place in 1988 under the FDN banner.[11] Unlike previous electoral reforms since 1977, which aimed to make the election process more competitive and guarantee representation for smaller parties (most significantly through the allocation of seats based on proportional voting), this reform was designed to limit competition.

The intent of the 1990 electoral reform was in keeping with Salinas's record on political reform in general. The Mexican case provides yet another example from Latin America that economic and political liberalism are not necessarily coterminous. Modernization under Salinas meant deep structural reforms in the national economy and a reorientation in international relations (principally concerning changes in economic relations with the United States).[12] Significant reform efforts, such as changes in Mexico's corporatist relations, were often publicized as democratic reforms but are more accurately seen as necessary for Salinas's vision of a modern Mexican economy. Salinas never backed away from economic reform as the priority of his administration; the pace of democratization would always be dependent upon the successful restructuring and stability of economic development. Opposition forces of the Left and Right not surprisingly pressed for both economic and democratic reforms, and that the latter should not be held hostage to the former. The Left was the more emphatic in insisting that economic reforms in an authoritarian context would essentially guarantee that the economic system would be unjust and authoritarian. In this war of wills, Salinas clearly gained the upper hand, as electoral reforms during this period were kept to a minimum and postponed

11. Prior to the 1990 reform, it was possible for individual candidates to run on more than one ballot line. Cárdenas's powerful showing in 1988 was a result in part of his running on a number of ballot lines. The new code prohibited this practice. That this reform was directed specifically at undermining Cárdenas and the PRD was lost on no one.

12. Modernization was Salinas's theme song. Essentially, all actions, policy, and reforms were defended and promoted in terms of this agenda. Salinas aspired to push Mexico into the community of modern nations, leaving behind those institutions, practices, policies, and beliefs deemed to be anachronistic and a hindrance. Modernization theory, popularized in the United States during the 1950s and 1960s by Seymour Martin Lipset (1967), Kalman Silvert (1967), John Johnson (1958), Daniel Lerner (1958) and others, was never particularly popular in Mexico at the time it was written about. Much more in fashion was the interpretation of development referred to as dependency theory and made popular by Celso Furtado (1970) and by Fernando Henrique Cardoso and Enzo Faletto (1979). This began to change during the 1980s, with Presidents de la Madrid, Salinas, Zedillo, and Fox all embracing many of modernization theory's basic tenets.

until the Zedillo administration. While the PAN favored significant electoral reforms, it was willing to bargain with Salinas on this issue and, in the
process, help to ensure that those reforms that did pass would be particularly unsympathetic to Cárdenas and the PRD. Meanwhile, Salinas succeeded in deepening the neoliberal transition to the point of no return.

Salinas's success in undermining the unity that was reached at the zenith
of the 1988 protest cycle, was, in my view, aided particularly by the PRD
leadership's decision to focus on contesting elections and pressing for
political reforms. The success in shifting the political opportunity structure toward the party-building arena was decisive in Salinas's ability to
ensure that neoliberalism would survive the threats posed to it by the
1980s protest cycle. So effective was Salinas at dividing the opposition, and
so incapable was the opposition at unifying for a regime transition, that the
most significant obstacles to the Salinas modernization were traditional
elements within the PRI itself.

The growing influence of popular movements during the de la Madrid
administration had the paradoxical affect of generating the very program
that would most undermine the united opposition of political parties and
popular movements to the regime. PRONASOL was the primary tool of the
state to regain votes for the PRI, as Carlos Ramírez made clear in 1991:

> The political current of Solidarity will be determinant to winning
> the 1991 elections. In itself, the Solidarity program has become a
> parallel PRI; its delegates are the new political class of *salinismo;*
> they arrive with power and money. . . . As long as it lasts, . . . Soli-
> darity will be the new instrument of control of the current gov-
> ernment. Many will enter politics as representatives of the Soli-
> darity Party. The presence of this program will be key, because it
> will invest money into opposition areas to regain the vote for the
> PRI. That's why the voice of Solidarity . . . at the hour of deciding
> candidates will be fundamental. (Cited in Dresser 1991, 43)

Assisting Salinas in his political recovery was the United States; the
U.S. failure to pressure for democratic reforms and to challenge the high
incidence of violence against PRD supporters in the 1988–91 period aided
Salinas in limiting the protest cycle. President George Herbert Walker
Bush's recognition of the Salinas victory even before official results were
complete and, later, the U.S. direct intervention in Mexico's renegotiation

of its national debt both served to shore up the regime. More important than the modest economic relief the United States provided was the political capital gained by Salinas in his demonstrating his ability to extract concessions from powerful international actors. The successful completion of the NAFTA agreement further bolstered his national image as a strong leader in international affairs.

Political recovery was strengthened by a modest economic recuperation. The table below, constructed by Manuel Pastor Jr. and Carol Wise, clearly illustrates the recovery. My argument is that the boom of the late-1970s through the early 1980s, followed by the bust of the de la Madrid years, fueled the protest cycle. Later, the Salinas-period economic recovery helped to deflate the protest cycle. Finally, the bust economy that faced Zedillo in 1995 increased pressure to introduce the serious electoral reforms that contributed to the Fox victory in 2000.[13]

In assessing the changing balance of power between Salinas and the Left opposition, it is crucial to understand that the regime enjoyed control over the vast majority of public resources, the legislature, and the judiciary. Even though de la Madrid had been unable to use these resources to effectively curtail the protest cycle, in the hands of the more politically adroit Salinas, aided by an improved economy and international support, they became lethal tools. These tools, together with Salinas's effectively incorporating some social movement representatives directly into his administration, allowed him to manipulate public opinion despite the implementation of policies—such as wage and price controls—that were opposed by large sectors of the population.[14] Meanwhile, Cárdenas and the PRD were confronted with chronic shortages of funds, internal divisions, lack of functional organization (particularly on the state level), and an inability to bring out the vote or defend PRD victories in localities where they alleged that fraud had taken place.

In municipalities where the opposition had won, Salinas applied a four-part strategy: (1) employing selective use of state repression; (2) creating delays in the normal flows of resources, delays that undermined a local government's ability to implement public works; (3) directing extra

13. For an excellent analysis of the 1995 Mexican political economy, see Castañeda 1995.

14. According to the Banco de México, the minimum salary in Mexico City declined 23 percent (in real terms) between December 1987 and April 1990. Enrique Dussel Peters calculates that between in 1998, "real wages and real minimum wages equaled only an estimated 57.0 percent and 29.5 percent of their respective levels in 1980" (2000, 161).

Table 1 Mexican macroeconomic indicators since 1980

	1980	1981	1982	1983	1984	1985	1986	1987
GDP annual growth (percent)	8.4	8.8	-0.7	-4.1	3.7	2.7	-3.9	1.9
Inflation rate (percent, Dec.–Dec.)	29.8	28.7	98.9	80.8	59.2	63.7	105.7	159.2
Trade ($U.S. mil.)								
Exports	18,031	23,307	24,056	25,953	29,101	26,758	21,803	27,599
Imports	21,087	27,184	17,009	11,848	15,915	18,359	16,784	18,813
Trade balance	(3,056)	(3,877)	7,047	14,105	13,186	8,399	5,019	8,786
Investment flows ($U.S. mil.)								
Foreign direct investment	2,090	3,078	1,901	2,192	1,542	1,984	2,036	1,184
Portfolio investment	60	996	645	(519)	(435)	(595)	(517)	(1,002)
Total reserves less gold ($U.S. mil.)	2,960	4,074	834	3,913	7,272	4,906	5,670	12,464
Real exchange rate (1980 = 100), controlled rate	100.0	91.1	134.6	143.8	124.3	120.0	149.0	148.6

Table 1 *(cont'd)*   Mexican macroeconomic indicators since 1980

	1988	1989	1990	1991	1992	1993	1994	1995
GDP annual growth (percent)	1.3	3.5	4.3	3.9	2.8	0.4	3.8	–6.2
Inflation rate (percent, Dec.–Dec.)	51.7	19.7	29.9	18.8	11.9	8.0	7.1	52.0
Trade ($U.S. mil.)								
Exports	30,692	35,171	40,711	42,687	46,196	51,885	60,879	79,543
Imports	28,081	34,766	41,592	49,966	32,130	65,366	79,346	72,454
Trade balance	2,611	405	(881)	(7,279)	(15,934)	(13,481)	(18,467)	7,089
Investment flows ($U.S. mil.)								
Foreign direct investment	2,011	2,785	2,549	4,742	4,393	4,389	10,972	6,963
Portfolio investment	1,001	354	3,369	12,741	18,041	28,919	8,185	(10,140)
Total reserves less gold ($U.S. mil.)	5,279	6,329	9,863	17,726	18,942	25,110	6,278	16,847
Real exchange rate (1980 = 100), controlled rate	119.1	112.8	105.4	92.4	82.5	77.5	79.5	115.2

SOURCES: World Bank, World Data, 1995; IMF, International Financial Statistics, December 1995, March 1996, September 1996 (CD-ROM); CEPAL, Economic Panorama of Latin America, 1996; author estimates.

NOTE: Following the new IMF practice, trade figures include *maquila* exports and imports; thus, this table may differ from other historical tables that treat the net earnings of the *maquila* sector as part of the current balance in services.

resources to some opposition governments in efforts to bribe officials, some of whom later faced charges of corruption; and (4) reducing budgets (Alejandro Lueveno, interview by the author, March 1999). As a result of this assault, as well as a hostile media and often ineffective local leadership, the PRD found it very difficult to hold power from one municipal presidency to the next.

All these political difficulties culminated in Cárdenas's dismal performance in the 1994 presidential elections. Despite an economic recession beginning in the second half of 1993, deep divisions within the PRI, and the emergence of the Zapatista rebellion in the southern state of Chiapas, the PRD performed poorly and received less than 20 percent of the vote, whereas the PAN nearly doubled its 1988 totals. Although the PRI won with barely more than 50 percent of the vote, this time the results were achieved without widespread allegations of massive fraud.[15]

The decision to form a party and not pursue massive civil disobedience meant that Cárdenas and his supporters were without the power of a movement that could effect policy process and outcomes. While the PRD certainly early on prepared some rather sophisticated documents containing alternative proposals and policy recommendations on a host of issues, including economic reform, the perception on the part of many Mexicans (encouraged by the media) was that the PRD had little to offer except a return to the past and sharp criticisms of the Salinas administration, neoliberalism, and the authoritarian political system. In my judgment, a review of the evidence suggests that the PRD had much more to offer than its critics charged.[16]

The Salinas Project in Comparative Perspective

When Salinas took office as president on December 1, 1988, against the backdrop of a highly mobilized opposition, the language of democracy, which the opposition claimed for itself, and that of authoritarianism,

15. For an excellent and succinct critique of Cárdenas's 1994 presidential bid, see Castañeda 1995. For a much more detailed account, see Aguilar Zínser 1995.

16. On the early PRD documents, see, for example, PRD 1990a, 1990b, 1990c, and especially 1990d and 1991.

There were also a number of North American academics who sought to paint Cárdenas as anachronistic and simple-minded at best. See, for example, Baer 1991.

ascribed to the clientelist party/state regime, dominated political discussions in Mexico.[17] Under de la Madrid, the regime had lost its near monopoly on the effective use of revolutionary imagery, symbols, and rhetoric—key resources in the Mexican battle for votes and legitimacy. Previous to the 1980s, popular movements and leftist parties had chewed away at the edges of this monopoly but had failed to make significant inroads on a national scale.[18] The Cárdenas campaign and response to the Salinas "victory" had given leftists and populists a national stage upon which they claimed, with considerable success, that the party/state had abandoned the revolutionary project and its ideals in pursuit of an export-led, antipopulist, pro–United States (and thus anti-Mexican) development model.

Salinas never attempted to return to precrisis definitions of Mexican nationalism but rather endeavored to redefine Mexican nationalism to include neoliberalism and a foreign policy that embraced the neighbor to the north.[19] Salinas's program of political modernization also extended to efforts at using competition to reform what he perceived to be moribund corporatist sectors of the PRI itself. This was most dramatically pursued in the urban popular sector of the party, CNOP, through including urban popular movement organizations in the competition for PRONASOL funds. Improving relations with popular movements was also pursued as a means for legitimating the modernization process. As mentioned previously, top

17. Salinas was "awarded the presidency" through the constitutionally mandated procedure of legislative ratification without any support from the opposition. Only his own party members voted for the legality of the presidential succession in 1988. His gaining only 51 percent of the popular vote, followed by the narrow margin of 263 to 237 in the constitutionally mandated ratification by the House of Deputies, represented the weakest formal beginning for any president in the postrevolutionary era.

18. While prior to the 1980s the opposition adopted revolutionary imagery for their uses, I am suggesting that the demonstrated capacity of the Cardenista opposition to wrestle away from the regime's key revolutionary symbols was something very special and unique in twentieth-century Mexican history. For a short period, the FDN was seen by many if not most Mexicans as the legitimate bearer of the revolution.

19. The Salinas record is full of political concessions to the United States that can reasonably be interpreted to be the cost of pursuing the economic integration required by the neoliberal strategy. These examples are found in Mexico's voting patterns in multilateral institutions, such as the United Nations and the Organization of American States, in which Mexico had clashed with the United States in the past. Changes also took place in Mexican bilateral relations with the United States, particularly in relation to drug trafficking and migration. Salinas was greatly assisted by the end of the Cold War, and the decline in U.S. military intervention in Central America, which had caused de la Madrid considerable tension with the Reagan administration.

appointments of people with long track records in working with popular movements was an important factor in Salinas's successes in these directions.

Once in office, Salinas lost no time in establishing himself as an activist president who was willing and able to take bold actions. Motivated by a perceived need to establish a popular image, and insisting on loyalty from elites who backed his modernization scheme, he moved against powerful business leaders and union corporatist kingpins.[20] He was aggressive in removing from office, oftentimes in dramatic fashion, members of political elites who either questioned his authority and direction or were unable to contribute to a "new PRI."[21]

Salinas's efforts to reform the Mexican party machine were aimed less at democratizing it than at building a reformed, more efficient authoritarianism and were consistent with his modernist critique of historic political practices as being incapable of maintaining regime support. However, party reform was one of his least successful efforts, demonstrating the depth of resistance to change from powerful economic and political interests both within and outside the formal party/state institutional structure, and that Salinas was wise enough to recognize that the regime still needed the party and that he could only go so far.

Contrasting the serious political challenges faced by Presidents Luis Echeverría and Carlos Salinas de Gortari is instructive here. In many ways the men were polar opposites: Echeverría (1970–76) launched himself as a preeminent spokesman for the global South and positioned himself as being acutely distrustful of the United States, while Salinas sought to "move beyond" the nationalism and anti–United States rhetoric of old. However, there were important commonalties. Both men entered the presidency in an

20. The most famous and influential cases of Salinas moving against union leaders came early in his administration, when establishing a reputation for decisiveness and strength was at a premium. The first strike was directed at the oil workers union. In a dramatic show of strength, which ended in a shoot-out between federal troops and an oil worker militia, Salinas imprisoned the union's secretary of social works and "moral leader" Joaquín Hernández Galicia (known as "la Quina"). This move against one of Mexico's most well known and powerful *caciques* (political bosses) went far in establishing Salinas's credentials. The forced resignation of longtime leader of the Teacher's Union Carlos Jonguitud, after a period of sustained protest by the intraunion reformist movement represented by the National Coordinating Committee of Education Workers (CNTE), is another example of Salinas's removing political strongmen.

21. Among his most important early political "removals" were those of the governors of Michoacán (Luis Martinez Villicaña), Baja California Norte (Xicotencatl Leyva), México (Mario Ramon Beteta), and Yucatán (Victor Manzanilla Schaffer)—all locations of opposition strength where the standing governors apparently did not demonstrate the political efficiency demanded by Salinas.

atmosphere of "lost consensus" and a need to better incorporate regime detractors. Whereas Salinas's legitimacy suffered from the 1988 elections, Echeverría was extremely preoccupied with the fallout from the 1968 massacre of Mexico City students and mounting opposition emanating from journals, newspapers, universities, popular movements, and an armed insurgency. Echeverría endeavored to incorporate critical social actors into a somewhat reformed fold, enhancing legitimacy for his presidency and the regime while at the same time effectively undermining coordination and unity within the newly invigorated Mexican Left (Hellman 1988, 158–59).[22] Manuel Villa stresses that Echeverría used the "mobilization-manipulation" populist technique, a time-honored strategy in which a political boss intervenes in an existing conflict by supplanting the existing balance of power with the introduction of new actors who are loyal to him or her (or with the incorporation of previously independent actors). This allows the power holder, in this case the president, not only to control outcomes, but also to reserve for himself the role of "grand arbitrator" in the dispute (n.d., 8).

Salinas exercised this tradition through the multiple policy tools and programs that were administered under the rubric of *concertación social* (social reconciliation). An orchestral concert offers an apt metaphor. In Salinas's case, the score to be played was neoliberalism. As conductor, Salinas saw his job as urging society to play this new music well. While the musicians may be unionized, thereby limiting his capacity to hire and fire at will, he was empowered to spend political capital in selective rearrangements of the players, which he achieved through demotions and promotions within the PRI. He then did something more novel: he allowed a number of state programs to direct finances to social movement actors who remained outside the PRI. So while he did not disband the union, he took away its ability to control the entire workforce.[23]

22. For book-length treatments of union activism during the 1970s, see Basurto 1983 and M. Camacho 1984.

23. López Portillo also began his administration with efforts at reconciling divisions that had been handed down from the previous president. Indeed, López Portillo did spend a considerable amount of his presidency, particularly the early years, overcoming the distrust of business groups generated by Echeverría's populism. It is also true that López Portillo handed de la Madrid his own last-minute stunt, the nationalization of the banks. What makes the similarities between Echeverría and Salinas so important is that the national contexts of 1970 and 1988 led both men to actively court important leftist individuals and organizations, incorporating important actors from the Left, or risk the emergence of a popular resistance potentially capable of forcing a regime breakdown. In this sense, there is an important distinction between Echeverría and Salinas on the one hand, and de la Madrid on the other; de la Madrid perceived no such necessity during his tenure.

For those who view Salinas's concertación strategy as simply the modern face of state corporatism, its origins can be dated back to at least the 1930s. But even if concertación is similar to the long-standing strategy of incorporation, its particularities are recent and represent a different phase in Mexican corporatism. Jonathan Fox (1990a) traces the beginnings of concertación to the Sistema Alimentario Mexicana (Mexican Food System [SAM]), the rural food-distribution program that functioned temporarily in the very early 1980s in de la Madrid's government. Fox provides one of the more generous independent interpretations of concertación social, recognizing that it can be effective in encouraging autonomous organizations to mitigate poverty as well as be a productive political tool aimed at the modernization of corporatist relations. Indeed, the two need not be mutually exclusive. He sees concertación social as a useful tool in encouraging alliances between progressive social forces and state reformers. Many critics, unwilling to make this distinction, limit their comments to the "dark" side of concertación social. Sergio Zermeño states the view of many when he argues that "[t]his new reconciliation, which in Mexico is now called the 'ideology of *concertación*,' is really one of the privileged mechanisms of destruction of the collective identity of mobilized groups, and is turning into a new channel of bureaupolitical ascent" (1990, 178). Fox argues that "'traditional' *concertación* agreements serve the existing power structure" (1990b, 158), and Neil Harvey, while acknowledging that *concertación* was "nothing new in Mexico," claims that what made the 1980s distinct was that "the targeting of opposition grassroots organizations [had] become increasingly important." Harvey advances the view common to most critics that concertación and democracy are antithetical:

> [E]lectoral democracy is being resisted by the PRI and the government, while new, more direct relationships are being established between the State and popular organizations. These relationships may be significantly more democratic than before, but at the same time they reproduce the familiar pattern of political bargaining between State and sectors within civil society. . . . the democratization of corporatism is constraining the democratization of the system as a whole. . . . Is it not just a strategy of containment, giving the PRI time to reform itself while squeezing out the Cardenista alternatives? (1990, 2, 4)

The argument is often made that concertación, as practiced by both the de la Madrid and the Salinas administrations, represented a new and insidious form of neocorporatism. Many popular movements—especially those closely aligned with the PRD—claimed that concertación, not party building, was contributing to the decline of the protest cycle. Concertación, rather than assisting civil society to "think for itself" and develop its ability to make demands on the state (political as well as economic), strengthened the hand of the state and undermined the autonomy of civil society. Armando Bartra expresses the concern felt by many movement activists when he concludes that "[i]n times of crisis and political transition, to *depoliticize* negotiations with the state and promote deep reforms outside the arena of the new opposition, tends, by omission, to legitimize the existing political system and can end up as neoclientelism; a technocratic and 'modern' corporatism but as oppressive as the previous system" (cited in Harvey 1990, 18).

The different approaches adopted by the de la Madrid and Salinas administrations to these issues had major political implications. De la Madrid proceeded to initiate a paradigmatic shift from state-led capitalism to neoliberal capitalism while relying on the durability of existing political arrangements and institutions. Salinas continued and in fact deepened and made more permanent the neoliberal model by accelerating the pace of privatization, negotiating and signing NAFTA, and pushing through other measures. However, Salinas's economic policy was accompanied by a studied attention to regaining regime legitimacy, which had been so badly eroded during the de la Madrid years. Salinas did no less than move aggressively to renovate and redefine the system of state alliances. That is, he shored up, on a selective basis, some of those relationships that had been damaged, and he also moved to form new relationships with actors who were previously outside the regime. His most innovative Machiavellian move was to renovate and innovate in ways that undermined his most serious and personally abhorrent challenger: Cuauhtémoc Cárdenas. And to this end, all other efforts pale in comparison with that of PRONASOL.

PRONASOL

The theory that participation by beneficiaries in grassroots development projects actually strengthens the political system had been of considerable interest to Salinas for years (Salinas de Gortari 1984). While participation in development programs is hardly new to Mexico, Salinas brought a degree of sophistication to the process, thus maximizing political gains to a degree unmatched since the 1930s under Cárdenas.[24] The most significant differences between the de la Madrid and Salinas policies for the poor are not to be found in content but rather in form and packaging. Although both presidents' policies were painful to the poor, Salinas successfully presented himself as quite distinct from his predecessor, in the process undermining the Left rather than enhancing their structure of political opportunities, as had occurred under de la Madrid, who disdained populist rhetoric and practices. Salinas's use of a modern populist style—characterized by skillful attention to presentation, image, publicity, and media coverage—served him well.

PRONASOL contributed to the relative ease with which Salinas postponed significant democratic political reforms while getting on with neoliberal economic reform. Salinas and his top aides correctly reasoned that PRONASOL need not significantly compensate for the severity of the austerity measures and economic crisis experienced by the country during the de la Madrid and his own administrations; rather, a carefully targeted and well-administered program that ensured the maximization of political gains was necessary to address political vulnerabilities.[25] This was achieved by well-orchestrated public ceremonies that received sustained and favorable media attention.

PRONASOL provided the lubricant that enabled the political machine to prosper for the duration of his administration and was a—if not the—central tool employed to legitimize the deepening of neoliberalism. PRONASOL was designed to substantiate the claim that neoliberalism was in the national interest and would benefit not only the wealthy. PRONASOL

24. Examples of high-profile development programs that emphasized the participation of beneficiaries would include the Caminos de Mano de Obra program of Echeverría or the Coordinación General del Plan Nacional de Zonas Deprimidas y Groupos Marginados (Central Coordination of the National Plan of Economically Depressed Regions and Marginalized Groups [COPLAMAR]) program of de la Madrid.

25. During Salinas's second State of the Union address, in which he showcased Solidarity, he also made clear that strict wage controls would be continued to control inflation. Consequently, prices for electricity and water skyrocketed and the principal outlet for subsidized food, CONASUPO, had its operations cut back. According to one calculation, subsidies decreased by 66.4 percent in real terms between 1989 and 1990 (Grupo de Economistas y Asociados, cited in Dresser 1991, 11).

was also the most important expression of Salinas's efforts to modernize corporatist relations through the reform of existing relationships and the creation of new—some would call neocorporatist—relationships with powerful social actors outside the inclusionary system's boundaries.

Glowing reports of PRONASOL accomplishments filled the media throughout Salinas's six years in office. The promotional blitzkrieg that the PRI (as distinct from the state) administered through the airwaves in support of PRONASOL, which was frequently promoted as the symbol of the "new PRI," sharply contrasts with the scarce electronic media access gained by PRONASOL critics. It also demonstrates that Salinas's expressed intention of reforming the PRI's preferential access to the media was a hollow promise.

Weekly, the president traveled to a PRONASOL site to unveil yet another example of the administration's commitment to grassroots development.[26] By using resources derived from the privatization of state properties to fund PRONASOL, Salinas gained credibility and deflected the PRD's claims regarding both privatization and PRONASOL. PRONASOL projects included efforts to generate employment, increase agricultural production, improve health-care delivery, and provide low-income housing and classroom space. By directing a large proportion of allocated funds to municipal governments, PRONASOL was promoted as evidence of the president's commitment to decentralization, long a political buzzword in Mexican politics. Rojas argues that PRONASOL "makes the constitutional reforms to strengthen the free municipality a reality" (C. Rojas et al. 1991, 38).

Such claims have been studiously investigated and found to be wanting. For example, John Bailey uses the term "recentralization" to describe how Salinas actually reversed the minor progress made by de la Madrid to "at least deconcentrate" (1994, 176). PRONASOL returned to the executive branch (from state government) many elements of decision making. PRONASOL reduced local discretion in two ways. First, some PRONASOL funds came from programs that had previously provided at least some local-spending authority. Second, when local officials were required to

26. "In Mexico, there's a backlog of more than a million homeowners waiting for land titles. In the 16 years prior to Salinas's administration, the agency that resolves title questions delivered 300,000 titles. Already Salinas has handed out 775,000 land titles" (D. C. Scott 1991). Quoting one of the beneficiaries of this program, Scott highlights an aspect of the Salinas political genius: "I don't care if the PRI or the PRD is behind Solidarity. I've been waiting years for this and Salinas gave it to me."

invest in PRONASOL projects, they could not use these funds to pursue their own development initiatives, undermining local-spending authority.[27]

The disbursement of PRONASOL funds was politicized in many instances to the advantage of the PRI.[28] As noted by Dresser, it is impossible to even know how much money was spent, where it went and who benefited:

> Given the increasing visibility and scope of PRONASOL programs, there is evidence to argue that the program operates with a much larger pool of resources than those presented in the Public Account. It is virtually impossible, however, to gauge the extent of off-budget funds provided to PRONASOL by the sale of public enterprises and relabeled old categories of social/infrastructure spending at the state level. . . . Executive groups directly under presidential supervision coordinate and centralize the work (and funds) of existing social welfare institutions to suit PRONASOL's purposes. This parallel institutional network enables Salinas to use vast amounts of resources and carry out significant programs without the scrutiny of Congress and the pressures of party politics. Resources from "the president's private pocket" thus can be targeted strategically according to electoral calendars and specific political needs throughout the country. (1991, 16–17)

However, this is not the whole picture. One of the most significant innovations of PRONASOL was its allowing non-PRI actors—including social movement actors in competition with the PRI, such as in the case of the CDP in Durango and the Coalición de Obreros, Campesinos y Estudiantes del Istmo (Coalition of Workers, Peasants, and Students of the Isthmus [COCEI]) in Oaxaca—to compete with the PRI for these funds. Although this did have the intended affect of contributing to discord within the Left, it also put development funds into the hands of actors that

27. In my view, nobody has a comprehensive national understanding of what the program meant on the ground. There are two primary problems. First, PRONASOL included thousands of small projects. Second, the goals of PRONASOL were multiple, and different published analyses have focused on specific portions. Broad studies that try to get at the gestalt of the program are useful but lack grassroots details. Case studies are also useful, but one cannot generalize from what happened in a set of communities or even several states. The best single reference is the anthology edited by Cornelius, Craig, and Fox (1994).

28. See, for example, the cases documented in Dresser 1991 and Moguel 1990a, 1990b. For the best macro analysis, see Molinar Horcasitas and Weldon 1994.

were more likely than the PRI to assist the intended beneficiaries. Thus, while the Salinas policies did not significantly help the poor in macro terms, there were many instances in which economic relief was enjoyed by PRONASOL beneficiaries. And one of the most significant groups that benefited were low-income people associated with popular movement organizations that negotiated PRONASOL agreements with the Salinas administration.

Critics are right to claim that the PRONASOL budget was totally inadequate given the program's goals and rhetoric, which verged on promises to eradicate extreme poverty. It never reached much beyond 1 percent of GDP (Lustig 1994, 89), an amount of money far too small to seriously mitigate Mexico's poverty. Furthermore, critics questioned the extent to which PRONASOL funds actually reached the "poorest of the poor." For example, Levy claims that little more than half the U.S.$900 million spent in PRONASOL's rural food and health programs actually reached the very poor (1991, 78). Moguel argues that the cap of U.S.$17,000 for projects carried out under the municipal Solidarity program severely limited a community's ability to devise effective integrated development programs that had a chance of truly changing economic prospects (1990a, 9–10). He also points out that "if PRONASOL's budget for 1990 had been divided by 365 days and by the 17 million people in Mexico who live in extreme poverty, each would have received only 15 cents a day" (1991b, 9).

Critics never tire of pointing out that PRONASOL outlays were but a fraction of what was being expended to pay interest on the foreign debt and point to data analysis that shows clearly that funds were directed to areas with the greatest political threat from the PRD (Molinar Horcasitas and Weldon 1994). In a different political context, such critiques could potentially have had the effect of mobilizing large numbers of people around a common cause—the bankruptcy of the president's war on poverty. However, the lack of a united opposition, and an increasingly united political elite, determined that such a mobilization did not occur. PRONASOL was everywhere. Although the programs were often small in light of the magnitude of the problem, the airwaves were constantly bombarded with the image intended by Salinas: that the government was attending to their needs. The opposition working outside PRONASOL funding could not begin to compete with this.

The success of the party/state in persuading the public that PRONASOL supported the administration's claim that "modernization is for everyone" worked well in concert with the effort to entice important FDN supporters to participate in the program. PRONASOL divided the Left by creating tensions between those who participated and those who chose not to, as well as between those who participated and those who attempted, but were unable, to gain access to significant funding. The decision of whether to participate generated cleavages within the peasant movement, the independent labor movement, the urban popular movement, and others.[29] Many movement opponents argued that PRONASOL's strategy of dividing organizations one from the other was made possible by the fact that each organization signed its own separate agreement (convenio), and thus the state was able to pit movements against one another for scarce resources. Some critics designed and advocated strategies that would encourage movements to form a solid bargaining bloc, at least at the sectoral level (urban poor, peasants, and so on) as a way of building cohesiveness and of pressuring Salinas to make more funds available. The strategy failed because it is very difficult to get social actors, each dealing with a powerful state actor, to agree on the terms of their resistance. This is especially true when the costs of ending bargaining with the state are high and when the potential for holding the coalition together and actually achieving the larger prize is far from guaranteed.

PRONASOL even created internal splits within individual organizations. The Unión Nacional de Organizaciones Regionales Campesinas (National Union of Autonomous Regional Peasant Organizations [UNORCA]), which replaced CNPA as the lead rural organization in the mid-1980s, is a case in point. In 1990 a difference emerged between, on the one hand, sectors willing to tone down protest specifically directed at Salinas in order to participate in PRONASOL and, on the other, those not willing to pay this cost. While the details vary, PRONASOL caused similar internal problems for CONAMUP and the OIR-LM. When the most powerful actor within the regime, the Office of the President, offers a deal, especially one that did not require explicit affiliation with the PRI, it was extremely difficult to refuse. Because this was a tough call for many movement organizations, the lack of unity should not come as a big surprise. How organizations dealt with these differences of opinion also varied, with some organizations splitting apart and others managing to hold together.

PRONASOL's unofficial goal of luring popular movements away from the Cárdenas camp required that the program be promoted as a government

29. These splits were often exacerbations of previously existing rifts between political currents.

program and not as a PRI program. Although politicians and movement actors were well aware that the government was drawing a sharp distinction between the PRI and the state, the situation was complicated by media promotions of the program that continued the more usual practice of intentionally blurring the distinction. Predictably, those movement organizations that chose to participate in PRONASOL would emphasize the distinction, while those who opposed participation used the blurring in the media as part of their argument about why others should not.

This distinction made it possible for social Left participants to develop rationales for accepting public funds in the name of their rank and file.[30] The most commonly heard argument was that their gaining PRONASOL funds was a function of a concessionary act on the part of the government, which was deferring to the power and influence of popular movement organizations. They claimed, with some justification, that it was they who best represented the interests of the poor, far better than could any arm of the regime or any other nongovernmental organization (NGO). The development of such a rationale would have been difficult, if not impossible, if the program had a closer relationship with the PRI.

While de la Madrid's technocratic leadership and decision-making style favored bureaucratic rationality in the disbursement of public funds, even when this carried with it certain political liabilities such as the estrangement of local political elites, PRONASOL reversed this tendency during the Salinas administration. Disbursement of PRONASOL funds, managed by Carlos Rojas Gutiérrez with the involvement of President Salinas himself, was characterized by a very personalistic leadership. Leaders of popular movements such as the CDP of Durango and FPTYL who enjoyed long personal relationships with Rojas fared particularly well under PRONASOL.

The PRD argued that the disbursement of PRONASOL funds was highly politicized and that PRD municipalities were discriminated against. While not all of the PRD's claims have been substantiated by independent analysts, existing independent scholarship certainly supports the general contention

30. The list of popular movement organizations that chose to participate in Solidarity programs is a long one. Many of these organizations' leaders argued that participation had not meant a sacrifice of their autonomy or their credentials as members of the revolutionary opposition (interviews by the author). Some of the more important PRONASOL participants were the National Union of Autonomous Regional Peasant Organizations (UNORCA), the Democratic Peasant Front of Chihuahua, the Independent Federation of Agricultural Workers and Peasants, the Plan de Ayala National Coordinator, and important sectors of CONAMUP such as the CDP of Durango and Tierra y Libertad of Monterrey.

that many PRD municipalities (as well as others that were out of favor) were discriminated against by PRONASOL and other forms of discretionary state spending (Bruhn and Yanner 1995; Fox and Moguel 1995; Bailón 1995).

The PRONASOL program also encouraged movement organizations to relegate national considerations to a lower priority in favor of concentrating on their own organizational development. Participating organizations clearly reduced their tendency to comment critically on national affairs, most important, of the president himself. But Salinas also achieved this by encouraging the creation of new political parties, beginning with the formation of parties focused on the state level.

Popular movements can act in ways that encourage the elite conflict that is so often a precondition to significant political reform or they can allow or even encourage greater elite cohesion. One way to deflate elite conflict is for protest movements to split among themselves, decrease their support for those leaders attempting to form a national front, or both. This is what happened in Mexico over the course of the Salinas years of 1989–94. Social movements, once virtually united in their support for Cárdenas and the FDN became fragmented, with some continuing to support Cárdenas and the PRD, while others became neutral and still others became active critics of the PRD.

The history of postrevolutionary Mexican politics is replete with successful implementations of these divide-and-conquer methods of political control over the Left. In the contemporary period, the 1970s electoral reforms divided the Left over the costs and benefits of pursuing a parliamentary strategy. In the summer of 1984, the Partido Mexicano de los Trabajadores (Mexican Workers' Party [PMT]) was "awarded" electoral registration, thereby increasing intraleft competition, particularly between the PMT and the PSUM. PRONASOL was a dazzling stroke of political brilliance, one of the most significant in the postrevolutionary period. Although it certainly did not allow the regime to completely recover and reestablish its hegemony over the medium term, it did make a fundamental contribution to prolonging the period of regime transition. It also ensured that when the regime was forced to finally abdicate the presidency in 2000, power was transferred to the Center-Right candidate Vicente Fox rather than to the Center Left, led by Cárdenas. In other words, it allowed for the deep institutionalization of neoliberalism.

One of the reasons that the regime failed to reestablish political hegemony over the longer run was that it was not successful in its efforts to modernize the PRI. PRONASOL officers, and the president himself, argued from the outset that programs would be awarded on the basis of need and the merit of proposals. While the state certainly did not keep to its rhetoric that PRI affiliated groupings would receive no special considerations, evidence exists that PRONASOL funding of popular organizations increased scrutiny of PRI-linked organizations in some localities. However, this clearly did not lead to the type of modernization that Salinas hoped for.

CNOP/UNE

Early on in the Salinas administration, the reform of the PRI's popular sector received considerable attention when modernizers were placed in key positions in the National Confederation of People's Organizations (CNOP). Despite the fact that changes in this PRI institution did not live up to the rhetoric, it went through enough of a shift to be significant in an understanding of urban poor politics.

CNOP was formed in 1943, several years after the labor and peasant corporatist federations, to offer a contrast to Cárdenas's "anti-urban" policies of the 1930s, which favored the peasantry and industrial labor as the most reliable allies for the PRI (Davis 1994; Perló Cohen 1981). It was, and continues to be, a very heterogeneous group that includes professionals (such as doctors and teachers), street vendors, small-business people and, very important, government employees. CNOP functioned relatively well for decades, processing political talent and discouraging independent organization. However, beginning in the late 1970s, the rise of urban popular movement organizations and their coordinating body, CONAMUP, presented a direct challenge to CNOP. As middle-class social movement activity increased in the 1980s and provided support to Cárdenas, regime reformers realized that CNOP needed an overhaul. Its name was changed to UNE: Ciudadanos en Movimiento (ubiquitously referred to in Mexico as UNE) and its operating procedures and political mission were restructured. These efforts were ultimately stymied by traditionalists who saw their own interests threatened by the reforms. True to form, Salinas backed the reformers, but when stiff resistance emerged, he pulled back, preferring to work outside the party.[31]

31. The term *UNE* comes from the verb *unir* (to unite). It is not an acronym. The battle between political elites in favor of modernizing reform and traditionalists (sometimes derisively called dinosaurs) was central to all reform efforts in existing PRI institutions. During the Salinas administration, this elite infighting received significant press attention. Missing

The UNE was divided into five sections, or movements.

1. The Gremio Movement (Movimiento Gremial), consisting of guildlike unions and organizations that produce goods and services; among its members were taxi drivers and groups of small-business people and street vendors.
2. The Union Movement (Movimiento Sindical), whose most important members were employee unions of the federal government but also other public servants from the state and municipal levels. The Mexican state, despite fiscal and regulatory shrinkage, remained a major employer, and personnel grew between 1982 and 1988.[32] Some government employees were members of unions that belong to UNE and others did not. Some unions renounced their UNE affiliation.
3. The Movement of Professionals and Technicians (Movimiento de Profesionales y Tecnicos), composed of highly trained people who were expected to help a reformed UNE to regain lost legitimacy and better incorporate important social actors and sectors into the fold.

The preceding three groups were the old base of CNOP, and while they remained important, two new sectors of the organization were added:

4. The Urban Movement (Movimiento Urbano), embodying the PRI's efforts to establish its own "Urban Popular Movement" through establishing squatter settlements, or *colonias populares*. A key mechanism was building new and better working relationships with existing movement organizations and local leaders representing the urban poor.
5. The Citizen Movement (Movimiento Ciudadano), incorporating groups and individuals that did not fit easily into the preceding categories. Particularly important were those people who were not part of one of the first three categories or who had established antagonistic relationships with the party/state system. Examples of groups that had been particularly antagonistic included ecologists, human rights workers, disabled people, and feminists.

---

from most of the analyses, however, was that while Salinas generally favored the positions of reformers, he was very careful not to allow the splits to create opportunities for the opposition.

32. The total number of personnel employed by the central government was calculated to have risen from 1,583,771 in 1982 to 2,179,136 in 1988. A detailed account is presented in Albina Garavito and Bolívar 1990, 273.

While the Citizen Movement was seen as having great potential to incorporate important new actors into the fold, UNE officials, urban popular movement leaders, and cuadros in Mexico City agreed that the most important part of UNE's work during its first year was focused on the colonias populares in a hundred prioritized municipalities (interviews by the author).[33] A strong showing by the electoral opposition in July 1988 in areas where urban popular movements had made organizational inroads were the most important requisite for prioritization. Top officials within UNE were matter of fact in their admission that (1) the earthquake emergency response and reconstruction within the Federal District was dominated in large part by independent movements, (2) the events surrounding the earthquake fed directly into the PRI's losses in 1988, and (3) all this came as a shock to officialdom (interviews with the author).

Modernizers within UNE were quite aware that working within low-income neighborhoods had never been a primary focus of CNOP activities. Reformers emphasized repeatedly that the goal of UNE was to reverse this trend and regain these areas for the PRI. A key policy strategy was to channel UNE's most valuable professional human resources (lawyers, architects, engineers, accountants, and so on) into neighborhoods that housed the urban poor with the goal of assisting them to make better use of available resources, such as PRONASOL. In this way, party reforms and the introduction of innovative programs—most notably PRONASOL—dovetailed. When asked how UNE planned to "encourage" professionals to work in areas occupied by people who were unable to pay them and perhaps from whom many professionals would feel cultural distance if not react with disgust, one UNE respondent interviewed during the "heyday" of the reformers put it this way:

> Look, in the past, as everybody knows, CNOP operated primarily as an electoral machine in the sense that it proposed candidates for offices. It became a place where people from CNOP-type professions

33. Craske points out, "With *colonias populares* clearly identified as an area of weakness for the PRI, the first change for the CNOP was the development of a national organisation for the residents' committees" (1994, 15). Thus, "phase one" of the modernization plan was celebrated in April 1989, when the PRI held its first national meeting of "residents' committees" and consciously aped CONAMUP's format. As detailed in Chapter 6, this effort to copy the style of the urban popular movement had a variety of local manifestations, including the appropriation of popular symbols, such as Superbarrio, the "masked hero" character developed by the Asamblea de Barrios to lead the fight against exploitation and discrimination by slum lords and unresponsive government administrators.

came to get electoral posts. In the past, these professionals did not have to demonstrate that they had much presence in the community but only that they had climbed up the correct way through the party. This worked OK, in an immediate functional sense, as long as there was no real electoral competition, but it is clearly no longer adequate now that opposition has emerged. The situation since 1988 is a different one, and it has become increasingly important for candidates from the popular sector to have contacts in their localities, that is, to have a presence in the communities from which they are trying to be elected. Obviously, this is more important in colonias with significant organized opposition. We [the reformers within UNE] are trying hard to ensure that winning in these areas carries with it political benefits that can be used in future efforts by these people to advance themselves in party politics. (Interview by the author, February 1991)

Efforts were introduced in the priority municipalities, first at the neighborhood level, coordinated through municipal committees, which were reportedly promised a significant voice in the selection of candidates (interviews by the author, 1991).[34] In addition to bringing qualified personnel into the community, efforts were introduced to identify "natural leaders" within the community for positions of responsibility in CNOP. In my observations, it appeared that UNE reformers worked hard to create the impression that this kind of "rejuvenation" gave flesh to the promises of PRI reform so often referred to by party leaders and the president himself.

In the past, the work of CNOP began after the elections in terms of giving the elected officers credibility, doing their public relations work. This has changed dramatically since 1988, for we must now get involved actively in the campaigns themselves. We are changing from an organization run by political parasites into a sector actively contributing to the political rejuvenation of the party and the country. Of course, there remain grave questions regarding the future success of this reform effort. There is considerable resistance to internal reforms, just changing the name was a terrible struggle. (PRI official, interview by the author, February 1991)

34. It is my impression that this effort to develop new recruiting mechanisms was a sticking point with traditionalists within the party, although I could never get anyone I identified as a traditionalist to say as much, even in off-the-record interviews.

By 1991, the reformers had managed to push through an organizational restructuring whose result, in contrast to CNOP's historic structure, was clearly motivated by a concern for enhancing the mobilization and organization of new citizen identities (ecologists, women, human rights groups, and so on) and the urban popular movement. Not surprisingly, the 1991 reorganization unleashed a turf battle between modernizers who energetically proposed new—perhaps even more democratic—forms of party/ neighborhood relationships and traditionalists who argued that the root of the problem faced by CNOP had been the economic crisis and sharp declines in corporatist spending patterns.[35] The solution for the traditionalists was for UNE to position itself well vis-à-vis the new public-works projects of Salinas, ensuring that the PRI's political fortunes were associated with the new clientelism represented most importantly by PRONASOL.

Debates between traditionalists and modernizers raged within the PRI during the early 1990s. The most interesting possibility arose when José Parcero López, a key modernizing figure involved in the founding of UNE, was directed from the highest levels to develop what Craske describes as "a new model of collective action" (1994, 21). This was to be nothing short of a full reconfiguration of the PRI into "three social supports": the Popular Sector; a combined Confederación de Trabajadores de México (Confederation of Mexican Workers [CTM])–CNC Worker-Peasant Pact; and the new territorial organization designed to undermine the independent urban popular movements, the Movimiento Popular Urbano Territorial (Territorial Urban Popular Movement). However, substantial reforms such as this did not materialize. The popular sector did experience yet another name change, becoming the Frente Nacional de Organizaciones y Ciudadanos (National Front of Organizations and Citizens [FNOC]) in 1991, but without any of the more serious reforms proposed by the modernizers to make it more democratic (more participatory and less corrupt) and competent (through recruitment of candidates and management of program monies).

The failure to reform the entire party apparatus or even the urban sector meant that political recovery would have to come from elsewhere. The

35. Craske (1994) makes the interesting observation that "[t]he modernizers want to focus on the 'new leaders' [grassroots, organic leaders, especially those who have developed outside the PRI], whilst the traditionalists want to concentrate on stopping any disenchantment and apathy among long-term members" (34). Interviews with local and regional popular sector leaders in the state of Jalisco led her to observe that these functionaries remained mystified about the connection between the "democratization" that the reformers kept preaching and the economic betterment of their charges, which they had always been trained to keep uppermost in mind.

"urban problem" was the most serious for the regime, and thus the weight of this responsibility would fall to PRONASOL. When assessing the recovery of the urban vote in 1991 and 1994, the overwhelming majority of observers gave substantially more credit to PRONASOL than they did to the cosmetic reforms of the PRI's Popular Sector (interviews by the author).

In 1989, when efforts at party reform were just under way, noted Mexican historian Lorenzo Meyer published a paper in which he referred to serious reform of the PRI as a "mission impossible." He of course turned out to be right, in that despite efforts by sincere modernizers, the attempt to overturn a huge institution with sixty years of momentum behind it turned out to be much more difficult than simply creating a new set of organizational relationships. PRONASOL's directive to bypass institutional resistance and do what had to be done to recover legitimacy and votes—high-level delivery of basic services and resources targeted to urban voters and urban organizations that otherwise would likely continue to support Cárdenas—turned out to be a "mission possible."

The Role of Repression

The final ingredient in the temporary political recovery of the regime under Salinas was his selective use of repression. It is important to remember that one of the major differences between regimes (democratic, inclusionary authoritarian, and exclusionary authoritarian) relates to the use of force. Democratic regimes, at least ideally, use force only in strict accordance to the law, and when state actors use force illegally, these abuses are investigated and remedial action taken. What differentiates inclusionary authoritarian regimes such as Mexico's from exclusionary regimes such as Chile's and Argentina's during the 1970s is that the former uses repression much more selectively than does the latter. However, even if abuses are fewer, inclusionary authoritarian regimes do not routinely investigate abuses as do democratic regimes. Thus, the investigation and possible prosecution of past abuses had to await the democratic election of President Fox.

Repression, and the credible threat of repression, has a tremendously important influence on the emergence and character of collective dissent. For decades in Mexico, this threat, in concert with the existence of inclusionary channels, was widely credited as effectively explaining the long duration of the regime. This conception probably always discounted the amount of violence actually used by local elites (who may not follow the national party's conventional wisdom). Moreover, studies suggest that, as political discontent was increasingly channeled through organizations that were potentially able to ignite a regime crisis in the late 1980s, repression increased significantly, contributing to the protest cycle's decline. A 1990s America's Watch report argued that a wide array of abuses "[had] become an institutionalized part of Mexican society"; these included killings, torture, mistreatment by police, disappearances, targeting of opposition organizations, and violations of freedom of the press.[36] The report, consistent with claims made by a variety of independent human rights organizations, asserted that what was new in Mexico was not human rights abuse but the fact that the frequency of this abuse was increasing and that abuses were now also associated with elections as never before. The violence was explicitly directed toward those associated with the PRD.[37] In early state elections, while the PAN's victory was recognized in Baja California,

> PRD victories in Michoacán and Guerrero went unrecognized. Peasants, workers, and students occupied several government municipal offices. Salinas sent in the army to take them back. At least sixty PRI opponents, mostly PRD activists, were gunned down in 1990. A near-repeat occurred in Michoacán's disputed 1992 elections, resulting in six more deaths. Mexico's "national security forces," including paramilitaries and police, continued gunning down PRD members: some 300 were killed in 1994–1996 alone. (Cockcroft 1998, 300, 332)

36. The report explicitly sought to undo the image of Mexico as a "relatively benign version of authoritarianism," an image promoted by apologists for the regime. "More often than not, Mexico is overlooked when lists of countries that violate internationally recognized human rights are compiled. That this is so is more a testament to the Mexican government's careful cultivation of its pro–human rights image than its care to ensure that individual human rights are respected" (America's Watch 1990, 1).

37. The PRD has a credible estimate of 310 deaths during the 1988–91 period, of which, Alejandro Lueveno estimates, 70–75 percent were a result of local municipal conflicts, most notably in the states of Michoacán, Chiapas, Oaxaca, Guerrero, and Morelos. Of these, a large number occurred in local elections soon after the 1988 presidential elections, which had left many parts of the south highly mobilized and angry. Notably in Michoacán and Guerrero, municipal offices were held for two or three months by *campesinos* armed with single-shot rifles and machetes when official results of 1989 and 1990 elections were shown to profit the PRI. These conflicts were often resolved violently, leaving deep scars along with the casualties (interview by the author, March 1999).

This pattern of violence resulted directly from the fact that the PRD had overstepped the regime's "acceptable bounds of behavior" by mobilizing power with the potential to seriously undermine the legitimacy and thus the continuation of the regime. The Mexican regime has always been particularly reluctant to unleash violence in ways that are likely to become very public. The use of force against the PRD has a lot in common with other dramatic uses of force, for example, against the striking railroad workers in 1959 and against the students in 1968. In all three of these cases, the opposition refused to negotiate with the regime and held firm to its original demands. In such life-threatening circumstances, the regime has proved itself willing to use substantial force to not only weaken those already mobilized but also, importantly, to discourage others. In my many interviews with urban popular movement actors during this period, it was clear that this message was not lost on them. For many, it contributed to their preference to work with the president and PRONASOL and, in the process, to distance themselves from the PRD.

Conclusion

Salinas accomplished a political recovery for the Office of President, the party/state system and the inclusionary authoritarian regime in general. The fact that this recovery did not prevent the steady erosion of the PRI's electoral domination during the Zedillo administration and the eventual democratic transition in 2000 should not obscure its importance. As argued earlier, the most profound legacy of the Salinas reforms was that they stalled the momentum of the Left, thereby providing time for the deep institutionalization of neoliberalism. In addition, the Salinas reforms should be credited with contributing to the fact that when democratic transition did occur at the ballot box, the victory went to the neoliberal PAN candidate.

The success of the Salinas strategy was already clear by the 1991 midterm elections, in which many 1988 losses were overturned. Despite the fact that the standard of living did not improve for the Mexican poor on a national level, moderate economic recovery and a well-articulated media campaign contributed to a sense that the worst was over and that Salinas was in control of the economy and the country. While economic recovery may have not been generalized for the urban poor, significant

resources were directed to areas of political vulnerability by the administration, resulting in significant political recovery. The PRD's poor showing
in the 1991 and 1994 elections certainly provides evidence in support of
this contention.

While the Left far from folded up shop and went home, a number of
important developments took place that strengthened the regime. Despite
concerted efforts to form an electoral alliance between the PAN and the
PRD, this failed to gel, as seen most notably in the inability to produce a
common presidential candidate. By contrast, the PAN reached important
agreements with the PRI on a number of key issues. The PRD was largely
unable to win elections or disrupt the taking of office by PRI candidates
who the PRD claimed had been fraudulently elected. While some movement organizations continued to support Cárdenas, others, attracted by
the possibilities of PRONASOL and the penalties associated with continuing
to support Cárdenas, did not.

Although Salinas was able to postpone a regime transition, he clearly
was not capable of preventing its eventuality. Despite rave reviews from his
international backers, notably members of the administration of President
Bill Clinton, Salinas left office in the midst of a firestorm. The year 1994
was one of revolutionary challenge (from the extremely popular Zapatista
rebels in the southern state of Chiapas); murder and scandal (there were
assassinations of the PRI's presidential candidate Luis Donaldo Colosio and
the party's general secretary); and the revelation late in the year that Salinas's financing of the neoliberal recovery had been constructed on shifting
sands. Deep socioeconomic problems that created economic instability
and downward mobility across much of Mexico's class structure continued
and fueled the opposition message. What the regime needed was a sustained economic recovery that the regime's political operatives could turn
into a political message that would dampen civil society's growing appetite
for regime change. Clearly, this did not materialize.

Salinas was unable to make deep and long-lasting urban reforms. Neither his political reforms nor his efforts to modernize the Mexican economy through fiscal changes, export orientation, and the promotion of foreign investment and better relations with wealthier nations altered the
deep structural problems of urban areas. In fact, given the militarization of
the Mexico–United States border and other results of legislation passed in
1996 to discourage migration to the United States, pressures on Mexico's
cities increased even further. Barkin (1978) has concluded that the failure

of regional planning to better distribute population and income had occurred primarily because the policy of national development inevitably encouraged income concentration and centralization; at the close of the Salinas years, Barkin's conclusion remained true.

Mexico is certainly not the only developing country to have experienced rapid rural-to-urban migration without also providing basic services and subsistence employment. At the close of 1994, it was, however, one of the only such countries to have endured such shifts without regime change. Mexico's system of single-party domination was a declining breed in a world caught up in a democratic wave of seismic proportions. As demonstrated by the results of the 1997 and 2000 elections, Mexico is now clearly on a trajectory to establish a more pluralist politics. The increased willingness of the urban poor to vote for opposition candidates is a decisive factor in this transition.

In the Introduction, reference was made to the literature on the urban poor during the 1960s and early 1970s. Reflecting a reality found in most of Latin America, the Mexican urban poor were characterized by political docility. The majority voted for the PRI, worked the PRI's clientelist networks as best they could, and generally acted in ways supportive to the regime. Those forms of opposition that existed were small local affairs without much consequence.

As described in Chapter 2, this changed so that by the late 1970s, a Mexican urban popular movement had emerged that was truly national in scope, with powerful organizations operating in a large number of locations across the country. As discussed in Chapter 1, social movements often have lead organizations that shape the messages and behaviors of the larger movement in highly significant ways. We now turn to a detailed exploration of what were arguably the two most important lead urban popular movement organizations in the country: The Comité de Defensa Popular de Durango (Popular Defense Committee of Durango [CDP]) located in the central northwest section of the country and the Asamblea de Barrios (Assembly of Neighborhoods [AB]) of Mexico City.

These movements had shared roots in the social Left that emerged out of the 1960s student movement, and their leaders knew one another and in fact participated in collaborative projects. However, as will also become clear in the pages to follow, they ended up taking very different, in fact contradictory, political and strategic decisions during the height of the 1980s protest cycle, the implications of which were significant not only for them but also for the Mexican Left more generally.

FOUR

The Comité de Defensa Popular de Francisco Villa de Durango

We are a poor people. It takes no particular genius to see that. It is not so much that we expect the CDP to lift us from this poverty, although making it easier to suffer is always welcome. But, more than anything, we wish and expect that we will manage our poverty with dignity, thereby making life worth living. That we will live lives that require no apologies.
—CDP ACTIVIST

The real question has never been: Does the end justify the means? The real question is and always has been: Does this particular end justify these particular means?
—SAUL ALINSKY, *The Professional Radical*

The violent repression of the 1960s student movement produced three political tendencies in the Mexican New Left, tendencies embodied in three different entities. The first was an armed revolutionary movement with both rural and urban wings, neither of which could sustain their operations, and the movement succumbed relatively quickly to the search-and-destroy policy of President Echeverría in the early 1970s. The second was a group that began work on a democratic project, believing that the time was right to focus on developing an electoral path to political power. The third was a group that was attracted to the political opportunities and moral imperative that it saw among the poor. Guided by the concept of "returning to the people," this last group set out to construct new forms of social power through grassroots efforts.

The story of the urban popular movement in Durango represents the historical trajectory of what is undeniably one of the most significant expressions of this return to the people. Not only did the Popular Defense

For both Alinsky and the CDP, pragmatism was a quality to cultivate, not a sin or sign of betrayal. Strict adherence to the moral imperatives of academic leftists was rejected as politically counterproductive and, thus, morally wrong. Alinsky and the CDP understand the goals of ethically sound radical action to be self-evident: a redistribution of power and resources in favor of the working and poorer classes. Both evaluate the strategy and actions of specific movement organizations in terms of this objective. Even the public disclosure of errors is done with an eye toward the goals of power.

Committee (CDP) build the largest social base of all Mexico's urban popular movement organizations; from the early 1970s to the late 1990s it was also central to movement coordination efforts (CONAMUP), one of the most important political currents on the left (OIR-LM) and a founding organization of the PT.

The antecedents to the organizing in Durango were Mexico's student movement and Política Popular, which adapted Maoist revolutionary strategy to the country's structure of political opportunities (Hernández Navarro 1991a). Política Popular's emphasis was on overcoming what it perceived to be a disconnect between leftist leaders and the majority of the Mexican population. In keeping with Left traditions around the globe, Política Popular was convinced that the true interests of the lower classes lay in a socialist transformation. The group resolved to create powerful mass movements through developing a grassroots practice capable of transmitting revolutionary praxis to Mexico's poor and working classes. Theory was to be brought to the masses and then refined through practice. As had been true in China, "mass politics" of "the people" was not limited to the industrial proletariat but extended to include the rural and urban poor. Their ultimate goal was to develop a Party of the Proletariat, which, according to Maoist theory, can only occur once the Left has united with the people.

From 1972 to 1978, emissaries of Política Popular went to the northern city of Durango and mobilized for their first urban actions, moving on to land invasions and the creation of "free neighborhoods" (colonias populares). The organizational structure they developed was called the Unión Popular Independiente (Independent Popular Union [UPI]). From the inception of the group, and throughout all its organizational formations, the Maoists of Durango maintained complex relationships with the regime at the local, state, and federal levels. The nature of these relationships varied, from hostility escalating to violence, to Machiavellian exchanges of interests. The theme has been played out throughout history in the complicated dance of politics: a social movement trying to exacerbate and exploit elite divisions at the same time as elites endeavor to use the movement to their advantage.

The CDP was founded in 1979; by 1985 it had become a strikingly powerful social actor, demonstrating increasing sophistication in its mix of mobilization and negotiation strategies. Its move into electoral politics in 1986 reflects a particular reading of the political opportunity structure. The

CDP motto "Llegó la hora de ser gobierno" (The time to be the government has arrived) first came into use in 1986. Shortly after the implementation of PRONASOL in 1989, the CDP became a key player in the creation of the PT. In 1992 and 1995, the electoral strategy was consummated with the dramatic CDP/PT victory in Durango's municipal elections, when it became *un partido de gestion*—"a party of public works" with broad multiclass appeal.

What were the implications of the transition to electoral politics on the part of a social movement for Mexican democratization; and what were the implications for "the people," who were considered the moral protagonists by Política Popular? As explained in Chapter 1, this can best be examined through the lens of relationships, with detailed attention paid to changes within the movement and the interrelationship between internal and external forces.

Piven and Cloward (1992, 317) ask two important questions concerning the value of enduring formal organizations for poor people's politics: "[C]an those with few resources form influential organizations successfully? Indeed, do they even have the resources to form stable formal organizations, influential or not?" The CDP certainly built an influential organization that persevered far longer than Piven and Cloward indicate is the norm (317–18). The CDP achieved high levels of success in building movement identity and solidarity and in extracting significant government resources for the basic needs of Durango's poor. The durability of the CDP depended in part on the provision of material payoffs to its members in ways that overrode the free-rider problem while also building solidarity and identity on bases not contemplated in Mancur Olson's (1965) paradigm of human nature and politics. The CDP survived, and often prospered, for almost of two decades because of its ability to induce and sometimes coerce participation—a power generally reserved for unions. The longevity of the CDP depended on and thus was conditioned by its extremely complex relationships with state actors that empowered the movement's ability to attract rank-and-file participants and influence the contours of Durango's political economy.

In essence, the enduring challenge to the CDP was to balance the tension between accommodation with state elites and the ongoing commitment to structural reforms. The legitimacy of the CDP depended on its leadership's ability to maintain this tension within acceptable boundaries. Going too far in an oppositional direction ran the risk of state repression, which could ultimately lead to the demise not only of individual targets of repression but also of the organization itself. In addition, in a society such as Mexico's in which the state continues to be a vital source of material goods, the CDP also was required to maintain working relationships with the state so as to gain access to material resources, which were translated into material gains for their rank-and-file bases. Going too far in the direction of accommodation with the regime risked the loss of its reformist not to mention its revolutionary, commitments.

The CDP's decline in the late 1980s was the combined result of its leaders' decision, first to collaborate closely with the Salinas administration's concertación strategy and, second, to opt for building a political party at the expense of the movement. Despite its impressive successes, its history also illustrates how vertical integration with state elites invites "the destructive forces of oligarchization, cooptation, and dissolution of indigenous support" (McAdam 1982, 55). In the following chapter, we will see how this contrasts with the history of the AB, also a lead urban popular movement organization, but one that opted for maintaining a dual strategy of pursuing party politics while also preserving the movement.

Beginnings: The Student Movement and Política Popular

The origins of the CDP can be traced to the Mexican student movement as well as to a French interpretation of the Chinese Cultural Revolution.[1] The violent repression of Mexico's 1968 student movement caused most young people to cut short their activist careers short as they realized that radical action carried with it real risk and costs. However, some of the most committed were attracted to a key idea in Mao Zedong's Little Red Book: that real revolutionary activity was born out of face-to-face work with the people. This radical democratic ideal proposed that the best revolutionary ideas came from those who lived, worked, and suffered with the poor.

Política Popular, which was formed in 1969, was one of three Maoist groups operating independently in Mexico, and the brainchild of Adolfo Oribe Berlinguer, whose graduate study in France exposed him to the

---

1. Barbosa (1984), Bennett (1995a), Núñez (1990), and others correctly emphasize that the creation of Política Popular in 1968 was also influenced by earlier experiences and thinking. The most relevant antecedents are the Liga Comunista Espartaco (LCE) (particularly the Ho Chi Minh section was most associated with doing grassroots organizing work). The origins of the LCE are found in the 1958 internal rupture of the Communist Party. As noted by Bennett, "While it is true that the Maoist groups were something new, their existence constituted a response to long-standing debates at the heart of the Mexican left" (1995a, 92).

ideas and political activism of Charles Bettelheim.[2] Oribe and other Mexican Maoists chose to focus on the creation of one of the three pillars critical for Maoist revolutionary struggle—a popular front—arguing that the other two pillars, a revolutionary army and a political party, were not viable options in Mexico's configuration of political opportunities. They proposed that the army and the party would eventually and naturally evolve from the popular front experience. In part because of the influence of Maoist theory and the experience of the Chinese Revolution Oribe's original preference was to work in rural areas, and in the very early 1970s, he sent young radicals to places in the countryside that were deemed ripe for organizing.[3] These original rural efforts sometimes failed, often leading the young activists to shift their focus to the urban periphery.

In December 1969, Política Popular wrote that it sought to construct an organization that must "fundamentally reject all forms of dogmatism, sectarianism, and closed thinking, and in their place, instill the constant use of imagination, intelligence, and inventiveness." The group's manual refers to Marxism as a "guide to action," rather than as a bible to be strictly adhered to, and repeatedly insists that internal democracy must be practiced, as a source of strength in the struggle against economic, social, cultural, and political authoritarianism.[4] These ideals remained important throughout the history of the CDP and its sister organizations.

The Formative Years of Social Struggle, 1972–1978

The most important for putting an end to bourgeois attitudes and ideas is to eliminate the concepts of the private, the individual, the egoism. . . . If the concept of the private is not annihilated, it will not be possible to establish the concept of the public, of absolute disinterest and the abandonment of the other, related inferior

2. The other two Maoist groups operating in Mexico were the Sección Ho Chi Minh, called the Ho, and the Organización Regional Compañero. Compañero, as the latter was most commonly known, was to give birth to the UCP, perhaps the single most important urban popular movement operating in the Mexico City area during the 1970s. The Ho would later join with sectors of Política Popular to form the OIR-LM.

Adolfo Oribe is the son of political elite member Adolfo Oribe Alba, who held a number of high-level political positions beginning with the Calles administration of the 1920s. During the Echeverría administration, Oribe Sr. headed up a large state-owned enterprise and enjoyed close ties with the president.

3. The most important locations of the first organizing wave were in the states of Durango, Zacatecas, San Luis Potosí, Tlaxcala, and Nayarit and the state of Mexico.

4. The direct citations from *Sobre el desarrollo de Política Popular y sus cuadros medios* as well as the subsequent quote from *Por una línea de masas* are as they appear in Bracho 1995 (78, 80).

preoccupations. To arrive at the former, the fundamental is to bind with the masses and coexist with the people in their struggles, but also one has to study the revolutionary theory. . . . Our service must be total and sincere to the people, a practice of absolute disinterest without the least preoccupation for ourselves, casting our lot with the people . . . daring always to struggle and to know that in the long run the enemies of the people will be conquered by the people.

—POLÍTICA POPULAR, *Por una línea de masas*, MARCH 1974

Early in 1972, *Política Popular* sent a small group of young "missionaries" to the capital city of Durango, La Victoria de Durango.[5] The city and surrounding state was, and in many ways still is, a very traditional place, where the Catholic Church exerts a strong, conservative influence. The local political and economic ruling class is also conservative but tends to be weak.[6] The mainstay of regime power was consolidated in the PRI-controlled trade union, the Confederation of Mexican Workers (CTM), dominated by local strongman Don Antonio Ramírez.[7] This context left a considerable opening for Política Popular, as the corporatist PRI organization

5. This small group of enthusiastic, committed, and inexperienced revolutionaries included Jesús Vargas Valdez and his wife, Marcela Frías; Carlos Cruz Martínez, alias Marcos (who became one of the two most powerful leaders within the CDP); Rodrigo Durán Martínez, alias Ramón; and Alberto Escudero Gómez.

    For the sake of convenience, I refer to the capital city as Durango, which is how it is commonly known in Mexico. With a municipal population of more than a half million, Durango is an important population center in northern Mexico, a region characterized by low population density. Despite its history as one of the silver capitals of New Spain, and its timber and mineral potential, Durango during the 1980s was an economic backwater, producing less than 1.5 percent of Mexico's GDP and receiving less than 1 percent of total federal investment (Canudas 1991, tables 3, 8, 9). The state of Durango, with a population of 1,352,156, contains only 1.67 percent of the country's population, down from 2.4 percent in 1950 (Gobierno 1987). Census figures from 1990 show Durango municipality with an urban population of 348,036, of a total municipal population of 413,835. According to Arzaluz Solano (1995, 203), poverty levels worsened considerably during the 1980s economic crisis, with Durango ranking among Mexico's poorest. Durango's poverty is linked to the region's economic stagnation, which is exacerbated by its landlocked status and lack of transportation systems.

    6. The weakness of Durango's economic and political elite can be traced in part to the devastation caused by the Mexican Revolution, when the state's population fell drastically. Durango was strongly loyal to Pancho Villa, and when he lost, so did the state. Many prerevolution elites lost their fortunes and their positions. Many of those who survived (literally or figuratively) opted for relocation, leaving Durango "sin dueno" (without owner). For a detailed, nuanced account of the revolutionary period, see Martínez Guzmán and Chávez Ramírez 1998. For an analysis that extends into the first postrevolutionary decade, see Martínez Guzmán 1998.

    7. The absence of a strong local political class has meant that PRI political talent is regularly imported in Durango, principally from Mexico City and Monterrey. This has made the city vulnerable to strong opposition figures, as demonstrated in the PAN municipal presidency

(CNOP) responsible for incorporating the urban popular sector into the regime was very weak. Moreover, despite the local conservative culture, urban movements of dissent had arisen before.[8]

In June 1972, the young Maoists divided the city into the zones that they identified as most auspicious for organization and began the long and often arduous task of persuading poor renters in PRI-controlled or unorganized neighborhoods to work to create colonias populares, which were conceived of as "liberated zones" for the urban poor.[9] These colonias were to be formed by land invasions and used as "bases" from which the revolutionaries could expand—partly through building horizontal ties to radicalized peasant groups. While the details varied, the basic idea of land invasions was to organize renters and homeless people to occupy and then purchase a particular piece of land from the owner, either before or after the occupation at a price and on terms that very low income people could pay. While the material appeal of these colonias was home ownership, a substantial number of participants were also attracted by the political vision (interviews by the author).[10] The Maoists were wise enough—particularly

victory in 1983 and the CDP/PT victories in 1992 and 1995. Since the 1970s, politics have been strongly influenced by the distaste displayed by presidents, particularly Echeverría and Salinas, for the "backward" nature of Durango's political elite. These splits between the local and the federal elite enhanced opportunities for the opposition.

8. Although both the Movimiento del Cerro del Mercado in 1966 and the Movimiento Popular de 1970, led by student leaders, failed to achieve their demands, they raised the possibility of oppositional politics in Durango. The 1966 movement, called the Frente Civico Durangueño, sought to develop a local steel industry so that more profits and employment would remain in the state. The government was able to disband the multiclass front with small concessions and promises of future studies, which never took place. In the view of Miguel Palacios, director of the Institute of Social Sciences at the Universidad Juarez del Estado de Durango (UJED), the failure to achieve more was a result of inexperienced student leaders simply being out-negotiated by the state (interview by the author, 1991). The 1970 student-led movement was based on a labor dispute at the university, conflict over increases in property taxes, and a corruption scandal involving the governor. Once again, the student leaders who headed the multiclass front, the Frente Popular de Lucha, were out-negotiated if not simply bought off by federal negotiators. In the end, the governor created several industrial parks, some new employment was generated, and several unpopular members of his government were removed. For more on the 1966 movement, see Borrego Rodríguez 1984. For the 1970 movement, see Ornelas Navarro 1984.

9. These were a variation on the themes promoted by Oribe. Whatever reservations he might have had about changes in plan from rural to urban, they were not sufficient to prevent him from financing the Maoists in Durango.

10. CDP leadership consistently asserted that in the early years of the movement the rank and file was much more ideologically motivated than it was by the late 1980s. The most common explication is that in the early years the leadership spent long hours in political education with the rank and file. As the organization grew, sustained interaction between leadership and

given their poor performance in rural Durango—to understand that developing people's confidence in them and their ideas would not be easy. After all, both the urban and the rural poor were deeply influenced by a conservative church in which acquiescence to temporal realities was seen as a virtue. Despite wide distribution of personal invitations and fliers, only thirty people, most of them women, turned up to the UPI's first general assembly in August 1972 (Escudero Gómez and Cruz 1986, 17).

Then local water rates increased, providing the Maoist organizers with a tool to use against this ideology of political passivity. They undertook an intensive effort to mobilize for a second meeting in the collective housing projects, known as *vecindades*. Their work paid off: this meeting was attended by four hundred people (20) and eventually led to a successful protest against the water-price hike. For most of these people, this was the first experience of raising a public challenge to authority—an electrifying experience for some, less so for others.

One woman told me: "We lived in a poor *vecindad*. . . . Here we were, for the first time in our lives, standing up to these sons of bitches, who thought they could raise prices on the poor and put the money in their pockets without us saying a word. . . . They would kick us and we would just move out of the way and let them have their way. But this time we said no; thanks to the *compañeros* [the Maoists] we finally took a stand" (interview, 1990). Another woman explained: "I was scared. Who knew what would happen? But my neighbor told me if we did not go we put the entire *vecindad* at risk. And if we didn't go, maybe they would take us off the list. So, we went, but I didn't like it. When they got really excited, and starting yelling, I liked it even less. I was of course very happy when we heard the good news" (interview by the author, 1990).

At this point, the UPI was characterized by a confrontational style of mass mobilization, charismatic leadership, revolutionary ideology, and the fact that married women made up the majority of the rank and file.[11] Fresh from this victory, the Maoists recognized that "the most important thing, without

rank and file became far less frequent. Although middle-level activists, or cuadros, were ostensibly charged with bridging the gap between leadership and the bases, they never reached their anticipated potential, which critics of the CDP argue was not entirely unintentional, as it served to enhance the current leadership's power via prevention of the rise of more capable competition.

11. This is true of the overwhelming majority of Latin American urban popular movement organizations. However, this presence among the rank and file does not extend to leadership positions, which are overwhelmingly male dominated.

any doubt, was that the masses felt that the small victories were thanks to their mobilization" (Martínez Guzmán, 1998, 60). They spent the remainder of 1972 working in more than 150 *vecindades* and the smaller *casas de renta* (rental houses) and particularly with the water rates committees they had formed. Long hours were spent in mostly small-group discussions with renters, in which, slowly and with persistence, the young radical Maoists successfully overcame the low expectations and the fears of reprisal.

During this time, President Echeverría began to intervene in Durango's politics, as he was concerned about CNOP's failure to effectively incorporate the urban poor into the regime and thus was willing, as was Salinas years later, to "make arrangements" with at least some popular movement organizations, including the young Maoists. Early in 1973 at the behest of the president, Governor Páez Urquidi, who was widely considered a particularly bad governor, proposed changes in the state's constitution that asserted that all inhabitants had the right to a decent dwelling, that monopolizing urban property was against the public interest, and that the state could expropriate properties deemed to be in the public interest.[12] Needless to say, such a proposal not only created a local ruckus but also raised concerns nationwide. While pressure from elites around the country managed to tame down what finally passed, the proposal nonetheless sent a signal of encouragement to the Maoists in Durango.

This facilitated the UPI's quick ascendancy and ability to challenge the social assumptions and political habits of an extremely conservative and provincial part of Mexico. In February 1973, the UPI led six hundred people to invade unoccupied land that was slated for a PRI low-income housing project, leading to eight arrests (Escudero Gómez and Cruz 1986, 24; Manuel Rosas Santillan, interview by the author, 1990). This action made it clear that the UPI was intent on direct confrontation with the local regime. In early March, it led one thousand people to invade land owned by "a gringo." This time, when faced with forced eviction, the group backed off and camped in the main plaza, where, despite arrests, its members remained for almost two months. In meetings with senior officials of the state government, the UPI leaders, dressed in humble clothing and accompanied by a strong showing of rank-and-file support, struck a sharp contrast

12. Not only was Urquidi "more businessman than politician" and a nonnative unfamiliar with the state; he compounded this liability by constructing a team made up almost entirely of people from Mexico City. With his classic wit, Martínez Guzman wrote of Páez Urquidi: "Of the 900,000 people living in the state, he knew only three . . . and they all lived in Gómez Palacio" (Durango's second largest city) (1998, 31).

with government officials, in their tailored suits and with every hair in place.[13] On May 3, the judicial police took back the central plaza, beating people and detaining several members of the leadership, who were beaten again and then relocated to different parts of the country (Durán 1991, 17). These leaders made their way back to Durango "shaken but not deterred" (interviews by the author, 1989, 1990). Finally in September, after much negotiation, they received 20 hectares (49.4 acres), which they would pay for over five years. With this land they created Durango's first colonia popular, División del Norte.

This was but the first of many colonias populares that were successfully formed by the Maoists in Durango. While each colonia has its distinct details, the strategy was to build working relations with federal agencies while using mass mobilizations to pressure local power holders into negotiating agreements. As popular organizations will almost inevitably lose in any direct confrontation with private landlords or state firepower, identifying and effectively exploiting intragovernmental elite splits was central to the CDP's strategy. While the Maoists effectively gained increasing amounts of political space from *neopopulismo echeverrista* (Echeverría's neopopulism) over time, they were simultaneously contained by the repressive policies of Durango's governor.

The UPI as an organization ended in 1973 with the creation of División del Norte as an organization. For the following two years, División del Norte concentrated on gaining services for the colonia and imbuing the "revolutionary lifestyle" with meaning. People who experienced this period describe the creation of a collective living distinct from that of the mainstream. Police did not enter the *colonia*, because they felt unwelcome and superfluous: "We policed ourselves. If somebody got out of line, we took care of it our way—and let me tell you, it usually didn't happen again" (resident of División del Norte, interview by the author, 1990).

At this point, there was a deepening of the relationship between the Maoist outsiders and the rank-and-file inhabitants of the colonia. As one

---

13. Bringing the rank and file had a number of positives. It often served to discombobulate public officials. It also allowed the movement's participants to witness their leaders stand up to governmental power and, consistent with a long-held Maoist value, experience it themselves. Another, very practical, objective was to have witnesses to whatever promises or verbal agreements were made by government officials. Many rank-and-file members often commented that hearing about these actions contributed to their initial decision to join and explained that participating in such actions both solidified their loyalty to the organization and its goals.

resident explained: "Sure, [the Maoists] were different. They were more educated than we were. But they made a real effort; do you know what I mean? They dressed like us, they ate what we ate . . . they lived with us. When we went somewhere, we went together in the same vehicles. They fell in love with our women [smile]. They participated in the work brigades. They got to know us, and we got to know them. They were unlike any leaders any of us had ever known" (interview by the author, 1989).

When asked if rank-and-file members ever criticized the leaders in public, they gave the following representative answer:

> Sure, we criticized them. They never stopped asking us to. You see, we were organized by street and by sector.[14] And we had lots and lots of assemblies, assemblies by neighborhood, and assemblies by sector. We were living together, so of course there were problems. And sometimes the problems were with *los jovenes* [literally, the young people, in reference to young Maoist leaders] and sometimes they were with some guy who thought he was a big shot from the neighborhood. Whichever, we let 'em have it. And I remember really well, that especially with *los jovenes*, they took it pretty well. Better than I would have if I had been one of them. I mean, it takes a lot of personality to be someone who has not had a lot of power and then once you get it not to abuse it. (CDP rank-and-file member, interview by the author, 1989)

If a *compañero* (comrade) from the colonia had a work problem, that person was no longer limited to the PRI-controlled CTM labor tribunals, which many viewed as being as arbitrary and antiworker as the owners were. The Maoists formed a Labor Committee whose members listened to the complaint, and if it was determined to be legitimate, they went to the work site to resolve the issue. If the problem persisted, they would resort to direct action—and they had two thousand households to draw from. Sometimes they would help themselves to some portion of the owner's property or set up a "plantón indefinido" (an encampment of undetermined duration) on the doorstep of the owner's home, complete with nightly bonfires, loud chants and laughter, and perhaps a loud radio in the mix. As

14. Durán explains that all forty streets were organized into a neighborhood association (*asamblea de vecino*) and that the highest authority was the General Assembly, where everyone was entitled to participate in decisions (1991, 22).

one participant told me: "Before, we would have to go through all this paperwork, hassle, and expense—and after all that, as often as not, we lost. If you were in a union, it was the CTM. And how they treated you depended on if you were in good with them. No, when we took the power of the colonia to them, then they listened like they never had before. We liked it. We liked it a lot" (interview, 1989).

This challenge to the CTM and, more generally, to the etiquette of power long established in Durango was no doubt facilitated by the new governor, Héctor Mayagoitia, who had been handpicked by President Echevarría. According to CDP leader Martínez Guzmán, when the local power elite would complain about the Maoists' frequently illegal tactics, he would "indulge them with a face that revealed the smile of the Mona Lisa" (1998, 84). Taking advantage of the new brand of urbanism promoted by Echeverría, the Maoists began to form new colonias themselves without suffering the violence they had experienced earlier. The competition from the Maoists stimulated the PRI's CNOP to also initiate land invasions, and they established sixteen PRI-controlled colonias during this period.

For the División del Norte, 1976 was an important year. The organization, and as a result the people of the colonia, experienced a split over a combination of political ideology, strategy, tactics, and personal power. The debates in Durango mirrored those taking place within Política Popular on a national level, most notably in Monterrey between Alberto Anaya (who would go on to lead Línea de Masas) and Adolfo Oribe (who became the head of Línea Proletária), the two men accusing each other of authoritarianism. Anaya and his supporters, who had been successful in urban areas, in a sense provoked the struggle by challenging the dominant leadership position of Oribe, who was becoming less interested in the urban periphery movement and wanted to shift the focus to labor organizing.[15] In Durango, Marcos Cruz allied with Anaya and established himself as the local leader. When new opportunities arose in 1976 to develop colonias, he quickly organized two successful land invasions in what became among the most important CDP colonias, Emiliano Zapata (two thousand home-sites) and Lucio Cabanas (eight hundred).[16]

With the presidential transition from Echeverría to López Portillo in 1976, the Maoists' fortunes declined, along with collaboration from the

15. This split led those from Proletaría to essentially integrate themselves into the regime during the 1980s and 1990s, while Línea de Masas remained more independent.

16. From this point forward, Línea de Masas is the focus of the present study and the history of Línea Proletaría moves to the background.

presidency.[17] As a result, Marcos Cruz and other leaders dedicated themselves during the 1976–78 period to the consolidation of their two new
colonias.[18] The decline in federal-level access pressured the Maoists to
improve relations with state-level officials and meant that they negotiated
from a somewhat weakened position. This helps to explain why Marcos
Cruz was willing to make a deal with the governor to stay out of peasant
organizing. While Cruz reportedly "cheated" on this deal from time to
time, he did so only cautiously. As the capital city continued to grow, new
colonias formed and there were even some land invasions on *ejido* properties.[19] Territorial turf battles between the PRI and the Maoists to form and
politically control these colonias were common, although the Maoists generally proceeded cautiously, primarily because they had lost their strong,
reliable federal allies. While the PRI had far more resources at their dis-
posal in this struggle, the weakness of CNOP and the dominance of the CTM
in Durango undermined the effective targeting of these resources to the
new colonias. The Maoists were able to take advantage of this, forming
committees of supporters within the PRI-controlled and the new politically
independent colonias.

The Formation of a Formidable Organization: The CDP, 1979–1989

By 1979, the Maoists concluded that the time had come to present a common front. In August, six hundred people, representing twenty-two colonias

17. Mexico's concentration of power and resources in the presidency meant that transitions
always generated intense strategy deliberations within popular movement organizations because
the president had such an enormous influence on the structure of political opportunities.

18. Many popular movement organizations experienced a decline in the political opportunities associated with this presidential transition. See, for example, the case of the Union of
Ejidos "Lázaro Cárdenas" (UELC) in the state of Nayarit as reported in Fox 1990a. The history of the CDP strongly supports the hypothesis that when the political leadership takes an
aggressive stand against a particular movement, the movement is forced to shift political
alliances to different governmental officials. If this fails, often the movement's very existence
is threatened.

19. The *ejido* is part of a land-tenure system set up under the Mexican Revolution
whereby the *campesino* "caretaker" has a right to work the land. The *ejidatario* may not sell the
land, however; nor does the *ejidatario* possess mineral rights. The state retains the right to
"repossess" *ejido* land at its discretion in order to serve the "national interest." In their original conceptualization, *ejidos* were intended to be tracts of land, which would be cultivated in a
cooperative fashion. The *ejidos* ranged in size from very large tracts with many members to
very small tracts worked by a small number of families. For a variety of sociological, economic, and political reasons, the majority of present-day *ejidos* have been divided into individual plots run by single families at subsistence or near-subsistence levels.

and two small independent organizations—the Frente Popular de Lucha (Front for Popular Struggle) and the Frente Popular Independiente de Fincas Urbanas (Popular Independent Front of Urban Farms)—formed the Comité de Defensa Popular Francisco Villa (Francisco Villa Popular Defense Committee).[20] They made a very clear decision to resist the "bait" of the political reforms enacted by the López Portillo administration, which meant in practice that the CDP would not affiliate or cast votes as a bloc for a political party.

The lack of political opportunities with the hard-line López Portillo administration resulted in the fact that CDP leadership devoted time and effort toward improving its relationships with state-level officials. When the governor and head of the PRI's CNOP, Tejada Espino, arrived at Colonia Zapata to dedicate a medical clinic, it signaled that a working relationship had been established: prior to this, it had been extremely rare for public officials to set foot inside Maoist colonias. The event also signaled to the urban poor that the Maoists were people of power who had to be reckoned with and who could get things done.

Soon after, Mayagoitia received a national appointment and Dr. Salvador Gámiz Fernandez, who was sympathetic to the social Left, was appointed as interim governor. Gámiz Fernandez was the best thing that had ever happened to the Maoists in Durango. In nine months, the CDP established three new colonias in the capital and carried out two land invasions in the municipality of Durango and one in a neighboring municipality. In the particularly dramatic case of Colonia Tierra y Libertad, when the owners refused to accept the price and terms offered by the CDP, the governor issued a decree of expropriation. Never before had the CDP received this kind of support from any government official.

With the arrival of the new governor, Armando del Castillo Franco (1980–86), the CDP's political maneuverability declined, but the group adjusted in ways that demonstrate how popular movement organizations are often characterized by their close, detailed, intelligent interpretations of the complex power relationships in their political environment. While good relations with state actors can be propitious for the fortunes of popular movements, at least in terms of short-term material goals, whether such close relations with state actors also become a liability is an important question for both social movement theory and the political strategy of

20. *Urban Farms* refers to agricultural producers on the outskirts of urban areas.

exiting movement organizations. Between 1980 and 1986, ten new CDP*ista* colonias were founded and the CDP became increasingly skillful in its negotiations with federal and state authorities.

The CDP's terrain of action was certainly influenced by dramatic fluctuations in Mexico's economy. Particularly important were the ways in which the 1982 economic crisis favored the CDP's political opportunity structure as unemployment increased and more people moved into the informal economy. Of special relevance were street vendors, known as *plataformeros*. These workers were not popular with the middle class, and they were particularly disliked by the shopkeepers with whom they competed. The PRI was notorious for driving them away and confiscating their wares, while the conservative Partido Acción Nacional (National Action Party, PAN), to the extent that it weighed in at all, supported the shopkeepers, who were part of its political base. This created an opening for the CDP, and the *plataformeros* were mobilized, adding an important base. Another significant important CDP expansion occurred in 1986, when the Union de los Pueblos de Emiliano Zapata (Union of the People of Emiliano Zapata [UPEZ]) was formed as an organization of rural communities within the CDP.[21] The CDP also sent emissaries to establish beachheads in the Laguna region, Durango's industrial center, located in the eastern part of the state, and to a select number of rural communities. The organization also developed a law office (Bufete Jurídico) that not only defended CDP members for nominal fees but also was available to nonmembers, thus promoting an image of the CDP as a group that served the broader community. On the national level, the CDP was one of three organizations that founded CONAMUP. In 1983, the CDP was fundamental to the founding of the political tendency OIR-LM.

In 1984, the CDP took on the PRI labor giant CTM and its head boss, Don Antonio Ramírez, when they sided with the musicians' union and its dissident leader, Juan Lira Bracho, against the PRI.[22] Obviously, this trespassing

21. For a history of the UPEZ, see Moguel 1991a, 50–61.

22. While governors came and went, Don Antonio Ramírez, along with the archbishop, were widely regarded as permanent fixtures of political power in Durango. If you wanted to do business in Durango, you had to come to an agreement with Don Antonio. Without such an agreement, which most often included paying a monthly tribute personally to Ramírez, labor trouble was essentially guaranteed.

Juan Lira Bracho, who challenged the regime first in the late 1950s, contested Don Antonio's exclusive right to designate the head of the musicians' union (for more on the 1950s movement, see Stevens 1974). While Lira had the temerity to challenge one of the most powerful men in Durango, he also recognized that he would need outside support. He first approached the rival union confederation, the CROC, but they were unwilling. Lira then

into a labor dispute would not please Don Antonio, who was none too used to people challenging his authority.

For the first two years under Governor Castillo Franco (1980–86), relations between the CDP and his administration were very conflictive. Fortunately for the CDP, at that point the governor appointed the accountant Sergio González Santacruz to the position of state treasurer, and Castillo Franco, most notorious for robbing state coffers, faded into the background as the treasurer took over more and more of the day to day operations. At the same time, the CDP was building organizational capacity while CNOP was floundering, unable to sustain the rejuvenation it had experienced during the Echeverría years with López Portillo as president. The crisis in corporatist structures caused by the economic bad times in the early 1980s further weakened CNOP.

In a provincial state lacking a strong political class, the CDP leadership became politically adept at mobilizing popular people power and translating this into political pressure that brought results. Their well-honed negotiation skills and mastery of existing dynamics and relationships all levels of government were impressive, and they carefully calculated their moves in reference to the existing elite configuration. Negotiations with political elites were often held prior to or simultaneous with mass mobilizations and achieved extensions of preexisting colonias, as well as extensions of low-interest housing credits and services, principally water, electricity, and drainage.

Internal Organization and Leadership: Ostensible and Real

By 1986, a formal decision-making procedure had been formulated for the CDP. It involved a six-member permanent elected commission; a thirty-five-member elected political commission (made up mostly of the CDP's most important activists); and functional working groups centered on basic consumer goods, women, culture, and propaganda. There was a detailed

---

contacted the CDP and found a partner who put two thousand to three thousand people onto the main streets of town. Lira eventually gave up challenging Ramírez inside "his union" and created an independent union affiliated with the CDP, but after months of constant aggression against the new union, he was assassinated in 1986. While martyrs generally did not play a crucial role in the symbolism of the national urban popular movement or the CDP, Lira was invoked as a symbol of the regime's injustice, to the costs of defying it, and to the courage that sustained the struggle.

structure and set of formal procedures, down to the neighborhood level, embedded with mechanisms ostensibly designed to ensure democratic decision making and collaboration between the rank and file and leadership. Like many, if not most, other popular movement organizations in Mexico, the CDP did not foster collaborative decision-making processes as much as it counted on rank-and-file consultation and ratification for leadership decisions sent down through the organization. The lack of participation is most noticeable around key strategic decisions—such as political alliances, with the rank and file most active in decisions pertaining to particular CDP colonias. For the CDP, more important than democratic decision-making processes was its persistent ability to form broad-based consensus within the organization.[23] On those rare occasions that consensus could not be built around leadership decisions, adjustments were made until support was achieved. Through 1989, the CDP avoided forging ahead without a rank-and-file consensus.

This structure made leadership extremely important in the CDP, and during the early years, Marcos Cruz was in charge. In 1979, at age twenty-three, Gonzalo Yáñez moved to Durango from Mexico City, and very quickly he made his way to the highest levels of the organization, sharing power with Cruz. No decisions were taken that were not worked out between Yáñez and Cruz, which is not to say that a wider debate did not occur. Formally, high regard was given for the general assembly, which was touted as being a high-quality exercise in democracy. In practice, as I observed, these assemblies mostly confirmed positions previously decided upon by top leadership. Occasionally the midlevel activists known as cuadros would take strong stands in opposition to the leadership, and while their positions would never prevail, these opinions were taken into account by Cruz and Yáñez. Sometimes those with dissenting views were pressured out of the organization or quit in disgust. While complaints being muttered about the power of top leadership was common, this never led to changes in the internal decision making or moved it in a fundamentally more democratic direction. As will be discussed in Chapter 5, this differs from the relationship between cuadros and leadership in the AB.

The predominance of authoritarian decision making in the CDP had enormous consequences. First, and perhaps foremost, it worked against

23. Important elements of the dissident teacher's organization, CNTE, appear to be a marked exception to this social Left norm, with the more democratic locals being the most successful. See, in particular, Cook 1996.

the emergence of new leadership, either from the CDP base, or from among its midlevel activists, or from outside the organization. This stymied the generation of new talent during the CDP's life span. It also meant that once the CDP leadership moved into party politics, the demise of the CDP would be quick in coming.

Consultations with the bases also featured prominently in formal descriptions of power and decision making. Unlike the assemblies, however, these consultations, often carried out with impressive organization, inclusiveness, and efficiency, sometimes shaped decisions. While these consultations were used to secure support and legitimacy for leadership decisions, they also permitted the leadership to grasp the complex dynamics of their growing organization. For example, when the results of the 1986 elections made it clear that the CDP colonias had voted for both the PRI and the PAN, the leadership initiated an intensive consultation process based on a carefully designed questionnaire and intensive discussions.[24] In the 1990s, when this same leadership no longer engaged in this type of consultation with the grass roots, the movement's strength eroded.

The Cultural Project: Developing the Revolutionary Consciousness Among the Masses

In 1983 the Centro Cultural Jose Revueltas was formed, promoted by Gonzalo Yáñez who was better read and always more highly motivated by political theory than was Marcos Cruz or were any other of those who held top leadership positions. Yáñez interpreted critical social theorists such as Michel Foucault and Gramsci to suggest the importance and difficulty of creating the "revolutionary subject." Yáñez was never shy about his respect and admiration for the people he led and his dismay at their lack of "revolutionary consciousness" and the difficulties of "instilling it." The cultural project and the

24. The PAN made major advances in the northern part of the country during the early 1980s. In Durango, their candidate Rodolfo Elizondo Torres won the municipal presidency, and they claimed that they had won the governor's race only to have their victory stolen from them through corruption. Protests by PAN supporters ended only after recourse to repression, ordered by the standing PRI governor. Some CDP rank-and-file members and even some cuadros were drawn to the citywide buzz that the PAN campaign generated, and to the fact that the PAN campaign rhetoric that harshly criticized the *priísta* status quo resonated with their own positions, even if the alternative to the PRI represented by the PAN was hardly consistent with the kind of Left revolutionary positions embraced by the CDP.

development of revolutionary consciousness were one and the same for the CDP and for the Mexican urban popular movement in general. Fulfilling or perfecting the Mexican Revolution was present in the PRI's cultural project as well, and the political culture of twentieth-century Mexico was dramatically shaped by different conceptualizations of the "revolutionary." The Left regularly competed over who was able to claim the revolutionary mantle, and in Durango, as elsewhere, considerable energy focused on wrangling this away from the PRI and the institutionalized regime. In general, the Mexican Left claimed for itself the proper mantle of that which was "revolutionary" and did all it could to undermine the regime's ability to legitimize itself with reference to its revolutionary credentials.

Yáñez's understanding of the obstacles to the cultural project included an appreciation of the difficulties involved with breaking from a materialist Marxism that historically had not given much attention to this dimension. So even when a decision was made, as it was in Durango in 1983, to prioritize this project, its success was undermined by a lack of enthusiasm and skill in implementing it (interviews by the author; Barrera 1986, 41–42). Neither the cultural center nor the cultural project more generally ever met Yáñez's expectations, although he never gave up on the importance of cultural meanings as an essential aspect of revolutionary praxis, and he later attributed some of the failings of the CDP to a lack of attention to it. He could lead the effort, but he could not accomplish a cultural transformation alone (interview by the author, 1998).

In the 1983–86 period, projects for youth and for women were top priorities, in a recognition that existing gender relations were frequently sexist both in the colonias and in the CDP's own relations of power. When the CDP hosted CONAMUP's Primer Encounter Nacional de Mujeres del Movimiento Urbano Popular (First National Meeting of Women of the Urban Popular Movement), it did so with "great enthusiasm for educating ourselves regarding the special struggles of women and seeking solutions," even though this did not translate into significant results (Barrera 1986, 45).

Gender

While women had little influence in the top leadership circles of the CDP, they were critically important at the colonia level, sometimes having positions of authority, though never at the highest organizational level. Basic consumption, housing, potable water, electricity, drainage, schools, clinics, and the like, generally the domain of women, were priority issues for the CDP (observations and interviews by the author). Why, if the focus of the CDP was on issues that made women the base of the organization and active as cuadros, did women not rise to top leadership positions? Drawing on Julieta Kirkwood's (1985) work, Venegas Aguilera (1995) suggests that it is not direct discrimination by male leaders that discourages women from more frequently assuming leadership positions, but rather deep seated cultural norms held by the women themselves: "It seems that women have internalized the lesson that their place is in the home and with the family; when they venture into politics, they rarely pursue a personal objective" (101). However, the reality is that women's traditional identity is constantly reinforced by male attitudes and behaviors. Changing relations in gender roles is more likely when those in power (usually men) come into regular contact with women who express political self-confidence. Unfortunately, such interactions were extremely rare for most leaders of the Mexican urban popular movement.

The CDP certainly did not excel in challenging dominant patterns of discrimination by placing women in top leadership positions within the organization.[25] What the CDP did do was create opportunities for women at the neighborhood level to alter their social relations by providing them with opportunities to participate in public life in innovative ways. In part because the CDP insisted that the males accept this change in their roles, women found themselves in an opportunity structure that allowed them to escape traditional male domination.

The central role of married woman in the CDP's bases and their importance in the day-to-day operations in the colonias came about in part because most men worked and thus were not able to participate in events during the workday; such responsibilities fell to women. Moreover, when men cannot earn enough to support their family or have left, women assume a greater role, and participating in the CDP, which was successful in increasing social services and benefits, assisted women in fulfilling their

---

25. The CDP ran female candidates, most notably for municipal president of Durango in 1989 and then in 1994 as part of the PT when they ran a female candidate for president of the nation. However, neither these women nor any others ever had important positions within the movement or party organization itself. At CONAMUP meetings, the issue of unequal gender relations was a topic of hallway discussion that sometimes also made it into workshops, but not much further.

responsibilities. Because success in this effort was often crucial to family survival, the CDP's capacity to help women in this way generated deep loyalties.

In conversations with CDP women regarding gender relations, I was repeatedly struck by the wisdom of Alexandra Massolo's conviction, written with specific reference to the day to day realities of the Mexican urban popular movement, that political life begins in the home, that changing gender relations in public must first overcome resistance in the family (1983, 1987, 1988; interview by the author, 1989). The following statements demonstrate family reactions to women's decisions to participate in the CDP:

> Well, it caused trouble and confusion is what it did. On the one hand, they knew that it was important to do, that it needed to be done, and since they were not usually available, I had to do it. Also, because this was the situation in most homes, my husband and most of the others did not really want to go to the activities where they would have to work mostly with other women [laughs]. We built bonds with each other, and the men felt excluded. Isn't that a change! But even though they knew we had to go, the husbands did not like it. It made them feel uneasy. We were out somewhere out of their control, and they knew it. I mean, there was all the talk about women being just as good as men and all that. We heard that at the meetings all the time. But, doing it, well, that's another thing. When it is right there in your own life, it is a lot more difficult than just nodding your head when some leader says that is the way it should be. So, it would cause fights. Some *compañeras* had real difficulties, and we would encourage them, and sometimes warn their husbands that they better watch out [laughs]! So, it was a struggle, still is. Things like this don't change quickly. (Interview by the author, 1991)

Another woman explained:

> Where I come from, women are treated as slaves, as property. Men can beat us, and nobody figures anything is wrong—must be something we did. If they wanted to use up the money drinking, the wife can't say anything. The place of the woman was in the house, especially in the kitchen and taking care of the kids. If she

was out doing something else, the man felt the right to question her, including being hostile and even violent. Other men expected it of him. If he did not do it, other men would chide him for not being in control of his woman. The CDP gave us a chance to change this, it took power away from men that they never should have had and gave it back to us where it belonged. (Interview by the author, 1991)

This testimony raises the issue of solidarity between movement women. In the course of working with the CDP, these women forged strong friendships, and an atmosphere of sisterhood and solidarity emerged. Many women insisted that they were motivated as much by bonds of solidarity as by organizational pressure and the services the CDP provided. This solidarity was fundamental to the power of the movement, fostering a deep intelligence and increased knowledge regarding collective action. It solidified the movement's ideals, giving them a place to be carried out. It generated loyalty and affection for the movement and certainly contributed to the willingness of women to work hard over long periods, while serving as an important way to attract other potential members.

1986–1988: The Electoral Option

Before 1986, the CDP had argued that electoral involvement without a "true worker's party" could be nothing but an elitist bourgeois activity incapable of producing revolutionary structural change. In the 1983 elections, the CDP formally remained neutral regarding voting, although some activists did recommend that those rank-and-file members who wanted to vote should opt for the Unified Socialist Party of Mexico (PSUM) (interviews by the author). But when the results showed that the conservative PAN received the majority of votes in many CDP strongholds, the CDP's position began to shift, and by 1986 it entered its first formal electoral alliance as the senior partner with the Partido Revolucionario de los Trabajadores (Revolutionary Workers' Party [PRT]). With the CDP setting policy positions and controlling candidate selection, the PRT won two seats for *regidores* (council members) in the capital city of Durango—one in Suchil and one in Coneto de Cononfort—as well as one seat in the state legislature.[26] From this election on, the CDP increasingly projected itself as an organization that, while primarily focused on the low-income urban population, also worked in the interest of peasants and the urban working and middle classes on issues such as the environment, legislative reform, and "ridding public offices of official corruption." To achieve this change in its public image, it worked hard to reduce conflict with the police and change media coverage of its activities. Prior to 1986, when the CDP received press attention, it had most often been in the "nota roja"—the crime report.

The successful 1986 election of CDP candidate Gabino Martínez Guzmán to the state legislature was of particular importance to the organization.[27] Just as for members of the federal legislature, most state legislators did not initiate laws, but Gabino Martínez proposed important constitutional changes that earned him and the CDP grudging respect from even some of the organization's harshest critics (interviews by the author). Some initiatives centered on the *ejido* laws, others on laws governing church-state relations. He also introduced legislation designed to expose and limit payoffs between public officials and companies that were awarded public-works contracts, and he argued fiercely against proposed rate hikes for basic services. An articulate lawyer, historian and intellectual, he was possessed of an effective oratory style that greatly enhanced the aura of professionalism surrounding the CDP.

José Ramírez Gamero, son of longtime political strongman Don Antonio, was elected governor in 1986 just as the CDP was beginning its electoral ascendance.[28] His win was hotly contested by the PAN, which charged electoral fraud, holding a prolonged and angry protest in the main plaza. Ramírez Gamero inadvertently contributed to the CDP's political aspirations when he agreed to work with the CDP on public-works projects.

---

26. *Regidores* make up the "administrative cabinet" of municipal government and are appointed by party based on percentage of votes received for the Office of the Municipal President.

27. Martínez Guzmán was selected to occupy the one space the PRT had earned through proportional representation because neither Marcos or Gonzalo were qualified to serve in the legislature, since neither was born in Durango.

28. Palacios Moncayo (1999) points out that the president did not handpick Ramírez Gamero, in contrast to what had been the historic norm for such positions in Durango and in much of the rest of Mexico. Rather, he got the position because of his strong connections in Durango and because he was the "political godchild" of CTM leader Fidel Velázquez (10).

When he failed to complete them, the CDP garnered positive media attention by questioning the governor's commitment. He went on the offensive and took out full-page ads in local papers proclaiming that the CDP was controlled by criminal elements, a move that was viewed as not only factually inaccurate but also politically counterproductive. Although the CDP scored a public relations victory and in the process undermined the governor's reputation, Ramírez Gamero became determined to limit state funding to any projects that would benefit the CDP and its constituents, which made raising the standard of living within CDP colonias much more difficult. When state funds ran dry, and new federal sources could not be found, the CDP was considerably strained under the pressure. In 1988, it entered into a political alliance with the Partido Mexicano Socialista (Mexican Socialist Party [PMS]), supporting first Heberto Castillo for president and then, when he withdrew, Cárdenas. The key electoral victory was gaining a federal deputy seat for CDP founder and leader Marcos Cruz, which gave the Durango Maoists improved access to federal offices.

The CDP had evolved from a small group of students organizing in a semiclandestine manner in poor neighborhoods to an institutionalized popular movement capable of mobilizing thousands of people on short notice and able to negotiate with public officials at all levels of government. As late as 1976, the movement was still based in only one colonia, but by the late 1980s the CDP was in control of twenty colonias in which they were the major institutional and political force.[29] In addition to their solid bases in colonias of their own making, they also had made significant inroads in a number of other pre-existing colonias around the city. Together, this meant that by 1990, the CDP was drawing from a base of around 100,000 people or about a quarter of the miniciple poulation.

These early electoral victories were instrumental in the CDP's effort to erase its public and political image as that of a radicalized and somewhat dangerous organization. Its new role in government changed the public perception of the CDP; it was no longer thought of as a group "begging" for services but, rather, seen as to a political organization capable of presenting alternatives, negotiating publicly recognized successes, and implementing increasingly larger-scale and more sophisticated public-works

---

29. This estimate is calculated from the twelve thousand house sites listed in Appendix A, multiplied by six persons per house. Moguel estimated that the CDP's sixty bases, including other activities and locations in addition to CDP colonias, translated into 150,000 people (1990a, 16). My estimate would be somewhat lower, around 100,000. Even so, this made the CDP one of the very largest popular movement organizations in the country.

projects. Their success meant that "since 1986, [the CDP had become] the leading force and point of equilibrium among all of the urban popular movements of northern Mexico and the rest of the organized popular centers in the country" (Moguel 1991, 3).

As the CDP steadily gained more and more legislative experience, its ability to present public-works projects in a technically and politically effective fashion improved, and it gained new insights into the workings of local and state government. This helped the group's members in their self-appointed role as government watchdogs and to develop stronger campaign positions in the 1988 and 1989 elections. This in turn positioned them for the first time to negotiate terms with President Salinas.

The 1989 Convenio de Concertación

The failure of both the López Portillo and the de la Madrid administrations to effectively incorporate the growing urban popular movement into the regime reduced the state's ability to set the national political agenda. As movement organizations effectively radicalized large numbers of the urban poor to press their demands outside existing institutional channels, the PRI lost its ability to dominate electoral outcomes in poor urban neighborhoods. The most dramatic sign of this was the swell of nationalist populist support for Cuauhtémoc Cárdenas in 1987–88, which caught the country by surprise.

President Salinas quickly demonstrated that his administration would address the political liabilities brought about by neoliberal economic policies through constructing new institutions to build legitimacy and to incorporate, or reincorporate, a substantial percentage of the political opposition. The primary tool in this task was the National Solidarity Program (PRONASOL), instituted in 1989. Even before Salinas's inauguration, his transition team began making overtures to popular movements, and the CDP found itself competing with other political organizations, including the PRI, to deliver material benefits to its constituents. The CDP, again ratifying its position as a lead organization, was the first popular movement organization to sign a convenio with the new president to participate in PRONASOL, a strategy that Salinas replicated with other movement organizations in other parts of the country in subsequent months. The convenio with the CDP stipulated that federal, state, municipal, and CDP resources were combined to implement public-works projects and create CDP-owned and -operated businesses. The total investment of the 1989 agreement was valued at 3.2 billion pesos, or about a million dollars. Almost two-thirds of the funding was federal (61 percent); the state government committed 5 percent; and the CDP 30 percent (mostly in the form of in-kind contributions).

The convenio permitted the CDP communities to contribute their matching funds as cash, materials, or labor; as a result, the overwhelming majority of the CDP commitment was met by providing manual labor to the public-works projects.[30] This arrangement was not unique to Durango or to the CDP. Allowing poor people to make their mandatory contribution to this "shared development" via manual labor was vital to the program, for it allowed many more groups to participate than otherwise would have been possible. This type of labor also put a premium on the ability to organize local people, something that many popular movement organizations were in a better position to do than were their PRI counterparts.[31]

The initial agreement was but the first of several CDP convenios signed that year. In September, the Union of the People of Emiliano Zapata (UPEZ, the organization of rural communities within the CDP) signed an agricultural, water-resource, and credit convenio, and later a convenio was signed for an ecological project to reduce contamination levels in the Tunal River. In addition to receiving government funds, the CDP was backed by the owners of the major industrial concern of Celulosico Centauro as well as the U.S.-government-funded Inter-American Foundation.[32] The ecological project was particularly significant for the CDP because it represented an attempt to establish the organization's credentials as those of a responsible participant in Durango's future economic development.

30. The convenio provided funding for a long list of small projects, including the construction of fourteen primary-school classrooms; electrification in six CDP colonias; potable water and housing improvements in seven CDP colonias; basketball courts; potable-water projects in seven CDP colonias; three sewing shops; child-care centers; six small tortilla factories; a construction-materials supply house; construction of fifteen kitchens that would provide subsidized food in CDP colonias; and a carpentry workshop.

31. From the beginning, one of the Salinas goals associated with providing development funds to popular movements was to introduce an element of competition and thereby force moribund corporatist institutions to develop new capacities. When the president visited Durango on February 13, 1989, he not only signed a convenio with the CDP but also signed one with the PRI's CNOP. This convenio committed funds far in excess of the CDP agreement, more than 22 billion pesos. "From the standpoint of total amounts, the differences between the CDP and the CNOP projects were enormous. Nonetheless, most of the amount given the PRI-connected group was in the form of credit. Thus, in relative terms, there was practically no discrimination against the CDP *colonías*" (Moguel 1995, 228). As time went on, however, it became clear that CNOP in Durango simply lacked the ability to coordinate convenio projects.

32. For a more detailed discussion of this complex history, see Moguel 1991b, 39–50.

However, these CDP convenios led to open, deep splits in the urban popular movement (and popular movements more generally), only months after so many movement organizations had joined together in support of the Frente Democrático Nacional (FDN) and Cárdenas's presidential bid. Gaining concessions was one thing; openly signing agreements that legitimated the president and his administration, if not the political system itself, was quite another. Some movements were inspired to replicate the CDP strategy, and many of these went on to form the PT. Others refused to sign public convenios with the Salinas administration and joined ranks with the PRD. Others changed their positions over time. For example, well-known intellectual activists Julio Moguel and Luis Hernández Navarro both supported the CDP's 1989 decision but later became vocal critics of what they regarded as the CDP's loss of autonomy and the strengthening of its authoritarian tendencies.[33] Others within the PRD began as outspoken critics of those who signed convenios, only to later soften their position and give it more nuance, most notably in the second half of the Salinas term. These contrasting and often conflicting priorities between political parties and social movements are an important part of the democratization process.[34]

Different priorities—and distinctive strategies designed to pursue those priorities—result in part from the diversity of locations in the political system, which generates different political opportunities. This can result in conflictive agendas, even between actors that assert common political goals. While it was relatively easy for left-leaning political parties and social movements to form a strong consensus behind Cárdenas's 1988 presidential bid, not long after the election differing priorities and strategies rose to the surface. As the PRD took shape in 1989 and 1990 it became clear that its priorities were to be electoral, first in its contesting the 1988 election results and then in its participating in the 1991 state and federal elections. While there were instances of popular movement organizations remaining formally within the Cárdenas/PRD fold while also actively seeking and receiving PRONASOL funds, many others concluded that their movement interests could be better served by severing their formal support to the PRD.

33. As argued in Chapter 1, movement autonomy should not be thought of in purist terms, but rather gauged in terms of whether or not a movement in general or a particular movement organization retains sufficient autonomy from other key actors—in this case the Salinas administration—to make the majority of its key decisions internally. The argument made by these critics and others was that the CDP came to fail this test.

34. This theme will be addressed in a comparative fashion in the final chapter.

For the CDP, the deterioration in relations between the CDP and the governor increased the appeal of PRONASOL (CDP leadership, interviews by the author, 1989, 1990) and was consistent with its strategy of exploiting elite splits. Salinas offered the type of resources and concessions that the CDP, along with many other popular movement organizations, had long advocated. The decision to tone down its rhetoric, notably against the president, and moderate behavior that was deemed "radical" in exchange for resources was not a difficult one for most of the CDP leadership. They, and many others who would eventually become associated with the PT, argued that PRONASOL was an important victory. It was a recognition by the state that movement organizations were often more capable of promoting development and service delivery than was the PRI. CDP leadership, and those who agreed with them, viewed PRONASOL as a successful split between the state and the PRI that they were prepared to exploit to their organizational advantage. They were of course very aware that Salinas was initiating this process for his own reasons but remained confident—and were even cocky—that they would emerge stronger from the relationship (interviews by the author).

Participants in PRONASOL and their critics also differed in how they viewed the political potential of Cárdenas and the PRD. Movement organizations that remained within the PRD fold often argued that if the Left remained solidly in support of the PRD they had a good chance of forcing a democratic transition. And even if a regime transition did not occur in the short term, when it did occur, it would be led by a PRD that would be much more politically progressive than if the Left deserted the PRD and thus by default increased the presence and position of ex-*priístas* and other moderates who had migrated to the PRD. Those who participated in PRONASOL emphasized the importance of providing services and material benefits as a means of retaining and expanding the Left's base, emphasizing the paucity of other sources of funding.[35] Furthermore, they remained uninspired by

---

35. A promise of neoliberalism is that as the state shrinks from its historic role of providing public services and social wages, civil society will expand to substitute for it. In Mexico, with little tradition of corporate giving or of nonprofits with significant budgets, the slight movement in this direction has been unimpressive, as least from the perspective of popular movements. This is not to say that NGOs have not become increasingly important to some popular movements, particularly in Mexico City (see, for example, the case of the AB, as discussed in Chapter 5). But the fact remains that even in Mexico City NGO budgets are small and for the most part capable only of supporting skilled staff, not as a source of funds. As noted by Hernández Navarro and Fox, "Mexican NGOs have far to go before achieving the institutional life, the political or the social presence of their counterparts in Chile, Brazil, or Peru" (1995, 203).

Cárdenas and the PRD more generally and also skeptical regarding the party's future. Finally, CDP leadership argued that if fortunes moved in unanticipated ways, and the PRD did end up gaining the power its proponents hoped for and predicted, well then, the CDP could rethink its position and realign more closely with them (interviews by the author).

Durango's governor Ramírez Gamero and the state-level PRI were out of favor with Salinas and key modernizers within the administration. The reasons for this were twofold. First, there had emerged over the course of the 1980s an internal split within the PRI between the "modernizers" and the "dinosaurs." Modernizers such as Salinas argued that the PRI needed to update if it were to remain competitive. *Dinosaurs* was the term used by modernizers and a number of critics outside the party to refer in a derogatory way to those said to resist modernization. Ramírez Gamero and Durango's PRI certainly qualified. Second, the governor, strongly identified with the labor wing of the PRI, had openly and aggressively lobbied for a candidate other than Salinas. Although the Mexican president picked his successor, this did not stop some from openly agitating for one of the so-called pre-candidates—the publicly bandied around list of those in the running for the sitting president's favor. Many local political observers concluded that this situation contributed to Salinas's willingness to risk building an alternative political power base with the CDP. Furthermore, the CDP top leadership had personal ties to Salinas and PRONASOL director Carlos Rojas.

However, the CDP's strained relations with Governor Ramírez Gamero meant that it also faced stiff opposition from the federal representatives in charge in Durango who had close ties to the governor. To remain within the PRD fold provided the CDP with no financial or political support in dealing with these local adversaries and CDP leaders reasoned that remaining loyal to Cárdenas would have left them without Salinas as an ally in these disputes and might well have turned him into a new enemy (interviews by the author).

But the changing political fortunes of the CDP raise an even more significant political question. Were Salinas and like-minded elites willing to support the political empowerment of at least a limited number of popular movement organizations so that these could contribute to the political system's legitimacy and stability? Clearly, the fact that the PRI was weak vis-à-vis the urban popular sector, particularly in Durango, goes a long way toward explaining why Salinas was so willing to underwrite the CDP. With echoes of Echeverría, Salinas moved to challenge existing "old and in-the-way" politicians and politics by risking the creation of new political opportunities to actors previously working in opposition to the regime.[36]

The convenio, signed while the CDP was still in league with the Cardenista bloc, strained CDP-PRD relations on the national level and essentially doomed them in Durango. While Cárdenas was clearly opposed to anything that could be perceived to strengthen the president's legitimacy, there is no indication that he would have forced the CDP out of the electoral alliance that was to become the PRD. On the state level, however, the PRD response was extremely critical and accusatory, the party branding the CDP as traitors to the cause. The CDP leadership explained that their 1989 decision to form their own state-level party, the Partido del Comité de Defensa Popular (Party of the Committee of Popular Defense [PCDP]), was a result of their inability to come to a power-sharing agreement with the state-level PRD (interviews by the author). The specific issue that tore them apart was that of deciding who would be federal deputy.[37] Even though the CDP had more popular support, when it lost the battle to install Marcos Cruz as deputy, it broke from the alliance with the PRD. Observers critical of the CDP argue that the real reason for the break was that the Salinas administration made terminating the alliance an explicit prerequisite for the CDP to receive PRONASOL benefits and other favorable political interventions. This is vigorously denied by the CDP. However, it seems that, given the CDP's predisposition to garner the best deal possible with the state and always to attempt to exploit elite splits, it had no alternative but to cut its close ties with the PRD. The formation of its own state-level party accomplished this very well.

In order to award the CDP temporary party registration, the state legislature had to amend the state electoral code. Its willingness to do so for the PCDP prompted some political observers and opponents, including the PAN, to suggest that the Salinas administration, if not the president himself,

36. Salinas visited Durango fifteen times in six years, a statistic remarkable for a provincial backwater. Each time he visited he would give distinct priority to the CDP, sometimes coming into town and visiting CDP neighborhoods and projects, and then leave town without even visiting with the PRI.

37. Mexico's legislative bodies are made up of both direct and proportional voting. Some officeholders are there because they won the majority of votes in a particular district. Others are there as a result of what is called proportional representation. Based on the number of total votes received, each political party that received the necessary minimum number of votes overall in the election is awarded a certain number of seats in the legislative body. The parties themselves decide who is going to hold these offices.

had played a role in pushing through the registration. Soon after the CDP had gained its temporary registration it attempted to move back toward the PRD and develop an interparty electoral alliance with it.[38] The PRD formally refused to consider any such alliance, even on a case-by-case basis, arguing that the CDP had been "captured" by the party/state. It was in the context of these strained relations between the PRD and the CDP that the CDP made agreements with the Partido del Frente Cardenista de Reconstrucción Nacional (Party of the Cárdenas Front of National Reconstruction [PFCRN]), PPS, and PARM to support common candidates.

The CDP's 1989 campaign cycle was notable for its increased accessibility to funding and its effort to reach out to a broad cross section of voters. Its candidate for the municipal presidency, Horténsia Nevárez, the wife of a wealthy industrialist in Monterrey, was clearly chosen to further the more moderate image the CDP was cultivating. While she lost the election as expected, she advanced the strategy of widening the multiclass appeal of the PCDP, which proved quite successful during the 1989–92 period. The party gained two state deputies, two municipal presidents, and twenty *regidores* (city-council members). These elections led to a difficult situation for the CDP, as the rank and file tended to view the newly elected officials as "theirs," and after years of opposition to the corporatist system of PRI patronage, they understandably expected that it was now their turn to have privileged access to government. CDP elected officials were pulled between balancing demands for privileged access and distribution of public benefits with making good on campaign promises to rid the system of its corporatist legacies and to govern democratically without prejudice. CDP leaders understood that if they were going to continue to make electoral gains, they would have to develop a multiclass appeal extending well beyond the CDP's historic bases of support.

PRONASOL, 1990–1991

While the PRI preferred to use convenios to launch PRONASOL during its first year of operation in 1990, the situation began to change when Solidarity Committees were formed to target resources to specific programs

38. Permanent registration was contingent upon the PCDP's receiving 4 percent of the vote in the July 1989 election, which they did.

(for example, to allocate so much for health; education, or for particular groups, such as the CDP).[39] Federal and state officials charged with administering PRONASOL funds in Durango insisted that these programmatic and funding changes made the projects more systematic and rational (that is, less politicized), and that the state government retained more responsibility (interviews by the author). While the state government (namely, the governor) was perhaps able to exert a greater degree of discretion over the initial funding, subsequent authorizations demonstrated that project selection was still highly centralized in the Office of the President, at least for the state of Durango.[40]

While centralizing actions were no doubt part of the PRONASOL picture, there were elements of decentralization involved as well. Although the Office of the President retained most important policy decisions, in Durango the municipal president exercised a large degree of autonomy in determining which public-works projects to fund (not an apolitical decision). As a substantial portion of these funds would have been spent in the municipalities anyway, the overall level of funding clearly did not increase by as much as was routinely trumpeted by government officials who were eager to claim substantial new monies. However, this is not to say that funding levels did not increase. Equally important was that the balance of power tended favorably in the direction of the federal authorities and the local municipality at the expense of state government.[41]

Consider the municipality of Nombre de Dios, where the CDP won municipal elections twice in a row, in 1989 and again in 1992. In 1991, its municipal budget was 1.1 billion pesos and PRONASOL funds were an additional 1.2 billion pesos. While noting that this was not a significant increase in municipal funding, the CDP municipal president, Octavio

39. There were two major 1989 convenio processes in Durango, in addition to convenios signed with the CDP and CNOP. The first was a regional development project in La Laguna, Durango's prime agricultural area. The second was a project targeted to improve the standard of living among Durango's indigenous population in the highlands in the southeast portion of the state.

40. Numerous political observers ridiculed the notion that Salinas encouraged decentralization in the state of Durango. Constant references were made to a reoccurring Salinas habit: upon arriving in Durango Salinas held meetings with groups of businesspeople, in which he exhorted them to enter into joint investments with the federal government and foreign capital. In this view, the state government was increasingly left out of the process.

41. To my knowledge, there exist no comprehensive studies of the impact of PRONASOL on the distribution of funding by municipality. My efforts to construct a longitudinal study for Durango that could assess municipal spending "before, during, and subsequent to PRONASOL" was frustrated by an inability to gain access to reliable data sets.

Martínez, observed that for the first time he was free to allocate the money without interference from the state government—no small matter during the administration of then CDP foe Ramírez Gamero. When asked about federal interference, Martínez demurred at first, before admitting that the federal government had a say in how the money was spent. He emphasized that neither President Salinas (whom he met on several occasions) nor any other federal officials ever sought to undermine the political efficacy of his administration as he would have expected the governor to do. In fact, his impression was that they very much wanted him to succeed (interview by the author, 1991).

This all configures well with the overall intent of the Salinas reforms: create new alliances that undermine the appeal of Cárdenas and the PRD; in the process, strengthen new actors that will speak well of you while also introducing competition for existing party and state institutions in an effort to speed their resolve for the modernization project.

PRONASOL also handed over state resources directly to popular movement organizations. In CDP's case, its budgetary allocation from PRONASOL in 1990 was an impressive 5.7 billion pesos, supplemented by an additional 1.8 billion pesos allocated as part of the Laguna regional development project. While the 1990 allocation was a significant increase over the 1989 convenio, problems of implementation resulted in the cancellation of projects valued at a total of 3.5 billion pesos. The silver lining of the CDP's ability to effectively make use of such a sharp increase in funds in a very short period of time was that that resources not spent in 1990 rolled over to 1991 (interviews by the author and author's review of documents with PRONASOL officials in Durango, 1991).

Technical and organizational impediments to completing PRONASOL projects were much discussed during these years by those charged with implementing the programs on the local level. My interviews with technical personnel both in the CDP and within several municipalities revealed a common criticism that transcended political affiliation. While PRONASOL channeled increased funding to popular movements and municipalities across the country, it did not authorize monies for technical staff and equipment (including photocopiers, phones, and computers) that were adequate to successfully implement the programs. Opinions varied on the reasons for this problem, one that was both serious and unresolved, despite frequent complaints from these local implementers to higher-ups. Some defined it as an unintentional bureaucratic problem, while others argued that, intentional or not, it favored the PRI, which is relatively weak in its ability to organize community involvement in projects but relatively strong on technical expertise and equipment. Among those who thought it intentional, the logic was that failing to "technically empower" popular movements and municipal offices resulted in an indirect political subsidy to national and state leaders of PRI machines who had an interest in maintaining control over *priísta* municipal presidents and, of course, were interested in undermining confrontational popular movements. To the extent that this is the correct explanation, it certainly ran counter to Salinas's stated goals of decentralization and PRI reform through political competition.

The Creation of the Partido del Trabajo, 1989–1992: Co-optation or Democratic Empowerment?

CDP's tacit support for concertación social and its active participation in PRONASOL led it to moderate its criticism of government officials—first and foremost, President Salinas and his administration, and eventually Governor Ramírez Gamero as well, though it remained vocal in its opposition to the PRI and the PRI-state relationship. Regarding presidential policies, such as the support for NAFTA, the CDP sometimes supported President Salinas and sometimes remained noncommittal.[42] Changing relations with the state, and modifications in behavior that seemed to result directly from it, generated controversy within the urban popular movement. Some argued that the CDP's behavior could and should be defined as co-optation and a betrayal of the democratic movement. Others argued that the CDP's relationship with the state empowered an organization that used its new resources and power to benefit its constituency and, in the process, contributed to a liberalization of the regime itself.

As discussed in Chapter 1, the characteristics and implications of key relationships are at the center of movement life—including on the terrain of conflict. Here we have a debate about which relationships are acceptable and which are not: critics charged that the CDP's inappropriate relationship

42. In his assessment of changes in Durango's political culture, Palacios notes that Gonzalo Yáñez had led a rally protesting the visit of U.S. Ambassador John Gavin to Durango during the PAN municipal government of Elizondo (1983–86). This is the same man who, in his capacity as municipal president, hung a medal around the neck of U.S. Ambassador John Dimitri Negroponte (1999, 9).

with the Salinas administration not only ultimately hurt them but also hurt the broader movement and was thus a betrayal of common purpose.

Co-optation of a popular movement or movement organization as commonly defined in Mexico—complete loss of autonomy and incorporation into the inclusionary authoritarian regime's corporatist relations—does not adequately describe CDP political behavior between 1988 and 1992. Although the CDP's moderating its criticism of the Salinas administration was a significant shift in the direction of co-optation, the CDP claimed that this change stemmed from changes in the administration's behavior that were more conducive to the Left's social justice agenda. However, its muted criticism of the governor is more difficult to defend as anything but self-interest. If this was not classical co-optation, should it be characterized as a modified form of clientelism as well as co-optation? My conclusion is yes. The CDP leaders decided to throw its lot in with the Salinas administration in part because they determined that Cárdenas and the national project of the PRD had little chance of short-term success. Their inability to dominate PRD decisions on the state level reinforced this decision. In the process, the CDP forfeited one of the defining characteristics of social movements: it gave up its primary focus on acting in pursuit of a radical transformation. With the benefit of hindsight, we can now see that the Mexican Left was moving inexorably away from social movement activity and toward electoral politics. Some, such as the Zapatistas and their allies, resisted this movement, but most did not. This is particularly true of the urban popular movement wing of the social Left. The process clearly benefited the urban poor in material terms and the CDP as an organization. The CDP's dynamic performance in governing at the local level was also in the general interest, as it was a decisive improvement over previous administrations of both the PRI and the PAN. Both CDP municipal presidents Octavio Martínez Alvarez of Nombre de Dios and Jaime Sarmiento Minchaca of Suchil established themselves as able and honest administrators and contributed to the image of the CDP as an organization capable of governing. The CDP's inclusion of other party representatives in the municipal administration and the fair distribution of public projects furthered the CDP's mission of establishing itself as a mature, responsible political organization worthy of support, one that transcends social movement membership. These were all positive contributions to political liberalization in Durango.

That is not to say that the first CDP municipal governments were problem free. Because both were headed by local men recruited to the CDP ticket, the task of establishing power relations between the new municipal presidents and the CDP leadership in Durango proved difficult. Each of the municipal presidents combined forces with CDP members outside the inner circle in an effort to decentralize decision making. The new municipal presidents viewed their efforts as challenges to the CDP's top-down authoritarian decision-making culture, while the top leadership experienced these same efforts as direct challenges to their well-earned authority and superior judgment (interviews by the author). The conflict eventually got nasty and went public. For example, when CDP state legislator Gabino Martínez Guzmán headed up an effort to create a CDP newspaper, *Cambio*, that questioned certain leadership decisions and style, the paper was closed down by order of the top leadership.

The funding of the ambitious ecological and development project led to the arrival of several Mexico City intellectuals and seasoned activists who also resisted the authoritarian tendencies of the top leadership and eventually left in disgust. The building of institutional capacity was clearly creating pressures for pluralism. As the CDP moved from a militant urban movement organization to an organization focused on (some would say obsessed with) implementing economic-development projects in collaboration with government agencies, it was forced to expand its technical capabilities to people who demanded decision-making authority. These people, along with the CDP municipal presidents, demanded more decentralized decision-making power. They were challenging the "enlightened bossism" that had characterized the organization's internal power structure. The CDP top leadership wasted little time in demonstrating that there were limits to an internal democratization process and that they would continue to try to control the pace of such changes.

On the state level, the CDP became increasingly willing to arrive at agreements with Governor Ramírez Gamero. In December 1990, the two CDP deputies in the state congress, Gonzalo Yáñez and Alfonso Primitivo Ríos, voted in favor of the governor's 1991 budget (Ley de Egresos). In an interview, Yáñez explained to me that they had voted for this bill in exchange for concessions from the governor, such as a land credit fund controlled by the CDP, preschool facilities, and electrification of the CDP colonias.

While the CDP argued that this support demonstrated maturity and a move away from empty rhetoric toward a more realistic assessment of what was politically feasible, others viewed it as further proof of co-optation.

It became commonplace for CDP leadership to make favorable comments about President Salinas. Yáñez explained: "With respect to the government of Licenciado Carlos Salinas de Gortari, there exists a rather good relationship, one characterized by mutual respect, we have proposed various demands to the federal government and we have been given very favorable responses" (A. G. Yáñez 1991, 22).

The creation and registration of the Partido del Trabajo (Workers' Party [PT]) in December 1990 was an important factor in the changing balance of electoral power, which closely linked to the implementation of PRONASOL.[43] The formation of the PT produced a storm of commentary and criticism. The president of the PAN called the northern urban popular movements, *campesino* organizations, and union factions that were among the founding organizations "political merchants," and other observers charged that another "paraestatal" party had been created. Most of these organizations were closely associated with Línea de Masas, although there were some important exceptions, notably the CDP de Chihuahua.[44] "Well-known political commentator Luis Javier Garrido went so far as to accuse and condemn the CDP of Durango as "active collaborators of the PRI in frauds against the citizenry" (cited in Hernández Navarro 1991a, 21). The CDP leadership endeavored to preserve the legitimacy of its oppositional status by arguing that that it was acceptable to work with the state so long as autonomy from the PRI was preserved. Clearly, this was not acceptable to a number of critics who charged that the CDP's link to PRONASOL was tantamount to co-optation and trying to maintain a distinction between the PRI and the state was a fiction. The expeditious approval of the new

43. Twenty-two organizations signed the petition for party registration, addressed to Fernando Gutierrez Barrios, president of the Federal Election Commission, on December 11, 1991: the CDP of Chihuahua, CDP of Coahuila, CDP of Durango, CDP of Fresnillo, CDP of La Laguna, CDP of Torreón, FPTYL of Nuevo León, Organización Campesina Popular Independiente de la Huasteca Veracruzana, Sociedad de Solidaridad Social Hijos de Emiliano Zapata (of Morelos), a CNTE faction headed by Teodoro Palomino Gutiérrez called Alternativa Sindical (AS-CNTE), Frente Popular de Lucha de Zacatecas, Movimiento de Izquierda Revolucionaria de Guanajuato, Comités Populares del Valle de México, Uniones Unificadas de Vendedores Ambulantes de Toluca, Coordinadora Emiliano Zapata, UPVA 28 de Octubre (of Puebla), Comité Popular de Lucha Emiliano Zapata de Querétaro, Movimiento Vida Digna del Estado de México, Movimiento Campesino de San Luis Potosí, Movimiento Campesino de Guanajuato, and Unión de Crédito de Zacatecas.

44. The CDP of Chihuahua had been almost universally condemned by non-PRI forces following its working relationship with the PRI in opposition to the PAN municipality of the mid-1980s. Its inclusion in the PT did not do anything to further the party's credibility in opposition circles.

party's registration, the only one granted during this period, only served to fuel the accusations of co-optation. The PT was often referred to as the party of PRONASOL and as the "Partido Salinista," with many characterizing it as a Salinas creation, in the tradition of other state-sanctioned and -affiliated parties such as the PARM, PPS, and the PFCRN.

Deliberations over the PT's formation exacerbated internal splits within the OIR-LM and CONAMUP that had been present since the 1989 convenio signings. When the decision was made to form the PT, a number of movements split off, adding their numbers to those ex-OIR*istas* who had already broken ranks to join the Cárdenas forces. Two important labor factions that had previously participated in OIR-LM, Sindicatos de Universidad Nacional Autónoma de México (National Autonomous University of Mexico [UNAM]) and CNTE, refused to join the PT. Many opposition forces went further, condemning the decision to form the party.[45] The new party failed to receive 1.5 percent of the national vote in the midterm elections of August 1991, garnering only 263,000 votes out of the 23 million cast. Its best result was in Durango, where it received 11 percent of the vote, followed by Nayarit with 4.1 percent, Chihuahua with 3.7, Zacatecas with 3.5, and Nuevo León with 2.6. These states, not surprisingly, are those with the greatest OIR presence.

The initial decision to form the PT was motivated in part by the desire to gain access to the considerable amounts of money that the state doles out to registered political parties. Rumors abounded that Salinas added further incentives. While the PT did not expect to significantly alter national policy directions, it did accurately anticipate being a player in the political process of formulating policy with direct bearing on the Mexican poor and it frequently defended its position in these terms. Línea de Masas, and thus the CDP, always maintained that achieving governmental positions and influencing policy outcomes are not goals in themselves but means to a greater end—power. The CDP argued that revolutionaries should not feel obligated to observe the mandates of liberal democratic theory, of PRD elites with roots in the PRI, or of PRD intellectuals without experience in grassroots struggle (interviews by the author). The Maoist accumulation of power was done in the name of the Mexican poor and,

45. Hernández Navarro concluded that "[T]he bulk of activist Left from the Federal District, the state of Mexico, Veracruz, Guerrero, Morelos, Oaxaca and Tabasco as well as significant parts of the activist Left from the Laguna region and Zacatecas viewed the decision to obtain a national electoral registration as a mistake" (1991, 22).

subsequently, in the name of Durango's "citizenry." CDP leaders insisted that they continued to speak on behalf of the disadvantaged, oppressed, repressed, and marginalized.

For the CDP, practical considerations were paramount. Because of practical, not doctrinal, considerations, the CDP rejected the military option adopted much later by the Zapatistas of Chiapas. Similarly, the leadership determined that it help form the PT and participate actively in PRONASOL because it determined that conditions of political power dictated this course of action as the best that was available. In the short term, this pragmatism resulted in a significant increase in resources, which the CDP put to good use. Furthermore, the historical trajectory of the PRD during the 1990s supported the CDP position that it had hardly sidelined itself from being part of a transition to participating in a left-leaning democracy. However, this process is also accurately summarized as a case of neo cooptation. The CDP's political participation and record of public administration did result in some significant short-term benefits for the urban poor and for the broader society. However, it also contributed to Salinas's efforts to rebuild the regime's legitimacy. Changes of behavior that commenced soon after Salinas's election calls into serious question whether the CDP could still be characterized as a social movement as defined in Chapter 1. The following section of the definition is particularly worth recalling: Social movements may seek to secure distributive benefits for their members, but to maintain their status of a social movement rather than an interest group, they must not lose the drive to make transformative social change beyond benefiting their own members. With the creation of the PCDP and then the PT, clearly the CDP ceased to perform as a social movement.

State-Level Elections in Durango, July 1992

While the PRI's candidate, Maximiliano Silerio Esparza, won the governor's race in Durango's July 1992 statewide elections, the CDP won the municipal presidency of the capital city of Durango, leading political commentators to speak of a "new political equilibrium" in the state As a result of proportional voting, almost half the state legislature went to the opposition. Of the twenty-five state deputies, thirteen were from the PRI, and twelve came from the opposition: eight from the PAN, three from the

CDP/PT, and one from the PRD. The opposition also won some important municipal races.[46]

The CDP channeled substantial resources into the campaign, concentrating on the candidacy of CDP leader Gonzalo Yáñez for the office of municipal president, which is largely credited as the reason why he won the three-way election. His victory registered the monumental growth in CDP electoral strength since 1986. This led to credible charges that there could be no other source for this funding but under-the-table payments from the Salinas administration. However, Yáñez's abilities as an able and charismatic campaigner are beyond dispute. PRONASOL funding—the amount that passed to the CDP aboveboard as well as cash transfers that transpired beyond the boundaries of official public accounting—also contributed directly to the CDP's electoral power. It is highly unlikely that the CDP would have won the office of municipal president in the state's capital without the political legitimacy and organizational empowerment it achieved from concertación social and PRONASOL. Not unexpectedly, the election results were beset by controversy. For better or worse, they had become a different type of political animal, to be understood and evaluated according to a different set of criteria.

Yáñez's campaign evoked images of the PRI in better days. He traveled from campaign stop to campaign stop handing out millions of pesos in support of highly visible and popular public-works projects (such as church extensions, day-care centers, and health clinics). In each neighborhood, Yáñez pledged (in writing) to work steadfastly on the list of material demands put forward by each community. He told his audiences that the CDP, win or lose, would continue to work toward meeting their demands. The seed money left behind, along with the CDP's growing credibility for

46. The PRI's fall from electoral dominance began in the 1980s at the municipal level: with the COCEI in Juchitán, the PDM in Guanajuato, the PST in Ensenada, the PAN/Frente Cívico in San Luis Potosí, the PST in Ensenada and a string of victories for the PAN in the north, first in Chihuahua and Ciudad Juárez and then in Durango, Zamora, Hermosillo, and elsewhere. As noted by Rodríguez and Ward, "[U]ntil 1988 the PAN formed the vanguard of the [electoral] opposition and therefore was the foil and the focus of the PRI's attention" (1995, 6). Post-1988, opposition victories at the municipal and state levels picked up considerably. At least in part because of the fact that the Salinas administration came to accommodation with the PAN while working diligently to undermine the PRD, the PAN scored the majority of officially sanctioned victories during this time. The PAN won governorships in Baja California, Guanajuato, and Chihuahua along with many municipal victories, including the major cities of Saltillo, Mérida, San Luis Potosí, León, Mazatlán, San Pedro Garza García, Salamanca, and Celaya. The CDP's victory should be seen in the light of these broader developments.

getting things done, served to lure votes away from traditional politicians and parties. The PRD, without the CDP, had no chance whatsoever.

It must be stressed that the CDP's effort to establish itself as a capable administrator of public works did not begin with the advent of PRONASOL, even though these funds were responsible for CDP expansion into new areas, including into working- and middle-class neighborhoods that previously had been dominated by the PRI or the PAN. PRONASOL introduced a high profile program into a region where the traditional electoral powers were increasingly perceived as unable to match the CDP's ability to use the funds in the efficient implementation of public works, a—if not the—central concern for Durango's voters.

Vamos por la Dignidad de Durango

The 1992 campaign and election results raised interesting questions regarding the process of concertación social in the state of Durango.[47] Given that Yáñez's victory was in large part a result of the CDP's demonstrated ability to raise federal funds for public works at impressive rates, his administration had to continue this success if the PT hoped to continue the rapid pace of electoral power established during the 1989–92 period. Indeed, it was not unreasonable to expect that Durango's voters would hold the PT's elected officials to higher standards than they did those of the PRI (or even the PAN) because of their raised expectations. The PT had promised to be *dramatically* different, and people waited to see if it would prove to be so.

Yáñez's municipal council (referred to as a *cabildo*) had ten council members (*regidores*) from the PT, four from the PRI, and three from the PAN. Concerned to demonstrate that his administration was representative,

---

47. The heading of this section translates as "Let's work for Durango's dignity"; this was the PT's 1992 campaign slogan and it then remained the "publicized promise" of the CDP as social movement and political party. It is notable for, among other reasons, its multiclass appeal.

As noted by Martha Singer and Gustavo Leal (1993), Durango, along with Gazcón, Nayarit, Morelia, Michoacán, were the only state capitals governed by a party of the Left. While limited to an analysis of only the first five months of the new administration, the authors emphasized that the focus on public works came at the expense of legislative actions capable of restructuring political processes in the municipality. This critique would be restated by many voices from the Left throughout Yáñez's administration—and it has been leveled against the PT on a national level.

Yáñez ensured that the PT candidates were selected through a highly competitive internal party process. However, Yáñez had inherited a municipal government from the PRI that was highly indebted. One of the first actions taken by the new administration was to raise property taxes (*impuesto predial*). The tax increase was important for a number of reasons: it not only provided important funds that were necessary in implementing campaign promises but it also fit into the drive by the opposition (PAN, PRD, and PT) to make Mexican federalism a reality rather than a cruel constitutional joke. Knowing that raising taxes always carries the potential for political liabilities, Yáñez was nonetheless convinced that increased local taxes in concert with increased federal support would produce a dramatic, efficient, and politically popular increase in public works. Throughout 1993 and 1994 he continued to expand the budget. The percentage of overall municipal spending that was derived from locally collected taxes increased from 32 percent in 1992 to 42 percent in 1993 (Arzaluz Solano 1995, 228).

Winning the municipality gave the Maoists one more important organizational tool in leveraging public funds to support their relentless drive to control the largest percentage possible of the state's public works. Yáñez was creative in producing new programs and "institutes" that allowed him to take direct credit for projects that were mostly funded by PRONASOL. If part of the Salinas strategy for PRONASOL was to force a rejuvenation of the PRI by introducing competition for federal funding, the continued ability of CDP organizations to dominate so much of the funding represented a failure in meeting this challenge.[48]

By the summer of 1994, Yáñez was running for senator.[49] Throughout the campaign, he emphasized the importance of public works, proposed a redistribution of public spending, and argued that power was too centralized in Mexico. In a sharp distinction from what was claimed by the PRD,

48. In the case of Durango, PRONASOL officials expressed frustration at the amount of funding that went to the capital city, which necessarily reduced money for other areas (interviews by the author). The most glaring example of this was the fact that Gomez Palacio, the second population center in the state, received only about 5 percent of the PRONASOL budget. (It is perhaps not incidental that Gomez Palacio is where PRD power is greatest in the state.)

49. During the campaign, Jesús Dávila Valero acted as interim municipal president. It was clear that the loss of Yáñez from the office lowered people's enthusiasm for and interest in municipal government. His leadership was simply that important. People were noticeably relieved when the campaign ended and Yáñez resumed his responsibilities. Arzaluz Solano makes a similar observation (1995, 233).

Yáñez emphasized that Durango's future economic prosperity was dependent upon NAFTA. By August 1994, opposition to Yáñez centered on the increases in municipal expenditures. He responded by insisting that what made his government different was that the spending was being carried out in an honest and efficient way. His ultimate failure to win the senate seat demonstrated that while he was extremely competitive in Durango, he was unable to project his power over the entire state.

Although the Yáñez administration was certainly the focal point for the PT/CDP in the 1992–94 period, the PT also had received three seats in the Durango state legislature.[50] Juan Salazar, Octavio Martinez, and Juan Cruz were selected by an internal rank-and-file CDP vote. Salazar was a university-trained cuadro who, by virtue of his education and the fact that he was very popular among the rank and file and had demonstrated loyalty to the top leadership over the years, had climbed the organizational ladder. Martinez was the former municipal president of Nombre de Dios. Juan Cruz's major asset was his being the younger brother of Marcos Cruz.

The PT contingent in the legislature was important for reforming the municipal housing law so that Yáñez could recalculate the value of property. The legislative contingent also forced both the head of the state's judicial police and the head of Obras Publicas (Office of Public Works) from office on the basis of corruption charges, strengthening the CDP/PT's image as the leaders of a statewide anticorruption campaign. The CDP legislative contingent successfully changed the state constitution so that someone could run for governor with eight years of residency, obviously paving the way for a future bid by Yáñez. Clearly, given the majority position of the PRI in the legislature, passing these PT initiatives required gaining the governor's support. Such support never ceased to attract the criticism of both the PRD and the PAN. These and other legislative victories provided the CDP/PT with opportunities to amass legislative acumen, which many social Left actors contend was key to the democratization process in Mexico, arguing that upon the arrival of an opposition president, experience gained in the 1990s would be important to the success of that phase of Mexico's long democratic transition (interviews by the author).

Neither the country of Mexico nor the state of Durango had yet met the minimal requirements of political democracy. Changes in institutions,

50. Durango's state legislature has twenty-five seats. Its composition as a result of the 1992 elections was thirteen diputados for the PRI and twelve for the opposition: eight for the PAN, three for the PT, and one for the PRD.

laws, and practices were needed in Mexico to make the playing field level enough for the system to be called a democracy. The 1994 elections continued the recomposition of electoral power that had begun in the 1980s and demonstrated the changing balance of electoral power between the CDP/PT, the PAN, the PRD, and the PRI as well as their relative capacities to compete under semidemocratic conditions. The PRI, again, experienced a decline in its proportion of votes against the three main opposition parties. The PT clearly demonstrated its ability to continue its electoral assent with Yáñez's winning the urban vote in Durango's capital. This represented a twelve-thousand-vote increase over his 1992 vote for the municipal presidency and was seen as a positive sign of momentum.

Conclusion

Durango's experience supports the hypothesis that rapid urbanization, not industrialization, can be the underlying structural factor contributing to collective dissent. Since the 1970s, Durango, despite its lack of "industrial take-off" has "had one of the highest rates of rural-to-urban migration nationwide, due to the crisis and decreasing pace of capitalization in the rural areas" (Moguel 1991a, 7). Very high rates of un- and underemployment, high housing costs, and housing shortages, combined with CNOP's historical inability to channel the allegiance of the growing numbers of urban poor, provided a set of favorable conditions or opportunities for dissent. Although many Mexican cities shared these characteristics, not all of them hosted committed activists who were capable of exploiting these historical opportunities.

Piven and Cloward (1979) suggest that one of the key vulnerabilities of poor people's movements is that once disruptive mobilization has been cashed in for whatever benefits are to be derived from negotiation, it is next to impossible to regain historic levels of militancy. And militancy is at the heart of a movement's power to disrupt and thereby gain a strong negotiating hand. Movement organizations must carefully pick the optimal time for negotiation. When states are forced to negotiate, they will usually exchange policy outcomes that are desired by the movement organization for an agreement to mitigate militancy and disruption.

The best movement outcomes in the United States are constitutional, followed by entitlement programs, for these are the most difficult to undo.

The worse-case results are promises for change that fail to come to fruition once the threat of disruption has been erased. The Mexican system offered a different hierarchy of outcomes, as the constitution routinely goes unfulfilled and existing entitlement programs do not have the same place in public policy that they have in the United States. In Mexico, movements sought a change in regime and, failing that, to force the regime to direct resources to them. Was the obvious exchange of militancy and disruption by the CDP in exchange for increased control over public resources, party registration, and the opportunity to win elections "a good deal"?

In 1989 and 1990, the CDP leadership assured me that should the time come when a more militant position was again the most effective way to exploit existing opportunities, history would witness the "return of the radical." However, in discussions a decade later with CDP leadership and cuadros, with neighborhood activists and informed observers, I found that these same people tended to be much less sanguine about this possibility. Not only had the rank and file become dispirited about such tactics; more important, the grass roots now perceived that the leaders would never give up their privileged positions and state subsidies for a return to mobilizing on the ground. Clearly, if mobilization and institutional disruption is again to change the face of Durango's politics, it will come from sources other than the historic CDP leadership.

What history does suggest is that certain characteristics of Durango's CDP and PT became increasingly counterproductive. The charismatic and intelligent leadership of Marcos Cruz and Gonzalo Yáñez served the organization well during the 1980s to generate the loyalty of top lieutenants, cuadros, and the rank and file. This was not without its costs and periodic ruptures, but for the most part, divisions were contained with minimal damage. Such a concentration of power contributed to the decline of the CDP as a movement once the PT was formed and efforts to maintain a more dissident movement position were successfully discouraged by the top leadership. Meanwhile, the multiclass electoral support has shown serious signs of decline in the past few years, leaving in doubt the PT's electoral future, even in its key stronghold. Part of the electoral problem is a direct result of the centralization of power and the serious internal splits that have occurred in recent years as a result of that concentration. As is also the case with the AB of Mexico City, internal divisions that were successfully managed pre-Salinas fractured the movement organization during the process of party building.

The CDP's development of what Fox (1990a) calls "intermediate instances of participation" always remained marginal at best. "Intermediate instances of participation permit subgroups first to emerge, and then to communicate and coordinate among themselves. They refer more to processes than to particular events or formal institutions. Specifically, they are formal or informal opportunities for representative subgroups to exercise power within large organizations" (Fox, 1990, 7).

The CDP had a number of such subgroups, such as the *campesino* organization, the municipalities, the small-business association, individual colonia organizations, and cadres of technical-support personnel who worked on specific projects. However, they were unable to achieve the internal democracy attained by CNTE in the 1980s (Cook, 1996). As Fox notes, for subgroups to democratize internal decision-making processes, there must be a steady stream of information coming downward from the top— notably absent in both the CDP and the PT.

As argued in Chapter 1, the structure and quality of relationships is at the heart of politics. Central to the Salinas project of reversing the 1982–88 decline in the regime's political legitimacy was a recomposition of state alliances that included the forging of new political relationships with powerful social forces. Concertación via PRONASOL allowed organizations, including the CDP, to take advantage of the political and economic opportunities associated with "playing ball." In so doing, the CDP was able to preserve its autonomy—in terms of both identity and decision making—from the PRI but not from the state. As detailed earlier, this distinction was more meaningful to the CDP membership and its supporters than it was to its critics. Salinas and the CDP's top leadership entered into a relationship motivated by a complex self-interest, whose features were personal advantage, organizational and regime empowerment, and a furthering of their respective visions for the country's future. As Salinas left the scene, the obvious question was how the CDP/PT would fare without the support of the man who had been so fundamental to their transition to a political party, their early electoral successes, and their efforts to run local government more efficiently, aggressively, and honestly.

While the PT maintained strength in the capital city in 1995, winning the municipal presidency, again with Marcos Cruz as candidate, and when Yáñez became federal deputy in 1997, the lack of breath across the state was dramatically demonstrated in Yáñez's 1998 bid for the governorship, which he lost badly. Palacios Moncayo argues that the position of the PT deteriorated during the 1995–98 period, as Cruz failed to maintain the momentum initiated by Yáñez. Charges of corruption, already present during the administration of Yáñez became more frequent and more serious during the Cruz administration (1999, 23; personal conversations).[51]

Internal tensions arose within the organization as some members of the PT argued that the abandonment of the "social struggle" was a mistake and began to organize "as a movement." As a result, one of the leaders, longtime CDP cuadro Juan Salazár, was not selected as the PT candidate for municipal president in 1998 despite his high chances for success. In a purge of the disloyal, top leadership suspended not only Salazár but also three of the four sitting PT state deputies, who initiated a multiclass effort known as "El Central." Thus, the decline of the CDP and the transformation to political party resulted in the creation of new movement organizations.

A visit that I made to Durango in spring 1999 clearly revealed that not only had Maoism in Durango been radically transformed, the organization itself was in crisis. In interviews with many historic CDP cuadros, some of whom I had known for more than ten years, I was struck by their degree of disillusionment with a leadership they felt had abandoned them for a bankrupt strategy. Cuadros and local observers wondered where the "party of public works" would go now that it had lost its usefulness to its federal benefactors. Research by Bolos (1995) makes it clear that that this phenomenon was certainly not limited to the CDP. Reports from activists vary greatly in terms of describing how pervasive the abandonment of the bases by movement leaders has been once they take office (see, for example, Bolos 1995, 175, 185).

With the elections of 1998, the PRI regained its electoral and governing dominance in the state of Durango. Palacios Moncayo notes that the decisive PRI victory for municipal president in Durango cannot be explained by simply who spent more money in the campaign. By the close of the millennium, the Maoists were no longer Maoists, the CDP no longer existed, and the PT was of questionable value except to those who depended upon it for employment.

My telling of the story has been shaped in part by a methodological challenge well stated by Tilly: "The organization which concerns us most

51. Not all analyses of the PT's 1998 electoral fortunes are quite so glum. While it is true that they lost the municipal presidency, the total number of votes received did not decrease markedly. This was true despite the fact that their candidate was not well known, the campaign was by all accounts poorly run, and they were radically outspent by the PRI. Clearly, the major change was the remarkable recovery made by the PRI.

For a more specific view of electoral results, see the tables in Appendix C.

is that aspect of a group's structure which most directly affects its capacity to act on its interests. Clearly one of the problems is to determine which features of organization *do* make a difference" (1978, 7). Decision-making processes and leadership authority were always central to the CDP's record of affecting political outcomes. My conclusion is that the intelligence and commitment of the Maoist's authoritarian leadership style certainly contributed to the impressive initial gains, but in more recent years, the leadership characteristics contributed to significant problems.

Max Weber's third type of authority, what he calls charismatic authority, best describes the Maoists in Durango as well as in a number of other popular movements in Mexico. As noted by one veteran, Georgina Sandoval of the Mexico City NGO Casa y Ciudad, despite the intentions of democracy, in the end, the political culture, wherein the "leader is the leader" often prevails (cited in Bolos 1995, 121). An interesting paradox of the urban popular movement culture was a fierce antiauthoritarian rhetoric when it came to the regime, along with the exercise of a charismatic leadership style within the movement itself. Although the CDP leadership was legitimized by being voted into office, it is quite clear that the main source of their authority emanates from the organization's emphasis on charismatic leadership. Whereas the CDP long ago entered into what Weber calls the routinization (*Veralltaglichung*) of charisma, it has only more recently faced the problem Weber identifies as charismatic succession.

The decline of the CDP was certainly not only a product of the failure of leadership, as a diminished role for urban popular movements was the logical outcome of the social Left's move into electoral politics. The key questions concern whether CDP's top leadership made the wisest decisions in terms of its own rank and file and its contribution to Mexico's democratic transition. Answering this question is not easy, but on balance, I believe that it did not. The inability of the top CDP leaders to pass on the torch to new blood undermined the capacity of the organization and the party to continue to play a dynamic role in early twenty-first-century Durango. The Maoists made their mark in Durango and for years made a significant contribution to bettering the lives of the urban poor. They succumbed, however, as have many other groups, to the seductions of a powerful state. In giving up its autonomy, the CDP relinquished its militancy and its ability to create a transformative project. In so doing, it gave up its movement identity. When its members botched the transition to a new generation of leaders, they also undermined their ability as elected public administrators at the local and state level. In short, leadership decisions taken by the CDP's top *caudillos* to fundamentally alter their relationship with the regime resulted in a loss not only of vision but also of survival.

The importance of the CDP to its membership, to political culture in Durango, and to the Mexican urban popular movement and the Mexican Left is substantial. From its humble origins in the early 1970s, it grew to be one of Mexico's most important civil society actors. The CDP changed the consciousness and eased the poverty of many thousands of Duran-gueños. It played a vanguard role in the creation of OIR-LM and CONAMUP. The CDP's ability to create vision and to survive for more than twenty years is an accomplishment with few comparisons in the social movement world. Its history provides insight for students of social movements, at all phases of its existence, from birth to decline.

FIVE

The Asamblea de Barrios of Mexico City

Over and above their legitimacy in constitutional terms, the extent to which law and order can legitimately demand (and command) obedience and compliance largely depends (or ought to depend) on the extent to which this law and this order obey and comply with their own standards and values. These may first be ideological . . . but the ideology can become a material political force in the armor of the opposition as these values are betrayed, compromised, denied in the social reality. Then the betrayed promises are, as it were, "taken over" by the opposition, and with them the claim for legitimacy.
—HERBERT MARCUSE, "An Essay on Liberation"

Toda familia tiene derecho a disfrutar de una vivienda digna y decorosa. La ley estalecerá los instrumentos y apoyos necesarios a fin de alcanzar tal objetivo.
[Every family has the right to decent and proper housing. The law will establish the instruments and assistance necessary to achieve this objective.]
—MEXICAN CONSTITUTION, ARTICLE 4

In our country we live a surreal politics where public acts are not public acts. They appear to be public acts but only in the press. In reality they are private acts, done in obscurity.
—SUPERBARRIO GOMEZ, IN SILIVIA BOLOS, *Actores sociales y demandas urbanas.*

The Asamblea de Barrios (Assembly of Neighborhoods [AB]) emerged in 1987 during the height of the 1980s protest cycle, and it quickly became one of the lead urban popular movement organizations in Mexico. In the aftermath of the dramatic 1988 presidential elections, as President Salinas introduced the PRONASOL program—at least in part as a means of relegitimizing his regime and splitting the political and social opposition—the AB and the CDP were the two most important urban popular movement organizations in Mexico. In sharp contrast to the CDP, the AB sided with Cárdenas and the PRD and took a fierce stance of "no cooperation" with the Salinas administration. An examination of these two movements, taken together, reveals a great deal about the scope of the urban popular movement in Mexico during the 1980s protest cycle and its decline in the 1990s as movement activists moved decidedly into the electoral arena.

The AB and the CDP developed very different relationships with the Salinas administration and publicly debated each other about the wisdom of their respective choices. As will be detailed below, the AB was distinct not only from the CDP but from most of the urban popular movement in a number of other key respects as well. Among the most important are the timing of its emergence in the protest cycle, the relatively diverse class makeup of its membership, the importance of renters as opposed to shantytown dwellers who own their own small plots of land, internal organization, and its remarkably creative forays into the Gramscian project of counterhegemonic cultural creation.

As happened with the CDP in Durango, decisions by the AB leadership to enter into electoral politics eventually led to the decline of the organization. However, the historical trajectory was different in significant ways. Unlike the CDP, the AB did not quickly dissolve when a party strategy was adopted by its leadership, but rather the decision to participate in the electoral process exacerbated differences, eventually leading the organization to split in two. Although the AB was weakened by this process, the vitality of its midlevel activists allowed the AB to continue to function more effectively than the CDP.

Originally born from an internal split within the Coordinadora Unica de Damnificados (United Coordinating Committee of Earthquake Victims ([CUD]), an umbrella organization organized in response to the earthquake of September 1985, the AB was no stranger to intense organizational divisions and controversy. An examination of these internal splits and controversies illuminates the importance of internal relationships and the AB's dialectical relationship to other movement organizations, parties, and the state. As discussed in Chapter 1, viewing movements and their organizations as dense networks of relationships reveals a great deal both about the experience of a movement and about a movement's power to advance its values and interests.

The AB was formed only months before Cuauhtémoc Cárdenas began his 1987–88 presidential bid. As is true of all major urban popular movements, the AB had deep ties to political currents that predate the party formations of the late 1980s, specifically the Asociación Cívica Nacional Revolucionaria (National Revolutionary Civic Association [ACNR]) and Organización Revolucionaria Punto Crítico (Critical Point Revolutionary Organization, known simply as Punto Crítico). Just as with the CDP, these early organizational affiliations were fundamental to the ideological and political formation of the AB leadership. AB leaders determined that the time had come to end the negotiating practices and "deal making" with the state that were typical of many Mexican popular movements. Their reading of the political opportunity structure led them to decide that a democratic transition was now possible and that Cárdenas had the capacity to head the process. The AB felt that despite Cárdenas and other top PRD leader's PRI origins, both the social and political Left could influence the PRD, and the group pushed for democratic transition to become the focus for all sectors. Key to achieving this was a sharp rejection of presidential initiatives, most notably PRONASOL. The issue of how to relate to powerful state actors surfaces again later, as a crucial element in the internal AB split, reinforcing how profoundly problematic this issue is for many social movements. The experience of the AB illustrates how political positioning vis-à-vis state actors fundamentally shapes relations within entire movements and between specific organizations.

The AB supported Cárdenas early and never publicly wavered from this position. The AB was never in control of the PRD but rather always functioned within a party in which movement concerns were secondary. Power-sharing from a subordinate position within the PRD was difficult at times, but within the PRD, the AB has been a major player and its leaders have held seats on the national executive council and on the executive council of the Federal District—including chair. In August 1991, AB leaders were elected to important public offices on the PRD ticket, including gaining two federal deputy positions and a seat in the Mexico City Assembly. AB leaders have continued to play important roles as PRD officials, at the Mexico City and national levels. Although moving into the party and elected office forced these leaders to expand their priorities beyond the scope of the AB, they nonetheless continued to be strong advocates for the issues they had supported earlier. As a result, these issues remained more important within the PRD and in the policy-making process than would have been the case otherwise.

The case of the AB attests to the importance of timing in organization success. The political process approach suggests that movements that emerge during the stage of expanding opportunities in a protest cycle are likely to fare better than those that surface during the cycle's beginning or its decline. Early organizations often fight an uphill battle, since they cannot take advantage of momentum, and they often serve to pave the way for others (Tarrow 1994).[1] The AB's emergence well into the protest cycle, and

---

1. Organizations such as the CDP are not shy about pointing this out, and they often express dismay that they are not more generously acknowledged for persevering through difficult times and laying the groundwork that subsequent movements make use of in more auspicious times. Movement organizations that emerge later, particularly those that surface during

the unusually auspicious political opportunity structure present at that time, are fundamental to comprehending its unparalleled success during its first couple of years. However, these advantages and its key role within the PRD were not enough for the AB to escape the impact of declining opportunities during the 1990s. While groups of citizens continued to mobilize under the banner of the AB, by the mid-1990s the organization no longer played the lead role within Mexico City politics it once had. As emphasized by Piven and Cloward (1979), while history creates and limits the possibility of political change by social movements, the extent to which those possibilities are exploited is profoundly influenced by the theory, strategy, and tactics employed by the actors themselves. The story told here provides insight into this process.

The Earthquake and the Coordinadora Unica de Damnificados

The AB would not have come into existence without the devastating earthquakes that rocked Mexico City in September 1985. The enormous human and material toll of the earthquake was centered in the downtown area, exactly where the most dramatic popular movement upsurge occurred in the 1980s protest cycle. Three major groups of *damnificados* mobilized and organized in response to the regime's emergency response and initial reconstruction plans.[2] These groups were from three areas: (1) Tlatelolco and Colonia Roma, which were largely middle-class areas; (2) Multifamiliar Juárez, a public housing program that housed retired state bureaucrats and members of the middle class; and (3) the downtown colonias of El Centro, Morelos, Guerrero, Doctores, Obrera, Peralvillo,

---

a period of rapid acceleration in the protest cycle, as was the case of the AB, often respond with frustration that they have provided "radical flank effects" for selfish movements willing to forsake the larger democratic project for their own short-term goals.

Haines (1984) coined the phrase "radical flank effects" to describe the service provided by more radical movement organizations to more moderate ones. He shows, in reference to the U.S. civil rights movement, how more radical movements assisted moderate movements to gain legitimacy and funding from the state. In this case, the AB built on the foundation created by the CDP, which later used the AB and other PRD-affiliated movements to pressure the regime into providing them funding.

2. The literal English translation of *damnificado* is "damaged" or "injured." It was widely used to refer to the estimated 250,000 people who had been left homeless as a result of the quake.

Asturias, Nicolás, Bravo, and others, where workers and the urban poor lived (Cuéllar Vázquez 1990, 4–5; Massolo 1986, 196).[3] As so often is the case with social movement formation, the overriding sense among these groups of people was that if they did not gather forces and insert themselves into the decision-making process, the regime would initiate programs of reconstruction that favored interests other than their own.

On October 24, 1985, more than twenty territorially based urban popular movement organizations joined together to form the CUD; by November 9, forty-two organizations were affiliated. For the following year and a half, the CUD served as the primary coordinating body for earthquake victims and as the most dynamic expression of popular urban militancy. It incorporated existing organizations that were dedicated primarily to housing issues; the most important of these organizations was the Coordinadora Inquilinaria del Valle de México (Coordinating Committee of Renters from the Valley of Mexico).[4] Some AB leaders saw the coordinadora as "the backbone of the CUD during 1985" (Cuéllar Vázquez 1990, 11), others argue that the CUD was dominated by middle-class interests and was never led by the more radical factions.[5] While not all popular movement organizations

3. What is referred to here as Tlatelolco is located in Colonia Guerrero, on the outskirts of downtown. It is the site of a massive 1960s public housing project, that has seen some of the most contentious political conflict in the city, when thousands of people were forcibly relocated during construction (Coulomb 1986, 300–302). The student massacre of 1968, when police and military units killed hundreds of protestors also took place in Tlatelolco. The earthquake's destruction of one of the largest public housing high-rises generated considerable organizing, because residents had long petitioned the government to repair the building. The loss of life was very high, and residents and sympathizers accused the government of homicide, pressing for criminal charges to be brought against responsible officials (Monsiváis 1988, 56; Roberto Eibenschutz, director of FONHAPO, 1982–85, interview by the author, February 1991).

Damnificados from Colonia Roma were represented largely by the Unión de Vecinos y Damnificados 19 de Septiembre (UVYD), which also organized the residents of Colonia Condesa. Colonia Roma was where the renter's movement exploded in the quake's aftermath, as owners of damaged buildings attempted to evict residents and rents rose by as much as 300 percent with threats to evict those unwilling or unable to pay (UVYD, Boletín informativo, no. 3, December 1985, cited in Massolo 1986, 225).

4. The Coordinadora Inquilinaria, which was formed in 1983, never affiliated with CONAMUP because many of its leaders were associated with political currents, such as ACNR and Punto Crítico, which were uncomfortable with the degree of OIR-LM power within CONAMUP.

5. Some analysts, such as Eckstein (1990), have concluded that the CUD was dominated by the middle class and the interests of property owning members of the CUD overshadowed the concerns of those members from poorer neighborhoods, most of whom were renters (283–84). However, more radical CUD participants were active in shaping the behavior and political positioning of the CUD throughout the dynamic eighteen-month phase of October 1985 through April 1987.

representing damnificados belonged to the CUD, the majority of the most important did.

The drive to mobilize and organize collectively was initially motivated by the regime's farcical response to the earthquake. While it is certain that the disaster presented a crisis of such proportion that even governments of more wealthy nations would have had difficulties, initial official responses from the regime, from the local neighborhood political bosses to the president himself, aggravated the impact of the earthquake in ways that were not directly related to the lack of material resources. Political problems arose from the outset, when the government announced that there already existed sufficient housing to absorb all those left homeless (Eckstein 1990, 280). Subsequent government statements that downtown residents would be relocated to the periphery were widely perceived by the CUD and large sectors of public opinion as an attempt to use the disaster to gentrify the downtown area.[6]

At early meetings the head of the Secretaría de Desarrollo Urbano y Ecología (Ministry of Urban Development and Ecology [SEDUE]), Guillermo Carrillo Arena, informed representatives of popular organizations that they should merge themselves into corporatist channels. The following from a participant at one meeting is representative of the government's attitude:

> Carillo Arena wasted no time in informing us that he believed we would need to reorient our political affiliation if we expected to gain access to the funding he controlled. True to form, he acted as if the public monies he was charged with dispensing were to be dispensed according to his own political judgment and personal prerogative. It's as if it was his money, not the people's. What a surprise it turned out to be for him over time that we had amassed sufficient power to break his custom (Interview by the author, 1989)

Requests that the director assist the petitioners to obtain funds and help them in their efforts to repel the eviction plans of powerful landlords were

---

6. Large sectors of the historic downtown section were rented under a 1940s Rent Control Law that resulted in many long-term residents being able to pay next to nothing for their apartments. Buildings had seriously deteriorated due to the owners' reluctance to make improvements as long as the Rent Control Law was still in existence. Plans were drawn up in the 1970s for an ambitious urban renewal project that was never fully implemented, due to resistance by popular movements and a lack of resources (Eckstein 1990, 280–81).

met with derision. Urban popular movement organizations had of course long demanded that the state desist from granting priority to PRI organizations and treat all political and social organizations equally, but after the earthquake this demand took on increased urgency because popular movements were rapidly rising in public favor at the same time as the government's image was facing a prodigious decline. The earthquake provided an exceptional opportunity for opposition forces to confront and discredit the institutionalized linkages between the state and the PRI. Since the relationship between the two entities was absolutely fundamental to the legitimacy and functioning of the inclusionary authoritarian regime, to effectively confront this relationship was to strike at the heart of the regime's ability to continue. Activists on the left were very aware of the new opportunities presented by the earthquake and were highly motivated to exploit them to the fullest extent possible.

De la Madrid's inept response to the earthquake, both in the immediate aftermath and in the subsequent year of reconstruction, resulted in political costs and tensions that a more savvy strategy and demeanor could have avoided. The PRI proved ineffective as an intermediary between citizen and government, thereby contributing directly to the power of the urban popular movement (Villa, 1987, 44). Manuel Villa argues that government incompetence forced the unwilling politicization of social demands on the part of the damnificados (45), failing to recognize that radical leaders in organizations affiliated with the CUD had long dreamed of the type of improved opportunity structure created by the party/state's response to the earthquake. Radical CUD leaders moved swiftly and consistently to politicize reconstruction to the greatest degree possible, creating tension with more moderate CUD leaders who were more narrowly focused on housing projects.

Urban popular movement organizations called a protest march in early October, at which more than fifteen thousand people demanded that the reconstruction be "democratic" (namely, that it include non-priísta organizations), that the military pull out of neighborhoods severely affected by the quake where popular movement organizations were struggling with the PRI for political control, that tenants' rights be respected, and that evictions end. That afternoon, de la Madrid gave an audience to about a dozen urban popular movement leaders, at which Francisco Saucedo (later one of four top AB leaders) presented a document that articulated what would continue to be the core popular movement demands throughout the reconstruction process: expropriation of all condemned buildings and land and the creation of a "popular" and "democratic" reconstruction project that included the full participation of the popular movements. On October 11, the president announced the expropriation of 5,500 properties, covering 550 acres. This former number was subsequently reduced to 4,332, no doubt because of pressure from landlords and other powerful real estate interests (Ziccardi 1986, 173).

This kind of political experience, in which radical Left movement leadership has an audience with the president that results in a major governmental concession, was hardly the norm in Mexico in the 1980s, and the movement leadership was as surprised by it as anyone. As recounted by Saucedo:

> I was shocked. There we were, waiting among ourselves, starring at each other and the paintings on the wall, feeling out of place and awkward, but also in some strange way expectant, as if perhaps our time had come. . . . We handed over our materials, and the president looked at them briefly and passed them to an aide. . . . Time stood still for us, as we lost our sense of virginity and began to engage the president as the legitimate interlocutors that we had told ourselves we were but perhaps until that moment had not quite known to be true. (Interview by the author, 1990)

The presidential decree led to a landslide of expropriation demands from other colonias and their representatives (Massolo 1986, 202–3). It also contributed to an enhanced sense of self-confidence on the part of many Mexico City movement organizations in their ability to extract governmental concessions (author's interviews with movement leaders). As one movement leader told me:

> What changed is that overnight we found ourselves in a situation of negotiating with high regime officials about concrete project proposals. Even more astounding is that we kept walking out of meetings not only with the historic satisfaction of having eloquently stated our case but with authority and money in our hands to really do something. This was a new kind of power and responsibility. It was kind of a shock. There were setbacks of course, but the direction was clear. We were growing in competency and influence. (Interview by the author, 1990)

Public protest and mass mobilization designed to reform and expand official reconstruction efforts characterized the months following the earthquake. On October 26, the CUD (which had only formed two days earlier) held its first march, which was attended by thirty thousand people (Rodríguez Velázquez 1987, 3). The demands were already taking on a decisive political tone: they included that the government declare a unilateral debt moratorium and channel the savings into reconstruction and that key government administrators of the reconstruction effort resign. Tamayo notes that this first stage was characterized by "political contention" and suggests that the mix of popular resistance and poor government administration resulted in "political frictions" at the highest levels of the regime over how best to manage the resulting political fallout (1989, 58).

The regime realized that existing organizational structures were inadequate to addressing the scale of the reconstruction, and on October 14, the Programa de Renovación Habitacional Popular (Program of Popular Housing Renovation [PRHP]) was established, with José Parcero López as Director (Presidencia de la Republica 1986, 556). PRHP's first step was to identify all the damnificados and issue criteria for program participation. Renovation Councils (Consejos de Renovación) were established to administer this process. The councils quickly became locations of political conflict, particularly on those not infrequent occasions when participation was made contingent on joining or having previously belonged to the PRI. Parcero López, ex-secretary of CNOP and then federal deputy from a downtown district, was at the center of the stormy controversy regarding the politicization of reconstruction programs. CUD leaders defended their members' rights to receive impartial treatment under the program, regardless of political affiliation. Those not affiliated with the PRI were treated to bureaucratic runarounds and other obstacles, but those more willing to comply with the PRI were more promptly attended to (interviews by the author). As Eckstein notes, this led "some *vecindad* associations . . . to affiliate with the party because they thought their prospects of getting state assistance would thereby be improved" (1990, 284). Clearly while the earthquake served the Left in its efforts to politicize, mobilize, and organize barrio residents, in a few cases, it served the PRI as well.

Thus was set up a classic situation of competition between the social Left and the regime. A crisis occurred of such severity that it motivated large numbers of people to mobilize and intensify interactions with the regime. Both the regime and independent social movement organizations competed for the hearts and minds of potential recruits. The particulars at this historic moment created a particularly dangerous situation for the inclusionary authoritarian regime. As introduced in Chapter 2, the legitimacy and continuation of the Mexican political system was enshrined in its ability to co-opt and incorporate new actors, lest they otherwise affiliate with the opposition. The ability to maintain the existing fold, let alone expand to include new actors, had already been weakened by the economic crisis of the 1980s, for not only had that crisis undermined the legitimacy of regime competency, it had also, perhaps even more important, created a fiscal emergency under which it was simply much more difficult to administer state corporatism. This weakening of the corporatist regime created substantial new opportunities for the opposition. Although the regime was able to incorporate some actors by means of the reconstruction monies, the opposition was able to shift the balance of affiliation power to its side, at least until the election of President Salinas.

From late 1985 through the first quarter of 1987, the CUD remained the focal point in popular movement efforts to force the government to "depoliticize" reconstruction by "politicizing" the process to further the organization's own organizational and ideological interests. While few of the more far-reaching demands of the CUD were fully realized, partial victories were common. This is certainly not unusual when movements push very ambitious demands; they often lead to partial concessions.

As Piven and Cloward (1979) have persuasively argued, the proper assessment of a movement lies in determining what was historically possible and the degree to which strategy succeeded or failed to take advantage of existing political opportunities. Most important, Piven and Cloward argue that it is the job of movement leaders to encourage and effectively channel the power of mass mobilization whenever possible, because it is the institutional disruption caused by mass mobilization that forces governments to make important concessions to groups and classes that are not normally favored in public policy. Using this criteria, the CUD receives relatively high marks for its activities in the first months following the earthquake. However, its grade declines over time as more moderate voices within the CUD argued in favor of discouraging mobilization and in favor of acceptance of government offers *at such time* that further mobilization and institutional disruption was possible. As we shall see, this premature posture of accommodation with the regime led to the decision to form the

AB on the part of a group of militants who accurately read the historic moment; they saw the potential for further weakening the regime and gaining access to more state resources. The analysis now turns to a summary of this CUD history.

The CUD's demand that expropriated properties be controlled by collective ownership was not achieved, but the CUD was successful in gaining a large number of expropriations for its members, albeit considerably fewer than those formally petitioned for. Between 1986 and 1987, forty-four thousand units were constructed, representing "a housing construction program without national historical precedent" (Casa y Ciudad 1996, 29). Many renters became property owners as a result of these reconstruction projects, a key CUD demand.

Respect for property rights acquired previously by CUD members in negotiation with landowners as well as the continued respect of rent agreements negotiated prior to the earthquake was also achieved, thereby protecting individual CUD members from land and real estate speculation. Previous rental arrangements, however, were more vulnerable, and many CUD renters living in buildings not covered by the earthquake response were subject to substantial rent hikes.[7] This led to a wave of evictions, and resisting evictions became a defining characteristic of CUD's activities. Efforts to protect renters' interests in the area previously targeted for gentrification were for the most part soundly defeated. Demands for substantial reforms in the Rent Law failed and would remain a core challenge for organizations in renter's movements, including the AB.

The CUD's goal of acquiring favorable credit terms so that low-income members could pay for the repair and rehabilitation of their homes was largely successful and gained broad public support, despite pressure from real estate interests and high-ranking party/state officials. The fact that major international donors, such as the World Bank, supported such programs was certainly a decisive factor.[8] This success did not come easily or all at once. Nevertheless, the CUD's insistence that the rehabilitated housing be adequate in size and services was also largely met and many people

7. The Instituto de Investigaciones Sociales of the National University (UNAM) calculated that rents in the Federal District rose by an average of 40 percent one month after the earthquake (cited in Rivas 1989, 22).

8. "The World Bank financed the direct building costs of the housing program (US $15, 264.2 million) 57% of the program's total cost" (Eckstein 1990, 291).

receiving new housing ended up in homes that were major improvements over their preearthquake dwellings.

CUD attempts to reduce bureaucratic delays and halt corrupt government-construction company arrangements had only limited impact. Efforts to have technical reviews by nongovernmental organizations (NGOs) recognized in order to bypass the biased and often delayed actions by government agencies were also not accepted, but the CUD did have its own expert opinion recognized. The CUD also had mixed results in ensuring that residents were able to stay in their preearthquake neighborhoods, as in the later stages of reconstruction, most units were built on less valuable land outside the downtown area. The CUD's broader demand for some sort of debt moratorium, and a redirecting of these funds to housing programs, failed to produce results, as Mexico continued to meet International Monetary Fund (IMF) agreements and fulfill its obligations to foreign debtors. However, the replacement of the original government bureaucrats in charge of reconstruction, Carrillo Arena and Parcero López, with state reformers signaled a recognition by the de la Madrid administration that conciliatory figures were needed. The appointment of reformers did not completely reverse the political liabilities for the government, but their success not only contributed to their own professional mobility into the next administration under Salinas but also directly affected how Salinas dealt with popular movements. The CUD's ability to force changes in personnel to bring in more moderate actors was heralded as an important movement victory.

The initial elation soon gave way to the more plodding politics of implementation. Through persistence and public pressure, the CUD gradually increased its participation on key housing decisions, one of the more important political outcomes of popular movement mobilization and negotiation to take place during the 1980s protest cycle. While CUD failed to augment the overall number of expropriated properties, pressure on the de la Madrid administration to use the earthquake to redistribute real estate ownership in the downtown area was equally unsuccessful. Preventing expropriated properties from passing back into the hands of the previous owners through bureaucratic maneuverings was also a considerable concern of the CUD, but for the most part, it was prevented. When employers attempted to take advantage of the earthquake to declare the kind of extraordinary situation that would permit workforce reductions, the CUD defended these workers, calling for an end to what it termed "unjustified dismissals."

The CUD demanded that the government provide a salary or unemployment insurance for all workers who lost their jobs because of the earthquake and compensate families who lost members in the quake. The government did not respond to this demand in any specific way. Finally, the CUD demanded that the reconstruction program be seen as an opportunity to create a public-works project that in effect put to work those who had lost their jobs. Once again the government did not respond.[9]

Because of the multiclass nature of the CUD, it was impossible for the government to respond only to the CUD's middle-class interests while ignoring those of its popular-class constituency (interviews by the author; Eckstein 1990, 288). At the same time that the government determined that it could neither ignore the CUD nor deal with it in a traditional clientelistic fashion, the CUD decided that it would have to negotiate with the federal government if it was to gain concessions. In May 1986, in return for a truly extraordinary commitment to construct forty-eight thousand units benefiting 250,000 people in a little over a year, the government obligated each popular movement to sign the Convenio de concertación democrática para la reconstruction de vivienda (Democratic agreement for housing reconstruction). In the document it put in writing that the new housing units would respect the "urban characteristics and cultural identity" of the inhabitants from the city's center, decreed that beneficiaries would pay back loans at rates within their means, and recognized the importance of public participation in the design and implementation of the projects.

Not unexpectedly, interpretations of the significance of this highly publicized convenio de concertación, which included the signatures of 106 groups, ranged widely. Cuauhtémoc Abarca, a key CUD leader, represents one widely held view. He understood the convenio to be a concession by the state that the reconstruction could not happen without the independent movements. He emphasized the extent to which the convenio included the "immense majority" of CUD demands and saw it as a testament to what persistent mobilization and organization can achieve for those without significant resources (cited in Tamayo 1989, 61). Eckstein offered a different interpretation:

9. This summary of CUD demands and analysis was constructed with reference to Cuéllar Vázquez (1990, 25–26); a review of CUD, AB, and government documents; and a series of conversations and correspondence with participants and observers. I would like to thank Paco Saucedo and Angélica Cuéllar Vázquez in particular.

> *Damnificados* did not need to belong to a group that signed the *convenio* to get housing, but the principal groups that had actively mobilized for housing all had to sign; in so doing, they agree, in effect, to work with and not against the state. The accord therefore included all relevant groups in the resolution of the political crisis. . . . The state as well as the slum-dwellers benefited from the housing reform. To get housing, defiant groups had to agree to quiescence and to accept the terms of housing imposed by the government. Meanwhile, the government allocated housing in a manner that undermined the social base of the "new social movement" type groups. (1990, 290, 294)

Those that take Abarca's position miss the fact that the convenio is, by definition, a mutual concession on the part of all signers. Many CUD leaders insisted that they did not have to change their political behavior in a manner amounting to co-optation, as happened to those who later signed PRONASOL convenios, such as the CDP.[10] However, a review of activities after the convenio signing suggests that the CUD in fact did moderate its behavior. This was in part because individual movement organizations had their hands full overseeing the implementation of the housing programs, leaving less time for agitating for new government initiatives. Its moderation also stems from the constant threat the projects faced of being sidetracked or derailed by local PRI elites, real estate interests, and state employees who felt that their interests were threatened.[11] In such an environment, it is not surprising that popular forces would seek to avoid confrontation wherever possible. This situation also shows how interactions with the state can moderate the system-challenging behavior of opposition forces in complex ways.

---

10. One might wonder how AB members who participated in this earlier *convenio* could later become such fierce critics of later *convenio* signers, such as the CDP. AB leader Marco Ráscon argues it was different because the PRONASOL *convenio* signed by the CDP legitimized an illegitimate president (Salinas) who sought to undermine a united Left (the PRD). He contends that such charges could not be attached to the May 1986 signing (interview with the author, 1993).

11. Ken Green points out that "given that the *convenio* was signed at the time construction began, the CUD's apparent acquiescence may be essentially the result of fulfilled demands. After all, the economic demands were really the core, while the political demands were very broad, far-reaching, and somewhat ill-articulated" (personal correspondence). As is revealed below, the political demands became increasingly well defined after the initiation of the AB by a small group of the more radical CUD leaders.

Although popular movement activities may have been somewhat derad-icalized, as Eckstein suggests, there is ample evidence to support the CUD's insistence that they remained anything but "quiescent." While the govern-ment certainly endeavored to allocate housing in a manner that under-mined the social base of the new social movements, it did not succeed. Many convenio signers continued to participate openly in acts of collective dissent. On numerous occasions the CUD and other convenio signers spoke out against party and state officials, receiving considerable media attention and creating an important asset in the growing power of a Mexico City opposition, which Cárdenas capitalized on in 1988.

By July 1986, nearly eighty thousand housing units had been assigned, repaired, and constructed for the benefit of four hundred thousand habi-tants (Presidencia de la Republica 1987, 400). *This level of reconstruction and the way it was implemented would have never have occurred without the presence and skillful political maneuvering of a relatively unified urban popular movement.* While the CUD experienced internal divisions, derived from personal and ideological differences as well as struggles for organizational control, it successfully presented a unified front to the government. This was no small feat for an organization with middle-class representatives coexisting with ACNR and Punto Crítico radicals.

The Mexican earthquake occurred at a moment in the protest cycle in which government errors had already increased, opening up political opportunities. Preexisting popular movement organizations and their leaderships in Mexico City were able to seize and further expand these opportunities. The removal of some government hardliners and their replacement with state reformers assisted popular movement organiza-tions that were amalgamated with the CUD front to build their credibility and influence in Mexico City politics. The popular movement response to the September 1985 earthquake began a dramatic phase of more radical and politicized mobilization that culminated in the elections of July 1988.

The Asamblea de Barrios of Mexico City

Once the housing convenio with the government was signed, the CUD had in most respects met its raison d'être, as many of its member organizations had plans no more ambitious than the reconstruction project, and these demands were the glue that kept the CUD's disparate wings united. After signing, most organizations focused on the implementation of the program. However, four CUD organizations, associated with the political tendencies represented by Punto Crítico and ACNR and inspired by the United Nation's proclamation of 1987 as International Year of Shelter for the Homeless, began to discuss ways in which the housing struggle could transcend the limits imposed by the convenio.[12]

Punto Crítico was officially formed in 1983, but it had existed as a political and ideological current since at least 1972, when it founded the eponymous important Left magazine *Punto Crítico*. Like most other pre-party formations in Mexico, Punto Crítico championed grassroots work by social movements and warned against participation in elections. It argued that López Portillo's electoral reforms were designed to diminish the capacity of the Left to take advantage of the increasing interrelated crises of capitalism and the Mexican state. This assessment of elections changed over the course of the 1980s, even when Punto Crítico's leadership remained suspicious, because the Cárdenas candidacy was so popular with its membership that it was forced to support electoral participation. The ACNR was formed by a number of regional grassroots organizations from around the country in concert with small groupings of radical Left intellectuals.[13] While the ACNR no doubt created opportunities for the exchange of ideas and offered a training ground for the ideological formation of cuadros, it was never able to provide a detailed and sound national strategy (review of ACNR literature and interviews by the author).

The most common accounts of the AB's history trace its origins back to actions by leaders of two CUD member organizations, the Cuartos de Azotea de Tlatelolco (Azotea Quarters of Tlatelolco) and the Comité de Lucha Inquilinaria del Centro (Committee of the Downtown Renter's

12. These were the Coordinadora de Cuartos de Azotea de Tlatelolco, headed up by Marco Rascón, and the Comité de Lucha Inquilinaria del Centro (CLIC), led by Francisco Alvarado, both affiliated politically with Punto Crítico; the Unión Popular de Inquilinos de la Colonia Pensil, headed up by Javier Hidalgo, and a faction of the Unión de Vecinos de la Colonia Guerrero and the Unión Popular de Inquilinos de la Colonia Morelos–Peña Morelos, led by Francisco Saucedo, both affiliated politically with the ACNR. These four men, sometimes referred to as "the gang of four" together formed the top leadership of the AB.

13. "The ACNR is the result of a process of fusion that began two years previous by nine political organizations of the Mexican revolutionary Left: the Asociación Cívica Guerrerense, the Comité Promotor de Lucha Campesina-Popular, the Colectivo Democrático Revolucionario, the Grupo de Izquierda Revolucionaria–Espartaco, the Grupo Revolución, el Movimiento Cívico Jaramillista, el Movimiento Independiente de la Laguna, la Unión de Estudiantes Revolucionarios de Sinaloa y la Unión Revolucionaria Independiente" (ACNR 1983, 3).

Struggle [CLIC]). These movement leaders, who came from the ranks of the radical social Left, created a list of petitioners for housing from those not covered by either phase of the earthquake reconstruction. They were convinced that the time had come to force a fuller realization of the Mexican Revolution's promise of decent housing for all. They asserted, with the bravado often associated with movements on the rise, that they would not allow the government to give projects piecemeal but would press for a comprehensive response to a macro structural problem (Trejo 1987). While this demand was not new among movement organizations, the AB leaders insisted that they were different because they really meant it. "Meaning it" required that the new organization not play by the old rules of cutting selective deals with state agencies. Instead, the AB insisted that the state deal more comprehensively, and more legally, with basic rights and needs as defined in the Mexican Constitution.[14]

The founding concept of the AB was that a mass movement in support of the constitutional right of all Mexicans to decent housing had a good chance of yielding substantial results. This was the issue over which the AB split off from the more moderate CUD. AB leaders understood the "protection brigades" that were organized to prevent government eviction of residents, most of whom were not covered by reconstruction programs as opportunities to organize for more radical changes (AB leaders, interviews by the author). From the outset, the AB sought to inject a sense of magic, myth, and humor into their actions and accounts of them. It quickly set about reinforcing the idea that the defiant actions of the CUD had forced the government to listen and, though it would be difficult, it was certainly possible to gain more concessions.

On April 4, 1987, as the political protest cycle was reaching its crescendo on a national level, the AB was founded at a public meeting attended by four thousand families representing twenty-eight colonias. There was a high degree of faith and conviction that past obstacles to structural reform could be overcome. AB leaders stressed the importance of going beyond the CUD to demand *vivienda digna* (dignified housing) for all, proclaiming

14. My interviews with midlevel cuadros and project managers revealed frequent and deep suspicions that deed and word often separated here. There were frequent allegations, with varying levels of credible "proof" that extensive deal-making went on in the negotiation and building of specific housing projects. Nonetheless, the AB's behavior vis-à-vis the Salinas Administration was clearly distinct from those that openly embraced *concertación* as a principal and PRONASOL as a program.

that the AB would embrace the problems of renters. Although the organization always claimed to promote the concerns of the homeless, in actuality most homeless people had incomes too low for them to qualify for public housing programs and thus were largely excluded from AB activities. As was true of most of the urban popular movement organizations, there were sharp contrasts between the class origins, gender, education, and political socialization of AB leaders, cuadros, and rank-and-file members. Top leadership usually did not come from the barrio, and they were constantly designing plans and developing language and practices that were meant to secure the support of the base for strategy positions that they took in relative isolation from it.

Determining the basic socioeconomic composition of most urban popular movement rank and files is quite easily done, even without the aid of methodologically exacting surveys. Shantytown movement organizations located in downtown areas as well as movement organizations based primarily on the outskirts of urban areas (such as the CDP), are made up mostly of low-income rural-to-urban migrants and their descendents. The socioeconomic makeup of the AB is more differentiated, although it is not as diverse as is claimed by AB leaders. In fact, AB spokespeople routinely insisted that it is not really an urban popular movement organization at all, preferring to call it a citizen movement. A review of AB literature, AB leadership statements in the press, fieldwork observations, and personal interviews reveals a steadfast insistence that the AB is different. It is different because it was always resolutely determined not to repeat what it believed to be the rigid thinking and authoritarian practices endemic to both traditional Left parties and OIRista popular movements. It also claimed to be different because of its multiclass membership.

A sample survey of 2,593 AB families revealed that 74.84 percent lived on one minimum wage, 23.94 percent had the equivalent of two minimum-wage salaries coming into the household, and 1.22 percent had more (Rivas 1989, 29–32).[15] Greene (1991) found that AB members had a somewhat higher income than that found by Rivas (see Appendix F in the present volume). While both analyses belie the AB leadership's claim to a multiclass membership, they do indicate that the membership did have higher incomes than is typical for the shantytown movements common throughout Mexico. AB leaders have observed that the income level of the average

15. Minimum salary was based on the official figure for Mexico City: U.S.$3.44 a day.

AB member rose somewhat between 1987 and the early 1990s because the lowest-income people dropped out if they were too poor to benefit from the public housing programs managed by the AB. While the AB was forced to construct much of its housing outside the downtown area, it was still much too expensive for the poorest of the urban poor.[16]

The majority of AB members were women, but according to the calculations of an important female leader, this percentage dropped, from about 85 percent in the beginning to about 65 percent in 1991 (interview by the author). This is consistent with other urban social movements and one study calculated that women make up 80 percent of those who "actively participate" in the movement in the Mexico City area (Casa y Ciudad 1996, 5). Most female AB members worked in the home, whether they were married and living with their spouses or single mothers. There were, however, a not insignificant number of students, factory workers (including many from Mexico's infamous sweatshops), secretaries, members of the informal sector, and a smaller number of professionals.

The AB's demands focused on eight key points that demonstrate how the organization was both similar to and different from the type of urban popular movement characterized by CONAMUP:

1. The AB insisted on reducing payments on foreign debt, a demand consistent with other leftist or populist Mexican individuals and organizations.
2. The AB advocated a deep structural reform of the existing "collaborationist" regime.[17] In its stead, Mexico should install a democratic socialist regime. The central place given to democratization represents a significant shift not only for the AB but for most radical movements in Mexico.
3. The AB demanded an end to state-supported evictions of renters by private landlords. The focus on downtown renter issues distinguishes the

16. The level of income required to participate in AB housing programs was higher than programs gained by the CDP and most other urban popular movement organizations. While the CDP did some housing at expenditure levels roughly equal to the AB, most of its housing programs were much more modest; they typically provided services such as electricity and potable water and credit for land purchase, while the actual housing unit was self-built and very low cost.

17. Describing governments as collaborationist comes from the dependency literature that has had deep influence on many Latin American popular movements. It argues that countries such as Mexico are enduring neocolonialism, in which international relations (political and economic) still serve the interests of more powerful countries at the expense of their own.

AB from most other urban popular movements that are located in urban peripheries and that usually only have a minority of renters among their members.

4. The AB demanded that unused properties owned by the state or private speculators be expropriated and used to construct public housing. The AB made this its trademark and, far more than other organizations, developed impressive documentation on available sites and presented concrete proposals to state agencies.

5. The AB advocated reform of the Código Civil y de Procedimientos de 1984 (1984 Civil Code and Procedures) because, they claimed, it favored landowners over renters. Reform would include rent control and new procedures governing eviction processes. This demand was not unique to the AB, but it became the lead organization, pressuring, with some success, for the PRD to stress this issue.

6. The AB insisted that all *damnificados* were eligible for housing under the constitution. Phrases such as *damnificados por el sistema*, *damnificados eternos*, and *damnificados de toda la vida* became popular within the AB political dialect and distinguished the AB from the CUD.[18]

7. The AB demanded adherence to the laws formally outlawing preference of any particular political or social organization. This demand was a priority for all independent popular movement organizations in Mexico.

8. The AB insisted that the time had come to stop making under-the-table deals with the regime, arguing for a strategy that would force the state to follow the letter of the law. It believed that this strategy was capable of undermining the party/state's ability to divide and conquer the Left. This demand was characteristic of popular movements within the Cardenista fold, even though there was some gap between word and deed on this issue.[19]

---

18. The AB greatly expanded the term *damnificado* to include *damnificados por el sistema* (damaged as a result of the system), *damnificados eternos* (eternally damaged) and *damnificados de toda la vida* (damaged in all ways, or more colloquially, totally screwed). The focus of the AB was on housing, and in this way it was similar to the CUD, but its willingness to embrace people whose housing problems were not directly related to the earthquake sharply distinguished the AB from the CUD. The AB's embrace of poverty in general and belief in the state's responsibility to effectively address this problem are in keeping with the fundamental premises of the urban popular movement.

19. While most important Mexican popular movement organizations by 1989 were either supporting Cárdenas and the PRD or participating in PRONASOL, a third, smaller group remained outside the two main camps. These self-defined more radical movements often attacked both the other two as being reformist and thus counterrevolutionary.

Dynamics unleashed by the earthquake and the inability of more ambitious politicos to move the CUD to a broader mission together suggest that the emergence of a militant downtown popular movement was likely. However, de la Madrid's ambitious National Housing Program of 1987, announced in February, which was to benefit 1.7 million persons through the authorization of 350,000 housing credits, certainly contributed—at a minimum—to the timing of the AB's emergence in April that same year. This public policy program was the underpinning of what was to be the most ambitious year of public housing construction in Mexican history. The AB was a major player in the implementation of this program, instrumental in ensuring that poor people, particularly renters, were not excluded from the new housing credits. The belief was widespread among movement analysts and government functionaries alike that the impressive target figures were in large measure possible because of the efforts of AB and other popular movement organizations.

The AB, through championing the rights of renters to receive housing credits, was instrumental in the regime's formation of the Casa Propia (Home of One's Own) program, specifically directed at renters. This program was perhaps the AB's greatest housing victory, as it was the AB's popular mobilization in conjunction with skillful negotiation with key state reformists that quite clearly forced the government to establish the program. This is one of the few instances during the 1980s protest cycle when a movement's ability to affect state policy was so direct and unambiguous.

As impressive as these gains were, sympathetic critics of the AB point out that Casa Propia as much favored landlords looking for a solution to rent freezes as it was a concession to movement demands. Casa Propia's importance is also deflated somewhat by the fact that its budget always paled in comparison to the amounts needed to really implement it. Moreover, concerns surfaced that the AB used these funds in a highly clientelist fashion, and indeed, some of the fiercest differences between the four AB top leaders were over allegations of improper use of funds (interviews and field observations by the author).[20]

20. These types of problems and criticisms are more the rule than the exception, even in cases of highly successful movements with high ethical standards. I have a strong suspicion that when they are absent in movement histories this is more often a result of their being ignored by the historian than of no such problems having arisen. Politics, including the politics of transformative social movements, is not frequently inhabited by saints. The pressing question is the degree of integrity that can be sustained by a particular group of people operating in a political environment whose character is dominated by authoritarian relationships, rent seeking, and the like.

In its first few years, building on past movement experience and a fertile opportunity structure, the AB became one of the foremost procurers of housing projects.[21] The speed of its assent—which has no parallels in recent Mexican urban history—is a result of its propitious timing in the protest cycle, the earthquake that had put the PRI government on the defensive, and the rising opportunities resulting from the economic crisis.[22] Yolanda Tello, a midlevel AB cuadro, stated that as of 1994, the AB had overseen the construction of forty-six thousand housing units (cited in Bolos 1995, 265), mostly in downtown areas.[23] However, it is important to note that total number of units built in the periphery is much higher than the number in the center—a fact that, not surprisingly, was not broadcast in the AB's own promotional propaganda.

As argued in Chapter 1, relationships are at the core of politics. The stated need to change relationships is unusually intense in social movement politics, for, by definition, social movements believe the existing system to be in need of radical restructuring. In authoritarian settings such as Mexico during the 1980s, the focus was predictably on democratizing relationships. The AB pushed this campaign hard. It argued for it on the basis of the general proposition that democracy was superior to authoritarianism and also that democratization would be particularly beneficial to its constituency, which did not receive fair treatment by the existing regime.

The AB frequently advocated a broad language of regime transition in its rhetoric while in its day-to-day relationships with the state it worked more on the level of "democratizing" the relationship between specific state institutions and movement negotiators. This democratization meant first and foremost that the implementation of government programs would be directed at the intended beneficiaries without favoritism toward the PRI. Well-trained technical personnel with no love for what they would describe as the antiquated, authoritarian, and corrupt PRI were not necessarily convinced that social movement organizations really sought to replace this cronyism and inefficiency with a meritocracy. As one such Mexico City reformer with influence over project selection stated:

21. Greene points out that groups affiliated with the PRI remain the most powerful housing service providers, and among non-PRI groups, UPREZ still has more units because of their giant holdings in San Miguel Teotongo and Cabeza de Juarez (personal correspondence).

22. A relatively unknown fact is that the PRI began losing elections in Mexico City in the early 1980s when it lost the popular vote in the 1982 federal elections with 48 percent of the vote while the opposition garnered 52 percent (official figures from the Federal Election Commission as reported in Davis 1994, 330).

23. See Appendix E for more information on the distribution of AB housing projects.

Look, anybody with one eye to see and a willingness to objectively report what occurs with regular frequency in housing projects here can tell you that the PRI regularly wreaks havoc on the rational disbursement of funds. They come in here throwing their weight around, using their connections to channel funds in their own material and political interests. However, the movement leaders are often not so different, and I have always believed that the more power they get, the less different they will become. (Interview by the author, 1994)

Internal Organization

The AB had a somewhat more pluralistic and decentralized decision-making process than most other Mexican popular movement organizations. Because it grew out of several movement organizations affiliated with the CUD, was joined shortly after by other preexisting organizations, and then quickly spawned the birth of other affiliated organizations, the AB is best thought of as an umbrella organization itself, although as the experience of CONAMUP and other coordinadoras suggests, this does not automatically lead to high levels of internal democracy (P. Haber 1989; Bouchier Tretiack 1988). In the case of the AB, however, none of the founding organizations were willing to be subordinate to one another. Not that all member organizations possessed equal power over key decisions, but the balance of power required internal compromise and consensus. The relatively higher levels of education and class status within the AB generally also contributed, in my view, to a higher level of participation than is the case in most other Mexican urban popular movements.[24] This was most noticeable at the midlevel activist, or cuadro, level. Thus, power dynamics between cuadros and leaders were more equal than in other popular movement organizations that I observed.

I observed dozens of meetings of both the CDP and the AB that were attended by the full range of membership: leaders, midlevel management, and the rank and file. I was repeatedly struck by the high level of debate

24. Despite the higher level of participation, the four founding organizations continued to exercise considerable power through greater representation on the most important decision-making bodies. This led to discontent among AB affiliates that joined as groups of housing petitioners and whose members felt underrepresented. The result is a noticeable cleavage between these two "types" of AB members.

that occurred in the AB's general membership meetings. While most members had little formal education, there were often a half dozen or so outspoken participants who were well educated. In my view, there is no doubt that the more diverse socioeconomic makeup of the AB contributed to the relatively high degree of pluralism as contrasted with OIR-identified organizations, such as the CDP.

The sheer size of the AB target population lent itself to the implementation of one of AB's guiding ideological dictums: *autogestión*.[25] While no reliable data exists, the leadership claims that 1991 membership was around ten thousand families, or fifty thousand people, which I judge to be roughly accurate. The considerable size necessitated the empowerment of midlevel activists who were capable of making key decisions, mobilizing rank-and-file activities, negotiating with state officials, and interacting with the press. The fifteen central organizations that oversaw many of the housing projects demonstrated an organizational complexity and heterogeneity that encouraged more decentralized decision-making processes than is usual in a Mexican urban popular movement (Appendix D). Each of the ninety-six housing projects listed in Appendix E had its own internal structure and was run by an active and semiautonomous organization, but many of these were very small and did not exert much influence on important AB decisions.

The most crucial factor in resisting internal clientelist practices was the pressure levied by midlevel activists to open up the decision-making process.[26] They effectively insisted, loudly and persistently, on increased access to information and pressured for structural changes. The AB was also benefited by politically and technically astute NGOs with close links and influence on the thinking and political culture of the movement. This role was common for NGOs working with popular movement organizations such as the AB and they often served as a sort of brain trust. Their deep

25. The term *autogestión* can be loosely translated as "self-help." This definition, however, misses the philosophical richness that the term takes on within AB culture. The conceptual language of New Social Movement theory is common among AB leaders, activists, and, to a lesser but still impressive extent, rank-and-file members. The cultural practice of *autogestión* is understood to be essential to the creation of alternative subjects and the alternative identities necessary for the true Gramscian sociocultural as well as political/economic transformation of the country.

26. It is also important to point out that some of the more powerful of these middle-class activists attempted to set up their own local political machines based on clientelist control of resources (Ken Greene, personal correspondence).

knowledge base and the trust that movements placed in them helped keep Mexico City leaders more accountable and technically efficacious than they would have been otherwise.

From the outset, the AB formed semiautonomous groupings organized around different housing issues. The four principal groups were petitioners for housing, public employees entitled to housing but denied it because of delays in the state housing bureaucracy," groups of 24," and renters.[27] The AB also formed a number of other suborganizations: (1) barrio-wide organizations, (2) neighborhood organizations, (3) housing units, (4) youth groups, (5) women's groups, (6) groups of street vendors and small-shop owners. To manage these different kinds of groups, the AB developed a formal decision-making structure that encompassed the following:

1. Asamblea General de los Jueves. These Thursday-evening meetings were the primary location for constructing and reinforcing the AB's identity as an organization. Numbers fluctuated, with often a couple of thousand people in attendance, sometimes more. They included outside speakers, AB members expressing their own particular perspectives on "the struggle," impressive displays of music and theater, and information sessions about ongoing activities. While the AB literature referred to these meetings as the "maximum location of agreements and decisions," in reality, key strategic decisions were not made here, although they were periodically discussed and debated. Most key decisions were made by the four founding members, who also made up the political commission.

2. Comisión Política. This commission had four members, the founding leaders of the AB: Marco Rascón, Francisco Alvarado, Francisco Saucedo, and Javier Hidalgo. At least until early 1991, the commission was where all key AB decisions were taken. Between 1991 and 1993,

27. These public employees were essentially what gave the AB its multiclass character. The fact that people from this socioeconomic strata sought out the AB to aid them is a reflection of how capable the AB was in negotiating with the federal bureaucracy.

The "groups of 24" reflected a strategy designed to organize the vast numbers of housing petitioners. The number 24 was picked rather arbitrarily as manageable for a working group that would develop, with the assistance of AB "political and technical experts," a specific plan and strategy for accomplishing housing goals. While this form of organization was eventually phased out, it played an important role in the early stages. For example, in early June 1987, after only two months of organizing, the AB was able to petition for housing projects on behalf of 110 "groups of 24" (Cuéllar Vázquez 1990, 67).

the Comisión Coordinadora and Comisión Gobierno (see below) wrestled some of this power away from the top leadership.

3. Comisión Coordinadora. This commission began as a kind of information channel, meeting once a week to gather material in order to plan Thursday meetings. However, as a result of pressure from midlevel activists, it became focused on (1) the creation of intermediate levels of participation for which the top leadership were held accountable, (2) the detailed release of information from the leadership to the activists, and (3) a forum at which top leadership would take the concerns of "midlevel management" seriously.

4. Consejo General de Organización de la Asamblea de Barrios. These meetings, attended largely by activists and AB leaders along with various contingencies of rank-and-file members, were where issues could be debated at length. The AB literature describes them as sites for the exchange of information as well as for deliberation on and resolution of political and social strategy. The meetings also created openings for midlevel activists to debate the internal machinations of power with top leadership, on occasion resulting in actual reform. Five *consejos* were held between August 1988 and January 1991.[28]

5. Comisión de Gobierno. This commission was formed later than and to a certain extent took over the functions of the Comisión Coordinadora. It's members met weekly to plan the Thursday meetings and attempted also to coordinate the various commissions. In the AB literature of the early 1990s, it was described as where the most important planning decisions were taken. This commission, together with the Comisión Coordinadora, represented the efforts of midlevel activists to decrease the power of the Comisión Política.

6. Comisión de Vivienda. This commission functioned primarily as a technical-support group for the housing initiatives. As part of the 1991 decentralization efforts, it was given important powers to make specific and immediate decisions regarding housing issues without first consulting higher bodies. Its primary mission was to aid in the development of the *autogestión* capacity of individual housing groups. In practice, it functioned very closely with the Comisión de Gobierno with basically the same membership.

28. I attended two of these five meetings.

7. La Comisión Territorial. This commission was also a product of the internal reform movement. Its representatives were responsible, at least formally, for coordinating all territorial groupings and interactions with government bodies. It was also responsible for managing AB's alliances with other political and social organizations. It suffered from significant confusion regarding its mandate and authority (interviews by the author).

8. Comisión de Mujeres. This was the primary location for discussion, decision making, and action on women's issues, both within AB and the broader community. It was very involved in the electoral activity of the AB, from campaigns to the oversight of voting booths on election day. In contrast to what occurred in most other urban popular movement organizations, including the CDP, in which women did not posses much real authority above the neighborhood-activist level, in the AB, a number of women played important roles at a second tier of leadership.

9. Comisión Jurídica y de Derechos Humanos. This commission provided support for renter, civil, family, and criminal legal issues. It organized workshops and made a serious effort to capacitate "people's lawyers," who, while not having formal degrees, were empowered to make their way through the legal system on AB business.

10. Comisión de Formación. This commission was responsible for the political and social education of cuadros and the rank and file. It promoted both cultural and educational activities as well as distributed learning materials.

11. Comisión de Finanzas. This commission managed and reported on the AB's finances.

Superbarrio

AB's greatest cultural creation was Superbarrio Gómez. His character was the brainchild of the four AB founders, who took seriously the need for a cultural renaissance. Superbarrio was the representation of a masked man in a cape, who accompanied renters in their disputes with landlords, led marches, was present at AB negotiations with government officials, and even ran for president in 1988, receiving the vote of Cuauhtémoc Cárdenas.

The story of Superbarrio's "emergence" is known and cherished by many beyond the AB membership. In the tradition of Dickens, Superbarrio is an ordinary man, a street vendor by trade, who had been forcibly evicted from his home as a child. He later becomes profoundly disturbed by the government's incompetence and mean-spirited efforts to minimize the valiant citizen efforts taken during the emergency response to the 1985 earthquake. On June 12, 1987, as he heads to work early in the morning, his mind filled with thoughts of how the urban poor might better defend themselves, he finds himself engulfed in a sea of intense red-and-yellow light and a strong howling wind. When the wind and light subside, this representative of the exploited masses finds himself dressed in a bright red-and-yellow costume, replete with mask and cape. He does not understand what has happened until a booming voice informs him that "you are now Superbarrio, defender of the poor renters and scourge of the voracious landlords and corrupt authorities."

The creation of Superbarrio received impressive attention in the print and electronic media. He was the personification of the AB's popular struggle and a character with whom renters and housing petitioners could easily identify. He represented the popular will, the strength and determination to struggle for the AB's basic goals: housing and "una ciudad para todos." He also represented the spirit of Mexico's urban popular movements internationally. Superbarrio was like many other cartoon heroes, in that what made his victories against evil forces effective in changing attitudes and consciousness is that he fights "real problems" (Superbarrio's creators, interviews by the author). Part of the Superbarrio lore is that, in his previous incarnation as a street vendor, he had done some amateur wrestling. As Superbarrio he transforms this skill into fighting for "what is right" in public displays, such as when he fights the TV character Cataliño Creel in the ring.[29]

No to Evictions

Organizing resistance to evictions was certainly not unique to the AB, although its downtown location and the membership of many renters made this an issue that was critical to the organization in a way that it was not to most other urban popular movement organizations. While its ultimate

29. Cataliño Creel is a mean-spirited slumlord in the popular Mexican TV soap opera *Cuna de Lobos.*

goal was a new rental law, its skill at resisting evictions gained it an international reputation. Greene (1991) describes how the AB strategy mitigated the frequency of successful evictions in Colonia Guerrero:

> An elaborate alert system notifies residents of an eviction. Secret
> phones receive calls and begin a phone tree. For those without
> phones, three rockets are set off to alert of an eviction in progress.
> During the night local gangs keep an eye out for the presence of
> riot police, indicating an eviction. In the early morning those who
> work at the market monitor the immediate area for evictions. And
> in particularly difficult times, special resident patrols are organ-
> ized. (14)

One of the AB's most famous acts of resistance against a forced eviction
took place early in the AB's history, on June 17, 1987. Two hundred paid or
coerced thugs arrived at the Plaza Abasolo in the Colonia Guerrero (in the
AB heartland) intent on dislodging a single family. This family, aware that
such an occurrence was in the offing, fired three rockets into the night sky.
Within minutes, more than a thousand people confronted the would-be
evictors with sticks and rocks. The thugs retreated, to the wild cheers of
the crowd.

AB records report a decisive curtailment in the number of evictions over
the AB's life span (AB archives). Some of the decline is explained by the
decrease in attempted evictions during the 1987–93 period as a result of
earthquake-associated evictions coming to a close. Nevertheless, my own
observations in the field suggest that the AB's style of resistance had a part
to play in the success of a tactic that certainly contributed to the decrease
in forced evictions. The AB and Superbarrio's effective use of the media
forced property owners and government officials to reconsider their
actions. Superbarrio explains:

> We used the momentum of public opinion against evictions that
> arose from the 1985 earthquake. Before then, the middle classes
> had tended to believe the evictions were legitimate acts against
> poor marauders. The popular classes, unless they had independ-
> ent organization, had tended to believe that evictions were
> inevitable, if also unjust. The earthquake had the affect of chang-
> ing these attitudes, at least to a certain extent. The middle class no

longer assumed, at least to the same degree, that the poor were to blame and the poor lost some of their learned sense of resignation. We built on this. (Superbarrio Gomez, interview by the author, 1990)

The AB often did not simply resist the eviction, but worked with the landlords and renters to reach new agreements. While Mexico City has its share of slumlords, the AB recognized that many rental units are owned by working- or middle-class owners who depend on rents to cover their basic necessities. This perspective, which they publicized widely, contributed to the relatively high esteem the AB enjoyed among the Mexican middle class as well as strengthened their success rate in resisting forced evictions.

During my months of fieldwork with the AB in the late 1980s and early 1990s, I observed many such interactions. Perhaps most common was when those faced with evictions would come to the AB offices and explain their problem. AB representatives would be sent out to help mediate the situation with the landlord. Sometimes it worked; other times it did not. But in most cases I observed, the AB was able to negotiate some improvement of circumstances for those threatened with eviction. For example, in 1990, Superbarrio Gomez was asked to intervene in a situation in which renters who had organized collectively were being threatened with eviction following on their refusal to comply with a rent hike. Superbarrio set up a meeting with the landlord and the owner. Discussion ensued, and a compromise was reached, wherein the rent was increased, but the increase was cut in half, and the start date of the new rent was postponed by three months, so as to allow the renters to adjust to the new financial burden.

The AB efforts on evictions defined both its abilities and its limitations. While the successes served to strengthen its image and political strength and demonstrated its influence on the powerful coalition of landlords, politicians, and police, it remained unable to secure broader legislative victories or other means for institutionalizing renter protections. However, as was first argued in Chapter 1, the relative success of a movement must be judged in terms of what was historically possible at the time. In my judgment, the AB's marks in this area are extremely impressive. Their efforts gave hope to Mexico City's renting poor that through collective action an improvement in their situation vis-à-vis their vulnerability was possible. The AB regularly reinforced this hope by achieving concrete improvements in its interventions as mediators and advocates. Was there some strategy that the AB overlooked that would have allowed them to institutionalize even greater gains? In my judgment, no.

The Party/Movement Tension: The AB and Neo-Cardenismo

The AB entered electoral politics in November 1987, when, despite the leaderships' wariness, the organization's rank and file pushed strenuously for its participation in the 1988 presidential elections. Against a backdrop of dispute among nationalist and leftist forces over the selection of candidates, Superbarrio Gomez announced his candidacy for president.[30] This decision forced the AB to develop more sophisticated positions on issues that were beyond their traditional focus on housing and Mexico City democratization, issues such as ecology, income distribution, the foreign debt, U.S.-Mexican relations, unemployment, the federal budget, and the corrupt nature and illegal status of the PRI-state relationship.

> Being involved in the presidential campaign forced us to think in new ways. While a few of us had read and written on these issues earlier, most had been done in rather insular journals and, well, among people very much like ourselves. It is a very different thing to write for a small-circulation magazine than it is to develop positions that you hope to be taken seriously by the voting public. It forced us to think in new and, I would say, more serious ways. (AB leader, interview by the author, 1990)

The principal reason AB leaders gave for deciding to enter into electoral politics was their realization that, while they had a limited set of achievements (most prominently around housing), they had not succeeded in effecting structural reforms. While AB leaders, in common with virtually all other popular movement leadership, came from political currents that rejected electoral politics, by late 1987 this situation had been reversed

30. As of November 1987, the PMS was still running Heberto Castillo; the Corriente Democrática had proposed Cárdenas; and the PRT was running, and continued to run, Rosario Ibarra as its presidential candidate. For a detailed account of the AB's role in the FDN and the 1988 election campaign, see Tirado Jiménez 1990.

almost diametrically.[31] They were motivated by concerns that continued electoral abstention would make them miss a political opportunity to contest the PRI's recent adoption of their language and tactics, and they contended that participating in the campaign would allow them to present their own credentials and "expose the PRI as impostors."[32]

Superbarrio's entry into electoral politics also thrust the AB into the national limelight. He was interviewed on all major TV networks and received coverage in the major national dailies and on the radio. When he led a mobilization that forced the Mexico City office of City Bank to close, it was covered by the electronic and print media and regime officials were asked to comment. While being interviewed, like any good politician, *Superbarrio* always defined the AB's agenda in terms likely to appeal to the listening public.

In December 1987, formal negotiations began between the Cárdenas camp and the AB over participation in the July elections. When AB leaders suggested that it would be more "natural" for the AB to align with either the PRT or the PMS, given the similarities in their political positions, Cárdenas associate Profirio Muñoz Ledo offered to register AB candidates under the FDN banner (Cuéllar Vázquez 1993, 128). Realizing how attractive this offer was, the AB tried to bring in the PRT and the PMS, but the PRT was resolute, insisting that Cárdenas was nothing but a neo-*priísta*. Although the PMS eventually threw its support to Cárdenas, negotiating an arrangement with the FDN remained very difficult for the PMS. This led the AB to accept the Muñoz Ledo offer while simultaneously expressing regret that a more unified leftist position was unattainable.[33] Although the

31. Moguel (1987) offers a concise history of the Left's position on electoral participation up until the mid-1980s, including a discussion of Punto Crítico's position on abstention and electoral tactics. The ACNR, up until the early 1980s, held a position similar to that of Punto Crítico, as it distrusted elections as a matter of course and particularly the way in which they were conducted in Mexico (ACNR n.d.).

32. PRI efforts to appropriate the language of the urban popular movement were widely observed by both movement participants and outsiders. Perhaps nowhere was this trend more in evidence than in the AB's downtown territory. In early 1989, the PRI went so far as to create its own Superbarrio figure, which it named Super Pueblo. The language of Super Pueblo was strikingly similar to that of Superbarrio. (See, for example, *Metrópoli*, October 16, 1989, 3).

33. The fact that none of the AB candidates won their electoral races can be tied directly to the inability of the candidates to come to agreements with the other parties (the problems in presenting common candidates existed not only with the PRT and the PMS, but also with other parties, such as the PARM). As first argued in Chapter 1, alliances between social movements and between social movements and political parties are fraught with obstacles. While actors are attracted to the potential power that might come from them, differences over identity and power sharing often prevent their success.

platform presented by the FDN in January 1988 was more moderate than the AB would have wanted, the latter supported it. While the strength of this alliance was in the main responsible for the successes at the peak of the protest cycle, its weaknesses in part determined the limitations of what could be achieved.

During the campaign, Cárdenas went on four tours (*recorridos*) of the eleven electoral districts in which the AB was strong (Tirado Jiménez 1990, 52–67). While it was not solely responsible, the AB can take substantial credit for two elements of the FDN platform: the proposal to transform the Federal District into the state of Anáhuac[34] and "the necessity to promulgate a renter's law" (Tirado Jiménez 1990, 62). Cárdenas beat Salinas decisively by 49 percent to 27 percent in the Federal District, in no small part because competent election observers were placed in virtually all voting locations—a tremendous feat considering the city's size and one not duplicated anywhere else in the country. The AB was a lead organization in this effort in the eleven districts in which it ran candidates. This was a substantial achievement not only for the AB but also for the democratization effort more generally.

After the election, the AB was at the forefront of the popular movement resistance to the official results. It was also instrumental in the formation of the PRD and, unlike the CDP, was able to come to agreement on its own participation within the PRD as well as on party policy. AB leader Marco Rascón received a seat on the executive council, thus attaining the highest position of any urban popular movement leader. The AB was even more adamant than PRD leaders that participation in concertación social via PRONASOL was a strategic error as well as an insult to the opposition's democratic aspirations. While the AB never agreed with all PRD positions, it remained unwavering in the conviction that staying within the party and attempting to radicalize party policy was the best alternative for popular movements. While always unhappy about the influence exercised by the tight-knit group that surrounded Cárdenas, it decisively opted to remain within the party as a source of internal reform.

Although the AB had participated as individual members of the CUD in the convenio de concertación for earthquake reconstruction, it remained relentless in its critique of those popular movement organizations that left

34. The AB was without doubt the lead organization in the 1988 Convención de Anáhuac, which sought to establish an ongoing "popular parliament" to discuss Mexico City statehood as well as an open forum for discussing the city's problems (Rivas 1989, 85).

the Cárdenas camp and joined forces with Salinas through participation in PRONASOL. While some of its criticism was general, much of it focused on specific urban popular movement organizations, particularly the Popular Front Land and Liberty (FPTYL) of Monterrey and the CDP of Durango. These movements were singled out because of their early participation in PRONASOL through highly publicized convenio signings and the subsequent leadership role they took in the formation of the Workers' Party (PT), commonly called the "Partido de Salinas" or "Partido de PRONASOL" by AB members.[35]

These disagreements led to a split in the urban popular movement in 1989 when the AB acted as the lead organization in forming the Convención Nacional Urbano Popular (Urban Popular National Convention [CNUP]), an obvious split from CONAMUP.[36] Neither the AB nor most of its founding organizations were members of CONAMUP.[37] The AB had broken ranks with CONAMUP primarily over what the AB perceived to be domination

35. Despite this adamant public stance, there is significant evidence that some AB projects accepted PRONASOL funding, especially in the second half of the Salinas administration, when the PRD position vis-à-vis interactions with the Salinas administration and its programs mellowed somewhat. Greene asserts that there was PRONASOL funding used in the Ticomán project after Delegación Azapotzalco told them the "red de servicios urbanos" would not support the added strain and they would have to develop an alternative and secure their own funding. Desperate for cash, they secured a matching grant for half the cost form PRONASOL (personal conversation, 1997).

Other examples include Aeropuerto Arenal getting Christmas presents through Niños de Solidaridad; the CDB-Emiliano Zapata attempting unsuccessfully to get included in the Tortivale program (a tortilla subsidy program); and Barrio Nuevo Tultitlán applying for a variety of PRONASOL funds to complete several projects.

These and other, similar examples display the politics at play here. The AB's purist position on PRONASOL succumbed to the necessity of acquiring funds in a system so highly dependent upon federal funding during a time in which a substantial portion of such funding was being channeled through PRONASOL. Pressure to get the work done wore down the public position. Never publicly supporting PRONASOL meant that major funding was sacrificed; slippage in day-to-day project operations allowed for PRONASOL to be used as a subsidiary, secondary source of funds, with a premium placed on keeping the securing of such funds low key.

36. I attended the first meeting of the CNUP in December 1989. Over the entire course of the two-day meeting, Mexico City representatives of CONAMUP sent messages and came by the meeting place to hold talks with AB leaders in an attempt to limit the political fallout of the split. Attendance included about fifty organizations from sixteen states and the Federal District. While some peasant organizations participated, the overwhelming majority were urban movements.

37. ACNR-affiliated movements and leaders, including AB leaders Francisco Saucedo, had indeed been part of CONAMUP in its early stages but had broken ranks with it during the mid-1980s, primarily over what they perceived to be the domination of CONAMUP by OIR.

by OIR (interview by the author). But until 1989, none had attempted to form a parallel organization that would compete directly with CONAMUP. While the organizers insisted that the CNUP was made up of independent popular movements, their discourse was heavily Cardenista, and the man himself opened their founding conference in 1989 with a long speech, while explicit statements of support for him were pervasive throughout the two-day meeting.

The decision to enter into a political alliance with the PRD generated complex and often conflictive relationships within the AB. It could hardly have been otherwise, given the very different political histories and orientations. As one particularly astute PRD leader with origins in the social Left once remarked:

> One of our most serious failings is our ongoing inability to unite as a party. I can not tell you the number of hours we spend arguing among ourselves over doctrine, and seemingly more important at times, over which personality is going to have authority over what. It's not that I was surprised that this would happen at first, given our diverse backgrounds and orientations and just the natural competition for power and position. What dismays me, however, is our seemingly endless inability to learn and to better put these concerns aside in the face of the difficult and significant political challenges that face us. As if creating a viable electoral vehicle to transform neoliberalism was not enough. (Interview by the author, 1998)

As first discussed in Chapter 1, alliances between popular movement actors and parties are difficult to form and even more difficult to maintain. Mexicans from across the political spectrum were struck by the coalition of parties and civil society actors—including but not limited to social movements—that came together to form the FDN in support the Cárdenas's 1988 presidential campaign. As has been explored in previous chapters, this coalition was not able to preserve its unity much beyond Cárdenas's decision to form the PRD in 1989 and pursue an electoral strategy of regime transition rather than to mobilize the country through widespread protest and institutional disruption. Those social movement organizations that did stay within the Cárdenas fold found the experience difficult even if they also believed that it was the right thing to do on both strategic and ethical grounds.

There were a number of specific instances in which the AB came to political blows with high-ranking PRD members over the course of the PRD's first decade.[38] The AB gained some benefits from a close relationship with Cárdenas and the PRD by becoming the lead popular movement in what was—despite its problems—the most important political organization on the nationalist Left. But it also incurred significant costs from its association with the man whom Salinas targeted for political annihilation and from the more general dilemma that confronts any social movement entering electoral politics. Salinas targeted funds and political reforms in such a way as to maximize his ability to undermine the Cardenista opposition, and this included directing funding away from areas where the AB operated (Moguel 1990a; Dresser 1991, 42; interviews by the author). While the AB remained active in the construction of housing projects, most of these were started before Salinas, and their pace certainly declined when Salinas became president.

Just like the CDP, the AB struggled to maintain its social movement identity while implementing development projects that were necessary to maintain legitimacy with its cuadros and rank and file and when movement leadership moved into party leadership positions. This problem becomes even more acute when the social movement leadership is unable or unwilling to decentralize the decision-making process to incorporate cuadros or new leadership. Because the AB was not as centralized as the CDP, I originally thought that this challenge would be easier for it to overcome. However, the devolution of the AB into a number of splinter groups in the early 1990s, consistent with the generalized "process of fierce disarticulation" within the social movement sector during the period of 1991–94, (Casa y Ciudad 1996, 38) proved me wrong. Unlike the CDP, the AB did not completely disappear with the entry into party politics, but it became but a shadow of its former self.

38. Relations between party leaders and popular movement leaders often include elements of mutual animosity that seriously undermine efforts to build power through coalitions. Leftist party leaders have often been frustrated by movement leaders' reluctance to accept the unifying function of the party, and submit to, or at least coordinate, strategy within a party framework. Meanwhile, movement leaders traditionally accuse party leaders of attempting to submit movements to their own designs. Often there appears to be a lack of mutual respect for the "sacrifices and contributions of each to the socialist struggle" that fuels this animosity. While this personal dislike is in most cases insufficient to explain political frictions and strategic decisions to attack specific "political enemies," it is often a contributing factor to shaping the confrontation in important ways. This ongoing historic split between the social and political Left has certainly changed as increasing percentages of the social Left have joined the political Left.

As the top leadership entered party politics, the usual types of disputes—over strategy; balances of power within the AB between various projects, groups, and individuals; and money—proved impossible to resolve. This led to the breakup of the umbrella organization, with several territorial organizations continuing to operate under the AB banner, each claiming affiliation to the AB but no longer coordinating with one another. Other developments contributed to the decline of urban popular movement activity in the Mexico City area during the 1990s, such as control over housing funds shifting back to corporatist institutions that were extremely reluctant to deal with independent movement organizations (Casa y Ciudad 1996, 11–12). By 1995, housing programs in Mexico City were serving those who made at least 5.4 minimum salaries when it was estimated that less than 5 percent of central city residents fit this criteria (4, 39).[39]

By 1998, little doubt remained that the urban popular movement had declined relative to other social and political developments and that the AB's lead role was over. The focus had clearly shifted from the mobilization of specific social sectors (urban poor, the peasantry, and so on) in pursuit of revolutionary socialist ideals to participation in a politics based on the development of a democratic citizenry. Who wins and who loses in this shift is far from obvious. Among other dimensions to this complex question are sharp contrasts between the leaders who for the most part made these decisions by fiat and the cuadros and rank-and-file members who had to live with them. As one cuadro once quipped, "It might be good for democracy, I just don't know. But it sure ain't been so good for those of us who have had to live without the movement and all that it gave to us, day to day" (interview by the author, 1998).[40]

Conclusion

The AB's role as a lead organization during the 1980s protest cycle gave it the power to force government agencies to do what they otherwise would

39. Casa y Ciudad notes that "22 percent [of the economically active population] make salaries inferior to one minimum salary; 47 percent make between one and two times the minimum salary; 26 percent earn between two and five times the minimum salary and the remaining 5 percent surpass these levels" (1996, 4).
40. This issue will be discussed at greater length in the following chapter.

not have done. Without the AB, the entire Casa Propia probably would not have come into being. What distinguished the AB from other urban popular movement actors was its critical focus on the rental market, and especially on the problem of slumlords. The AB was also distinguished by the strength and tenacity of its midlevel activists who forced it to function in a more participatory manner than was true of most Mexican urban popular movements. In keeping with Maria Cook's (1996) analysis of internal democracy in her study of Mexico's dissident teacher's union, my judgment is that the AB's relatively more advanced democratic practice served the organization well. This internal structure enabled the AB to persist—albeit in a weakened state—after top leadership entered electoral politics. Furthermore, it encouraged a more active democratic practice, allowing more people within the movement organization to find, nurture, and benefit from a more actively democratic experience than was the norm within not only the inclusionary authoritarian regime but also within the urban popular movement.

Technical expertise, once not particularly important in the urban popular movement, became highly valued as the AB, again reflecting a broader movement trend, attempted to beat government agencies at their own game. As it did for the CDP, this process refocused strategy, moving it from a revolutionary Marxist–style confrontation with the state to negotiation for program benefits that then extended into the area of program implementation. Because of its membership, the AB was able to adopt strategies that were dependent on legal and technical expertise beyond the capabilities of most urban popular movement organizations. Admittedly, the AB was never able to win a high percentage of its legal cases, but that it was able to do competent battle on this front is impressive.

The AB played a decisive role among popular movement actors in the Cárdenas camp, first in the FDN and then again in the PRD. The organization maintained moral and practical superiority by insisting on elections while refusing government concessions. It attacked those groups, such as the CDP, which, in their judgment, continued to subject themselves to clientelist practices. In response, they were accused of being utopian by some and disingenuous by others.

In Chapter 1, the costs incurred by social movements in maintaining autonomy from the state were first raised. The most common costs include loss of political influence and of material benefits. This is particularly important in a setting such as Mexico where the state historically has dominated funding sources. Particularly relevant in this context is that maintaining autonomy from Salinas and PRONASOL funding had the great potential of undermining movement power by increasing discontent within the bases as they observed others gaining access to substantial material benefits. The AB countered that this was a cost worth paying, given the potential for forcing through a regime transition. Others countered that they could not afford such costs, adding, in some cases, that the AB's ability to resist PRONASOL was greatly facilitated the group's heavy focus on housing projects that were not funded by PRONASOL, some, in fact, being funded by World Bank sources.

The AB served, along with the UCP, as one of the lead urban popular movement organizations within the Cardenista fold that broke ranks with CONAMUP over the issue of PRONASOL and PRD party membership. While the AB insisted that PRD affiliation did not affect it, evidence suggests that, while there were advantages, costs were paid. First, internal tensions resulted from the AB's efforts to maintain itself as an active social movement organization while the leadership simultaneously invested large amounts of time and energy on party issues. Second, evidence suggests that the AB suffered in its ability to secure material concessions from the state by affiliating itself with a national leader who was singled out as the standing president's key enemy. These two costs contributed directly to the 1993 split and the AB's subsequent decline.

Chapter 1 concludes with a section titled "Vision and Survival." The argument is that experience demonstrates, at least in the Latin American context, that a neat distinction between these two core movement concerns—as sometimes appears in New Social Movement theory—is more a product of abstract theorizing than an accurate depiction of history. While many popular movement participants would counter Rivas's claim that there exist no historical precedents for the AB's struggle to democratize the city (1989, 17–18), it is beyond serious dispute that the AB was at the forefront of this effort between 1987 and 1991. Even more notable is perhaps that clean elections remained central to the AB's agenda throughout the 1989–93 period, at the same time as most other urban popular movement organizations were returning to the more traditional methods of organizational advancement and gaining of state concessions. While the AB's access to alternative funding sources certainly eased its ability to largely repudiate PRONASOL funding, its strident attacks on the regime and its insistence that democratic elections were part of Mexico's future has certainly been historically vindicated. Furthermore, its democratic discourse, leadership role in moving the subject of discussion on the left from revolutionary vanguard to citizenship, and imaginative cultural politics no doubt influenced the body politic to criticize the regime and to believe in and work toward the possibility of democratization.

SIX

Comparisons and Conclusions

[When] blacks [in the United States] won the vote in the South and a share of patronage in the municipalities of the North in response to the disturbances of the 1960s, black leaders were absorbed into electoral and bureaucratic politics and became the ideological proponents of the shift "from protest to politics."
—JAMES RUSTIN, IN FRANCES FOX PIVEN AND RICHARD CLOWARD, *Poor People's Movements: Why They Succeed, How They Fail.*

The central thesis that has governed the writing of this book is that it is important to understand the Mexican urban popular movement and other similar movements around the world from two perspectives. First, they are important to those who participate in and work with them. Significant social movements change significant numbers of lives in significant ways. Second, social movements of import change the culture and political economy in which they exist.

The urban popular movement and its organizations were important political actors in the fundamental changes that took place in Mexican politics between the 1970s and 1990s. The early risers of the 1970s, such as the CDP, developed repertories that were emulated and fitted to local conditions by the movement organizations that mushroomed in number and influence during the 1979–89 protest cycle. President Salinas responded to the challenge posed by these organizations with a dramatic effort to reestablish the regime's legitimacy between 1988 and 1994. In this complex process, urban popular movement organizations generated grassroots support for the new political parties as well as donating their leaders to party work and as candidates.

The organization and institution building of the UPI and then the CDP as well as the CUD and then the AB were made possible by widespread mobilization. Leaders combined forces with "regular people" who were willing to defy state and PRI authorities' notion of reasonable and just, and they effectively pressured regime officials to negotiate on different terms. The histories of both Durango and Mexico City movements demonstrate the power to do this—repeatedly. Of course, they were unable to revolutionize the system so that it approximated their visions, particularly those of their leaders. However, they came to be recognized as political and social subjects who were legitimate interlocutors with the state. Their mobilization forced government representatives to do what they would not have otherwise done: negotiate with actors unaffiliated with the existing PRI structure. The acquiescence that may have once adequately characterized the urban poor was replaced by something quite different.

The historical realities of the 1980s and 1990s are clearly distinct from those of the 1960s and 1970s as told by Fagen and Tuohy (1972), Cornelius (1975), Eckstein (1977b), Lomnitz (1977), and Montaño (1976). While the AB of Mexico City and the CDP of Durango may be atypical in terms of size and influence, they were far from the only important urban popular organizations. The inclusionary authoritarian regime failed to effectively incorporate this rich array of independent social organizations—which represented the largest single population sector in the country. The urban popular movement introduced, with force, important issues of social justice into the nation's discussion. It forced regime officials to respond, most notably in PRONASOL. PRONASOL—love it or hate it—clearly represented a significant shift from past policy. The migration of social movement leadership into political parties—love it or hate it—clearly resulted in an elevation of the concerns of the urban poor at the level of discourse. A combination of neoliberal economic policy making and relatively staid economic growth lessened the material advantages accrued to the urban poor during the 1990s.

The histories presented here provide ample evidence that skillful mobilization and negotiation, while unable to transform neoliberalism, did contribute to the creation of programs that mitigated the severity of economic restructuring. Without these organized and highly mobilized movement organizations, de la Madrid's concertación or Salinas's PRONASOL would not have been so substantial; nor would they have responded as well to the real material needs of the people. While the movements were unsuccessful in their efforts to combat the immense powers that drive the globalization of neoliberalism, they were able to shape some—if not enough—of its contours. Although they were unable to force a regime transition from the authoritarianism that has always been at the core of the nation's politics into a vibrant social democracy of their choosing, they were nevertheless successful in contributing to the pluralism that has increasingly characterized political debate and representation in Mexico at the local, state, and federal levels.

Most of the urban poor did not actively participate or clearly affiliate with social movement organizations. But the urban social movement profoundly changed the political atmosphere of many cities. Their work enhanced the ability of opposition parties to mobilize voters during the 1980s and 1990s, particularly in locations where the movement organization was of major significance, as was the case for the AB in Mexico City and the CDP in Durango. Although no conclusive empirical studies have probed the relationship between movement activity and opposition votes during the 1980s and 1990s, it is undeniable that it contributed significantly to electoral outcomes. In both cities, opposition candidates gained the top elected posts with strong support from urban popular movement organizations. While this relationship is most obvious in Durango, it is clear that the AB, along with other Mexico City organizations, played key roles in the democratic transition that has engulfed the politics of the federal district.

This book's findings challenge some of what Piven and Cloward (1979; 1992) predict on the basis of their deep knowledge of U.S. social movements. Most important, their contention that organization building during times of intense mass mobilization leads inexorably to demobilization does not hold true for either the CDP or the AB, in which organization building not only coexisted with continued social mobilization but actually facilitated the construction of progressive identities that, in turn, generated and rejuvenated mobilization. The history recounted here shows clearly that organization did not lead to demobilization until the late 1980s with the advent of PRONASOL and party building. PRONASOL in Durango clearly resulted in a moderation of militant activity by the CDP. As argued by Piven and Cloward, leaders make a key strategic decision when they decide to exchange mobilization and the institutional disruption it can cause for material and political reward. The CDP leaders clearly negotiated this deal with both President Salinas and the governor. Once this was done, the CDP was finished. In the case of the AB, once its top leadership merged into the PRD the AB came to be but a shadow of its former self. Thus, it is not organization building *per se* that leads to demobilization. The implication of this study for future research on this question is that *the analysis needs to focus on the details of what the specific organization building implies for specific mobilizations.* It can enhance or discourage. In the Mexican case, as more and more of the preexisting movement leaderships moved increasingly into the process of party building, the loci of social movement mobilizations and institutional disruptions were reoriented away from the urban popular movement to other dynamic sources, perhaps most notably to the Zapatista movement that emerged during the 1990s in the southern state of Chiapas.

Urban politics of the 1990s saw the emergence of a host of new actors, particularly in Mexico City, where citizen groups proliferated. As one veteran of urban politics put it to me:

> The urban popular movement is clearly not what it used to be. But look at the conversations occurring today: democratization of organizations and of the national economy and politics at large; the environment; gender; and of course the relationship between poverty and the national economic-development model. . . . The urban popular movement was at the early forefront of placing these issues in public debate. What we have today is better, because the urban movement was weakened by its all-too-frequent internal authoritarian practices, especially the *caciquismo* [political bossism] that pervaded. And it was also weakened by its reliance on a relatively narrow class base; by definition it could not lead the national transition. But what we are enjoying today is in part a legacy of what we in the urban popular movement generated, gave life to, after the student movement came to a close in the late 1960s and early 1970s. We should be grateful. We as Mexicans should remember. (Interview, 1998)

Social movement theorist and historian Manuel Castells (1983) was one of the first to put forward a conceptualization of a politics of consumption as distinct from a politics of production as the basis of revolutionary proletarian resistance. The history of the Mexican urban popular movement from the 1970s to the present demonstrates a clear focus on the politics of consumption. Political opportunities encouraged mobilization around issues of collective consumption: housing; basic services related to housing (water, electricity, drainage, and sewage); and health and educational services. For the new urban popular movement of the 1970s, the prime target was not private capital, although its participants engaged private capital as renters or in land invasions. For these movements, the primary target of reform was the state, which did not limit them to the confines of consumption politics when they sometimes ventured into the politics of production.

A good example is found in the CDP Labor Committees, organized to take direct action against employers. The formation of these organizations was propelled by consumption pressures arising from rapid rural-to-urban migration and the relatively weak mechanisms of political incorporation combined with radical political entrepreneurs looking for opportunities. It is important to note that the transition from classes to masses, from work-place mobilizations to neighborhoods, described in these pages in regard to Mexico was part of a broader trend in Latin America.[1] This focus by social movements on the state has not been a constant in Mexico. For example, in the famous renters movement in Veracruz in 1922, when the majority of city residents participated in a dramatic collective action aimed at forcing landlords to improve housing conditions, the *inquilinarios* (renters) "always addressed themselves to the landlord, to the exclusion of any call to state intervention for the regulation of rents" (Castells 1983, 47).[2]

Mexico's urban movement organizations have both similarities and sharp differences with the new social movements of Europe that are described by Melucci. In both, "the organizational forms of movements are not just 'instrumental' for their goals, they are a goal in themselves" (1989, 60). What this refers to is the importance given to internal organi-zational life: life for participants within the movement is supposed to be transformative and liberating. The history recounted here makes clear that efforts were made to do just this, despite the problems in implementation. In this way, the Mexican urban popular movement can be placed in the tra-dition of new social movements.

However, Melucci also claims that in Europe, "if the basis of contempo-rary conflicts has shifted towards the production of meaning, then they seemingly have little to do with politics" (71). Clearly, the Mexican urban popular movement was deeply concerned with politics. New social move-ments appear as extremely differentiated in Melucci's portrayal, with dis-parate power centers and logics operating within the same movement, which can lead to an inability to mobilize. The two case studies here pro-vide a sharp contrast not only between the two Mexican organizations and

1. For a particularly good statement of this transition with reference to Chile, see Gar-retón 1989.
2. As Castells claims, "The strike of the *inquilinarios* of Veracruz, Mexico, in 1922, . . . was probably the most important social struggle triggered by urban issues to take place in Latin America before World War II" (3).

those in Melucci's conceptualization but also between different groups within each movement organization. In Durango, the Maoist leadership determinedly resisted challenges to hierarchy and efforts to decentralize power and create new logics. This resulted in the stifling of creativity among the bases and cuadros and a reduction in the recruitment pool for new leadership. This contrasts with the situation for the AB, which, with its disparate logics and power centers, essentially guaranteed that the transition from movement to party would break up the unitary front that the AB had maintained, despite internal tensions for its first five years (1987–91). The extreme centralization of power within a small leadership contributed directly to the collapse of the CDP as soon as leadership entered party politics. By contrast, the AB's degree of decentralization determined that it would factionalize and continue to exist.

Interviews with movement activists in 1999 revealed the costs of disillusionment and "dropout" when faith in a transformative project was undermined by leaders' responses to changing opportunity structures. One woman with years of experience as a founder and leader of a CDP colonia, had this to say:

> The change has been horrible, devastating for me personally and for those I work with. We founded this colonia because we needed a good place to live, but we maintained it with a sense of optimism and a different way of living because we were CDP*istas*. We held ourselves and our leaders to a higher standard. We were proud of what we had accomplished and proud of who we were. When we went to our leaders they responded to us. They would come out and visit with us, attend our meetings. And we would together make a plan of action, and they would come through for us. If a *compañero* or *compañera* was in trouble, they would personally go to the police or the judge and help them out. If it was an issue with the government, they would lead us in the negotiation strategies. Now, they are big shots. Now they are the PT. They no longer listen to us, they no longer respond. They are rude, giving us the feeling that we should go away. In the past, when they would hold a meeting or a march, people of our colonia would be there in strength, waving our *mantas* [painted signs with a slogan]. Now, if they have a march or rally like they did the other day, very few go, and they only go if they are paid. (Interview by the author, 1999)

Such payment came in the form of actual cash payments, food for the day, or other things, in an adoption of a common PRI practice. To claim that the CDP/PT resorted to this *priísta* tack rather than relying on the support of its bases is to level a serious charge. While not all cuadros I spoke with were as pessimistic as this woman, many were. Some members of the top leadership recognized the problem and took steps to remedy it, steps that largely failed.[3] Gonzalo Yáñez singled out the leadership's inability to effectively manage the significant increases in money, power, and fame as leading to the organization's degeneration. Competition for party and government positions undermined solidarity and progressive consciousness. The increased number of electoral slots afforded the opposition, the sharp raise in salaries for these positions, and the increased government money provided to political parties were viewed by some as intentional efforts to produce precisely the negative effects that have occurred in Durango and elsewhere (interviews by the author, 1998, 1999).

Much of the 1980s and early 1990s literature on Latin American social movements took a very optimistic view of the power of movement. This literature tended to focus on the proliferation of identities that was said to characterize many social movements, to the exclusion of detailed analyses intent on evaluating the capacity of the movements to effect policy making and outcomes. However, another, much more pessimistic line of thought also made its way into the literature. A good example is found in Castillo Palma's (1986) evaluation of the urban popular movement in Puebla, Mexico. Palma condemned the Puebla movement for its inability to move beyond criticizing state policy. He was disillusioned by its inability to pursue a transformative idea of "the alternative city," by the clientelism of its leaders, and by the fact that its rank and file and cuadros were ill-informed and rarely participated in decision making.

The complex political dynamics of the movement that I observed during the 1980s and 1990s lead me to steer a course between these two

---

3. For example, Gonzalo Yáñez gave up his position as federal deputy to run for governor in 1998. At the end of the unsuccessful campaign, rather than resume his responsibilities as federal deputy he decided to stay in Durango and found (along with Armando Meza) a national school of training for the PT. The driving force of the school was to return to the historic values of social and political transformation that first motivated the movement. Interviews and personal observations since that time suggest that little if anything came of this effort. Juan Salazar, a prominent CDP cuadro, attempted to reignite the CDP, and when that failed, to bring the "best of the CDP" way of doing things to some union activities. These efforts, while well intentioned, were modest in their outcomes.

extremes. The Mexican urban popular movement of the 1970s to the 1990s achieved both stellar accomplishments in the realm of identity and consciousness and was on occasion able to use this new identity to *influence* specific policy processes and outcomes. Both the CDP and the AB, along with a host of other urban popular movement organizations, clearly helped to mitigate the difficulties associated with urban poverty in Mexico. Their achievements are truly impressive. However, it is just as true that the Mexican urban popular movement, alone or in alliance, was unable to *transform* policy process or outcomes.[4] Reforms, yes; transformation, no. While the election results of August 2000 indicated significant change, a non-PRI president certainly has not in itself meant the end of authoritarian politics. On balance, the successes and the failures of the Mexican urban popular movement in the 1980s protest cycle and the electorally focused 1990s, are neither black nor white, but can best be described as complex colorings of gray.[5]

Different Paths: The CDP and the AB

Structured interviews and many more open ended-conversations with a variety of movement participants and scholarly observers reveal a cross section of opinion regarding the degree to which the AB differed from the CDP. Clearly, the AB took a fierce stance in alignment with Cárdenas's no-negotiation policy early in the Salinas administration, while the CDP took a very public position of participation in concertación and PRONASOL. However,

4. The successful adoption of neoliberal policies that accompanied virtually all the democratic transitions (certainly in Latin America) demonstrates the inability of the social Left to fundamentally influence the policy process at this time. From my perspective, it is as wrong to dismiss the role of social movements in democratic transitions (Brazil and Chile being perhaps the most undeniable) as it is to pretend that they maintained significant influence during the period of democratic consolidation. For a literature review, see P. Haber 1996a.

5. A favorite relative of mine, Uncle Max, once a member, and always a sympathizer, of the American Communist Party, once said to me: "You know your trouble, Paul? You don't understand that the world is white and black. There are good guys and bad guys. Why are you always so bent on painting the world in shades of gray?" I remain unrepentant.

While this tendency to celebrate or disparage social movements is pronounced in the social movement literature, a number of authors paint well in shades of gray (see, for example, Starn 1992, 1995). The question of how much the relative degree of success or failure attributed to a movement derives from history and how much from the biases of the author is both intriguing and usually difficult to answer.

as argued in Chapter 5, evidence exists that some AB projects accepted PRONASOL funding, especially in the second half of the Salinas *sexenio*.

In fact, the AB always insisted that it was not really an urban popular movement organization at all, preferring to call itself a citizen movement. A review of AB literature, AB leadership statements in the press, and personal interviews reveals a steadfast insistence that the AB was different—in its resolute determination not to repeat what it believed to be the rigid thinking and authoritarian practices endemic to both traditional Left parties and OIR*ista* popular movements.

And the contrast between CDP and AP is striking. In the case of the CDP, it was unusual for either midlevel activists or the rank and file to do anything but support positions taken by the leadership. The history presented in Chapter 4 details a number of episodes in which the top leadership shut down such opposition to the detriment of the movement. Such action was detrimental because it made a lie of the CDP's claim to be a practicing democracy at home. And it was detrimental because it discouraged or killed good ideas that were presented and thus ensured that less would be forthcoming in the future as would-be leaders self-censored themselves. Finally, it was detrimental because it ensured that once top leadership moved into party politics, there would be no new leaders to take their place. As detailed in the history presented in Chapter 5, although the "gang of four" founding leaders of the AB certainly dominated many key decisions, the social makeup of the AB—more class diverse than that of the CDP—contributed importantly to the democratic flavor of internal debates within the AB and to the AB's reaping the benefits.

In contrast to the CDP, the AB insisted that the Mexican public, and most emphatically urban popular movement organizations, were morally obligated to pressure the regime to act legally and rationally, even if this resulted in forgoing possible advantages. The AB argued, loudly and often, that since the regime had made clear by its actions in the 1988 presidential elections, its refusal to "democratize from above," massive resistance from below was required. The CDP argued that the structure of political opportunities (or to use the phrase most common to movement participants themselves, balance of forces) was not optimal for massive resistance and that Cárdenas was not leading an effective mobilization but rather was party building himself. The CDP contended that AB positions were self-serving, since their position in the capital, and their close ties to Mexico City's mayor Manuel Camacho, gave them access to funding sources outside

PRONASOL. The CDP did not have these advantages, as their regime relationships were centered around PRONASOL head Carlos Rojas. The CDP argued that there was no small amount of disingenuousness involved in the AB position of superior moral authority on their no-negotiation position.

This deep split between the two most important lead urban popular movement organizations in Mexico, and its explication through historical narrative, provides the opportunity for significant insights. First, and perhaps most important, the political relationships of individual social movement organizations are absolutely fundamental. As true as the adage "Where you stand has much to do with where you sit" is "The terms of your relationships have much to do with your identity and action."

The AB and CDP's political opportunity structure and the ways they understood how best to exploit these opportunities were fundamentally shaped by their relationships. The CDP's relationship environment was Durango, an economically depressed area of Mexico. The organization got seriously into the act of mobilizing when the fundamental need was the creation of new housing for large numbers of recent rural-to-urban migrants and when the repertoire of land invasions and the construction of colonias populares was tolerated, if not outright encouraged, by President Echeverría. The CDP emerged before the onset of the 1980s protest cycle and quickly rose to prominence within it. It thus rapidly developed the dual stance of negotiating with the state, making allies or coming to accommodation with state actors while simultaneously taking the position of a radical social movement bent on the socialist transformation of Mexico. The creation of a large base in the capital city of Durango that over time spread to other localities in this rural state, with a weak capitalist class, which was run in the deep tradition of Mexican political bossism, fundamentally shaped the identity that the CDP developed and the political strategies that occurred to them and seemed to work best.

The AB's relationship environment and the timing of its existence shaped that organization just as fundamentally. While the CDP emerged in the 1970s in an environment with almost no political momentum for the opposition, the AB emerged on the crest of the 1980s protest cycle in the downtown area of Mexico's political, financial, and cultural capital. The AB emerged out of the CUD and all the momentum for the opposition that was created in Mexico City by the government's inept management following the 1985 earthquake at a time when the regime was in wholesale political crisis, largely as a result of the 1980s economic emergency. This meant that the AB was extremely likely to take on a stronger stance of "no negotiation" with the Salinas administration than was true of the long-accommodating CDP, which existed in a very different political landscape, one characterized by very different relationships with very different kinds of people and operating by means of very different political logics.

Even movement organizations in Mexico that at first appear to be the most democratic and transformative often upon close critical scrutiny reveal problems that reflect a broader Mexican culture and social relations. Clientelism, corruption, political bossism, factionalism and sectarianism, sexism, polyphony, intimidation, and even violence between conflicting movement factions are essential parts of movement history. The grassroots participants were both inspired and betrayed by their leadership. It is critically important to include the good, the bad, and the ugly in the telling of these stories, lest we reduce them to quaint folktales of virtue. In an authoritarian country with one of the worst distributions of income in the world, these people dare to dream and envision a better world. We must see their efforts as those of human beings and resist the impulse to make them saints. The urban popular movement of Mexico represents the flawed efforts of passionate human beings in pursuit of utopia—and making deals along the way.

One may favor over others certain positions and forms of behavior of these movement organizations and of others that followed. It would be my argument, however, that an adequate understanding of the different positions can be gained only by knowing the environments and relationship matrixes of the two organizations. Judgments made on the basis of political preference without regard to the relevant environmental and relational histories can be only superficial.

Another insight that the comparative study of these two movements provides is that the historical trajectories of specific organizations can be very different within the same movement. While major movements are usually composed of more than two significant organizations (the Mexican urban popular movement surely was), if two or three organizations are key within the movement, not only in the power they themselves display but also in their being representative of a large grouping or even of a majority of organizations, then the comparative study of these two or three key organizations offers an effective methodological path to pursue.

Repression and Co-optation

José Luis Reyna long ago observed that autonomous political mobilization in Mexico was "the Achilles' heel of the system" (1977, 164). While changes tend to be resisted by the powerful, comfortable, and satisfied, if change becomes inevitable, attention turns to managing it so that the status quo is disrupted as little as possible. This is why governments often are willing to make concessions, shifting the political opportunity structure to reward those who are willing to use a more regularized access to power. From the government perspective, it is better to reform than to risk the nightmare of uncertainty that powerful, disruptive social movements represent.

In these terms, the Salinas strategy was a brilliant success. He ensured that neoliberalism was established as the economic model, rebuilt the system of state alliances sufficient to maintain political stability, and successfully undermined much of the threat Cárdenas represented. Salinas consciously left the job of democratizing the political system to his successor, Ernesto Zedillo. When this democratization allowed for a PAN victory in the summer of 2000, the economic model Salinas implemented was firmly established and not called into question.

The electoral political reforms of late 1970s through the end of the 1990s were designed to seduce social actors to enter the electoral arena. Political opportunities were opened as a means to channel threats to the system's stability in the least disruptive way possible. In the political arena, the radical opposition was socialized into valuing the benefits of access to personal and organizational monetary resources. Access to decision making brings not only personal satisfaction but may also introduce real reforms that, while far short of the Left's historical goals, are still viewed as positive. As one seasoned social Left activist turned elected officeholder commented:

> Look, there comes a time when it is no longer sufficient or satisfying to simply articulate the utopia. There comes a time when it becomes urgent to take the reins of power, and in this country that means the state, and see what can be done. Does it tarnish the appeal of the dream? Of course it does. But like I said, there comes a time when one senses there is no choice but to go forward, pay the price, and do the best one can do in the reality of government and governing. (Interview by the author, 1998)

When the social Left enters into executive and legislative offices at the local, state, and federal levels, its priorities shift. Winning elections and gaining support for moderate reforms requires very different resources and political consciousness from what is needed for instrumental disruption by a social movement in the pursuit of radical change.

The changes brought by the 1979 electoral reform, designed to enhance the appearance of democratic elections, pale in comparison with the urgent reforms taken in the wake of the 1988 electoral shock. If the regime was concerned in the late 1970s with appearances and stability, by the late 1980s and 1990s, it was focused on survival. The FDN's success in 1988 demonstrated to the Left that electoral victory was a very real possibility. This shift in political opportunity structure resulted, predictably, in both the political and social Left moving increasingly into the electoral arena. The Mexican inclusionary authoritarian regime masqueraded as a democracy. Its ability to do so was conditioned by its moderation in the use of repression against domestic threats to its hegemony along with the holding of regular elections. The use of too much force or the blatant use of corruption to avoid electoral defeat would undermine the regime. Thus, it was imperative that Salinas be successful in restoring the impression of relatively competitive elections without recourse to excessive political repression. Some repression was possible, and it was exercised against the PRD. However, the Mexican regime clearly had to work within much tighter restrains than those of the exclusionary authoritarian regimes that, during the 1970s and 1980s, existed in much of Latin America (in Chile, Argentina, Uruguay, Nicaragua, and El Salvador, among other countries).

Salinas's task was to produce just enough electoral reform, combined with expertly publicized public policy successes, to restore confidence in the electoral option and resuscitate the PRI at the ballot box. As detailed in previous chapters, Salinas achieved this, and he did so primarily through three avenues of action. First, he relegitimated the electoral process by hiring left-leaning and fiercely independent intellectual José Woldenberg to head up a newly configured Federal Electoral Commission (IFE). The IFE oversaw a number of reforms that effectively produced federal elections that were relatively free of charges of fraud, in the midterm elections of 1991 and even more significantly in the presidential elections of 1994. This was augmented by a number of very successful policy initiatives and an economic recovery that lasted until the financial crisis of late 1994 and 1995 after Salinas had left office. No policy was more important in this program of political renewal than PRONASOL. PRONASOL served to both divide the Left and raise the social justice credentials of the regime, thereby undermining Cárdenas and the PRD's electoral appeal. Furthermore, Salinas came to an accommodation with the PAN that ensured that the PAN would be able to "secure its victories" when they truly happened at the state and local levels, an accommodation not attempted or reached with a PRD that found its local and state electoral efforts still vulnerable to the regime's dirty tricks.

From Movement to Party: Implications for Mexico's Democratic Transition

Rightly or wrongly, many within the social Left came to believe that their organizing model of the 1980s—to create sectoral coordinating bodies—in the words of one Mexico City activist, "exhausted itself," so that when the electoral logic of 1988 appeared, there was little alternative but to seize it. Feelings among the social Left regarding this shift were decidedly mixed at best. The following quote from Leopoldo Enzástiga of the Unión de Colonias Populares, one of Mexico City's veteran movement organizations, expresses a sentiment shared by many: "Today we are paying a high price in sacrificing the momentum gained in the age of the coordinadoras to create social subjects to work for politically democratic options. These movements have all but disappeared, they have in reality converted to parties. While many retain a dual identity of party and movement, they have lost the capacity to generate subjects equal to the task of confronting an ever more complex social reality" (cited in Bolos 1995, 261–62).

Enzástiga also makes a point that is heard less often, that the social initiative has passed from the movement to the NGOs. I am not sure that I would concur wholesale with this observation, but I would certainly agree that the precipitous decline in the urban popular movement has coincided with the initiative being transferred to the NGO sector that has continued to grow from the 1980s to the present.[6] What are the implications of this for Mexico's democratization?

---

6. One measure of the significant and growing NGO presence is the 568 organizations that met for the 1995 National Citizen Organizations Encounter. There was an impressive array of issue areas covered, including gender, human rights of various stripes, gay rights, AIDS, the environment, and poverty (San Juan Victoria 1995, 157). Such a meeting held ten years earlier would have attracted only a relatively small fraction of this number of attendees.

They are mixed. On the one hand, the accumulating experience of a proliferation of NGO organizations dedicated to issues of urban poverty in particular and the quality of urban life more generally is a positive contribution to the policy-making process, as such NGOs weigh in and contribute to the quality of urban policies. On balance, NGOs, in my view, help to ensure that public policy reflects the concerns of the poor and working classes, along with those regarding the natural environment, more than would be the case if only those with commercial interests had the ear of policy makers.

On the other hand, NGOs do not generally endeavor to elicit the widespread participation of large numbers of people, thereby aiding inhabitants to become informed citizens contributing to the public policy process. As a result, they do not serve as training grounds for citizens as, at least potentially, can social movements dedicated to broad-based participation.

Enzástiga goes on to direct attention again at differentiating movements from parties—although he is careful to explicitly state that this does not mean a return to old autonomous sectoral social organizations. Rather, "it should be an organization that integrates the political with the social, that the new social subject is the citizen, the civic; it is a new option, the new social movements should work toward this conception" (Bolos 1995, 262). He is speaking here to an issue analyzed in depth in Chapter 2 in the present volume: the coordinadora option faded—perhaps most notably for the urban poor—as CONAMUP proved incapable of effectively addressing the electoral question. As more and more member organizations were forced—sometimes by their own membership, as was the case with the CDP—to enter electoral politics on the side of Cárdenas, the option of staying mute on electoral participation and a more sophisticated position vis-à-vis specific public policies doomed CONAMUP to irrelevance.

Related to this is the imperative of collective identity as discussed by Melucci. He argues that the inevitable outcome of the failure to continue the "on-going process of construction of a sense of we" is the disintegration of the movement (1989, 218). Clearly, the "we" constructed by the Mexican urban popular movement during the 1970s and 1980s was seriously eroded by the process of party formation in the 1990s. One can certainly hypothesize that this has been replaced by a new collective identity and perhaps even solidarity in the recently formed Left parties. But given the logic of electoral competition and the necessity of appealing to more conservative voters, this would seem to be highly unlikely. The evidence presented in the case studies here certainly argues against this hypothesis. During the 1980s I disagreed with well-known Mexican sociologist Sergio Zermeño's pessimistic reading of societal anomie in Mexico, arguing that the disintegration he correctly observed to be emanating from neoliberalism was at least in part compensated for by the surge of rural and urban social movements.[7] With the decline in social movement activity, I have come to disagree with him less strongly today than I did ten years ago. The existence of widespread anomie, in Mexico and of course elsewhere, undermines the vitality of the democratic experience.

Several factors account for the movement's decline in favor of a party strategy. First, diverse, competing, and most important, nonregenerative political currents, such as represented by Política Popular, oir-lm, Punto Crítico, and acnr, always coexisted uneasily within the national urban popular movement. Differences and competition between these currents and the movement organizations they helped form often served to divide the fragile alliances, as the conflict between Política Popular and Línea de Masas in Durango shows. These currents were mostly led by the "generation of 1968" and they had developed crucial political skills—such as the art of mobilization and negotiation and alliances (including with state reformers). However, they failed to train a capable "second generation" of leaders from among their most talented cuadros, who too often were relegated to cheering sections. As a result, when the leadership moved into party politics, these currents ceased to function. Even worse, in some cases, such as Durango, the historical leadership showed an unfortunate penchant for undermining new leadership that had any kind of mind of its own.

Second, the 1988 election had dramatically transformed the urban political conversation into one focused on democratic transition. Within the urban popular movement, the discourse of identity construction shifted from discussion on developing the revolutionary subject (both collective and individual) to that on forming individual citizens who would work together for the common good. The transition from transformative actor to citizen caused significant confusion and conflict for leaders, cuadros, and bases, and the inability to respond effectively to this new discourse contributed to the movement's declining health. By the mid-1990s, elected officials, many of whom have deep roots in the urban popular movements themselves, reported the most clientelistic and authoritarian

7. See, for example, Zermeño 1990.

of their constituencies were the remaining urban popular movements. With their continued alienation from the newly formed parties—most notably from the PRD—the urban popular movement sector was reduced to grubbing for public services, sometimes, as in Mexico City and Durango, from officials who once were their leaders!

A third challenge emerged that has contributed significantly to this decline—the diverse interests, values, and identities existing within the movement: feminist demands to change gender relations and prioritize issues such as domestic violence and children; housing issues, including the differences between renters, self-built-housing owners, and those who live in public-housing projects; ecological concerns in oftentimes fierce battle with priorities for economic development and modernization. These differences were not simply those of material interest for different identities bringing with them different mythologies. The failure of the urban popular movement to respond to this shifting terrain contributed to its loss of centrality in the politics of the urban poor in the post-1988 period. These divisions, seen in individual movement organizations, as well as in full regalia at CONAMUP meetings during the 1980s, required the creation of a structure that could adequately accommodate the movement's obvious and growing diversity. The level of discontent regarding the gap between word and deed was palpable at CONAMUP meetings in the late-1980s, and deep frustration surfaced when leadership attempted to stifle these issues.

A fourth factor in movement decline is the process of ascendancy within the PRD. Building strong working relationships with collective movement actors has been devalued, while the ability to be influential in competition for party leadership positions has been prioritized. Thus, the rational actor seeking power, prestige, and position within the PRD is not encouraged to develop the movement-party relationship or, for that matter, to democratize the relationship between citizen and party. The shift from a movement to a party strategy was, in my view, both cause and affect of the protest cycle's decline. If Cárdenas had moved quickly following the 1988 election to become a credible symbol for a regime transition in the spirit of those of Eastern Europe or South Africa, there is little doubt that the vast majority of the urban popular movement would have supported him *con ganas* (with enthusiasm) and that leadership would have had no choice but to follow, regardless of its own personal preferences. As it was, the extremely ambiguous position of Cárdenas as national leader and the turn toward party construction opened up divergent possibilities and choices that ensured that a broad-based national agreement would not be forthcoming.

Not surprisingly, analysts of the transition to electoral politics are diverse, encompassing the optimistic, the depressed, and those who insist that it is too early to write the final chapter. Representative perspectives include the following:

> If we think of the urban popular movement as a set of specific organizations, yes, they have declined. They are no longer the focal point of action they once were. But if we step back and look at civil society in broader terms, we see a creative blossoming of identities that is enriching the country. (Former UCP leader, interview by the author, 1999)

> In 1988 we were at the threshold of a dream come true. The urban movements had contributed in important ways to setting the conditions for change. We had been on the front lines of resistance to authoritarian rule. We had been jailed and beaten. Some of us had been killed. But they could not deny our existence, and try as they might, they could not erase us from history. We persisted. And in 1988 we were on the precipice. Cárdenas gave us what we needed, a symbol to rally around. The regime was corrupt. Everyone knew that. What the people needed was a vehicle for hope. And what happened? They bribed us into complacency, drunk with the illusions that a few of us in minor positions can make a difference. But we are not making a difference; well, we are not making enough difference. It's disgusting to see *compañeros* who once were truly leaders that inspired solidarity now driving shiny cars and eating lunch with their PRI benefactors, all behind this facade of political maturity. It's bullshit. (Still-active movement leader, interview by the author, 1999)

> Some things have gotten better. We are running the government of the largest city in the world. On the other hand, we remain basically powerless to affect the most important policies that are still made by the president. If we are not able eventually to win that office I'm afraid that the best advantages will be limited to

those of us who have been able to find places in the government
or in the party. The majority of the people, even the majority of
the cuadros, remain on the outside. (High-ranking cuadro, interview by the author, 1999)

In my conversations with state reformers, they expressed interest in
shaping independent movement organizations in ways that facilitated the
implementation of effective programs and—in some cases—the progressive ideals they held. Movement actors were engaged in something quite
similar—attempting to shape the ideals and program dispositions of these
same state actors. These interactions were not just a negotiated exchange
of power, but one of ideals as well. They demonstrate one way that movements effect policy reform: by creating opportunities for political elites.
"Reform is most likely when challengers from outside the polity provide a
political incentive for elites within it to advance their own policies and
careers" (Tarrow 1994, 98). By joining forces with parties, and thereby
decreasing the power their disruptive role gives them, the movements
lower the incentives for elites to actually carry through with reforms.
Those who have made this shift, not surprisingly, argue to the contrary:
that by joining forces within the PRD or the PT, their ability to shape policy
is enhanced and makes up for the loss of movement power. In the political
opportunity structure after the "moment of 1988 had passed," without a
unified call for mass civil disobedience from Cárdenas, the option of a
highly mobilized and broad-based social movement faded, and "party
building became not only the best option, it was the only viable option"
(Former urban popular movement leader, interview by the author, 1999).
    Against this mixed performance and arguments of historical necessity
are a set of decidedly pessimistic views on the movement-to-party transition. By forsaking movement radicalism for party accommodation, this
argument goes, the social Left has vertically integrated itself with elites,
placing itself in a situation not unlike that of the incorporated unions,
namely, that while they may exercise local and sectoral options, they are
unable to steer the country. For those who believe that the most potent
force of poor people is mobilized disruption, this vertical integration with
elites is obviously a loss of power. However, given the structure of political
opportunities in Mexico in the late 1980s, it can be argued that no such
mobilized disruption was possible or foreseeable. If radical disruptive

activity by social movements is unlikely to produce significant results, then a reasonable argument can be made in favor of party politics.

The debate between social movement actors, as well as scholars, over what level of institutional disruption must be maintained in order to achieve greater results than with party accommodation has suffered from the absence of scholarship that argues a persuasive historical counterfactual.[8] Much more common is the argument developed by James Petras to explain why social movements and not political parties are primarily responsible for progressive change in Latin America since the 1960s. He describes the political class as composed of those with vocations that lean toward the electoral, whose

> norms of reciprocity and loyalties compromise their vertical ties with extra-parliamentary groups. Their ideological differences and conflicting interests within the political class tend to become secondary to their common support for the political rules of the game. . . . For those individuals who rise from the social movements and retain ties to them, entering the political class creates serious and continuing tensions between the conflicting demands, styles of politics, norms of political practice, and class/institutional interests. (1989, 179–80)

Writing in 1989, Petras was of course in no position to comment yet on the Mexican case. However, it seems unlikely that he would argue a decade later that the Mexicans had avoided the fate of the Brazilians:

> Insofar as the political leaders of the [Brazilian] PT gain access to state office and become members of the political class, they inevitably become enmeshed in the commitments and constraints of existing state power. They have a tendency to adapt to, and negotiate with, the existing economic elite, the politicians of the central government *whose every move is conditioned by the strategic task of separating the electoral officials from control by the social movements, of forcing them to assume greater "responsibility" or managing the "whole economy" and of jettisoning the radical structural changes propounded prior to their election.* (1989, 200; emphasis added)

8. For an excellent explanation and implementation of the methodological device known as historical counterfactuals, see Gaventa 1980.

Such pessimistic assessments of the shift of movements into party politics in the context of democratic transitions are in clear contrast to the more optimistic predictions of Charles Tilly and his collaborators. Tilly argues first that legalization of social movements is good, because it lowers the costs of mobilization (Tilly 1978, 167). Furthermore, legality leads to the "group's capacity to organize, accumulate resources, and form alliances," especially within the electoral system (Tilly, Tilly, and Tilly 1975, 285).

Many defenders of the party option argue that despite the lack of advances for the urban poor during the Salinas and Zedillo administrations, and whatever the liabilities of PT and PRD municipal and state governments, continuing on a movement course and ignoring electoral options would have brought an even worse fate (interviews by the authors). Many argue that political democracy is a prerequisite to economic and social democracy and that without it, social justice is impossible. This position stands on the hope that multiparty competitive elections and the rotation of power by party will result in elected officials willing to implement policy more conducive to the interests of the poor. Clearly, the results to date have not been that impressive. However, as of this writing, the election in Brazil of Luis Inácio Lula da Silva (Lula), a man of the social Left if ever there was one, supports this position, as does the fact that the current PRD mayor of Mexico City, López Obrador, is currently ahead in public opinion polls leading up to the 2006 presidential elections. Clearly, the last chapter in this ongoing debate has yet to be written.

Strong assessments of the decline of the urban popular movement and the rise of party politics in the 1990s should evaluate the performance of elected Left opposition governments. The published record is very thin on this topic and does not capture the immense complexity and diversity of a country in which, even before Cárdenas's 1997 electoral victory in Mexico City's mayoral elections, the majority of citizens lived in municipalities governed by the opposition.[9] When asked, "What difference does a PRD government make?" people whose roots are in the social Left most often answer, "Not enough." Particularly in establishing democratic relationships with the citizenry, where the PRD had argued it would excel, the performance has been weak at best. Most movement actors close to the process agree that the PRD differentiates itself from the PRI most notably in its

9. The PRI still holds a much larger number of municipalities, but the opposition, through control of larger population areas, actually governs more people.

intention to be democratic. The former sometimes even tried to introduce democratic practices, whereas the PRI did not (see, for example, Bolos 1995, 118, 124). A PRD commitment to establish local offices charged with democratizing party practice had been implemented in only a handful of cases as of spring 1999 (interviews by the author).

By March 1999, virtually every Mexico City movement leader and many of the activist academics I knew had a position in the Cárdenas government. On a visit to a city government building, I had to make my way through a loud protest against Cárdenas by a recently formed urban popular movement organization. I turned to my OIR*ista* friend, then an assistant to Cárdenas, and asked, "How does it feel to be on the inside?" He gave a wry smile and responded, "Strange," and then launched into a critique of current social movement leadership, emphasizing its inability to transcend sectoral concerns and support the broader changes being sought by the Cárdenas administration.

This protest was not unique. In June 1998, a broad-based and coordinated demonstration of urban popular movement organizations, including many prominent ones such as the AB, UPREZ, and UCP, demanded that Cárdenas attend better to their needs. A former UCP leader and federal deputy commented, "Unfortunately, they were demanding that their material needs be solved, not that the relationship between citizens and the PRD government be democratized" (interview by the author, 1999). Consistent with views I heard from others in the social Left who were now in government, his response gave the process of democratization and the form that the poor use to interact with government officials more weight than the government's degree of willingness to respond to the content of their demands. This suggested that social Left leaders who had chosen the party option were well aware that this choice had led to the end of the 1980s protest cycle and that to make this choice "worth it," the democratic road really had to pan out. Continuing to extract specific material demands from a position of weakness relative to the 1980s was, from this perspective, understandably unsatisfactory.

The less-than-stellar performance in PRD municipalities has occurred in part because so many PRD officials come from the PRI and have not necessarily become more honest, skillful, or committed to values of social justice or democracy just because they have changed party labels. This role of ex-*priístas* in the PRD produces genuine anguish on the part of many leftists, and they press for internal changes that would make it more difficult for

PRI members to simply jump ship and attach themselves to the PRD in blatant exercises of electoral opportunism. Mario Saucedo, a social Left leader (ACNR), ran unsuccessfully for the party presidency in March 1999 on the slogan of "No to PRIizing of the PRD."

Another difficulty is that those from the political and social Left with government positions are often inexperienced. As one put it to me, we are "unprepared to govern." The skills, knowledge, and disposition required of effective officeholders and policy makers are quite distinct from the skills, knowledge, and disposition that are optimal for radical social movement politics or sectarian party politics. The continued power of the president and his willingness to use this power to political advantage seriously undermined the PRD's ability to develop a strong public-administration track record at the local and state levels. This was most decidedly the case during the Salinas years.

Particularly important for the future will be changes in the relationships between political parties and social movements. The infancy of the Mexican competitive party system helps to contextualize many of the current problems. Many activists have noted with obvious irritation the lack of intelligent conversation regarding the movement-party relationship (see, for example, AB leader David Cervantes and UCP leader Bernardino Ramos in Bolos 1995, 157, 162).

Lidia Samano of UPREZ notes that even if imperfect, mechanisms of accountability often exist in movement organizations (cited in Bolos 1995, 186), but when movement leaders find their way to public office, the system of accountability breaks down. Rocío Lomera makes the claim that the elected officials from the social Left owe an accounting, not only to the citizenry as democratic representatives, but also to the movements, whose work over the many years has gained them the seats they now hold (cited in Bolos 1995, 187).

In assessing the move into electoral politics, the CDP/PT in Durango of course attracted considerable national attention. Even those in the social Left who were most critical of the PT admit—sometimes grudgingly—that the back-to-back victories of the PT in 1992 and 1995, along with its record in office, were impressive.

Finally, it is worth noting that in the politics of relationships, reconciliation is oftentimes possible. Despite the points of fundamental disagreement between the AB and the CDP, and between the PRD and the PT, Mexico's electoral history of the 1990s and the first years of the twenty-first century have included a reconciliation at least ample enough to allow for a joining of PRD and PT forces in a number of electoral contests at the local, state, and national levels and in their legislative work as well. Clearly, the history of this trajectory of transition from movement to party and NGOs is far from over.

The Future

Despite the claims of some New Social Movement theory in Europe and Latin America, class continues to be a primary basis of common identity in many if not most poor people's movements in Latin America.[10] Furthermore, this class basis helps to explain the inability of these movements to make more progress on their visions.

A primary obstacle for class-based movements, repeatedly demonstrated through history, is that most often they lack the necessary resources of power to affect anything approaching the normative changes they seek, especially at a national level. More often than not, it is only a collection of diverse actors working in concert to exert pressure from different class and identity locations that together have been able to create a web of power capable of achieving significant reform. In the United States, consider the abolition of slavery, the civil rights movement, and the movement to end the war in Vietnam. In Latin America, consider the successful democratization movements across the region. Even in cases that are clearly led by a particular class, such as the workers movement in the United States during the 1930s, close inspection of the movement history shows multiclass coalitions at work. This is common knowledge among many historically knowledgeable social movement actors, and it explains the ongoing appeal of broad-based coalitions. The difficulty of holding broad coalitions together long enough so as to amass enough power to achieve significant reform or even radical transformation provides great advantage to and thus helps to explain the power of historical continuity.

Both the AB and the CDP leadership, along with the coordinating bodies of teachers and peasants, as well as the urban popular movement's own CONAMUP, attempted to broaden their class appeal during the 1980s protest cycle. This trend has continued in Mexico to the present day, as

10. For New Social Movement approaches to Latin American social movements, see Escobar and Alvarez 1992 and especially Alvarez, Dagnino, and Escobar 1998.

movement actors emphasize a particular sector of society while simultaneously making efforts to broaden their appeal.[11] As the electoral strategy of
all the existing parties in Mexico is multiclass, to participate in politics is by
definition to force the collective action of the organized urban poor into
accommodation with other class and identity interests.

Parties and candidates that seek to be truly competitive must broaden
their appeal beyond the normative aspirations of sectoral or issue-driven
movements. I know this as much from my own personal experience in
party-building efforts in the United States as I do from my research in
Mexico. Successful party building often requires appealing to the working
and middle classes that are often quite conservative in terms of social, cultural, and political mores (P. Haber 2001). So, while appeals based on
democratic credentials, such as honesty, efficiency, and accountability in
office, are of course welcomed, as are moderate policy reforms, more radical notions such as democratic socialism are not. This encourages candidates to moderate their positions, not only in policy terms, but also in terms
of the society they envision. Cuauhtémoc Cárdenas's momentous decision
to embrace the electoral path to reform rather than to call the people to the
streets in open and widespread radical protest launched the country on the
path that it is still walking. In my judgment, the importance of this decision
is generally not appreciated. There has been no other decision that has
been more important in the past twenty years of Mexican history.

Protest cycles always come to an end. They are by definition extraordinary times. Their declines create opportunities for powerful historical,
philosophical, political, and phenomenological reflections on the part of
participants and engaged observers.[12] One can find evidence for the contention that the politicization and idealism does not end with the passing
of a movement, and one can also find tales of disillusionment. And one can
find reports of how movement people keep the faith even through dark
times, only to reappear when political opportunities again shift in their
favor (see, for example, Rupp and Taylor 1987, on the U.S. women's rights
movement).

11. An excellent example of this are the Zapatistas of Chiapas, who emphasize issues of
special concern to indigenous people but do so without losing sight of ideals and values such
as democracy and justice that have broad appeal. For an excellent concise summary of the
Zapatistas, see Stavenhagen 2003.

12. See, for example, the passionate reflections of Zolberg (1972) and Hirschman (1982)
as well as the detailed empirical accounts of McAdam (1988) and Rogers (1993).

One of the ironies of powerful radical social movements is that they tend to speak revolution and achieve reform. The diverse revolutionary currents in the Mexican urban popular movement held in common the aspiration to transform political power, social relations, economic owner-ship and distribution, and cultural meanings. I have spent countless poignant and inspirational hours with movement veterans who told per-sonal stories of joining forces with others who shared their ideals. Interest-ingly, the achievement of reforms often did not dull, but rather served to sustain, these ideals, as these movement militants were able to achieve small but real gains while also keeping their eyes on the prize.

While the debate continues regarding the wisdom of either participation in the PRONASOL program or the entry into or creation of political parties, there persists a sense that the revolutionary ideals of the Mexican Left have yet to find their inspirational replacement in the democratic discourse of the 1980s to the present. Most movement activists, NGO associates, and sympathetic scholars concur that the current goals of the urban popular movement are very unclear, not yet reconstructed after the Left's ideologi-cal destruction resulting from socialism's decline in the 1990s. Although understandings of socialism were not monolithic within the movement, it did provide an overarching vision and direction that the new consensus on constitutional electoral democracy has at least thus far failed to provide (see, for example, the comments of Georgina Sandoval in Bolos 1995, 173).

This is not, I hasten to add, an inherent trait of democracy, which has certainly shown its ability to inspire the imaginations and actions of people across the globe and across centuries. Rather, it is that in Mexico, and per-haps in Latin American more generally, often movement activists recog-nize that the democracy they seek is not a deep democracy that lifts the spirit and feeds the belly, but rather a pragmatic set of institutional changes that make political representation more inclusive.

It is not that this shift is unimportant. Rather, such reform is a very far cry from where these movement struggles began. The struggle for democ-ratization in Mexico is not generating the kind of solidarity that occurred in the urban poor movement politics of the 1970s and 1980s. The culture of democratic transition in the 1990s was far different from the movement culture of previous decades. For the most part, it did not require or even desire dedicated civic participation by the urban poor. As described in Chapter 4, to live in a CDP colonia is not what it used to be. There is a loss of identity and meaning born of pride, solidarity, and hope.

As the Mexican urban poor enter the twenty-first century, their fate is anything but certain. Both those with movement histories and those without them have in common a deep uncertainty as they listen to politicians explain their fortunes under neoliberal democracy. As one woman in her fifties put it:

> We poor people are used to listening to big shots tell us what we want and how they are going to get it to us if we only cooperate. If we follow them. When the CDP was exciting and healthy, I came to believe in them. And we worked together. Now we have lost that sense of working together. The leaders have moved away from us. I no longer feel them in my heart. It's the same with my friends. Something has surely been lost. And now there is all this talk of the new politics. I felt better when we had that sense of working together. I have this uneasy feeling when they tell us they are going to take care of us. It feels too much like the old song. I sure hope they can be trusted. I fear that they cannot. (Interview by the author, 1998)

Social movements are important because more often than not they have been the ones to introduce the most important ideas into the political discourse and the ones to push hard for their realization. They have played critical roles in the transitions from authoritarian regimes to democratic rule that figured so importantly in Latin America, Eastern Europe, and elsewhere during the 1980s and 1990s. The end of the Cold War combined with this democratic transition has resulted in a dramatic decline in the long-standing battle between socialism and capitalism. The at least temporary end of significant ideological battle in Latin America has meant that the focus has shifted to the building of democratic institutions and reforming capitalism so as to benefit a larger percentage of the population. This is a very new terrain for social movements, but one that I think is a transformative project around which they can mobilize. In fact, they already are. Expanding the democratic franchise and widening the percentage of people benefiting from an increasingly globalized capitalism are, along with environmental concerns, at the heart of progressive international efforts today.

A new urban popular movement that holds political parties and elected officials accountable to a new ecologically sound and deeply democratic capitalism has real potential. The very real human beings that peopled the urban and other popular movements of the 1980s protest cycle did not achieve their aspirations. But their resistance to the brutalities and abuses of Mexican authoritarianism were important struggles against exclusion and marginalization and for a democratic Mexico that makes good on the progressive promises of its Constitution. While not perhaps the harbingers of a deep transformation, they were part of the stubborn refusal of Mexico's majorities to be history's passive spectators and second-class citizens in a nation that promises equality for all.

APPENDIX A

CDP Strength in Durango, Dgo., by Colonia

Colonia	Year established	Number of lots
Emiliano Zapata	1976	2,000
Lucio Cabañas	1976	800
Tierra y Libertad	1980	1,000
Genero Vasquez	1980	400
Arturo Gamiz	1980	1,200
Jose Revueltas	1982	1,200
Manuel Buendia	1984	300
Juan Lira	1985	600
Isabel Almanza	1985	500
8 de Septiembre	1986	500
José Angel Leal	1987	1,400
Heberto Castillo	1987	100
Flores Magon	1987	100
Viciente Guerrero	1987	60
Frac. Fco. Sarabea	1987	400
Predio Canelas	1988	250
Predio Florida	1988	200
Marshall	1989	600
Carlos Luna	1989	300
Álayos	1990	90

NOTE: The totals are 20 colonias and 12,000 lots, for a population of approximately 70,000. In addition to being engaged in the CDP colonias populares shown in this list, by the late 1980s the CDP was active in committees in twenty-seven other colonias and housing developments in the capital city itself. The majority of these committees were located in lower-middle-class neighborhoods, which have standards of living somewhat above those of the CDP colonias. A half dozen of these—Insurgentes, Barrio de Anarco, IV Centarios, Tierra Blanca, and El Milagro—are more appropriately classified as middle-class neighborhoods; and Morga, Villa de Guadalupe, J. Guadalupe Rodriguez, and Asteca are poor colonias.

APPENDIX B

CDP Activities at the State Level, 1972–1991

Municipalities	Years	Nature of activities
Durango	1972–90	The focus of CDP activity as social movement and as political party
Canatlán	1986–89	One *regidor*
Coneto de Comonfort	1986–89	One *regidor*
Gómez Palacio	1984–present	Three colonias, six bases, one *regidor* in 1989
Ciudad Palacio	1985–90	Two colonias, seven bases, one *regidor* in 1989
Santiago Pap.	1986–90	Two colonias, three *comités*
Nombre de Dios	1971–90ᵃ	1989, won municipal elections; organizing in townships of Nombre de Dios, Constancia, Tuitan, and La Parrilla
Suchil	1986–90	1986–89, one *regidor*; 1989, won municipal elections
Mezquital	1985–90	Ecological groups
Tepehuanes	1985	Started strong; fell apart in 1986 when CDP participated in elections as PRT because most local leaders were PAN affiliated
Vicente Guerrero	1990	Early stages of organization
Villa Union	1990	Early stages of organization

ᵃIn 1992, the CDP/PT again won the municipal presidency of Nombre de Dios.

APPENDIX C

Election Statistics from Durango

Electoral Results for Municipal President of Durango, Dgo.

Year	PT	PRI	PAN
1986[a]	4,583	38,435	35,362
1989	12,824	35,751	26,113
1992	42,482	35,920	33,551

SOURCE: Palacios Moncayo 1994, based on data obtained from the Comisión Estatal Electoral.
[a]In 1986, the CDP ran as PRT candidates and in 1989 as candidates of the PCDP.

Elections in Durango, 1992

	Municipality of Durango	Governor	Directly elected deputies
PT	42,482	26,775	39,251
PRI	35,920	160,834	167,288
PAN	33,551	106,865	99,060
PRD	274	9,734	11,203

SOURCE: Singer and Leal 1993, based on data obtained from the Comisión Estatal Electoral.

Votes by Party and Electoral District in Durango for the 1994 Senatorial Election

	PAN	PRI	PRD	PT
I. Durango	36,503	39,892	5,045	39,424
II. Gómez Palacio	30,105	47,102	21,049	4,865
III. Canatián	10,114	36,287	2,148	5,722
IV. Guadalupe Victoria	10,103	38,858	4,319	7,546
V. Durango	17,073	45,633	2,892	22,561
VI. Lerdo	16,614	37,474	9,248	4,304
Total	120,512	245,246	44,701	84,422

SOURCE: Personal correspondence from Palacios Moncayo, based on official figures from IFE.

Votes by Party and Electoral District in Durango for the 1994 Presidential Election

	Total votes	PAN	PRI	PRD	PT	Others
I. Durango	127,072	49,419	51,359	6,940	14,200	2,091
II. Gómez Palacio	108,084	29,803	48,587	22,277	4,029	3,388
III. Canatián	54,845	10,766	37,188	1,870	4,267	754
IV. Guadalupe Victoria	60,761	11,659	39,886	4,645	3,824	747
V. Durango	90,526	22,508	50,427	3,782	12,374	1,408
VI. Lerdo	69,981	16,266	38,355	10,088	3,795	1,477
Total	511,296	140,421	265,802	49,602	42,489	9,965

SOURCE: Marín López and Palacios Moncayo 1995, based on official figures from IFE.

Votes by Party and Electoral District in Durango for the 1994 Election for Federal Deputies

	PAN	PRI	PRD	PT
I. Durango	45,052	51,803	3,947	20,311
II. Gómez Palacio	29,432	44,516	21,683	4,589
III. Canatián	9,884	36,396	1,744	4,907
IV. Guadalupe Victoria	10,384	38,778	4,377	6,825
V. Durango	17,602	48,155	4,413	18,027
VI. Lerdo	15,063	38,416	9,438	4,224
Total	127,387	253,001	45,602	58,884

SOURCE: Marín López and Palacios Moncayo 1995, based on official figures from IFE.

Votes Cast for Municipal President in the State Capital of Durango (Thousands)

	1992	1995	1998
PT	43	53	51
PRI	34	25	70
PAN	35	35	20

SOURCE: IFE.

APPENDIX D

Organizational Makeup of the AB

There were fifteen preexisting organizations that came together to form the AB. Although many new organizations came into being and associated with the AB, the following remained the most influential. Among other measurements of importance, these organizations oversaw the majority of the housing projects listed in Appendix E. The following list of semiautonomous organizations that together constituted the organizational core of the AB is suggestive of the organizational complexity of the AB, a complexity and heterogeneity that encouraged more decentralized decision-making processes than is usually to be expected from a Mexican urban popular movement. The first four listed are the founding members of AB and always enjoyed substantial influence on AB direction.

1. "Centro" (Comité de Lucha Iquilinaria del Centro [CLIC]). Deleg. Cuauhtémoc.
2. "Guerrero" (Comité de Defensa del Barrio "Emiliano Zapata" [CDB-EZ]). Deleg. Cuauhtémoc.
3. "Peña Morelos" (Uníon Popular de Inquilinos de la Colonia Morelos-Peña Morelos [UPICM]). Deleg. V. Carranza.
4. "Pensil" (Unión de Inquilinos de la Colonia Pensil [UICP]). Deleg. M. Hidalgo.
5. "Alvaro Obregón" (Unión de Vecinos de la Colonia Alvaro Obregón). Deleg. V. Carranza.
6. Comité de Defensa del Barrio "Benito Juárez" (CDB-BJ). Deleg. Benito Juárez.
7. Unión de Vecinos de Azcapotzalco. Deleg. Azcapotzalco.
8. Comité Popular Voces de Coapa. Deleg. Coyoacan.
9. Comité Popular Voces del Sur. Deleg. Xochimilco.
10. Iztapalapa. Deleg. Iztapalapa.
11. Martín Carrera. Deleg. Gustavo A. Madero
12. Unión de Inquilinos de la Colonia Anáhuac. Deleg. Miguel Hidalgo.
13. Colonia Federal. Deleg. V. Carranza.
14. "Aeropuerto-Arenal" (Comisión Coordinadora del Fraccionamiento Aeropuerto-Arenal). Deleg. V. Carranza.
15. Grupo en la Colonia Guadalupe Tepeyac. Deleg. Gustavo A. Madero.

APPENDIX E

Asamblea de Barrios Housing Projects

	Name	Delegation or Municipality	Number of Units	Financing Agency
1	Fracc. Cuatotonque	Azcapotzalco	24	Fonhapo
2	Flor de Geraneo	Azcapotzalco	8	Fonhapo
3	Naranja 1	Azcapotzalco	108	Fonhapo and Fase II
4	Naranja 2	Azcapotzalco	88	Fonhapo and Fase II
5	Nextengo (Arenal)	Azcapotzalco	61	RHP and Fonhapo
6	Tepantongo	Azcapotzalco	315	Fonhapo and Fase II
7	Comité de Defensa del Barrio "Benemérito Benito Juárez"	Benito Juárez	8	Casa Propia
8	Comité de Defensa del Barrio "Benemérito Benito Juárez"	Benito Juárez	7	Casa Propia
9	Esparta 13	Benito Juárez	10	Casa Propia
10	Aluminio	Cuauhtémoc	40	Fonhapo
11	Argentina 89	Cuauhtémoc	30	Fase II
12	Argentina 91	Cuauhtémoc	40	Fase II
13	Belisario Domínguez	Cuauhtémoc	8	Fase II
14	Bolivia 37-39	Cuauhtémoc	42	Fase II
15	Chabacano 115	Cuauhtémoc	152	Fase II
16	Chile 47 and 49	Cuauhtémoc	—	RHP and Fonhapo
17	Emiliano Zapata 115	Cuauhtémoc	48	Fase II
18	Limón	Cuauhtémoc	6	Fividesu
19	Manuel Doblado 67-a	Cuauhtémoc	9	Fonhapo
20	Montero	Cuauhtémoc	55	Fonhapo
21	Perú 74-86	Cuauhtémoc	20	Fase II
22	Comité de la Defensa del Barrio "Emiliano Zapata"	Cuauhtémoc	34	Fideicomiso
23	Mina 121	Cuauhtémoc	42	Casa Propia
24	Zaragoza 192	Cuauhtémoc	20	Casa Propia

Asamblea de Barrios Housing Projects (*cont'd*)

	Name	Delegation or Municipality	Number of Units	Financing Agency
25	Flores Magón 164	Cuauhtémoc	15	Casa Propia
26	Camelia 197	Cuauhtémoc	22	Casa Propia
27	Ogazón 7	Cuauhtémoc	20	Casa Propia
28	Cedro 323	Cuauhtémoc	34	Casa Propia
29	Camelia 189	Cuauhtémoc	62	Casa Propia
30	Izcabalceta 85	Cuauhtémoc	29	Casa Propia
31	Héroes 104	Cuauhtémoc	25	Casa Propia
32	Crisantemo	G. A. Madero	40	Fonhapo
33	Ticomán	G. A. Madero	120	Fonhapo
34	Una Luz en mi Camino	G. A. Madero	12	Fonhapo
35	M. Carrera 77	G. A. Madero	20	Casa Propia
36	C. de la Unión 91	G. A. Madero	20	Casa Propia
37	C. de la Unión 63	G. A. Madero	35	Casa Propia
38	C. de la Unión 87	G. A. Madero	38	Casa Propia
39	Oniquina 6245	G. A. Madero	20	Casa Propia
40	Oriente 233	Iztacalco	50	Fase II
41	Oriente 247	Iztacalco	50	Fase II
42	Pantitlán Zaragoza	Iztacalco	60	Fonhapo and RHP
43	Calle 5	Iztacalco	23	Fonhapo and RHP
44	Cerrada de San Pedro	Iztacalco	23	Fonhapo
45	Cabeza de Juárez	Iztacalco	70	Fividesu
46	Calle 11	Iztacalco	886	Fonhapo
47	El Moral	Iztacalco	120	Fonhapo
48	Unión Estrella	Iztacalco	32	Fonhapo

Asamblea de Barrios Housing Projects *(cont'd)*

	Name	Delegation or Municipality	Number of Units	Financing Agency
49	Bella Realidad 12 de Octubre	Miguel Hidalgo	24	Fase II
50	Buenos Aires	Miguel Hidalgo	9	Fase II and Cruz Roja
51	Cacamatzin	Miguel Hidalgo	18	Fividesu
52	Campeche	Miguel Hidalgo	30	Cruz Roja and Fonhapo
53	Carrillo Puerto 378	Miguel Hidalgo	38	Fase II
54	Carrillo Puerto 510	Miguel Hidalgo	30	—
55	Casa Amarilla 44	Miguel Hidalgo	12	Fonhapo
56	Cerrada de Allende	Miguel Hidalgo	53	Fase II
57	Cda. Lago Kolin	Miguel Hidalgo	16	Fonhapo
58	Golfo de California 24	Miguel Hidalgo	30	Fase II
59	La Pérdida	Miguel Hidalgo	8	Fonhapo
60	Lago Biwa 29	Miguel Hidalgo	42	Fonhapo
61	Lago Biwa 43	Miguel Hidalgo	32	Fase II
62	Lago Cortina 29	Miguel Hidalgo	30	Fase II
63	Lago Cortina 17	Miguel Hidalgo	8	Fonhapo
64	Lago Gran Oso 29	Miguel Hidalgo	24	Fase II
65	Lago Gran Oso 50	Miguel Hidalgo	87	Fase II
66	Lago Guanacacha	Miguel Hidalgo	6	Fividesu
67	Lago Ness 163	Miguel Hidalgo	32	Fividesu
68	Laguna de Guzmán 115	Miguel Hidalgo	21	Fonhapo
69	Maracaibo 5	Miguel Hidalgo	12	Fonhapo
70	San Joaquín 84	Miguel Hidalgo	54	Fonhapo
71	Wether 86	Miguel Hidalgo	20	Casa Propia
72	Wether 89	Miguel Hidalgo	9	Casa Propia

Asamblea de Barrios Housing Projects *(cont'd)*

	Name	Delegation or Municipality	Number of Units	Financing Agency
73	Lago San Pedro 72	Miguel Hidalgo	8	Casa Propia
74	Carrillo Puerto 549	Miguel Hidalgo	20	Casa Propia
75	Lago Viedma 104	Miguel Hidalgo	25	Casa Propia
76	Lago Patzcuaro 78	Miguel Hidalgo	25	Casa Propia
77	Lago Como 86	Miguel Hidalgo	42	Casa Propia
78	Lago Cardiel 33	Miguel Hidalgo	10	Casa Propia
79	Santa Úrsula	Tlalpan	200	Fonhapo
80	Congreso de la Unión	V. Carranza	105	Fonhapo
81	Gran Canal	V. Carranza	6	Fonhapo
82	Héroes de Nacozari	V. Carranza	12	Fonhapo
83	Magdalena Mixuca	V. Carranza	48	Fonhapo
84	Rotograbados	V. Carranza	6	Fonhapo
85	Trabajo y Prev. Social	V. Carranza	6	Fonhapo or Fividesu
86	Transvaal	V. Carranza	120	Fonhapo
87	Aeropuerto Arenal	V. Carranza	1,100	Fonhapo
88	La Noria	Xochimilco	58	Fase II and Fonhapo
89	Acueducto Siglo XXI	Xochimilco	81	Fonhapo
90	Apaches	Xochimilco	250	Fonhapo and Fovissste
91	Frente de Trabajadores Derecho–habientes	Xochimilco	170	Fovissste
92	Tultilán Barrio Nuevo	Ecatepec	600	Fonhapo
93	Profopec	Ecatepec	600	Fonhapo
94	Porvenir 87	Nezahualcoyotl	6	Fonhapo
95	Hormiga	Tlanepantla	120	Fonhapo
96	Artemisa	Tlanepantla	48	Fonhapo

SOURCE: E. E. Vega 1991

APPENDIX F

Asamblea de Barrios Family Income in Relation to the Minimum Wage

Salaries per household	CDB-EZ (percent)[a]	Calle 11 (percent)[b]	Cuadros medios (percent)[c]
< 1	2.1	2.0	—
1–1.9	41.7	42.0	36.4
2–2.9	39.6	42.0	40.9
3–3.9	6.3	2.0	9.1
4–4.9	6.3	2.0	13.6
5–5.9	2.1	2.0	—
6 +	2.1	10.0	—

SOURCE: Kenneth Greene, "Apuntes estadísticos sobre la Asamblea de Barrios de la Ciudad de México," mimeograph, 1991.

[a]CDB-EZ is the acronym for Comité de Defensa del Barrio–General Emiliano Zapata. It is one of the most important territorial organizations existing with the AB and is located in Colonia Guerrero.

[b]Calle 11 is the AB's largest housing project, with 933 units (number 46 in Appendix F).

[c]Cuadros medios are midlevel activists. The survey results are based a representative sample of 32.

BIBLIOGRAPHY

ACNR. 1983. "Declaración de Iguala." January 31.

———. n.d. *Nuestra táctica*. Mexico City: Ediciones Patria Nueva.

Adams, Richard. 1970. *Crucifixion by Power*. Austin: University of Texas Press.

Agger, Ben. 1998. *Critical Social Theories: An Introduction*. Boulder, Colo.: Westview Press.

Aguero, Felipe, and Jeffrey Stark, eds. 1998. *Fault Lines of Democracy in Post-transition Latin America*. Miami: North-South Center Press.

Aguilar Camín, Héctor, and Lorenzo Meyer. 1993. *In the Shadow of the Mexican Revolution*. Austin: University of Texas Press.

Aguilar Zínser, Adolfo. 1995. *Vamos a ganar! La pugna de Cuauhtémoc Cárdenas por el poder*. Mexico City: Oceano.

Albina Garavito, Rosa, and Augusto Bolívar, eds. 1990. *Mexico en la decada de los ochenta: La modernización en cifras*. Mexico City: Universidad Autónoma Metropolitana-Azcapotzalco.

Alemán, Ricardo. 1991. "Clase politica." *La Jornada*, January 26.

Alvarez, Sonia E., Evelina Dagnino, and Arturo Escobar, eds. 1998. *Cultures of Politics, Politics of Cultures: Re-visioning Latin American Social Movements*. Boulder, Colo.: Westview Press.

America's Watch. 1990. *Human Rights in Mexico: A Policy of Impunity*. New York: Human Rights Watch.

Anguiano, Arturo. 1975. *El Estado y la política obrera del cardenismo*. Mexico City: Ediciones Era.

Arzaluz Solano, Socorro. 1995. "Del movimiento ubano al gobierno local: El caso de la gestión del Partido del Trabajo en el municipio de Durango." In *La tarea de governar: Gobiernos locales y demandas ciudadanas*, ed. Ziccardi, Alicia. Mexico City: Instituto de Investigaciones Sociales, UNAM, and Miguel Angel Porrúa.

Baer, M. Delal. 1991. "North American Free Trade." *Foreign Affairs* 70, no.4:132–49.

Bailón, Moisés Jaime. 1995. "Municipios, Opposition Mayorships, and Public Expenditure in Oaxaca." In *Opposition Government in Mexico*, ed. Victoria E. Rodríguez and Peter M. Ward. Albuquerque: University of New Mexico Press.

Baily, John. 1994. "Centralism and Political Change in Mexico: The Case of National Solidarity." In *Transforming State-Society Relations in Mexico: The National Solidarity Strategy*, ed. Wayne A. Cornelius, Ann L. Craig, and Jonathan Fox. U.S.-Mexico Contemporary Perspectives Series 6. La Jolla: Center for U.S.-Mexican Studies, University of California, San Diego.

Barberán, José, Cuauhtémoc Cárdenas, Adrian López Monjardin, and Jorge Zavala. 1988. *Radiografía del fraude: Análisis de lost datos oficiales del 6 de Julio*. Mexico City: Editorial Nuestro Tiempo.

Barbosa, Fabio. 1984. "La izquierda radical en México." *Rivista Mexicana de Sociología* 46, no. 2:111–38.

Barkin, David. 1978. "Regional Development and Interregional Equity: A Mexican Case Study." In *Urbanization and Inequality: The Political Economy of Urban and Rural Development in Latin America*, ed. Wayne Cornelius and Robert V. Kemper. Beverly Hills: Sage.

Barrera, Marco. 1986. "Viva Villa Cabrones: Entrevista a Gonzalo Yáñez, dirigente del Comité de Defensa Popular de Durango." In *Llego la hora de ser govierno*, by Marcos Cruz et al. Mexico City: Equipo Pueblo and Editorial Praxis.

Basurto, Jorge. 1983. *En el régimen de Echeverría: Rebelión e independencia*. La clase obrera en la historia de México, no. 14. Mexico City: Siglo XXI.

Becker, Ernest. 1968. *The Structure of Evil*. New York: Free Press.

Bennett, Vivienne. 1995a. "Orígenes del Movimiento Urbano Popular Mexicano: Pensamiento político y organizaciones politicas clandestinas, 1960–1980." *Revista Mexicana de Sociología*, no. 3 (July–September): 89–102.

———. 1995b. *The Politics of Water: Urban Protest, Gender, and Power in Monterrey, Mexico*. Pittsburgh: University of Pittsburgh Press.

Berger, Susan. 1997. "Political Masks: The State and Social Movements in Guatemala." Paper presented at the annual meeting of the Latin American Studies Association, Guadalajara, Mexico, April 17–19.

Bizberg, Ilán. 1989. "Modernization and Corporatism in Mexico." Monograph, El Colegio de Mexico, Mexico City.

Bolos, Silvia, ed. 1995. *Actores sociales y demandas urbanas*. Mexico City: Universidad Iberamericana and Plaza y Valdés.

Borrego Rodríguez, Carlos. 1984. "Una aproximación al studio del Movimiento del Cerro de Mercado." Revised version of paper presented at the conference "Seminario Regional Sobre Movimientos Sociales en México, Región Chihuahua, Durango y Zacatecas," Instituto de Ciencias Sociales at the Universidad Juarez del Estado de Durango, Durango, Mexico, May.

Bouchier Tretiack, Josíane Cécile Olga. 1988. "La conamup: Una historia de odios y amores, encuentros y desencuentros entre organizaciones politicas." Undergraduate thesis, unam.

Bracho, Julio. 1995. "La izquierda integrada al pueblo y la solidaridad: Revisiones de Política Popular." *Revista Mexicana de Sociología*, no. 3 (July–September): 69–87.

Briene, Wini. 1982. *Community and Organization in the New Left, 1968–1982: The Great Refusal*. New York: Praeger

Brockett, Charles D. 1991. "The Structure of Political Opportunities and Peasant Mobilization in Central America." *Comparative Politics* 23 (April): 253–74.

Bruhn, Kathleen. 1997. *Taking on Goliath: The Emergence of a New Left Party and the Struggle for Democracy in Mexico*. University Park: Pennsylvania State University Press.

Bruhn, Kathleen, and Keith Yanner. 1995. "Governing Under the Enemy: The prd in Michoacán." In *Opposition Government in Mexico*, ed. Victoria E. Rodríguez and Peter M. Ward. Albuquerque: University of New Mexico Press.

Butler, Edgar J., and Jorge A. Bustamante, eds. 1991. *Sucesion Presidencial: The 1988 Mexican Presidential Election*. Boulder, Colo.: Westview Press.

Caldeira, Teresa Pires de Rio. 1990. "Women, Daily Life, and Politics." In *Women and Social Change in Latin America*, ed. Elizabeth Jelin. London: UNRISD/Zed Books.

Camacho, David, and Rafael Menjívar, eds. 1989. *Los movimientos populares en America Latina*. Mexico City: Siglo XXI.

Camacho, Manuel. 1984. *El futuro inmediato: La clase obrera en la historia de México*. Mexico City: Siglo XXI.

Camp, Roderic A. 1990. "Camarillas in Mexican Politics: The Case of the Salinas Cabinet." *Mexican Studies/Estudios*, no 1 (Winter): 87–107

———. 1999. *Politics in Mexico: The Decline of Authoritarianism*. 3d ed. Oxford: Oxford University Press.

Campbell, Joseph. 1988. *The Power of Myth*. New York: Doubleday.

Canudas, Rocío Carmen. 1991. *La modernización económica en Durango*. Durango, Mexico: Instituto de Ciencias Sociales, Universidad Juarez del Estado de Durango.

Cardoso, Fernano Henrique, and Enzo Faletto. 1979. *Dependency and Development in Latin America*. Berkeley and Los Angeles: University of California Press.

Carr, Barry. 1986. "The Mexican Left, the Popular Movements, and the Politics of Austerity, 1982–1985." In *The Mexican Left, the Popular Movements, and the Politics of Austerity*, ed. Barry Carr and Ricardo Anzaldúa Montoya. Monograph Series 18. La Jolla: Center for U.S.-Mexican Studies, University of California, San Diego.

Carrillo, Teresa. 1990. "Women, Trade Unions, and New Social Movements in Mexico: The Case of the Nineteenth of September Garment Workers Union." Ph.D. diss., Stanford University.

Carson, Clayborne. 1981. *In Struggle: sncc and the Black Awakening of the 1960s*. Cambridge, Mass.: Harvard University Press.

Casa y Ciudad. 1996. *La interacción entre las organizaciones sociales y los organismos no gubernamentales en las políticas públicas habitacionales de la Ciudad de México*. Mexico City: Casa y Ciudad.

Castañeda, Jorge G. 1993. *Utopia Unarmed*. New York: Vintage Books.

———. 1995. *The Mexican Shock*. New York: New Press.

Castells, Manuel. 1983. *The City and the Grassroots*. Berkeley and Los Angeles: University of California Press.

Castells, Manuel, et al. 1972. *Los campamentos de Santiago: Movilización urbana*. Santiago, Chile: Centro de Desarrollo Urbano y Regional.

Castillo Palma, Jaime. 1986. "El movimiento urbano popular en Puebla." In *Los movimientos socials en Puebla*, ed. Jaime Castillo Palma. Puebla, Mexico: Instituto de Ciencias, Universidad Autónoma de Puebla.

Centeno, Miguel Ángel. 1997. *Democracy Within Reason: Technocratic Revolution in Mexico*. 2d ed. University Park: Pennsylvania State University Press.

CEPAL. 1988. *Anuario estadistico de America Latina y el Caribe: Desarrollo social y bienestar social*. Santiago, Chile: United Nations.

Cloward, Richard A., and Frances Fox Piven. 1979. "Hidden Protest: The Channeling of Female Innovation and Resistance." *Signs* 4:41.

——. 1989. "Why People Deviate in Different Ways." In *New Directions in the Study of Justice, Law, and Social Control*, ed. Arizona State University School of Justice Studies Board. New York: Plenum.

Cockcroft, James D. 1998. *Mexico's Hope: An Encounter with Politics and History.* New York: Monthly Review Press.

Cohen, Jean L. 1985. "Strategy or Identity: New Theoretical Paradigms and Contemporary Social Movements." *Social Research* 52:663–716.

Coleman, James S. 1960. "Conclusion: The Political Systems of the Developing Nations." In *The Politics of Developing Areas*, ed. Gabriel Almond and James Coleman. Princeton: Princeton University Press.

Collier, David. 1976. *Squatters and Oligarchs.* Baltimore: Johns Hopkins University Press.

Comité de Defensa Popular de Durango. 1979. Documentos Basicos.

CONAMUP. 1983. "IV Encuentro Nacional del Movimiento Urbano Popular— Discurso de apertura." Mimeograph.

——. 1990. El combate a la pobreza: Lineamientos programáticos. Mexico City: El Nacional.

Cook, Maria Lorena. 1990. "Organizing Dissent: The Mexican Teachers Movement, 1979–1989."

——. 1991. "Restructuring and Democracy in Mexico: Twenty Years of Trade Union Strategies (1970–1990)." Paper presented at the Latin American Studies Association, April 4-6, Washington D.C.

——. 1996. *Organizing Dissent: Unions, the State, and the Democratic Teachers' Movement in Mexico.* University Park: Pennsylvania State University Press.

Córdova, Arnaldo. 1976. *La política de masas del cardenismo.* Mexico City: Ediciones Era, Serie Popular Era.

Cornelius, Wayne. 1972. "The Cityward Movement: Some Political Implications." In *Changing Latin America: New Interpretation of Its Society and Politics*, ed. Douglas Chalmers. Proceedings of the Academy of Political Science.

——. 1973. "Nation-Building, Participation, and Distribution: The Politics of Social Reform Under Cárdenas." In *Crisis, Choice, and Change: Historical Studies of Political Development*, ed. G. A. Almond, S. C. Flanagan, and R. Mundt, 392–485. Boston: Little, Brown.

——.1974. Urbanization and Political Demand Making: Political Participation Among the Migrant Poor in Latin American Cities." *American Political Science Review* 68, no. 3:1125–46.

——. 1975. *Politics and the Mexican Poor in Mexico City.* Stanford: Stanford University Press.

Cornelius, Wayne, Todd Eisenstadt, and Jane Hindley, eds. 1999. *Subnational Politics and Democratization in Mexico.* Center for U.S.-Mexican Studies, University of California, San Diego.

Cornelius, Wayne A., Judith Gentleman, and Peter H. Smith. 1989. *Mexico's Alternative Political Futures.* La Jolla: Center for U.S.-Mexican Studies, University of California, San Diego.

Cornelius, Wayne, and David Myhre, eds. 1998. *The Transformation of Rural Mexico: Reforming the Ejido Sector, 1998.* Center for US-Mexican Studies.

Cornia, Andrea Giovanni, and Sanjay Reddy. 2001. "The Impact of Adjustment-Related Social Funds on Income Distribution and Poverty." Discussion Paper no. 2001/1, World Institute for Development Economics Research, United Nations University.

Craig, Ann. 1990. "Institutional Context and Popular Strategies." In *Popular Movements and Political Change in Mexico*, ed. Joe Foweraker and Ann L. Craig. Boulder, Colo.: Lynne Rienner.

Craske, Nikki. 1994. *Corporatism Revisited: Salinas and the Reform of the Popular Sector.* London: Institute of Latin American Studies, University of London.

Crespo, José Antonio. 1995. "Governments of the Opposition: The Official Response." In *Opposition Government in Mexico*, ed. Victoria E. Rodríguez and Peter M. Ward. Albuquerque: University of New Mexico Press.

Cuéllar Vázquez, Angélica. 1993. *La noche es de ustedes, el amanecer es nuestro: Asamblea de Barrios y Superbarrio Gómez en la Ciudad de México.* Mexico City: UNAM.

Davis, Diane E. 1994. *Urban Leviathan: Mexico City in the Twentieth Century.* Philadelphia: Temple University Press.

Delgado, Gary. 1986. *Organizing the Movement: The Roots and Growth of acorn.* Philadelphia: Temple University Press.

Deutsch, Karl. 1961. "Social Mobilization and Political Development." *American Political Science Review* 55:493–514.

Díaz Thome, Hugo. 1989. "Intervención de Hugo Diaz Thome, Secretario de Coordinación de Fomento a la Vivienda, del PRI en el D.F. en la primeria asamblea de la coordinadora de defensa de vecinos e inquilinos del centro historico." Mimeograph, September 26.

Domingo, Pilar. 2000. "Judicial Independence: The Politics of the Supreme Court in Mexico." *Journal of Latin American Studies* 32, no. 3:705–35.

Dresser, Denise. 1991. *Neopopulist Solutions to Neoliberal Problems.* La Jolla: Center for U.S.-Mexican Studies, University of California, San Diego..

Durán, Ramon. 1991. "Durango: Veinte años de lucha de masas." May.

Dussel Peters, Enrique. 2000. *Polarizing Mexico: The Impact of Liberalization Strategy.* Boulder, Colo.: Lynne Rienner.

Eckstein, Susan. 1977a. *The Poverty of Revolution: The State and the Urban Poor in Mexico.* Princeton: Princeton University Press.

———. 1977b. "The State and the Urban Poor." In *Authoritarianism in Mexico*, ed. José Luis Reyna and Richard S. Weinert. Philadelphia: Institute for the Study of Human Issues.

———. 1989a. "Power and Popular Protest in Latin America." In *Power and Popular Protest: Latin American Social Movements*, ed. Susan Eckstein. Berkeley and Los Angeles: University of California Press.

———, ed. 1989b. *Power and Popular Protest: Latin American Social Movements.* Berkeley and Los Angeles: University of California Press.

———. 1990. "Poor People Versus the State and Capital: Anatomy of a Successful Community Mobilization for Housing in Mexico City." *International Journal of Urban and Regional Research* 14:2.

Eisinger, Peter K. 1973. "The Conditions of Protest Behavior in American Cities." *American Political Science Review* 67:11–28.

Elizondo, Carlos. 2003. "After the Second of July: Challenges and Opportunities for the Fox Administration." In *Mexico's Politics and Society in Transition,* ed. Joseph S. Tulchin and Andrew D. Selee. Boulder, Colo.: Lynne Rienner.

Enzástiga, Leopoldo. 1990. "El Movimiento Popular Cardenista a dos años de Julio." *Barrio Nuevo* (Mexico City), 1, no. 5.

Escobar, Arturo. 1995. *Encountering Development: The Making and Unmaking of the Third World.* Princeton: Princeton University Press.

Escobar, Arturo, and Sonia E. Alvarez, eds. 1992. *The Making of Social Movements in Latin America: Identity, Strategy, and Democracy.* Boulder, Colo.: Westview Press.

Escudero Gómez, Alberto, and Marcos Cruz. 1986. "Breve historia del Comité de Defensa Popular de Durango." In *Llego la hora de ser govierno,* by Marcos Cruz et al. Mexico City: Equipo Pueblo and Editorial Praxis.

Espinoza Valle, Víctor Alegandro. 1999. "Alternation and Political Liberalization: The PAN in Baja California." In *Subnational Politics and Democratization in Mexico,* ed. Wayne Cornelius, Todd Eisenstadt, and Jane Hindley. Center for U.S.-Mexican Studies, University of California, San Diego.

Fagen, Richard R. 1969. *The Transformation of Political Culture in Cuba.* Stanford: Stanford University Press.

Fagen, Richard R., and William S. Tuohy. 1972. *Politics and Privilege in a Mexican City.* Stanford: Stanford University Press.

Farthing, Linda, and B. Kohl. 2001. "Bolivia's New Wave of Protest." *nacla Report on the Americas* 34, no. 5:8–11.

———. 2003. "La policía se amotinó en La Paz y dejó desprotegida a la ciudad." La Paz, Bolivia, 12 February, http://ea.gmcsa.net/2003/02-Febrero/20030212/Especial/Febrero/esp030212a.html.

Ferree, Myra Marx. 1992. "The Political Context of Rationality: Rational Choice Theory and Resource Mobilization." In *Frontiers in Social Movement Theory,* ed. Aldon D. Morris and Carol McClurg Mueller. New Haven: Yale University Press.

Foweraker, Joe. 1993. *Popular Mobilization in Mexico: The Teacher's Movement, 1977–87.* New York: Cambridge University Press.

———. 1995. *Theorizing Social Movements.* London: Pluto Press.

Foweraker, Joe, and Craig, Ann L., eds. 1990. *Popular Movements and Political Change in Mexico.* Boulder, Colo.: Lynne Rienner.

Fox, Jonathan. 1990a. "Democracy and the Development Process: Leadership Accountability in State-Structured Peasant Organizations." Mimeograph, April.

———. 1990b. "The Political Dynamics of Reform: State Power and Food Policy in Mexico."

———. 1993. *The Politics of Food in Mexico: State Power and Social Mobilization.* Ithaca: Cornell University Press.

———. 1994. "Targeting the Poorest: The Role of the National Indigenous Institute in Mexico's Solidarity Program." In *Transforming State-Society Relations in Mexico: The National Solidarity Strategy,* ed. Wayne A. Cornelius, Ann L. Craig, and Jonathan Fox. U.S.-Mexico Contemporary Perspectives Series 6.

La Jolla: Center for U.S.-Mexican Studies, University of California, San Diego.

Fox, Jonathan, and Julio Moguel. 1995. "Pluralism and Anti-poverty Policy: Mexico's National Solidarity Program and Left Opposition Municipal Governments." In *Opposition Government in Mexico: Past Experiences and Future Opportunities*, ed. Victoria Rodríguez and Peter Ward. Albuquerque: University of New Mexico Press.

Fundación Arturo Rosenblueth. 1989. *Geografía de las elecciones presidenciales en México, 1988*. Mexico City: Fundación Arturo Rosenblueth.

Furtado, Celso. 1970. *Economic Development of Latin America*. New York: Cambridge University Press.

Gamson, William. 1988. "Political Discourse and Collective Action." In *From Structure to Action: Comparing Social Movement Research Across Cultures*, ed. Bert Klandermas, Hanspeter Kriesi, and Sidney Tarrow, 219–44. International Social Movement Research, vol. 1. Greenwich, Conn.: JAI.

———. 1992a. "Social Psychology of Collective Action." In *Frontiers in Social Movement Theory*, ed. Aldon D. Morris and Carol McClurg Mueller. New Haven: Yale University Press.

———. 1992b. *Talking Politics*. Cambridge, U.K.: Cambridge University Press.

Garner, Roberta Ash, and Mayer N. Zald. 1985. "The Political Economy of Social Movement Sectors." In *The Challenge of Social Control: Citizenship and Institution Building in Modern Societ. Essays in Honor of Morris Janoqitz*, ed. Gerald Suttles and Mayer N. Zald. Norwood, N.J.: ABLEX, 119–145.

Garretón, Manuel Antonio. 1989. "Popular Mobilization and the Military Regime in Chile: The Complexities of the Invisible Transition." In *Power and Popular Protest: Latin American Social Movements*, ed. Susan Eckstein. Berkeley and Los Angeles: University of California Press.

Gaventa, John. 1980. *Power and Powerlessness: Quiescence and Rebellion in an Appalachian Valley*. Urbana: University of Illinois Press.

Gay, Robert. 1994. *Popular Organization and Democracy in Rio De Janeiro: A Tale of Two Favelas*. Philadelphia: Temple University Press.

Giddens, Anthony. 1984. *The Constitution of Society*. Berkeley and Los Angeles: University of California Press.

Gitlan, Todd. 1980. *The Whole World Is Watching: Mass Media in the Making and Unmaking of the New Left*. Berkeley and Los Angeles: University of California Press.

Gobierno Constitucional de Los Estados Unidos Mexicanos y el Gobierno Constitucional del Estado de Durango. 1987. Plan Estatal de Desarrollo, Durango, 1987–1992.

Gómez Tagle, Silvia, ed. 1993. *Las elecciones de 1991: La recuperación oficial*. Mexico City: García y Valadés Editores.

González Casanova, Pablo. 1970. *Democracy in Mexico*. New York: Oxford University Press.

González Navarro, Moisés. 1965. "México: The Lopsided Revolution." In *Obstacles to Change in Latin America*, ed. Claudio Veliz. London: Oxford University Press.

Gramsci, Antonio. 1971. *Selections from the Prison Notebooks*. Edited and translated by Quintin Hoarse and Geoffrey Nowell Smith. New York: International.

Greene, Kenneth F. 1991. "The Asamblea de Barrios de la Ciudad de México, the Partido Revolucionario Democratico, and the Question of Democratization." Mimeograph.

———. 1994. "Complexity, Cohesion, and Longevity in an Urban Popular Movement: The Asamblea de Barrios de la Ciudad de Mexico." Mimeograph.

Grindle, Merilee. 1977. *Bureaucrats, Politicians, and Peasants in Mexico*. Berkeley and Los Angeles: University of California Press.

Grindle, Merilee S. 1991. "The Response to Austerity: Political and Economic Strategies of Mexico's Rural Poor." In *Social Responses to Mexico's Economic Crisis of the 1980s*, ed. Mercedes González de la Rocha and Agustín Escobar Latapí. Ja Jolla: Center for U.S.-Mexican Studies, University of California, San Diego.

Gurr, Ted R. 1970. *Why Men Rebel*. Princeton: Princeton University Press.

Guzmán, Gabino Martinez. 1998. *cdp: El Poder del Pueblo*. Durango, Mexico: Instituto de Investigaciones Historicas, U.J.E.D.

Haber, Paul. 1989. "Hacia dónde, CONAMUP? El X encuentro nacional de la CONAMUP." *Pueblo* 12, no. 148.

———. 1990. "Cárdenas, Salinas y los movimientos populares urbanos en México: El Caso del Comité de Defensa Popular, General Francisco Villa de Durango." In *Movimientos sociales en México*, ed. Sergio Zermeño and Aurelio Cuevas, 221–52. Mexico City: Centro de Investigaciones Interdiciplinarias en Humanidades, UNAM.

———. 1993. "Cárdenas, Salinas, and the Urban Popular Movement." In *Mexico: Dilemmas of Transition*, ed. Neil Harvey, 218–48. New York: St. Martin's Press.

———. 1994a. "The Art and Implications of Political Restructuring in Mexico: The Case of Urban Popular Movements." In *The Politics of Economic Restructuring: State-Society Relations and Regime Change in Mexico*, ed. Maria Lorena Cook, Kevin J. Middlebrook, and Juan Molinar Horcasitas, 277–302. La Jolla: Center for U.S.-Mexican Studies, University of California, San Diego.

———. 1994b. "Political Change in Durango: The Role of National Solidarity." In *Transforming State-Society Relations in Mexico: The National Solidarity Strategy*, ed. Wayne Cornelius, Ann Craig, and Jonathan Fox, 255–79. La Jolla: Center for U.S.-Mexican Studies, University of California, San Diego.

———. 1996a. "El arte de la reestructuración y sus implicaciones políticas: El caso de los movimientos urbanos populares." In *Las dimensiones políticas de la reestructuración económica*, ed. Maria Lorena Cook, Kevin J. Middlebrook, and Juan Molinar Horcasitas, 333–70. Mexico City: cal y arena.

———. 1996b. "Identity and Political Process: Recent Trends in the Study of Latin American Social Movements." *Latin American Research Review* 31, no. 1:171–88.

———. 1997a. "Social Movements and Social Change in Latin America." *Current Sociology* 45, no. 1:121–40.

———. 1997b. "Vamos por la dignidad de Durango: Un estudio de poder sociopolítico." In *Movimientos Sociales y Democracia en el México de los 90s*, ed. Sergio

Zermeño. Mexico City: La Jornada ediciones and Centro de Investigaciones Interdiciplinarias en Humanidades, UNAM.

——. 1998a. "Import-Substitution Industrialization," In *Encyclopedia of Mexico: History, Society, and Culture,* ed. Michael Werner. Chicago: Fitzroy Dearborn.

——. 1998b. "Neoliberalism." In *Encyclopedia of Mexico: History, Society, and Culture,* ed. Michael Werner. Chicago: Fitzroy Dearborn.

——. 1998c. "Popular Organizations." In *Encyclopedia of Mexico: History, Society, and Culture,* ed. Michael Werner. Chicago: Fitzroy Dearborn.

——. 2001. "Party Time? Building a Progressive Electoral Movement: A Case for the New Party." In *Forging Radical Alliances Across Difference: Coalition Politics for the New Millennium,* ed. Jill M. Bystydzienski and Steven P. Schacht. Rowman and Littlefield.

Haber, Stephen R. 1989. *Industry and Underdevelopment: The Industrialization of Mexico, 1890–1940.* Stanford: Stanford University Press.

Haines, Herbert H. 1984. "Black Radicalization and the Funding of Civil Rights, 1957–1970." *Social Problems* 32:31–43.

Hamilton, Nora. 1982. *The Limits of State Autonomy: Post-revolutionary Mexico.* Princeton: Princeton University Press.

Handleman, Howard. 1975. "The Political Mobilization of Urban Squatter Settlements: Santiago's Recent Experience and Its Implications for Urban Research." *Latin American Research Review* 10, no. 2:35–72.

Harvey, Neil. 1990. "The Limits of Concertation in Rural Mexico, 1988–1990." Paper presented to the research workshop "Mexico in Transition: Elements of Continuity and Change," Institute of Latin American Studies, London.

——. 1993. *Mexico: Dilemmas of Transition.* New York: St. Martin's Press.

——. 1998. *The Chiapas Rebellion: The Struggle for Land and Democracy.* Durham: Duke University Press.

Hellman, Judith Adler. 1988. *Mexico in Crisis.* 2d ed. New York: Homes and Meier.

——. 1992. "Latin American Social Movements and the Question of Autonomy." In *New Social Movements in Latin America: Identity, Strategy, and Democracy,* ed. Arturo Escobar and Sonia Alvarez, 52–61. Boulder, Colo.: Westview Press.

——. 1994. "Mexican Popular Movements, Clientelism, and the Process of Democratization." *Latin American Perspectives,* vol. 21, issue 80, no. 2: 276–94.

Hernández Navarro, Luis. 1986. "The SNTE and the Teacher's Movement, 1982–1984." In *The Mexican Left, the Popular Movements, and the Politics of Austerity,* ed. Barry Carr and Ricardo Anzaldúa Montoya. Monograph Series 18. La Jolla: Center for U.S.-Mexican Studies, University of California, San Diego.

——. 1991a. "El Partido del Trabajo: Realidades y perspectivas." *El Cotidiano,* no. 40 (March–April): 21–28.

——. 1991b. "El Partido del Trabajo: Recuento de una derrota." *El Cotidiano,* no. 44 (November–December): 70–75.

Hernández Navarro, Luis, and Jonathan Fox. 1995. "Mexico's Difficult Democracy: Grassroots Movements, NGOs, and Local Government." In *New Paths to Democratic Development in Latin America: The Rise of ngo-Municipal Collaboration,* ed. Charles A. Reilly. Boulder, Colo.: Lynne Rienner.

Hillman, James. 1983. *Inter Views: Conversations Between James Hillman and Laura Pozzo on Therapy, Biography, Love, Soul, Dreams, Work, Imagination, and the State of the Culture.* New York: Harper and Row.

Hirschman, Albert. 1982. *Shifting Involvements: Private Interest and Public Action.* Princeton: Princeton University Press.

Hoare, Quintin, and Geoffrey Nowell Smith, eds. 1971. *Selections from the Prison Notebooks of Antonio Gramsci.* New York: International Publishers.

Huntington, Samuel. 1968. *Political Order in Changing Societies.* New Haven: Yale University Press.

Jenkins, J. Craig. 1983. "Resource Mobilization Theory and the Study of Social Movements." *Annual Review of Sociology* 9:527–53.

———. 1985. *The Politics of Insurgency: The Farm Worker Movement in the 1960s.* New York: Columbia University Press.

Jenkins, J. Craig, and Charles Perrow. 1977. "Insurgency of the Powerless: Farm Worker Movements (1946–1972)." *American Sociological Review* 42, no. 2:249–68.

Johnson, John J. 1958. *Political Change in Latin America: The Emergence of the Middle Sectors.* Stanford: Stanford University Press.

Joseph, Gilbert M., and Daniel Nugent, eds. 1994. *Everyday Forms of State Formation: Revolution and the Negotiation of Rule in Modern Mexico.* Durham: Duke University Press.

Karl, Terry Lynn. 1990. "Dilemmas of Democratization in Latin America." *Comparative Politics* 23, no. 1:1–21.

Katz, Fredrich. 1998. *The Life and Times of Poncho Villa.* Stanford: Stanford University Press.

Keck, Margaret, and Kathryn Sikkink. 1992. "International Issue Networks in the Environment and Human Rights." Paper presented at the Seventeenth International Congress of the Latin American Studies Association, Los Angeles, September 25.

Kielbowicz, Richard B., and Clifford Scherer. 1986. "The Role of the Press in the Dynamics of Social Movements." In *Research in Social Movements, Conflict, and Change.* Vol. 8, ed. L. Kriesberg, 71–96. Greenwich, Conn.: JAI.

Kirkwood, Julieta. 1985. "Feministas y política." *Nueva Sociedad* (Venezuela), 78:82–91.

Klandermans, Bert. 1988. "The Formation of Mobilization of Consensus." In *From Structure to Action: Comparing Social Movement Research Across Cultures,* ed. Bert Klandermans, Hanspeter Kriesi, and Sidney Tarrow. International Social Movement Research, vol. 1, 173-96. Greenwhich, Conn.: JAI.

———. 1992. "The Social Construction of Protest and Multiorganizational Fields." In *Frontiers in Social Movement Theory,* ed. Aldon Morris and Carol McClurg Mueller. New Haven: Yale University Press.

Klandermans, Hanspeter Kriesi, and Sidney Tarrow, eds. 1988. *From Structure to Action: Comparing Social Movement Research Across Cultures.* International Social Movement Research, vol. 1., 219–44. Greenwich, Conn.: JAI.

Klesner, Joseph. 1998. "An Electoral Route to Democracy? Mexico's Transition in Comparative Perspective." *Comparative Politics* 30, no. 4:477–97.

Knight, Alan. 1990. "Historical Continuities in Social Movements." In *Popular Movements and Political Change in Mexico*, ed. Joe Foweraker and Ann L. Craig. Boulder, Colo.: Lynne Rienner.

———. 1994. "Cardenismo: Juggernaut or Jalopy?" *Journal of Latin American Studies* 26, no 1:73–107.

Kuhn, Thomas. 1962. *The Structure of Scientific Revolutions*. Chicago: University of Chicago Press.

Laso de la Vega, Jorge, ed. 1987. *Corriente Democrática: Hablan los protagonistas*. Mexico City: Editorial Posada.

Lau, Rubén, and Víctor M. Quintana Silveyra. 1991. *Movimientos Populares en Chihuahua*. Ciudad Juárez, Mexico: Universidad Autónoma de Ciudad Juárez.

Lerner, Daniel. 1958. *The Passing of the Traditional Society*. Glencoe, Ill.: Free Press.

Lerner de Sheinbaum, Bertha. 1989. "El movimiento neocardenista: Perspective a corto plazo." Paper presented at the Fifteenth International Congress of the Latin American Studies Association, Miami, Florida.

Levy, Santiago. 1991. "Poverty Alleviation in Mexico." Mimeograph.

Lichbach, Mark I. 1987. "Deterrence or Escalation? The Puzzle of Aggregate Studies of Repression and Dissent." *Journal of Conflict Resolution* 31 (June).

Lipset, Seymour Martin. 1967. "Values, Education, and Entrepreneurship." In *Elites in Latin America*, ed. Seymour Lipset and Aldo Solari. Oxford: Oxford University Press.

Lodhi, Abdul Qaiyum, and Charles Tilly. 1973. "Urbanization and Collective Violence in Nineteenth-Century France." *American Journal of Sociology* 79 (September): 296–318.

Lomnitz, Larissa Adler. 1977. *Networks and Marginality: Life in a Mexican Shantytown*. New York: Academic Press.

López Portillo, José. 1975. *Elevación y caída de Porfirio Díaz*. Mexico City: Porrúa.

Lustig, Nora. 1994. "Solidarity as a Strategy of Poverty Alleviation." In *Transforming State-Society Relations in Mexico: The National Solidarity Strategy*, ed. Wayne A. Cornelius, Ann L. Craig, and Jonathan Fox. La Jolla: Center for U.S.–Mexican Studies, University of San Diego.

McAdam, Doug. 1982. *Political Process and the Development of Black Insurgency, 1930–1970*. Chicago: University of Chicago Press.

———. 1988. *Freedom Summer*. Oxford: Oxford University Press.

McAdam, Doug, John D. McCarthy, and Mayer N. Zald. 1988. "Social Movements." In *Handbook of Sociology*, ed. Neil J. Smelser. Beverly Hills, Calif.: Sage.

McCarthy, John D., and Mayer N. Zald. 1977. "Resource Mobilization and Social Movements: A Partial Theory." *American Journal of Sociology* 82:1212–141.

Magaloni, Beatriz, and Guillermo Zepeda. 2004. In *Dilemmas of Political Change in Mexico*, ed. Kevin J. Middlebrook. London: Institute of Latin American Studies, University of London.

Mainwaring, Scott. 1987. "Urban Popular Movements, Identity, and Democratization in Brazil." *Comparative Political Studies* 20, no. 2: 131–59.

Malloy, James J., ed. 1977. *Authoritarianism and Corporatism in Latin America*. Pittsburgh: University of Pittsburgh Press.

Marín López, Héctor, and Miguel Palacios Moncayo. 1995. *Las Elecciones Federales de 1994 en Durango*. Durango: Instituto de Ciencias Sociales, Universidad Juarez del Estado de Durango.

Martin, Everett D. 1920. *The Behavior of Crowds*. New York: Harper.

Martínez Guzmán, Gabino. 1997. *Los anales de Durango, 1900–1930*. Durango: Instituto de Investigaciones Históricas, U.J.E.D.

———. 1998. *cdp: El poder del pueblo*. Durango, Mexico: Instituto de Investigaciones Historicas, UJ.E.D.

Martínez Guzmán, Gabino, and Juan Ángel Chávez Ramírez. 1998. *Durango: Un volcán en erupción*. Mexico City: Fondo de Cultural Económica.

Massolo, Alejandra. 1983. "Las mujeres en los movimientos sociales urbanos de la ciudad de México." *Iztapalpa* 9 (June–December): 152–67.

———. 1986. "'Que el gobierno entiedna, lo primero es la vivienda!': La organización de los damnificados." *Revista Mexicana de Sociología* 48, no. 2.

———. 1987. "Haciendo y deshaciendo paredes: La mujer en la reconstrucción de la vivienda." FEM 52 (April).

———. 1988. *Memoria del Pedregal, memoria de mujer: Testimonio de una colonia*. Mexico City: Mujeres para el Diálogo.

Mazza, Jacqueline. 2001. *Don't Disturb the Neighbors: The United States and Democracy in Mexico, 1980–1985*. New York: Routledge.

Melucci, Alberto. 1989. *Nomads of the Present: Social Movements and Individual Needs in Contemporary Society*. Philadelphia: Temple University Press.

Meyer, Michael C., and William L. Sherman. 1995. *The Course of Mexican History*. 5th ed. New York: Oxford University Press.

Meyer, Lorenzo. 1989. "Democratization of the PRI: Mission Impossible." In *Mexico's Alternative Political Futures*, ed. Wayne A. Cornelius et al. Monograph Series 30. La Jolla: Center for U.S.-Mexican Studies, University of San Diego.

Meza, Armando. 1994. *Movimiento urbano popular en Durango*. Mexico City: Centro de Investigaciones y Estudios Superiores en Antropología Social, Ediciones de la Casa Chata.

Middlebrook, Kevin. 1986. "Political Liberalization in an Authoritarian Regime: The Case of Mexico." In *Transitions from Authoritarian Rule: Latin America*, ed. Guillermo O'Donnel, Philippe C. Schmitter, and Lawrence Whitehead. Baltimore: Johns Hopkins University Press.

Migdal, Joel S. 1984. *Peasants, Politics, and Revolution: Pressures Toward Political and Social Change in the Third World*. Princeton: Princeton University Press.

Moguel, Julio. 1987. *Los caminos de la izquierda*. Mexico City: Ed. Juan Pablos.

———. 1989. "El Comité de Defensa Popular de Durango, sus luchas actuales y el PRD." *El Cotidiano*, issue 30 (July–August): 20–23.

———. 1990a. "National Solidarity Program Fails to Help the Very Poor" *Voices of Mexico* (UNAM, Mexico City), no. 15.

———. 1990b. "El programa nacional de solidaridad. Para quien?" Mimeograph.

———. 1991a. "Local Power and Development Alternatives: The Experience of the Urban Popular Movement in a Region of Northern Mexico." Paper prepared for the Sixteenth International Congress of the Latin American Studies Association, Washington, D.C.

——. 1991b. "Poder local y alternativas de desarrollo: La experiencia del movimiento urbano en una region del Norte de Mexico." Paper prepared for the Inter-American Foundation.

——. 1995. "Local Power and Development Alternatives: An Urban Popular Movement in Northern Mexico." In *New Paths to Democratic Development in Latin America: The Rise of ngo-Municipal Collaboration*, ed. Charles A. Reilly. Boulder, Colo.: Lynne Rienner.

Moguel, Julio, and Rosario Robles. 1990. "Los nuevos movimientos rurales, por la tierra y por la apropiación del ciclo productiv." In *Historia de la cuestión agraria mexicana*, ed. Julio Moguel. Vol. 9, pt. 2. Mexico City: Siglo XXI Editores and Centro de Estudios Históricos del Agrarismo en México.

Molinar Horcasitas, Juan, and Jeffrey A. Weldon. 1991. "Elecciones de 1988 en México: Crisis del autoritarismo." Mimeograph.

——. 1994. "Electoral Determinants and Consequences of National Solidarity." In *Transforming State-Society Relations in Mexico: The National Solidarity Strategy*, ed. Wayne A. Cornelius, Ann L. Craig, and Jonathan Fox. La Jolla: Center for U.S.–Mexican Studies, University of San Diego.

Monsiváis, Carlos. 1988. Entrada libre: Crónicas de una sociedad que se organiza. Mexico City: Ediciones Era

Montaño, Jorge. 1976. *Los pobres de la Ciudad y los asentamientos humanos*. Mexico City: Siglo XXI.

Moore, Barrington. 1969. *Social Origins of Dictatorship: Lord and Peasant in the Making of the Modern World*. London: Peregrine Books.

Morris, Aldon D., and Carol McClurg Mueller, eds. 1992. *Frontiers in Social Movement Theory*. New Haven: Yale University Press.

Morris, Stephen D. 1995. *Political Reformism in Mexico: An Overview of Contemporary Mexican Politics*. Boulder, Colo.: Lynne Rienner.

Mueller, Carol McClurg. 1992. "Building Social Movement Theory." In *Frontiers in Social Movement Theory*, ed. Aldon D. Morris and Carol McClurg Mueller. New Haven: Yale University Press.

Muñoz Ledo, Porfirio. 1988. *Compromisos*. Mexico City: Editorial Posada.

Musacchio, Humberto. 1994. "Palomino denuncia: Cecilia, la recomendada de Patrocinio." *Mira*, July 18, 7–10.

Núñez, Oscar. 1990. *Innocaciones democratico-culturales del movimiento urbano-popular.* Mexico City: Universidad Autonoma Metropolitana.

Obershall, Anthony. 1973. *Social Conflict and Social Movements*. Englewood Cliffs, N.J.: Prentice-Hall.

O'Donnell, Guillermo A. 1973. *Modernization and Bureaucratic-Authoritarianism: Studies in South American Politics*. Berkeley: Institute of International Studies, University of California.

Offe, Claus. 1985. "New Social Movements: Challenging the Boundaries of Institutional Politics." *Social Research* 52, no. 4:817–68.

OIR-LM. 1982. "Estatutos, resoluciones, y estrategia." Mimeograph.

Oliver, Pamela E. 1989. "Bringing the Crowd Back In: The Nonorganizational Elements of Social Movements." *Research in Social Movements, Conflict, and Change* 14:1–30.

Olson, Mancur. 1965. *The Logic of Collective Action*. Cambridge, Mass.: Harvard University Press.

Olvera, Alberto J., ed. 1999. *La sociedad civil: De la teoría a la realidad*. Mexico City: El Colegio de México.

Ornelas Navarro, Carlos. 1984. "Durango 70." Paper presented at the conference "Seminario Regional sobre Movimientos Sociales en México, Región Chihuahua, Durango y Zacatecas," Instituto de Ciencias Sociales at the Universidad Juarez del Estado de Durango, Durango, Mexico, May.

Oxhorn, Philip. 1995. *Organizing Civil Society: The Popular Sectors and the Struggle for Democracy in Chile*. University Park: Pennsylvania State University Press.

Oxhorn, Philip, and Graciela Ducatenzeiler, eds. 1998. *What Kind of Democracy? What Kind of Market? Latin America in the Age of Neoliberalism*. University Park: Pennsylvania State University Press.

Palacios Moncayo, Miguel. 1999. "Durango, clase politica, partidos y elecciones." Mimeograph.

———. 1994. "Durango." Excelsior (Seccion Ideas) 1 de Julio de 1994.

Palencia Alonso, Víctor Samuel. "Las finanzas municipales." *El Sol de Durango*, August 2.

Pastor, Manuel, Jr., and Carol Wise. 1998. "Mexican-Style Neoliberalism: State Policy and Distributional Stress." In *The Post-nafta Political Economy: Mexico and the Western Hemisphere*, ed. Carol Wise. University Park: Pennsylvania State University Press.

———. 2003. "A Long View of Mexico's Political Economy: What's Changed? What Are the Challenges?" In *Mexico's Politics and Society in Transition*, ed. Joseph S. Tulchin and Andrew D. Selle. Boulder, Colo.: Lynne Rienner.

Pérez Arce, Francisco. 1990. "The Enduring Struggle for Legality and Democracy." In *Popular Movements and Political Change in Mexico*, ed. Joe Foweraker and Ann L. Craig. Boulder, Colo.: Lynne Rienner.

Perlman, Janice E. 1976. *The Myth of Marginality: Urban Poverty and Politics in Rio de Janeiro*. Berkeley and Los Angeles: University of California Press.

Perlo, Manuel. 1980. "Politica y vivienda en Mexico, 1910–1952." *Revista Mexicana de Sociologia* 42:1.

Perló Cohen, Manuel. 1981. "Apuntes para una interpretación en torno al proceso de acumulación capitalista y las políticas urbanas del Distrito Federal, 1920–1980." Mimeograph, Instituto de Investigaciones de la UNAM.

Petras, James. 1989. "State Terror and Social Movements in Latin America." *International Journal of Politics, Culture, and Society* 3, no. 2:179–212.

Piven, Frances Fox, and Richard A. Cloward. 1979. *Poor People's Movements: Why They Succeed, How They Fail*. New York: Vintage Books.

———. 1992. "Normalizing Collective Protest." In *Frontiers in Social Movement Theory*, ed. Aldon D. Morris and Carol McClurg Mueller. New Haven: Yale University Press.

Política Popular. 1968a. *Hacia una Política Popular*. Mexico City: Política Popular.

———. 1968b. *Sobre el desarrollo de Política Popular y sus cuadros medios.* Mexico City: Política Popular.

———. 1974. *Por una línea de masas.* Mexico City: Política Popular.

Poniatowska, Elena. 1971. *La noche de Tlateloco.* Mexico City: Ediciones Era.

———. 1995. *Nothing, Nobody: The Voices of the Mexico City Earthquake.* Philadelphia: Temple University Press.

Popkin, Samuel L. 1979. *The Rational Peasant.* Berkeley and Los Angeles: University of California Press.

PRD. 1990a. *Crítica a la política del govierno.* Mexico City: Grupo Parlimentario de Partido de la Revolución.

———. 1990b. *Crítica y alternative a política económica.* Mexico City: Grupo Parlimentario de Partido de la Revolución.

———. 1990c. *Lucha parlamentaria por la reforma electoral democrática.* Mexico City: Grupo Parlimentario de Partido de la Revolución.

———. 1990d. "Voto particular del group parlamentario del PRD en contra del dictamen del presupuesto de egresos de la federación corrrespondiente a 1991." Mimeograph, Mexico City.

———. 1991. "1990: Situación nacional (balance y ropuestas)." Mimeograph, Mexico City.

Presidencia de la Republica, Unidad de la Cronica Presidencial. 1986. *Las rezones y las obras: Cronica del sexenio, 1982–1988.* Trecer Año. Mexico City: Presidencia de la Republica/Fondo de Cultura Economica.

———. 1987. *Las rezones y las obras: Cronica del sexenio, 1982–1988.* Cuarto Año. Mexico City: Presidencia de la Republica/Fondo de Cultura Economica.

Prieto, Ana Maria. 1986. "Mexico's National Coordinadoras in a Context of Economic Crisis." In *The Mexican Left, the Popular Movements, and the Politics of Austerity,* ed. Barry Carr and Ricardo Anzaldúa Montoya. Monograph Series 18. La Jolla: Center for U.S.-Mexican Studies, University of California, San Diego.

Punto Crítico. 1980. "Mexico: Class Struggle and 'Political Reform.'" *Contemporary Marxism* (Spring): 73–79.

Purcell, Susan Kaufman. 1975. *The Mexican Profit-Sharing Decision: Politics in an Authoritarian Regime.* Berkeley and Los Angeles: University of California Press.

Regaldo Santillán, Jorge. 1997. "Lo que quedó del MUP." In *Cultura Política de las organizaciones y movimientos sociales,* ed. Jamie Castillo and Elsa Patiño. Mexico City: La Jornada Ediciones and Centro de Investigaciones Interdiciplinarias en Humanidades, UNAM.

Reilly, Charles A., ed. 1995. *New Paths to Democratic Development in Latin America: The Rise of ngo-Municipal Collaboration.* Boulder, Colo.: Lynne Rienner.

Reséndiz, Jesús, and Roberto Zamarripa. 1992. "Durango formalizó nuevo equilibrio político: El PT estrenó alcaldía." *La Jornada,* September 10.

Reyna, José Luis. 1977. "Redefining the Authoritarian Regime." *In Authoritarianism in Mexico,* ed. José Luis Reyna and Richard S. Weinert. Inter-American Politics Series, vol. 2. Philadelphia: Institute for the Study of Human Issues.

Reyna, José Luis, and Richard S. Weinert, eds. 1977. *Authoritarianism in Mexico.* Philadelphia: Institute for the Study of Human Issues.

Reynolds, Clark W. 1970. *The Mexican Economy: Twentieth-Century Structure and Growth*. New Haven: Yale University Press,.
——. 1978. "Why Mexico's 'Stabilizing Development' Was Actually Destabilizing." *World Development* 6, no. 7/8.
Rivas, Manuel. 1989. "La Asamblea de Barrios." Mimeograph.
Rodríguez Garza, Francisco Javier. 1993. "El Maoismo de Salinas." *Topodrilo* 29 (July–August): 24–31.
Rodríguez, Victoria E. 1997. *Decentralization in Mexico: From Reforma Municipal to Solidaridad to Nuevo Federalism*. Boulder, Colo.: Westview Press.
Rodríguez, Victoria E., and Peter M. Ward, eds. 1995. *Opposition Government in Mexico*. Albuquerque: University of New Mexico Press.
Rodríguez Velázquez, Daniel. 1987. "Cronologia de la Coodinadora Unica de Damnificados (septiembre de 1985–mayo 1987)." Mexico City, May, Mimeograph.
Rogers, Kim Lacy. 1993. *Righteous Lives: Narratives of the New Orleans Civil Rights Movement*. New York: New York University Press.
Rojas, Carlos, et al. 1991. *Solidaridad a debate*. Mexico City: El Nacional.
Rojas, Rosa. 1989. "Geografía de las elecciones: Análisis y resultados." *La Jornada*, January 25.
Rubin, Jeffrey W. 1997. *Decentering the Regime: Ethnicity, Radicalism, and Democracy in Juchitán, Mexico*. Durham: Duke University Press.
Rule, James, and Charles Tilly. 1975. "Political Process in Revolutionary France: 1830–1852." In *1830 in France*, ed. John M. Merriman. New York: New Viewpoints.
Rupp, Leila J., and Verta A. Taylor. 1987. *Survival in the Doldrums. The American Women's Rights Movement, 1945 to the 1960s*. Oxford: Oxford University Press.
Sachs, Wolfgang, ed. 1992. *The Development Dictionary: A Guide to Knowledge as Power*. London: Zed Books.
Salinas de Gortari, Carlos. 1978. "Public Investment, Political Participation, and System Support: Study of Three Rural Communities in Central Mexico." Ph.D. diss., Harvard University.
——. 1982. *Producción y participación política en el campo*. Mexico City: Fondo de Cultura Económica.
——. 1984. "Production and Participation in Rural Areas: Some Political Considerations." *The Political Economy of Income Distribution in Mexico*, ed. Pedro Aspe and Javier Beristain. New York: Holmes and Meier.
——. 1989. Primer Informe, Statistical Index. Mexico City: Office of the President.
San Juan Victoria, Carlos. 1999. "Tendencia de la sociedad civil en México: La puja del poder y la sociedad a fin de siglo." In *La sociedad civil: De la teoría a la realidad*, ed. Alberto J. Olvera. Mexico City: El Colegio de México.
Schmitter, Phillippe C. 1974. "Still the Century of Corporatism?" *Review of Politics* 36, no. 1:85–131.
Schneider Cathy Lisa. 1995. *Shantytown Protest in Pinochet's Chile*. Philadelphia: Temple University Press.
Scott, David Clark. 1991. "Mexican President Wins Plaudits with Aid to Poor." *Christian Science Monitor*, February 28.

Scott, James C. 1985. *Weapons of the Weak: Everyday Forms of Peasant Resistance.* New Haven: Yale University Press.

SEDESOL. 1993. *Solidaridad Sintesis Nacional: Resultados 1992.* México City: SEDESOL.

———. 1994. *Solidaridad: Seis años de trabajo.* México City: SEDESOL.

Silvert, Kalman H. 1967. "The Politics of Social and Economic Change in Latin America." Sociological Review Monographs 11. London: University of Keele.

Singer, Martha S., and Gustavo Leal F. 1993. "Governando desde la oposición: Ayuntamiento de Durango 1992–1995." *El Cotidiano*, no. 54 (May): 90–100.

Smith, Peter. 1979. *Labyrinths of Power: Political Recruitment in Twentieth-Century Mexico.* Princeton: Princeton University Press.

Snow, David A., and Robert D. Benford. 1992. "Master Frames and Cycles of Protest." In *Frontiers in Social Movement Theory*, ed. Aldon Morris and Carol McClurg Mueller. New Haven: Yale University Press.

Snow, David A., E. Burke Rochford, Jr., Steven K. Worden, and Robert D. Benford. 1986. "Frame Alignment Processes, Micromobilization, and Movement Participation." *American Sociological Review* 51.

Snyder, David, and Charles Tilly. 1972. "Hardship and Collective Violence in France, 1830–1960." *American Sociological Review* 37.

Snyder, Richard, ed. 1999. *Institutional Adaptation and Innovation in Rural Mexico.* Center for U.S.-Mexican Studies, University of California, San Diego.

Starn, Orin. 1992. "I Dreamed of Foxes and Hawks: Reflections on Peasant Protest, New Social Movements, and the Rondas Campesinas of Northern Peru." In *The Making of Social Movements in Latin America: Identity, Strategy, and Democracy*, ed. Arturo Escobar and Sonia E. Alvarez. Boulder, Colo.: Westview Press.

———. 1995. "To Revolt Against the Revolution: War and Resistance in Peru's Andes." *Cultural Anthropology* 10:547–80.

Stavenhagen, Rodolfo. 2003. "Mexico's Unfinished Symphony: The Zapatista Movement." In *Mexico's Politics and Society in Transition*, ed. Joseph S. Tulchin and Andrew D. Selee. Boulder, Colo.: Lynne Rienner.

Stepan, Alfred. 1978. *State and Society: Peru in Comparative Perspective.* New Haven: Yale University Press.

Stevens, Evelyn P. 1974. *Protest and Response in Mexico.* Cambridge, Mass.: MIT Press.

Stokes, Susan. 1995. *Cultures in Conflict: Social Movements and the State in Peru.* Berkeley and Los Angeles: University of California Press.

Street, Susan. 1989. "The Role of Social Movements in the Analysis of Sociopolitical Change in Mexico." Paper presented at the Fifteenth International Congress of the Latin American Studies Association, Miami, Florida, December 4–6.

———. 1992. *Maestros en movimiento: Transformaciones en la burocracia estatal (1978–1982).* Mexico City: Casa Chata.

Tamayo, Jaime. 1990. "Neoliberalism Encounters *Neocardenismo*." In *Popular Movements and Political Change in Mexico*, ed. Joe Foweraker and Ann L. Craig. Boulder, Colo.: Lynne Rienner.

Tamayo, Jaime. 1989. "El programa de renovación habitacional popular (Análisis sin eufemismos)." *Revista Ciudades*, no. 1 (January–March).

Tarrow, Sidney. 1988. "National Politics and Collective Action: Recent Theory and Research in Western Europe and the United States." *Annual Review of Sociology* 14:421–40.

———. 1994. *Power in Movement: Social Movements, Collective Action, and Politics.* Cambridge, U.K.: Cambridge University Press.

Teichman, Judith A. 1995. *Privitization and Political Change in Mexico.* Pittsburgh: University of Pittsburgh Press.

———. 1997. "Democracy and Technocratic Decision Making: Mexico, Argentina, and Chile." Paper presented at the Twentieth International Congress of Latin American Studies Association, Guadalajara, Mexico, April 17–19.

———. 2001. *The Politics of Freeing Markets in Latin America: Chile, Argentina, and Mexico.* Chapel Hill: University of North Carolina Press.

Tejada Espino, Ángel. 1996. *Durango a través de sus gobernantes.* Durango, Mexico: Editora Tiempo de Durango.

Tilly, Charles. 1978. *From Mobilization to Revolution.* New York: Random House.

———. 1986. *The Contentious French.* Cambridge, Mass.: Harvard University Press.

Tilly, Charles, Louis Tilly, and Richard Tilly. 1975. *The Rebellious Century, 1830–1930.* Cambridge, Mass.: Harvard University Press.

Tirado Jiménez, Ramón. 1990. *Asamblea de Barrios: Nuestra batalla.* Mexico City: Editorial Nuestro Tiempo.

Trejo, Sofía. 1987. "Del rumor a la asamblea." *Patria Nueva* 1 (August–September).

Tulchin, Joseph S., and Andrew D. Selee, eds. 2003. *Mexico's Politics and Society in Transition.* Boulder, Colo.: Lynne Rienner.

Turner, Ralph H., and Lewis M. Killian. 1987. *Collective Behavior.* 3d ed. Englewood Cliffs, N.J.: Prentice-Hall and Killian.

Vanderschueren, Franz. 1971a. "Popladores y Conciencia Social." *Revista Latinoamericana de Estudios Urbano-Regionales* 1:95–123.

———. 1971b. "Significado Político de las Juntas de Vecinos en Poblaciones de Santiago." *Revista Latinoamericana de Estudios Urbano-Regionales* 1:67–90.

Vega, Edna Elena. 1989. "Movimiento urbano popular en México." In *Estancamiento economico y crisis social en México 1983-1988: Tomo II, Sociedad y Política,* ed. Jesús Lechuga and Fernando Chávez. Mexico City: Universidad Autonoma Metropolitana.

———. 1991. "Proyectos gestionados por la Asamblea de Barrios en el area metropolitana de la Ciudad de México." Mexico City: CECODES.

Venegas Aguilera, Lilia. 1995. "Political Culture and Women of the Popular Sector in Ciudad Juárz, 1983–1986." In *Opposition Government in Mexico,* ed. Victoria E. Rodríguez and Peter M. Ward. Albuquerque: University of New Mexico Press.

Vernon, Raymond. 1963. *The Dilemma of Mexico's Development: The Roles of the Private and Public Sectors.* Cambridge, Mass.: Harvard University Press.

Villa, Manuel A. 1987. "La politización innecesaria: El régimen politico mexicano y sus exigencies de pasividad ciudadana a los damnificados." *Estudios Demográficos y Urbanos* 4 (January–February).

——. n.d. "La política en el gobierno de Miguel de la Madrid." Mimeograph.

Villarreal, René. 1977. "The Policy of Import-Substituting Industrialization, 1929–1975." In *Authoritarianism in Mexico*, ed. José Luis Reyna and Richard S. Weinert. Philadelphia: Institute for the Study of Human Issues.

Walton, John. 1989. "Debt, Protest, and the State in Latin America." In *Power and Popular Protest: Latin American Social Movements*, ed. Susan Eckstein. Berkeley and Los Angeles: University of California Press.

Williams, Mark Eric. 2001. *Market Reforms in Mexico: Coalitions, Institutions, and the Politics of Policy Change*. Lanham, Md.: Rowman and Littlefield.

Wolf, Eric R. 1969. *Peasant Wars in the Twentieth Century*. New York: Harper and Row.

Womack, John. 1969. *Zapata and the Mexican Revolution*. New York: Alfred A. Knopf.

World Bank. 1986. *Poverty in Latin America: The Impact of Depression*. Washington, D.C.: World Bank.

Yáñez, Alejandro González. 1991. "Reflexiones de Diputado Alejandro Yáñez." *Contacto Durango*, no. 283 (February 3).

Yáñez, Gonzalo. 1993. *Primer informe de gobierno*. Durango, Mexico: Municipio de Durango.

Zeitlin, Maurice. 1970. *Revolutionary Politics and the Cuban Working Class*. Princeton: Princeton University Press.

Zermeño, Sergio. 1978. *México: Una democracia utópica*. Mexico City: Siglo XXI.

——. 1990. "Crisis, Neoliberalism, and Disorder." In *Popular Movements and Political Change in Mexico*, ed. Joe Foweraker and Ann L. Craig. Boulder, Colo.: Lynne Rienner.

——. 1997. *Movimientos sociales y democracia en el México de los 90s*. Mexico City: La Jornada Ediciones and Centro de Investigaciones Interdiciplinarias en Humanidades, UNAM.

Ziccardi, Alicia. 1986. "Política de vivienda para un espacio destruido." *Revista Mexicana de Sociología* 48, no. 2.

——, ed. 1995. *La tarea de governar: Gobiernos locales y demandas ciudadanas*. Mexico City: Instituto de Investigaciones Sociales, UNAM, and Miguel Angel Porrúa.

Zínser, Adolfo Aguilar. 1995. *Vamos a ganar! La pugna de Cuauhtémoc Cárdenas por el poder*. Mexico City: Oceano.

Zolberg, Aristide R. 1972. "Moments of Madness." *Politics and Society* 2:183–207.

INDEX

AB (Asamblea de Barrios)
  Anáhuac proposal and, 205
  class composition of, 174, 190–91,
    195–96, 197 n. 27, 221
  compared and contrasted with CDP,
    173–76, 186 n. 10, 188 n. 12, 190, 191
    n. 16, 196, 199, 205, 208, 210, 218,
    220–23
  cuadros, 174, 188–90, 194, 196, 199,
    208–10
  cultural project of, 174, 189, 196 n. 25,
    199–200, 212
  decision-making, 195–99, 209
  decline, 208–9, 211, 215
  elections and, 173–75, 188, 199, 203–5,
    210–11
  evictions and, 178–79, 183, 189, 192,
    200–203
  housing projects and, 193–94, 196,
    209–10, 222
  internal conflicts of, 175, 193, 207
  as lead organization, 173, 176, 192,
    205–6, 208–11, 222
  leadership and internal organization,
    174, 188 n. 12, 190, 195–99, 208
  media and, 200–201, 204
  mission statement of, 191–92
  negotiations and, 174, 180, 183–85, 189,
    189 n. 14, 193–97, 199, 204, 210
  NGOs and, 197
  origins of, 182–83, 189–90
  police and, 177, 201–2
  political opportunity structure and,
    175–76, 179, 187, 194, 204, 222
  precursors to. See CUD
  PRONASOL and, 175, 189 n. 14, 205–6,
    206 n. 35, 211
  protest cycle and, 174–75, 189–90,
    193–94, 222–23
  rank-and-file, 190, 196, 198–99, 203,
    208–9
  relationship with: Cárdenas and the PRD,
    173, 175, 188, 200, 204–8, 210; CDP,
    92, 206, 210, 221–23, 235–36; Mexico
    City government, 175, 205, 215; Sali-
    nas, 173–74, 186 n. 10, 189 n. 14,
    205–6, 208, 211, 223

  renters (tenants), 174, 177, 183, 189–93,
    197, 199–202, 205, 210
  street vendors and, 197, 200
  Superbarrio, 199–204
  women and, 191, 197, 199
Abarca, Cuauhtémoc, 185–86
ACNR (Asociación Cívica Nacional Revolu-
    cionaria), 70, 91 n. 4, 174, 177 n. 4,
    187–88, 204 n. 31, 206 n. 37, 228
Aguilar Camín, Héctor, 34
Alinsky, Saul, 123
alliances, 11, 22 n. 11, 25, 41–43, 63 n. 19,
    73, 83, 91 n. 4, 139, 199, 204 n. 33,
    205, 220, 228, 233. See also coalitions
  electoral, 94–95, 121, 144, 146, 152–53,
    207
  legislative, 77
  multiclass, 42, 53, 72, 81, 236
  problems of, 42
  special importance to urban popular
    movement, 41
  state, 62, 85–86, 104–5, 135 n. 18, 155,
    168, 224, 86
Alvarado, Francisco, 188 n. 12, 198
Alvarez, Rafael, 41
Alvarez, Sonia, 21 n. 8, 30 n. 23, 236 n. 10
America's Watch, 55 n. 12, 56, 119
Anaya, Alberto, 69 n. 30, 134
ANOCP (Asamblea Nacional de Obreros y
    Campesinos Popular), 71–72
authoritarianism, 1–2, 4, 33 n. 30, 38 n. 34,
    42, 48, 82, 139, 170. See also inclusion-
    ary authoritarian regime; post-revolu-
    tionary Mexican politics
Aztecs, 47

Bailey, John, 107
Barkin, David, 121–22
Bartra, Roger, 34, 105
Bennett, Vivienne, 5 n. 3, 126 n. 1
Bettelheim, Charles, 127
Bolos, Silvia, 12 n. 9, 41, 161
Bush, President George Herbert Walker,
    96–97
business
  businessmen, 9 n. 7, 50, 58
  class, 53, 83, 86

business *(cont'd)*
Lázaro Cárdenas and, 52
leaders, 102
organizations, 52, 83, 103 n. 23
small, 113–14

Cabañas, Lucio, 33
caciques (local political bosses), 64, 102 n. 20
caudillismo (political bossism), 40, 91, 171
Calles, Elías, 51–52
Camacho, Manuel, 221–22
Campbell, Joseph, 6 n. 6
Cárdenas, Cuauhtémoc, 14, 39, 76–82. *See also* neo-Cardenismo
decision to form PRD, 90, 92–93, 100, 237
"electoral fraud" strategy, 93–94, 96
1994 election, 100
1997 election, 233
relationship with popular movements, 79–80, 150–51, 229–30, 234
split with the PRI, 77
Cárdenas, Lázaro, 52–53, 59 n. 15, 77, 106
Carranza, Venustíano, 51
Casa y Ciudad, 12 n. 9, 170, 209 n. 39
Castells, Manuel, 8, 30 n. 24, 37 n. 33, 38, 41 n. 39, 216–17
Castillo, Heberto, 77, 146, 203 n. 30
Castillo Palma, 216
Catholic Church, 11, 48–49, 52, 128, 130
CDP (Comite de Defensa Popular)
Colonias populares, 129, 132–40, 146, 148, 158, 168, 218, 222, 238, 241
cuadros, 130 n. 10, 139–40, 142, 165, 167, 169–71, 218
cultural project, 140–41, 219 n. 3
decision-making, 133 n. 14, 138–40, 158, 168–70
decline, 126, 167–71, 215, 218–19
de-radicalization, 136, 145–46, 161, 167
ecological project, 148, 158
emphasis on public works, 125, 157–58, 162–64, 169
governors: Armando del Castillo Franco, 136, 138; Gámiz Fernandez, 136; Héctor Mayagoitia and, 134–36; Páez Urquidi and, 131; Ramírez Gamero and, 145–46, 151, 155–56, 158; Silerio Esparza, 161
internal conflicts of, 134, 157–58, 167, 169

labor committees and, 133–34, 217
land invasions and. *See* land invasions
leadership and internal organization, 125, 133, 138–42, 147, 158, 164 n. 49, 167–68, 170–71, 173, 213, 218–19, 221, 222, 228
López Portillo and, 134–36, 138, 147
media and, 145–46
negotiating skills, 124, 129 n. 8, 132, 136–38, 146–47, 166
1972–78 (formative years), 127–35
1979–89 (movement organization building), 135–47
1986–88 (electoral option), 144–47
1992–94, 163–66
1992 (state-level elections), 161–63
Nombre de Dios and, 154–55, 157, 165
peasants and, 129, 135, 145
police and, 132, 145, 165, 218
Política Popular and, 124, 126–29
political opportunity structure and, 124, 127, 137, 149, 218, 221–22
precursors to, 129 n. 8, 136. *See also* UPI
PT and, 125, 156–69
rank-and-file, 129–33, 139, 144, 153, 160, 165, 167, 169–70, 218–19
relationship with PRONASOL, 14, 163, 168; 1990–91, 153–56; convenio de concertación (1989) 147–54; financing of, 154–55; motivations for participation in, 150–52, 161–62, 150, 222; political moderation as a result of, 150, 153, 156, 158–59, 215; Yáñez municipal administration and, 164–65
relationships with: C. Cárdenas, 146–47, 149–52, 155, 157; Echeverría, 127 n. 2, 131–32, 134–35, 151, 222; inclusionary authoritarian regime, 124–26, 157; López Portillo, 134–136, 138, 147; PAN, 137, 140, 144, 152–53, 156 n. 42, 157, 159, 161, 163–65; PRD, 149–53, 157, 160–65; Salinas, 126, 147–52, 154 n. 40, 155–57, 159–62, 164, 167–68; state government, 135–36, 158–59, 161–62, 165, 169–71; unions, 133–34, 137–38
renters, 129, 131
reservations regarding elections (prior to July 1988) 68, 144
street vendors and, 137
violence and, 124, 132, 134

women and, 130, 133–34, 141–44, 153
Central America, 47, 101 n. 19
CIOAC (Central Independiente de Obreros
    Agrícolas y Campesinos), 91 n. 4
citizenship, 43, 216, 240
  AB and, 43, 190, 209, 212
  technocrats and, 61–62
civil disobedience, 72, 100, 231
civil society, 16, 24–25, 31, 43
  in Mexico, 1, 4, 14, 62, 64–65, 71, 86,
    104–5, 121, 150 n. 35, 171, 207
class
  AB and, 174, 190–91, 195–97, 201, 221
  business, 53, 83, 222
  compromise, 52
  conflict, 47–48
  middle, 1, 31, 41–42, 83, 87, 113, 137,
    145, 163, 176–77, 185, 187, 201–2,
    237
  multiclass, 27, 41–44, 71–72, 74, 76, 79
    n. 40, 80–81, 125, 129 n. 8, 153, 163
    n. 47, 167, 169, 185, 191, 236–37
  political, 96, 128 n. 7, 138, 232
  politics of, 123, 217, 236
  popular, 123–24, 182, 185, 201, 227
  relations, 31 n. 24
  ruling, 49–51, 128
  structure, 48–50, 51, 121
  structure, 48–50, 77 n. 39, 121, 216
  upper, 52
  working, 49–50, 52–53, 62, 87, 124, 227
clientelism, 4, 7, 9 n. 7, 41, 101, 122, 223
  AB and, 193, 196
  neo-, 105, 117, 157
Clinton, President William Jefferson, 121
Clouthier, Manuel J., 80, 83
CNC (Confederación Nacional Campesina),
  53
CNOP (Confederación Nacional de Organizaciones Populares), 64, 101–2,
  113–17. See also UNE
  Durango, 129, 134–36, 138, 148 n. 31,
    154 n. 39
CNPA (Coordinadora Nacional Plan de
  Ayala), 64–65, 67, 110
CNTE (Coordinadora Nacional de Trabajadores de la Educación), 32 n. 26, 64,
  66–67, 102 n. 20, 139 n. 23, 159 n. 43,
  160, 168
coalitions. See also alliances
  electoral, 38–39, 76–77, 87, 90, 207

multiclass, 76, 80, 236
  problems of, 38, 110, 208 n. 38
  sector, 13
COCEI (Coalición de Obreros, Campesinos y
  Estudiantes del Istmo), 44 n. 2, 72
  n. 33, 91 n. 4, 108, 162 n. 46
Cockcroft, James, 47–48
colonias populares
  CDP and, 124, 129, 132–40, 146, 148,
    158, 168, 218, 222, 238, 241
  definition of, 75 n. 36
collective
  action, 7, 22 n. 12, 24, 30, 36 n. 32, 117,
    133
  dissent, 35, 37, 74 n. 35, 81, 118, 166,
    187
Colosio, Luis Donaldo, 121
Communist Party, 58, 69, 72 n. 34, 91 n. 4,
  126 n. 1
CONAMUP (Coordinadora Nacional del
  Movimiento Urbano Popular), 42,
  113, 115 n. 33, 64, 67–68, 72–73,
  75–76, 110, 227, 236
  AB and, 177 n. 4, 191, 195, 206–7, 211
  CDP and, 111 n. 30, 124, 137, 141, 142
    n. 25, 160, 171
concertación social, 86, 92, 103–5, 126, 156,
  162–63, 168, 205, 220
consciousness
  Mexico City earthquake and, 74
  political, 23, 28, 74, 225
  popular movements and, 17, 19, 26, 44,
    46
  the study of, 20 n. 6, 22, 26, 28
  urban popular movement and, 4, 13,
    140–41, 171, 200, 219–20
convenios de concertación, 92, 110, 147–53,
  185, 205, 220
Cook, Maria Lorena, 25, 39, 67 n. 27, 139
  n. 23, 210
co-optation, 4, 42, 58, 65, 126, 156–61, 186,
  232
  in relationship to repression, 35–37, 43,
    125–26, 224–26, 230
coordinadoras, 56–58, 62–73, 195, 226–27
COPLAMAR, 106 n. 24
Cornelius, Wayne, 9–11
corporatism, 4, 10–11, 38 n. 35, 52–58, 60,
  62, 82–83, 87, 104, 153
  neocorporatism, 4, 95, 101–7

Corriente Democrática, 77, 90 n. 4, 203
    n. 30
corruption, 100, 223, 225
    anticorruption policies, 62, 80, 165
    Durango and, 129 n. 8, 142 n. 14, 145,
        165, 169
Cortés, Hernán, 47 n. 1
Craig, Ann, 79 n. 40
Craske, Nikki, 115, 117
Cruz, Marcos, 69 n. 30, 128 n. 5, 134–35,
    139–40, 146, 152, 165, 167–69
CTM, 117, 128, 133–34, 137, 145 n. 28
CUD, 75, 176–190, 192–93, 195, 205–6

damnificados, 176–79, 181, 186, 192, 192
    n. 18
debt, international, 59–60, 84, 97, 109
    AB position on, 181, 184, 191, 203
decentralization, 107, 154, 156, 158, 195,
    198, 218
de la Madrid, Miguel Hurtado, 60–63, 72,
    74–80, 83, 147
    AB and, 179–80, 184, 193
    contrasted with Salinas, 37, 86, 97, 101,
        103 n. 23, 104–6, 111, 214
    Reagan Administration and, 101 n. 19
democratic opening of the 1970s (apertura
    democrática), 10, 112
democratic transition
    AB and, 175, 194, 211, 215–16
    CDP and, 170, 215
    popular movements and, 2–3, 105, 165,
        207, 214, 220 n. 4, 226–36, 239–40
    Salinas and, 96, 120–21
    urban poor and, 3, 122, 238
    urban popular movement and, 216,
        228–29
democratization
    AB and, 191–92, 194–95, 203, 205,
        211–12, 221
    Cárdenas and, 78, 91, 205, 234
    CDP and, 158, 165, 221
    poor people and, 21, 239–40
    popular movements and, 41, 48, 125,
        149, 168, 238–40
    PRD and, 234, 229–30
    of the PRI, 78, 104, 117–18
    radical ideals of, 126, 191–92, 213–14, 223
    Salinas and, 95, 102, 224
    urban popular movement and, 40–41,
        216, 226–36

War of Independence and, 48–49
dependency theory, 33, 95 n. 12
Díaz, Porfirio, 1, 49
Dresser, Denise, 108
Durán, Ramon, 128 n. 5, 133 n. 14
Dussell Peters, Enrique, 97 n. 14

Echeverría, Luis Alvarez, 56–59, 82, 102–3,
    123, 222
    CDP and, 127 n. 2, 131–32, 134–35, 151,
        222
    contrasted to Salinas, 102–3, 129. n. 7,
        131, 151–52
Eckstein, Susan, 9 n. 7, 10, 62, 177 n. 5,
    181, 185–87
economy. See also neoliberalism; ISI
    boom and bust, 59–60, 97
    informal, 52, 55, 137
    macroeconomic indicators, 59–60 ,
        98–99
    Mexican Revolution and, 49
    1940–80, 54
    1980s economic crisis, 54, 59–60, 62; as
        political opportunity for social move-
        ments, 62, 71–72, 83, 97, 137; infla-
        tion, 76; worsening conditions for
        low-income people, 57–58, 60
    1995, 89, 97
    oil and, 59 n. 15
    popular movements and, 51, 213, 216,
        232
    recovery (1988–94), 87–88, 97
    student movement and, 59 n. 14
    urban, 55
    wage and price controls, 97
ejido, 135, 145
elections
    fraud, 1, 65, 80, 87, 93, 97, 100, 121, 225
    as legitimating acts, 1–2
    1985, 72
    1988, 1, 79–82, 205, 228
    1989, 93
    1991, 88, 93, 96, 118, 120, 225
    1994, 100, 118, 166, 225
    1997, 122, 233
    1998, 169 n. 51
    2000, 1, 89–90, 122, 220
electoral reforms, 224
    COFIPE (1990), 94–95
    1970s, 58, 69, 72 n. 34, 112, 136, 188, 225
    1980s, 95–96

1990s, 86, 88–89, 94–97
elite splits, 14, 25, 74, 76–77, 124, 128 n. 7,
    132, 150–52, 181
Elizondo Torres, Rodolfo, 140 n. 24, 156
    n. 42
El Salvador, 2, 68, 225
Enzástiga, Leopoldo, 90–91, 226–27
Escobar, Aruturo, 21 n. 8, 30 n. 23, 236
    n. 10

FDN (Frente Democrático Nacional)
    creation of, 38–39, 77–80
    electoral performance (1988), 93, 95, 225
    as legitimate bearer of the revolution,
        101 n. 18, 147
    relationships with: AB, 203 n. 30, 204–7,
        210; CDP, 149
    undoing of, 90, 112
federalism, 4, 55, 164
FNOC (Frente Nacional de Organizaciones y
    Ciudadanos), 117
Fox, Jonathan, 37, 104, 168
Fox, Vicente, 66, 87–90, 97, 112
FPTYL (Frente Popular Tierra y Libertad),
    68, 111, 159 n. 43, 206

Gramsci, Antonio, 26, 69 n. 31, 140, 174
Guerrero, Javier, 34

Haines, Herbert H., 176 n. 1
Harvey, Neil, 65 n. 23, 104
Hellman, Judith Adler, 50, 79
Hernández Galicia, Joaquín ("la Quina"),
    102 n. 20
Hernández Navarro, Luis, 66, 67 n. 26, 68
    n. 30, 69 n. 30, 149, 150 n. 35, 160
    n. 45
Hidalgo, Javier, 188 n. 12, 198
Hidalgo, Miguel, 48–49
human rights, 31, 55, 114, 117, 119, 226 n. 6

Ibarra, Rosario, 80 n. 41, 203 n. 30
ideological hegemony, 26
IFE (Instituto Federal Electoral), 88, 225
Import Substitution Industrialization (ISI),
    54, 61, 85. See also state-led capitalism
International Monetary Fund (IMF), 59–60,
    78, 184
inclusionary authoritarian regime, 51–56,
    82–83, 147, 181–2. See also postrevo-
    lutionary Mexican politics

absence of checks and balances, 55
    contrasted to exclusionary authoritarian
        regimes, 35, 53, 118, 225
    democratic pretenses, 55, 225
indigenous people, 47–48, 55 n. 12, 65
    n. 25, 154 n. 39, 237 n. 11
inequality, 48, 54, 59–60, 83
Inter-American Foundation, 148
Iturbide, Agustín de, 48–49

Jonguitud, Carlos, 102 n. 20

Klesner, Joseph, 2–3
Knight, Alan, 79 n. 40

labor unions
    CDP and, 133, 137–38, 151, 217
    de la Madrid and, 62
    independent, 37–38, 38 n. 35, 64
    industrial, 41, 113
    official corporatist, 37–38, 52–53, 55,
        64–66
    role in 1980s protest cycle, 66, 78
land invasions, 58, 124, 129, 131–33,
    134–36, 216, 222
land reform, 51, 64
Leal, Gustavo F., 163 n. 47
Left (Mexican), 14, 20, 71–72, 95, 122, 141.
    See also Salinas de Gortari
    Cárdenas and, 70, 77–78, 82
    divisions within, 69–71, 108–12, 122,
        150, 160 n. 45, 163 n. 47, 165, 207,
        208 n. 38, 209
    elections and, 1–2, 58–59, 72, 81, 121,
        170, 203–4, 224–26
    electoral reform and, 188, 224
    Mexico City earthquake and, 180–82
    movement to party, 157, 170, 226–36
    political Left, 71, 91 n. 4, 208 n. 38, 227
    social Left, 57–59, 62–63, 65, 88, 91 n. 4,
        111, 122, 220 n. 4, 170, 181, 225–26,
        231, 234
Levy, Santiago, 109
Línea de Masas, 134, 159–60, 228
Línea Proletária, 134, 228
Lira Bracho, Juan, 137, 137 n. 22
Lomera, Rocío, 235
Loaeza, Soledad, 34
Lomnitz, Larissa, 10
López Portillo, José, 56–61, 103 n. 23,
    134–36, 138, 147

Madero, Francisco, 49–50
Mainwaring, Scott, 42 n. 40
Maoism and Maoists in Mexico. *See also*
    Pólitica Popular
    decline in the 1990s, 160–71, 218
    Echeverría and, 132
    López Portillo and, 134–35
    organizations, 68 n. 30, 126–27
    strategy, 124, 127, 134–36, 164
    theory, 124, 127, 132 n. 13, 160–61
MAP, 91 n. 4
Martínez Álvarez, Octavio, 154–55, 157,
    165
Martínez Guzmán, Gabino, 131 n. 12, 134,
    145, 158
Marxism, 32–33, 127, 141, 210
Massolo, Alexandra, 143
Mayan people, 47
media, 18, 20, 22, 74
    AB and, 200–201, 204
    access to, 23, 89
    bias of, 65, 87, 100
    CDP and, 145–46
    PRI and, 107
    PRONASOL and, 107, 109
    Salinas and, 106–7, 111, 120
    social movements and, 27 n. 18, 187
Melucci, Alberto, 5 n. 5, 217–18
Mexican Constitution, 44, 50–51, 58, 73,
    167, 173, 240
    AB and, 189, 192
    reforms of, 50 n. 4, 88, 107
Mexican protest cycle (1979–94), 13–14, 27,
    37–38, 59, 63, 173–74, 184, 193, 220,
    240
    decline (1988–94), 39, 86–90, 105, 119,
    209, 215–16, 219, 234
    Mexico City earthquake and, 73–76, 176,
    179, 187, 201
    sharp deflation (1989–91), 39, 86
    zenith (1987–88), 76–77, 79 n. 40, 122,
    173, 189–90
Mexican Revolution (1910–20), 49–51
    revolutionary ideals, 50–51, 55, 58,
    82–83, 141, 189
Mexican structure of political opportunities,
    12, 14, 37, 62, 70, 76, 83, 216,
    224–25, 231–32
    AB and, 175–76, 179, 187, 194, 204, 222
    CDP and, 124, 127, 137, 149, 218, 221–22
    Salinas' influence on, 96, 106, 152

Mexico City
    earthquake (1985), 73–76, 176–79;
        reconstruction programs, 76, 115,
        176–77, 179–89
    Federal District Assembly, 79
    population, 55,
    strength of the PRD, 91
Meyer, Lorenzo, 118
migration (rural-to-urban within Mexico),
    9–10, 54–55, 80, 122, 166, 217
MOCER (Movimiento Obrero, Campesino,
    Estudiantil Revolucionario), 68 n. 30
modernization theory, 33 n. 30, 95 n. 12
Moguel, Julio, 65 n. 23, 67 n. 27, 69 n. 30,
    109, 146 n. 29, 149, 204
Montaño, Jorge, 9, 11–12
Monsiváis, Carlos, 34
Morelos, José María, 48–49
MRP (Movimiento Revolucionario del
    Pueblo), 68, 72
municipal government
    CDP and, 125, 153–55, 157–58, 161–66,
        168–69, 233
    PAN (in Durango) and, 124 n. 7, 140
        n. 24
    PRD, 93–94, 111–12, 119–20, 233–35
    PRONASOL and, 107, 109, 111–12, 154–56
    Salinas and PRD, 97–100, 115–16, 119
Muñoz Ledo, Porfirio, 77, 204

NAFTA, 87–88, 97, 105, 156, 165
Narro, José, 69 n. 30
nationalism, 52, 76–78, 87, 101–3
neo-Cardenismo, 80, 83, 90–94, 203–9
    weaknesses of, 97–98
neoliberalism
    anomie and, 228
    austerity measures, 62, 71 n. 32, 72, 76,
        85, 106
    definition of, 60–61, 60 n. 17, 150 n. 35,
        157
    de la Madrid and, 61–63, 74, 77–78, 83
    failures of, 21
    popular movements' ability to influence,
        214, 220
    privatization, 61, 63, 89, 105, 107
    PRONASOL and, 106, 112
    Salinas and, 96, 101, 103, 120, 224
    structural adjustment program, 60–61
Nevárez, Horténsia, 153

NGOS (nongovernmental organizations), 39, 111, 150 n. 35, 197, 226–27
Noriega, Manuel, 53
Núñez Acosta, Misrael, 66

Obregón, Alvaro, 51
oil, 54, 59, 67, 82, 102 n. 20
OIR-LM (Organizacón de Izquierda Revolu-cionaria–Línea de Masas), 68–70, 72–73, 76, 86, 91 n. 4, 110, 124, 127 n. 2, 137, 160, 228
AB and, 177 n. 4, 190, 196, 206–7, 221
Oliver, Pamela, 3, 32
Olson, Mancur, 125
Organización Revolucionaria Punto Crítico, 91 n. 4, 174, 177 n. 4, 187–88, 204 n. 31, 228
Oribe Berlinguer, Adolfo, 126, 126–27, 129 n. 9, 134
Oxhorn, Philip, 17

Pacheco, José, 34
Palacios Moncayo, Miguel, 129 n. 8, 145 n. 28, 156 n. 42, 168–69
PAN (Partido Acción Nacional)
de la Madrid and, 62, 83
Durango and, 128 n. 7, 137, 140, 144–45, 152–53, 156 n. 42, 157, 159, 161, 163–65
electoral outcomes of, 81, 89–91, 100, 119–20, 128 n. 7, 140, 144–45, 162 n. 46, 224
history of, 89
PRD and, 80, 121, 226
Salinas and, 85–86, 94–96, 120, 226
social movements and, 71
Parcero López, José, 117, 181, 184
PARM (Partido Auténtico de la Revolución Mexicana), 77, 90 n. 4, 93 n. 8, 153, 160, 204 n. 33
Pastor, Manuel, Jr., 60 n. 16, 97
PCDP (Partido del Comité de Defensa Popu-lar), 152–53, 165
Perlman, Janice, 9 n. 7
peasants
in cities, 9
demographics of, 1
difficulties of, 21, 166
division within, 110
movements of, 13, 28, 32, 41 n. 39, 64–65, 236

relationship with Cárdenas, 119
relationships with: CDP, 129, 135, 145; Echeverría, 56; PRI and state, 38, 53, 55, 113
rights of, 50
Petras, James, 232
PFCRN (Partido del Frente Cardenista de Reconstrucción Nacional), 90 n. 4, 93 n. 8
Pinochet, Augusto, 54
Piven, Francis Fox and Richard Cloward, 5–6, 22 n. 11, 23–24, 30 n. 22, 35–36, 47, 65, 125, 166, 176, 182, 215
PMS (Partido Mexicano Socialista), 91 n. 4, 146, 146, 203–4
PMT (Partido Mexicano de los Traba-jadores), 72 n. 34, 112
political culture, 33–34, 48, 141, 156 n. 42, 170–71, 197
political party system, 2, 4, 13, 16, 28, 89, 94, 235
Política Popular, 68, 124–27, 134, 228. See also CDP
poor people, 1, 10, 13, 148, 166, 193, 239
social movements, 30, 42, 44, 125, 166, 231, 236
urban poor, 122, 161, 215
populism, 147, 191
anti-populists, 101, 106
developmentalist, 86 n. 2
Echeverría's version, 103, 103 n. 23, 132
progressive populism, 70, 76, 101
Salinas' version, 106
post-revolutionary Mexican politics, 41, 50–52, 65–66, 74, 81, 112. See also Inclusionary Authoritarian regime
PPS (Partido Popular Socialista), 77, 90 n. 4, 93 n. 8, 153, 160
PRD, 70, 89–97
composition of, 90 n. 4
municipalities controlled by, 93–94, 97–100, 111–12, 115–16, 119–20, 233–35
PAN and, 80, 121, 226
position on PRONASOL, 92, 111–12, 149
relationship between ex-priístas and the Left, 90–92, 150, 234–35
relationships with: popular movements, 229–31, 234–35. See also AB, CDP
violence against, 96, 119–20, 225
weaknesses of, 20, 100, 235

PRHP (Programa de Renovación Habitacional Popular), 181
PRI
  basic characteristics of, 52–53, 56, 141, 219
  challenges to, 64, 110–11, 147, 162 n. 46, 166
  compared to other parties, 71, 77, 85
  Cuauhtémoc Cárdenas and, 76–80, 90, 94, 104
  domination in party system, 4, 11, 89
  Durango, CDP and, 128 n. 7, 134–37, 151, 156, 159, 163–66, 168–69
  elections and, 1, 93, 80–82
  ex-priístas and, 90–91, 150, 234–35
  internal divisions of, 117, 151
  media and, 107
  Mexico City, AB and, 91, 179, 181, 186, 194–95
  "New PRI," 102, 107
  PAN and, 94–95
  peasants and, 55, 65, 85
  PRONASOL and, 96, 107–8, 110–11, 117, 148, 153–54, 156
  relationship to state, 71, 73, 110, 150, 156, 203
  Salinas and, 85, 103, 112–13, 151–52, 224
  unions and, 67, 78, 133
  urban poor and, 55, 113–15, 122, 128, 147, 204 n. 32
  weaknesses of, 12, 57–58, 100, 115 n. 33, 118, 148, 150–51
Prieto, Ana Maria, 65 n. 23, 71 n. 32
PRONASOL
  AB and, 175, 189 n. 14, 205–6, 206 n. 35, 211
  affects on federalism, 107–8, 154
  beneficiaries of, 108–9
  CDP and. See CDP, relationship to PRONASOL
  CNOP/UNE and, 115, 117–18
  critics of, 109–11, 159–60
  description of, 14, 112, 118, 226
  financing of, 87–88, 107–8, 154–55
  implementation problems of, 155–56
  leadership of, 86, 107, 111
  media coverage of, 107, 109
  municipalities and, 107, 109, 111–12, 154–56
  official objectives, 107, 112–13
  political benefits realized, 88, 96

  popular movements and, 87, 94, 109–13, 120–21, 149–51
  PT and, 92, 150, 159–60
  Solidarity Committees and, 153–54
  states and, 107, 154
  strategy designed to undermine Cárdenas and PRD, 87, 105, 109–12, 226
  urban popular movements and, 101, 112, 214
proportional representation, 81, 95, 145 n. 27, 152 n. 37, 161–62
PRT (Partido Revolucionario de los Trabajadores), 72 n. 34, 80 n. 41, 144–45, 203 n. 30, 204
PSUM (Partido Socialista Unificado de México), 69, 71, 72 n. 34, 91 n. 4, 112, 144
PT (Partido de Trabajo), 70, 92, 124–25, 149–50, 156–69

race and racism, 48, 82
railroad workers' strike (1959), 10 n. 8, 56, 120
Ramírez, Antonio, 128, 137–38, 145, 151
Rascón, Marco, 188 n. 12, 198, 205
renters (tenants), 75, 216–17, 229
  AB, 174, 177, 183, 189–93, 197, 199–202, 205
  CDP, 129, 131
repression, 36 n. 32, 56, 63–65, 68, 72–73, 230
  as contribution to Salinas' political recovery, 118–20, 224–25
  as incentive to form alliances, 72
  in relationship to co-optation, 35–37, 43, 125–26, 224–26, 230
Reyes Heroles, Jesús, 58
Reyna, José Luis, 224
Rios, Alfonso P., 69 n. 30
Rivas, Manuel, 190, 211
Robles, Rosario, 69 n. 30
Rodríguez, Victoria E., 162 n. 46
Rojas Gutiérrez, Carlos, 86, 94, 107, 111, 151, 222
Rubin, Jeffrey, 4 n. 2, 5, 44 n. 42

Salazar, Juan Álvarez, 165, 169, 219 n. 3
Salinas de Gortari, Carlos, 1, 14, 39
  contrasted with: de la Madrid, 37, 86, 97, 101, 103 n. 23, 104–6, 111, 214; Echeverría, 102–3, 129 n. 7, 131, 151–52

economic: recovery and, 85–88, 97, 120–21, 225; reforms trump political reforms, 95–96, 106
governing style, 85–86, 100–106
modernization theme, 95, 101–2, 109, 112–18, 151
political: recovery, 86–88, 94–100, 118, 120, 224–26; reform efforts, 107, 112–18, 121, 164, 184, 195, 225–26
presidential succession, 101 n. 17
PRI reform efforts, 85, 101–2
relationships with: big business, 86; Cárdenas and PRD, 85, 87, 96, 105; CDP, 126, 147–52, 154 n. 40, 155–57, 159–62, 164, 167–68; Left, 14, 97, 106, 120, 226; PAN, 85–86, 96, 226; social Left and social movements, 86–88, 94, 96–97, 103, 111–12, 184, 213; United States, 85–88, 95–97, 101–2; urban popular movement, 86, 94; Zapatistas, 88
SAM (Sistema Alimentario Mexicana), 104
Samano, Lidia, 235
Sandoval, Georgina, 170, 238
Saucedo, Francisco, 179, 180, 188 n. 12, 198, 206 n. 37
Saucedo, Mario, 235
Seccional Ho Chi Min, 68 n. 30, 126 n. 1
SEDUE (Secretaría de Desarrollo Urbano y Ecología), 178
Selee, Andrew E., 88
Singer, Martha S., 163 n. 47
SNTE (Sindicato Nacional de Trabajadores de la Educación), 32 n. 26, 66–67
Somoza, Anastasio, 53
social movements. See also theory and method
    activity during the 1979–88 period (summary), 62–63
    autonomy, 37–39, 56–57, 73, 149 n. 33, 159, 168, 210–11
    assessing the importance of, 7–9
    challenges to PRI/state's revolutionary credentials, 73, 141, 213
    cultural project, 70, 140–41, 174, 189, 196 n. 25, 199–200, 212, 219 n. 3
    definition of, 30–33, 161
    as distinct from interest groups, 30–31
    electoral participation, 2 n. 1, 58–59, 68, 78–83, 144–47, 157, 215
    gender, 141–44

institutional disruption, importance of, 31, 231–32
intellectuals, 49, 69
internal: democracy (and lack thereof), 67 n. 27, 39–41, 127, 168, 223; organization, 39–41, 138–40
leadership, 3–5, 7, 20, 39–40; charismatic leadership, 32, 162, 167, 170; struggles, 40
movement to party, 157, 170, 226–36
rationality and non-rational dynamics within, 34
relationships, 125, 174, 194, 222; with political parties, 43, 70–71; with state reformers, 231. See also AB; CDP; C. Cárdenas; PRD; Salinas de Gortari; theory and method
solidarity, 14, 19–20, 31–32, 69 n. 31, 74, 125, 144, 238
vision and survival, 43–45
social movements and social movement organizations (the distinction between), 3, 32
Spanish Conquest of Mexico (1519), 47
state-led capitalism, 60 n. 17, 83, 105. See also ISI
Stevens, Evelyn, 10
strategies. See also theory and method; Maoism and Maoists in Mexico; PRONASOL
    AB, 174, 188, 190, 192, 197–98, 201, 203, 205, 207–10
    CDP, 124–25, 132, 139, 149–50, 153, 169, 218, 222
    social movements and, 23–26, 32–34, 43–44, 73, 76, 83, 135 n. 17, 215, 228–29, 232
student movement (in Mexico 1960s), 1, 32, 10 n. 8, 56, 59, 81–82, 120, 123–24, 177 n. 3, 216

Tamayo, Jaime, 181
Tarrow, Sidney, 22 nn. 11, 12, 25 n. 14, 31 n. 25
technocrats, 61–2, 76, 105, 111
    "técnicos vs. "políticos" 77, 86
Tello, Yolanda, 194
Tenochtitlán, 47
theory and method (for the study of social movements), 4–7, 15–45. See also social movements
    comparative study of, 223

theory and method (*cont'd*)
cycles of protest, 8, 24–25, 63 n. 20, 175, 237. *See also* Mexican protest cycle
determinism and agency, 21, 23
experience (phenomenology) of movement, 6–7, 15–20, 28, 45
ethnography, 16, 20, 28
free rider problem, 24, 125
importance of access to the movement by the researcher, 4–5
issue framing, 26 n. 17
lead organizations, 3, 32, 122, 213. *See also* AB and CDP
mobilization and negotiation, 166, 214
militancy and institutional disruption, 167, 170, 182–83, 207, 215–16
mobilizing, divesting, and reframing acts, 27
mobilization vs. organization, 92–93, 213–15
new social movement theory, 15, 19, 21, 43, 211, 217, 236
political: process model, 15, 19, 22–28, 39; opportunity structure, 13, 23–25, 27–28, 63 n 19, 76, 135 n. 17, 149, 182. *See also* Mexican structure of political opportunities
relationships, 28–30, 156–57, 194
resource mobilization theory, 19
strategy, 6 n. 6, 7, 13–14, 23–26, 28, 37, 39, 43, 123, 136, 176, 182, 215
syncretic model, 16–22
Tilly, Charles, 22 n. 11, 169–70, 233
Tulchin, Joseph S., 88

UNAM (Universidad Nacional Autónoma de México), 160, 183 n. 7
United States
Mexico and, 36, 50, 55, 121
Salinas and, 85–88, 95–97, 101–2
urban poor in Mexico, 122, 161, 215
the 1970s literature 9–13, 214
urban popular movement, 67 n. 27, 83, 170, 217, 219, 223, 227–28
goals, 33, 70, 170, 228
housing and, 131, 217
importance of, 4, 214, 216, 220
leadership structure and hierarchy, 20, 28, 170
splits within, 206–7, 222, 228–29
future of, 238

UCP (Unión de Colonias Populares), 12 n. 9, 68, 72, 91 n. 4, 127 n. 2, 211, 234
UNE (Ciudadanos en Movimiento), 113–18. *See also* CNOP
UNORCA (Unión Nacional de Organizaciones Regionales Campesinas), 65 n. 23, 110, 111 n. 30
UPEZ (Unión de los Pueblos de Emiliano Zapata), 137, 148
UPI (Unión Popular Independiente), 124, 130–32, 213
UPREZ (Unión Popular Revolucionaria Emiliano Zapata), 12 n. 9, 20, 91 n. 4, 194 n. 21

Venegas Aguilera, Lilia, 34, 142
Villa, Manuel A., 103, 179
Villa, Pancho, 50

War of Independence (1810–22), 4849, 82
Ward, Peter M., 162 n. 46
Weber, Max, 170
Wise, Carol, 60 n. 16, 97
Woldenberg, José, 225
women, 229
AB and, 191, 197, 199
CDP and, 130, 133–34, 141–44
World Bank, 65 n. 24, 183, 211

Yáñez, Gonzalo
as candidate, 162–66, 168, 219 n. 3
as federal deputy, 168, 219 n. 3
as movement leader, 69 n. 30, 139–41, 156 n. 42, 158, 167, 219
as municipal president, 156 n. 42, 163–65, 169
as state deputy, 158–59

Zapata, Emiliano, 50–51, 64, 73, 134, 136–37
Zapatistas
followers of the Mexican revolutionary, Emiliano Zapata, 36 n. 32, 64
"New Zapatistas" of the 1990s to the present, 33 n. 29, 36, 65 n. 25, 100, 121, 157, 161, 216, 237 n. 11
Zedillo Ponce de León, Ernesto, 50 n. 4, 61, 86, 88–89, 95 n. 12, 96–97, 120, 224, 233
Zermeño, Sergio, 3, 104, 228

www.ingramcontent.com/pod-product-compliance
Lightning Source LLC
Chambersburg PA
CBHW021853020426
42334CB00013B/313